FIGHTING AMPHIBS
The LCS(L) in World War II

With Illustrations

Donald L. Ball

Mill Neck Publications
Williamsburg, Virginia

Library of Congress Catalog Card #97-73465
ISBN #0-9659055-0-0

Cover by Markley Rizzi.
Maps by Karen McCluney
Book design by Candace Clifford, Cypress Communications
Front cover illustration from a painting by John Hamilton, courtesy John F.
Lehman; back cover illustration courtesy Ray Baumler

Copies available from the publisher: Mill Neck Publications
                                         1 Cole Lane
                                         Williamsburg, VA 23185
                                         (757) 229-5450

TO

The thousands of officers and men who served their country on the LCS(L)s in World War II. And to the memory of those LCS shipmates who gave their lives for their country in the Great War.

The memory of H. Richard Rhame, LCS Flotilla One Staff Member and pioneer editor of the National LCS(L) 1-130 Association Newsletter, who inspired veterans to submit contributions to the invaluable collection that bears his name and made this book possible.

Ray Baumler, LCS 14 machinist and pioneer historian and archivist of the Association, whose love for LCS(L)s and his LCS shipmates shines through in everything he does to reveal and promote the history of those 130 gunboats and their crews.

Author's Foreword

Like Coleridge's Ancient Mariner I feel compelled to tell a story, a 'history,' if you will, that will probably not, in its fullness, otherwise be told, or its contents be known to the world at large. It is the story of what 130 amphibious gunboats and their crews did in World War II.

The story of these gunboats designated Landing Craft Support (Large) is worth telling because, in many respects, their situation was unique—they were amphibious support ships and their crews were trained for this, but they were also much more, and they served in areas completely out of the amphibious world.

On the one hand, they were an effective weapon in amphibious operations, designed and built to support invasions by protecting the landing troops and bombarding the landing beaches with massive gun and rocket fire. On the other hand, they were combatant seagoing ships capable of serving on patrols of all kinds, of escorting and protecting larger and smaller vessels in coastal waters and on the open sea, of destroying enemy targets on the beaches themselves, and by directing the heavy gunfire of larger ships, of serving with destroyers and other ships on radar picket patrol on the high seas, destroying scores of enemy kamikaze planes and suicide boats and swimmers.

They were also capable of demolishing thousands of floating mines over large areas of open and coastal seas, of successfully fighting dangerous fires on larger ships and at ammunition dumps on the beach, of providing crucial damage control to larger stricken ships on radar stations, even keeping them afloat until they could be towed off for repairs, of caring for hundreds of wounded men from the stricken and sunken ships, and of rescuing thousands of their survivors.

LCS crews proved that they were capable of all these varied tasks in the most positive way possible. By doing them!

Their story needs to be told if only to record their achievements in firefighting, providing damage control, caring for the wounded, and rescuing survivors. In the histories of ships receiving aid from LCS crews appearing in the *Dictionary of American Naval Fighting Ships,* these achievements are nowhere mentioned. That LCS crews rescued just under 400 survivors from the sinking destroyers USS *Bush* (DD 529) and *Colhoun* (DD 301) and treated severely injured men from the *Bush* on April 6 at Okinawa is not mentioned. The dictionary's account of DD 579 *William D. Porter's* sinking on June 10 ends with this sentence: "Miraculously not one man was lost when the ship went down." The *miracle* was four LCS crews who rescued every member of the *Porter* crew after they had sent damage control parties aboard her to help keep her afloat and to salvage her vital records and equipment. No mention is made of LCS crews rescuing survivors of the *Braine* (DD 630) on May 21 by throwing out life rafts, at the same time avoiding being run down by the wildly circling, out-of-control ship. After the *Braine* ran her crazy course, LCS crews put out her raging fires. No mention is made of LCS damage control parties literally keeping the *Aaron Ward* (DM 34) and the *Hugh Hadley* (DD 774) afloat on May 3 and May 11 until they could be towed off by fleet tugs.

This book will correct these and other similar omissions of history and do much more to illustrate what the LCS ships and their crews did in World War II.

Two recent books, Bill Sholin's *The Sacrificial Lambs* and Paul Thurman's *Picket Ships at Okinawa*, describe the battle for Okinawa against the massive kamikaze air raids and enumerate in some detail the severe losses of ships and men in battle. Their authors credit LCSs on the picket stations with rescuing several hundred men from six sinking ships and providing vital assistance to three stricken ships. But as my story will illustrate, this is but a fraction of the support that LCSs provided to stricken destroyer-type vessels on the stations as well as to other ships, large and small, in the Okinawa area. One author, Thurman, does refer to the landing vessels (primarily LCSs, LSMs, and LSM(R)s) that supported the larger picket line ships as "life-saving craft"—"a Godsend."

Even though more than half a century has passed since LCS crews served in World War II, the full story of their actions and achievements has yet to be told. There are partial histories and a relatively brief summary history, which is presented with a number of useful personal accounts. There are several excellent published ship histories, including one written as a novel. There are also several informative videos showing LCSs in action. One major naval historian, Samuel Eliot Morison, has incorporated the combat actions of some of the LCSs into his important history of World War II naval operations.

But there is no reasonably complete history in which the actions of the ships and their crews are illustrated and described in some detail. The purpose of this book is to meet that need.

In my title I am using 'Fighting Amphibs' generically, and I am by no means claiming, or even implying, that LCSs were the only fighting amphibs in World War II. Far from it. From the very beginning of their invaluable service in the war, the crews of every armed amphibious vessel were 'fighting amphibs'. They fought with every bullet and shell of every caliber that they were able to fire. A beautiful example of the amphibs' fighting spirit is the LCT *33* crew's action on their way to Algiers on April 20, 1943: a large German bomber (a Junker 88) had made a bombing run on them and missed. When the bomber started its second run, presumably to finish them off, the LCT gunners shot it down, and it crashed in flames against a nearby mountain. And this happened when amphibious vessels were allowed only minimal armament for their own protection!

It was not until after the invasion of Tarawa in November 1943 that a number of the larger amphibious vessels were converted from troop and tank carriers to combatant vessels that would protect the landing troops and bombard the landing beaches before and during invasions. LCIs were armed with guns, rockets, and mortars, and rockets were installed on LCTs and LSMs.

These combatant amphibious vessels that were fighting amphibs in every sense of the word served valiantly throughout the remainder of the war. Their successes encouraged the Navy to design and build a combatant ship armed with guns and rockets to serve some of the same purposes as the converted ships and to fight alongside them. This new ship was the LCS(L). These ships and the 130 crews that manned them are the subject of this book.

My primary source for this book is the H. Richard Rhame Collection of materials on LCSs and their crews housed in the Operational Archives Branch at the Naval Historical Center at the Navy Yard in Washington. LCS veterans have been contributing to this invaluable collection since 1988.

The material in this collection is extensive in scope and varied in nature. It includes such official documents as war histories of the LCS flotillas, action reports of ships, war diaries, deck logs, official ship histories; and such unofficial writings as articles and personal accounts (some of which were published in the National LCS(L) 1-130 Newsletter and in newspapers), unpublished articles and 'sea stories', informal and personal ship histories, itineraries, and logs; diaries and notebooks of LCS sailors. In writing this book, I have used over a hundred separate items from this wealth of non-published sources, along with 18 letters from LCS veterans.

I have incorporated into my text quotations from four excellent books that are combinations of personal accounts and individual ship histories: Earl Blanton's *Boston to Jacksonville,* John Rooney's *Mighty Midget-USS LCS 82,* Frank Korany's *LCS(L) 14—One of the Mighty Midgets,* and L.E. Guillot's *How Did We Ever Win the War?* I have also incorporated into my text a series of excellent narratives by Richard H. Lewis, who was gunnery officer and executive officer on my ship. I have used Samuel Eliot Morison's *History of U.S. Naval Operations in World War II* and other histories for historical background and for accounts of LCS actions at Iwo Jima and Okinawa in particular. I have also made use of the books listed in my endnotes. When possible I have used accounts written at the time of the action described by the person involved.

I have tried to include descriptions of actions and comments from as many of the 130 ship crews as possible. In the few cases where there is absolutely nothing in the Rhame Collection about a particular ship (in spite of my making a series of appeals for information in the Association Newsletter over a three-year period), I have tried to discover from the accounts of other ships' crews, as well as from division, group, and flotilla reports, what those 'unpublicized ships' were doing. I have not been successful in every instance. To a great extent the amount of information presented here about the ships' and crews' activities depends on how much crew members have written and sent to the Rhame Collection. In this book LCS sailors have written a good bit of their own history.

Notes founds at the end of each chapter provide bibliographical information primarily to acknowledge and express thanks to the scores of people who have contributed to the history. The frequency of some notes' appearances demonstrates how substantial many of the contributions have been. I have also provided a separate bibliography of book-length publications used as sources and references and recommended for further reading.

In the appendix are names of LCS sailors killed in World War II, the LCSs sunk and damaged in action, and the individual LCSs that have received awards. Concerning awards to individuals, when the account I have used has included these, I have put them in the text. Because, however, no official list of awards to individuals exists and querying several thousand officers and men is well nigh impossible, I have not attempted to describe such awards.

I would like to acknowledge: the National LCS(L) 1-130 Association and its director Jeff Jeffers, which publishes the association newsletter and sponsors annual reunions, and without which the invaluable Rhame Collection would not exist; Ray Baumler, pioneer historian of the Association, who provided much useful information as well as constant and helpful encouragement along the way; Mary Louise Clifford, my editor, whose help and timely advice were extremely useful in writing and producing this book; those of my friends and LCS shipmates who have contributed photographs so that this book could be "illustrated"; and my wife Barbara who did extensive typing and retyping of the manuscript and provided constructive criticism of the text and unflagging encouragement from the start.

Abbreviations

AA - Anti-aircraft
AGS - Surveying vessel
AKA - Attack cargo vessel
AM - Minesweeper
APA - Attack transport
APD - Destroyer transport
ASW - Antisubmarine warfare
ARS - Salvage vessel
B-24, B-29 - Medium and heavy
　bombers
CAP - Combat Air Patrol
CV - Aircraft carrier
CVE - Escort carrier
Corsair - Navy-Marine fighter plane
DD - Destroyer
DE - Destroyer escort
DM - Light mine layer
DMS - High speed minesweeper
DUWK - Amphibious truck
GQ - General Quarters (battle-ready
　condition)
LC(FF) - Flotilla flagship
LCI - Landing craft infantry;
　(G),(R),(M),(D) added to LCI
　mean gunboat, rocket, mortar, and
　demolition
LCM - Landing craft, mechanized
LCS - Landing craft support; (L),(S)
　added to LCS mean large, small
LCT - Landing craft tank
LCVP - Landing craft, vehicle and
　personnel
LSD - Landing ship, dock
LSM - Landing ship, medium; (R)
　added to LSM means rocket

LST - Landing ship tank
LVT - Landing vehicle, tracked; (A)
　added to LVT means armored
OOD - Officer of the Deck
P500 - portable pump capable of
　pumping 500 gallons a minute
PA - Transport
PBM & PBY - Navy patrol bombers
PC - Patrol craft
PCE - Patrol craft, escort
PCS - Patrol craft, minesweeper
PGM - Motor gunboat
PT - Motor torpedo boat
R and R - Rest and recreation
SC - Submarine chaser
TU - Task Unit
TG - Task Group
TF - Task Force; (C) before TU, TG,
　or TF means commander (CTF
　51.7)
UDT - Underwater demolition team
YMS - Motor minesweeper

Contents

List of Illustrations

Maps

Chapter 1

The Fighting Amphibs[1]

The genesis of the fighting amphibs that are the subject of this story and whose designation is Landing Craft Support, Large, can be traced back to the November 1943 invasion of Tarawa at which the need to protect the landing troops and to provide greater firepower against enemy defenses ashore became sharply apparent. In this invasion the landing Marines were decimated.

Admiral Richmond K. Turner, Commander of Amphibious Forces, Pacific, called for fire-support protection for the troops moving into the beaches and for much heavier and more sustained pre-invasion bombardments of the landing beaches.

Up until that time none of the amphibious vessels provided adequate gunfire protection for the landing troops. The vessels in service—the tank- and vehicle-carrying Landing Ship Tank (LST), Landing Ship Medium (LSM), and Landing Craft Tank (LCT), and the troop-carrying Landing Craft Infantry (LCI)—were all armed but only minimally so, primarily for their own protection. Smaller vessels, such as Landing Craft Support (Small), a 37-foot support craft armed with machine guns and rockets, accompanied the boat waves into the beach, but could not provide the strong protection needed. Also all pre-invasion beach bombardment was done by larger fleet ships (destroyers, cruisers, and battleships) firing from some distance from the beach because of their deep drafts.

The need to protect landing troops was acknowledged earlier; an experiment was tried in October 1943, one month before Tarawa. At that time two Landing Craft Infantry, which fired only 20mm guns, were armed with three 40mm machine guns in addition to their 20s. These ships participated successfully in an assault on the Treasury Islands, adjacent to Bougainville in the Solomons.

The success of these 'experimental LCI gunboats' and the stimulus of heavy losses at Tarawa led, in January 1944, to the conversion of 24 LCIs to LCI gunboats, designated LCI(G). During the next six months approximately 200 of the over 900 LCIs in service were converted to LCI(G)s and armed with 20mm and 40mm machine guns as well as six racks for launching 4.5-inch rockets.

The successes of these converted LCIs led to the further specialization of a number of LCIs into 36 rocket-launching LCIs, designated LCI(R)s, and a similar number of mortar-firing LCIs, designated LCI(M)s. A relatively small number of LCI(G)s were equipped to cover underwater demolition teams (UDT) and were designated LCI(D)s, for demolition. Although they were never designated as such, a number of LCIs were equipped to serve as firefighting and salvage ships.

Not only did these specialized gunboats with their greatly increased firepower provide the much-needed protection for the landing troops, they contributed substantially to meeting the other need cited by Admiral Turner after Tarawa—for much heavier and more sustained pre-invasion bombardment of the landing beaches. Because of their relative smallness (158 feet long, displacing approximately 390 tons) and their flat bottoms, the gunboats were able to bombard and fire on the beaches at a much closer range than the larger ships with deeper drafts.

The gunboats could fire their shells and rockets from near-vertical trajectories. According to Rear Admiral W. H. P. Blandy, Chief of the Naval Ordinance Department at the time, this was more effective in destroying enemy defenses than the near-horizontal trajectories of shells fired by the larger ships at greater range. As Admiral Blandy pointed out, shells from near horizontal trajectories often did not inflict adequate damage to Pacific atolls and islands just a little above sea level; at times the shells ricocheted off the targets altogether. Shells and rockets fired in near-vertical trajectories, on the other hand, came much closer to producing the effect of bombs being dropped directly on the targets. Admiral Blandy's belief that the use of small, heavily armed flat-bottomed ships could significantly improve the Navy's fire-support of amphibious assaults was confirmed time after time by the successes of the specialized gunboats and the LCSs at invasions and assaults throughout the war in the Pacific.

The specialized LCI gunboats served their country well in the last two years of the war. Their crews performed courageously under fire on a number of occasions. The value of the LCI(G)s has been especially noted by historian Samuel Eliot Morison, a major naval historian: "LCS(G)s proved to be the answer for the fire support of assault troops delivered close to shore . . . the 'Elsie Item Gunboats', as they were nicknamed, proved their worth in every later operation of the Pacific war."[2]

The successes of the specialized LCI gunboats in both supporting invasions and providing effective pre-invasion bombardments led naval and civilian architects and engineers to design and build a new class of large amphibious support ships in the summer of 1944. This ship would incorporate the features of the LCI gunboats and serve some of the same needs.

Up until this time, all the alterations required to make the LCIs into efficient fire-support and beach-bombardment ships had been done with ships whose hulls were designed to carry and land troops. The new design provided for a ship with a basic gunboat structure, allowing ample open deck space for both single and twin gun mounts and their directors and for rocket launchers, as well as for ready and efficient ammunition storage.

This new class of ship was Landing Craft Support whose full designation was Landing Craft Support, Large, Mark 3—USS LCS(L)(3). The USS prefix indicated that it was a commissioned ship of the United States, even though it was designated 'craft'. The designation 'Large' was to differentiate it from the LCS(S) mentioned above.

Since the British, who had designed and built a large number of landing vessels, had two (Mark 1 and Mark 2) models of the LCS, 'Mark 3' was necessary to distinguish the new American model. Those of us who served on them disagreed with the 'C' for Landing 'Craft' Support in the above designation. We thought it should be 'S' for 'ship'. We firmly believed that our vessel was a ship because it had all the features of a ship. It was fully commissioned with a crew of over 70. It was able to go anywhere in the world on its own: 5,500 miles at 12 knots before needing replenishment of any kind. It could not be taken apart in sections (as could the LCT) to be transported on a larger ship.

The LCS, with an LCI hull 158-feet long, was also of ocean-going size. That LCIs were capable ocean-going vessels was established early in 1943 when 24 LCIs crossed the Atlantic Ocean in the dead of winter. They left Little Creek, Virginia, on February 15, stopped in Bermuda, and arrived safely at Gibraltar over a month later on March 23. They ran into cold, snow, fog, and bad weather.[3] But the crews stuck it out, and in effect established a standard for all LCI and LCS sailors to maintain for the rest of the war.

Basically, LCSs were designated 'C' for 'craft' because the 'C' in LCI is for craft, and the LCS has the same hull dimensions and roughly the same displacement (390 tons). Curiously, the principles used in 1944 and 1945 for the classification of landing vessels do not clearly place the LCI/LCS ships in either the 'craft' or the 'ship' category.

According to these principles, as stated in the introduction to the Office of Naval Intelligence publication *Allied Landing Craft and Ships in World War II*,[4] Landing 'Craft' applies to non-oceangoing vessels of less than 150 feet overall, and Landing 'Ship' applies to ocean-going vessels of more than 200 feet. As 158-foot-long ocean-going vessels, LCIs and LCSs were in between 'ship' and 'craft'. Since they did not qualify as ships, they were designated 'craft'.

Naval historian Samuel Eliot Morison, who, like others, objected to calling the LCI a craft, provides us with a historical explanation of why this was done: "It is an anomaly to designate these 158-foot vessels (LCIs) 'C' (for Craft) instead of 'S' for Ship; but originally it was planned to ship them across in sections and assemble them at the theater of operation."[5] For a brief period after the war, LCSs were classified Landing Ship Support, Large, but this was terminated by the 500-ton displacement requirement for all Navy ships (LCSs displaced 390 tons). So even though the LCS was very much a ship in the eyes of its sailors, the Navy could never bring itself to call it that.

The newly designed LCS would incorporate major features of three variations of the specialized LCI gunboats. Its three 40mm guns[6] with directors and four single 20mms gave it the capabilities of the LCI(G). Its ten racks for launching 120 4.5-inch rockets gave the new ship the basic features of an LCI(R). With several stationary and portable water pumps, the ship could produce up to 2,600 gallons of foam and water per minute. Its hoses and attachments gave it the capabilities of the LCI firefighting and salvage ship.

Because shipyards still had LCIs in production, it was decided to use the LCI hull. This 158-foot hull had a flat bottom, which allowed the LCS to beach, and provided it with a shallow draft, allowing the ship, like the LCI, to work and to fire its guns and rockets very close to the shore.

This same flat bottom also meant that, like the LCI, the LCS rode the high seas very roughly. When the ship was underway in a rough sea and its bow rising 15 to 20 feet and then plunging down an equal distance or more, the ship's flat bottom did not cut the water like a knife as do the keeled bottoms of larger ships. It smacked it like a frying pan.

The whole ship shuddered and all the crew braced themselves and held on for dear life. Those below tried to keep from being thrown out of their bunks; those stationed topside were in danger of being pitched overboard. They felt like they were caught in the midst of an unending life-and-death struggle between King Neptune and Mother Nature and neither side could win.

The LCIs' and LCSs' shallow drafts also made survival in typhoons on the high seas difficult for them. When the waves were so big that the ship was forced to run with the storm (keeping the waves at its stern) to survive, the ship became a roller coaster scooting violently down the slope of one wave and up over the next. In the pilot house two helmsmen were constantly spinning the ship's wheel to keep the ship from veering sideways and capsizing in the valleys. In the engine room two men were busy, desperately shifting engines—reducing the props' RPMs when the ship's screws came up in the water, and increasing RPMs when the ship's screws were digging in. On the conn, officers anxiously gave orders and hung on for dear life.

More rapidly perhaps than their counterparts on the larger, more stable seagoing ships, LCS sailors became seasoned seamen, practicing seamanship skills never dreamed of back in the training bases and surviving unforgettable drama never to be repeated again in their lives.

In addition to using the basic LCI hull, engineers and builders utilized the LCI's propulsion machinery of eight six-cylinder diesel engines producing 1600 to 1800 horsepower to give the LCS a sustained cruising speed of 13 knots and a flank speed of 15 to 16. Four of the eight engines (a quad) turned each of the ship's two screws, and because the screws had variable pitch control, the number of engines turning the screws could be varied from one to four. Also the engines never had to be reversed.

Two more diesel engines, similar to those used for main propulsion, generated electrical power for the ship. The propulsion system provided for great flexibility in operation because one, two, three, or four engines per quad could be engaged at different pitches for each screw. The ship's engineering department had the formidable challenge of keeping 10 six-cylinder engines in good running condition, sometimes for sustained periods. In addition to these 10 engines, there were five gasoline engines, three of them six-cylinder, used for fire pumps and raising the anchor, and two main electric generators as well as electric motors for ventilation and other purposes and several smaller fire pumps.

In practically every other way than using the LCI hull and engines, the LCS had new and different arrangements, both internally and externally. Instead of large troop compartments occupying most of the main deck, there was a relatively small deck house with a circular pilot house and conning tower (open bridge) above it. Aft of the pilot house on top of the deck house was a small open signal deck. The deck house contained a radio room, the ship's galley, the officer's and men's heads, and storage space for ammunition/electrical equipment.

All other living accommodations, along with propulsion and generating machinery and storage spaces—in fact, practically everything 'inside' on the whole ship—was on the first platform at the waterline. Here everything was compact to the Nth degree with every cubic inch utilized and without portholes, and with ventilation that was barely minimal in the tropical Philippines.

A crew of 71 crowded the new LCSs. A large crew was required to operate all the ship's guns and rocket launchers and to operate and maintain a moderately complicated vessel. Most ships of comparable size, such as the standard LCI, had crews of approximately 25 men with ample accommodations.

Berthing and eating spaces on the LCS totaled 1,430 square feet for the crew of six officers and 65 men. This averages out to approximately 20 square feet per person, which is not very much when you figure that the average person lying flat with his arms close by his side occupies at least 15 square feet. And when you compare 20 square feet with the 400 square feet that each member in a family of four has in a small home of 1,600 square feet today, you get a feel for how tight LCS living quarters were.

The enlisted men slept three and four deep in three compartments on metal-frame bunks of stretched canvas with thin pads for mattresses. They were lucky if the shipmate above them did not sag down and keep them from turning over to sleep on their sides. There was no privacy for the men anywhere on the ship. The officers fared somewhat better, but their privacy too was almost nonexistent. They had four double bunks with standard mattresses in two tiny staterooms. All officers had roommates; even the captain shared his cabin with two or three other officers.

While officers had a steward's mate to attend them in their tiny wardroom, eating for the men was a challenging event even in calm weather or tied to the dock. Each man had to pick up his loaded tray at the galley dutch door on the main deck and then make his way down a ladder (Navy term for very steep metal stairs) to the mess hall that could seat, on crowded benches, only about a third of the men at a time. Part of the mess hall's bulkheads were 'decorated' with loaded 20mm gun magazines.

After his repast, each man made his way back up the ladder to the outside deck aft of the deck house, where he deposited his tray's leavings in a GI can. It does not take much imagination to picture this event in even slightly rough weather or when the ship's bow was rising and falling 20 feet in heavy seas.

Sanitary facilities on the ship were basically adequate but downright primitive in certain areas. One such area was the men's head, a popular place for rolling the dice in the wee hours of the night. Instead of flush toilets for defecation, the men were provided with wooden seats over a metal trough through which sea water flowed. A favorite prank on some of the ships was to set afire a small raft of crumpled paper and sail it down an occupied trough. Needless to say, the hapless victims emerged with fire in their eyes.

Another primitive facility was the one and only clothes washing machine for the 71 crew members. Clothes drying had to be done on lines on the aft deck and fantail, which added immensely to the amount of clutter already crowding the aft deck. Some men washed their clothes by putting them overboard on lines to be dragged along behind the ship. The results of these operations were generally satisfactory, but the owners often discovered that their sea-washed dungarees came back stiff as a board.

Those of us who served on LCSs became aware of the cramped living quarters very abruptly. We discovered sooner than we wanted that meeting a shipmate almost anywhere inside the ship required that both persons give way and momentarily stand aside. We were pleased to have a head just for the officers, but it was so tiny that you practically stood in one place to shower and to shave. Deck space was so limited in the sleeping quarters, both enlisted and officer, that the bunk occupants could not all stand up at the same time. Even our larger compartments, such as the enlisted men's mess hall, were small and cramped. The officers ward room was so tiny that not over three of the six officers it seated at the table could stand in it at one time. There simply was not enough deck space inside the ship.

As I have pointed out above, the crews quarters were cramped because the ship was designed for supporting invasions and bombarding the beaches, not for the comfort of the crew. So much open main deck space was needed in the new gunboat for guns, gun tubs, ready boxes, rocket launchers, directors, firefighting equipment, and other gear that crew accommodation space was necessarily limited. It would have been very helpful, however, to have a somewhat larger deck house so that the galley and mess hall could be on the same level to facilitate the crew's eating.

After observing that the LCIs at Solomons were steered by a hand crank (reminding me of the trolley cars back in Richmond), I was pleased that our ship had a wheel for steering. To me, having to steer with a crank seemed to allow the helmsman absolutely no leeway or freedom when making turns. As it turned out later, however, a number of LCSs, including ours, had considerable trouble with their steering apparatus—cables would break or get twisted and motors would fail so that the steering would have to be done using radio communication by two men in the uncomfortable after steering compartment directly over the screws and rudders. Was the steering wheel a luxury that we could not afford?

When LCSs were designed and built, it was not envisioned that they would serve extensively on the high seas and that a number of them would support larger ships fighting the kamikaze planes off Okinawa and would need radar directed fire control for their guns. (As it turned out, their serving as support for ships off Okinawa was the result of a last-minute decision by Admiral Richard K. Turner.) Nor was it envisioned that they would desperately need smaller 50-caliber machine guns that would fire into the water at suicide boats and swimmers attacking them. Ironically LCSs were amphibious vessels built with flat bottoms to provide close-in support for invasions, but they had to go thousands of miles on the high seas to get to the invasions. In the process they were found to be useful in a number of situations. That LCSs were sometimes inadequately equipped for what they were called on to do should not be blamed on American industry. By and large American industry did wonders for those of us at the front in World War II. I am sure that we could not have won without them.

While the LCS was not quite as crowded topside as it was 'inside', its main deck had very little open space anywhere. In addition to the seven primary (40mm) and secondary (20mm) guns and the rockets, there was, as mentioned above, the necessary supportive gear for maintaining them and firing them. At the bow on some of the ships was a manifold for seven fire hose outlets for fighting fires.

On the small signal deck were two large flagbags. Just behind the tower that houses the pilot house and conn (open bridge) above it was the ship's mast with signal lights, flag halyards, and radar antenna (in 1945, still an official secret; all photographs were censored when the ship was built) and flag halyards. Hanging on either side of the deck house were life rafts, fire hoses and nozzles and attachments, stretchers, and other safety appliances. On the front of the conning tower was a director's tub for the forward 40mm twin gun. Along both

The LCS—a full topside view. Courtesy of Ray Baumler.

sides of the deck were bitts and chocks for eight manila lines, four on each side, for securing the ship to the dock.

On the deck on either side of the deck house were two portable gasoline fire pumps (P500s); further aft were two stationary Hale fire pumps, powered by six-cylinder Chrysler Marine engines. In the center of the deck a hatch led down to the engine room with the ship's 12-foot wherry (also called a dinghy) lashed to it. Above the hatch was the elevated director's tub for the aft twin 40.

Also in the after deck area were the ship's anchor cable and an engine for raising the large stern anchor (one of the few genuinely amphibious features of the ship), tanks of gasoline, clothes lines in season, a wooden potato locker, and at the very stern, the engineer officer's nightmare—the fog generator. Curiously, the most valuable object on the deck of LCS *15* when it was sunk at Okinawa was the wooden potato locker: it kept a number of the crew members afloat in the water until they were rescued.

The ship's guns were placed strategically. Two of the three primary (40mm) guns were in line forward of the conning tower with the second gun one level higher than the first. The third gun on the fantail had close to a 330-degree range. The four 20mm guns were two to each side, one set on either side of the conning tower, and the second set just forward of the aft primary gun.

This arrangement allowed at least five of the seven primary and secondary guns to be fired broadside at the beach after the rockets had been launched forward in pre-invasion bombardments. Also, in anti-aircraft fire at least four of the guns could quickly be brought to bear on passing and incoming planes. While on radar picket patrol against kamikaze planes at Okinawa, LCS captains found that one of the best defenses was to maneuver their ships so as to bring all guns possible to bear on the enemy planes before they could get into their suicide dives.

Fifty-caliber machine guns were installed on most of the new LCSs by individual ships' crews at stopover points between San Diego and the Philippines and Okinawa. The need was for guns that could be depressed to fire into the water. Ships in the forward areas had learned the hard way that they could not depress their 20 and 40mm guns low enough to fire on suicide boats ('skunks') and suicide swimmers attacking them.

Ships' crews obtained these guns from Navy, Army, and even Army Air Corps installations, sometimes by 'midnight requisitions'. Most ships utilized from four to six of these guns and found them useful in a number of ways, such as in the demolition of floating mines. One ship found them so useful that its crew installed an even dozen, giving them tremendous 'small fire' firepower and an imposing appearance.

Most of the men assigned to serve on LCSs found their shipboard experience a unique one. In the first place, they had never been on a ship or a boat where, while standing on the ship's side, a man was just five or six feet above the water. On a ferryboat or a yacht, he might be as close as three or four feet to the water over the side, but there would always be a short steel or wooden wall or partition between him and the water. And he would not be riding the ferry or yacht for weeks at a time on the high seas halfway around the world.

In the second place, because they were so open and close to the water, LCSs took water and spray on their decks in even moderately rough seas. Because of this, the ship was wet with standing water in places much of its time at sea.

Men who left their compartment ventilators even partially open sometimes found themselves 'drowned out' by one or two waves over the deck.

Finally, the ship took the sea so roughly that some men became seasick as soon as their ship put to sea and, if the seas continued rough, stayed sick for several days, unable to stand watch or do their work, much to the chagrin of the rest of the crew. And, as is pointed out above, the men's shipboard eating accommodations were not conducive to getting over seasickness quickly.

Although the LCS's primary mission in invasions was to neutralize enemy shore defenses and support and protect landing troops by massive gun and rocket fire, their participation in landing operations was by no means limited to this. Before invasions, LCSs protected minesweepers and demolished mines. They also protected underwater demolition teams and hydrographic and survey reconnaissance parties. During an invasion and afterward, LCSs put out dangerous fires on invasion ships and transports and on the beach, salvaged damaged and adrift landing craft, and provided rocket and gunfire to the beach to support the troops ashore.

LCSs also served in ways not directly related to amphibious operations: they served on patrols of various kinds; they escorted ships and provided them with anti-aircraft protection; they served as screens and generated fog (smoke) to cover larger ships; they guided ships through dangerous waters. After the surrender they demolished hundreds of mines in waters around Japan, Formosa, Korea, and China. On radar picket patrol at Okinawa LCSs destroyed enemy suicide planes, aided stricken and sinking ships by putting out fires, providing them with damage control parties, treating their wounded and dying, and rescuing hundreds of men from the water and the ships.

Taking into account what the LCSs did on radar picket patrol at Okinawa and their other non-amphibious activities, we can see that a good number of their actions were not directly related to amphibious operations. Even though they were technically amphibious ships, they were actually much more.

Because of their widespread activity in their relatively short career, LCSs acquired nicknames, some from known sources and some unknown. Admiral Richmond K. Turner in a May 13 congratulatory message to LCSs at Okinawa called them " . . . our Mighty Midgets."

Tokyo Rose, the Japanese radio spokeswoman who kept telling those of us at Okinawa that we would die, called LCSs "Miniature Destroyers." Other nicknames were "Vest-Pocket Battleships," "Spitkits," "Small Boys," and

"Liberty Boats." Destroyer sailors on radar picket patrol at Okinawa called LCSs "Angels of Mercy" and "Pall Bearers."

The first LCS, appropriately *Number One*, was commissioned in June 1944. The last, the 130th ship, inappropriately numbered *78* (because the different builders had different sets of numbers), was commissioned in the following March 1945—almost exactly nine months after *One*. Because it took just 30 days to build, the LCS was called 'The Thirty-Day Wonder'.

LCS *One* was designed and built by George Lawley and Sons Corporation of Boston, who also built LCSs *Two* through *25* and *109* through *130*—a total of 47 ships. The other ships were built in Portland, Oregon—52 of them (numbers *26* through *47* and *79* through *108*) by the Commercial Iron Works, and 31 ships (numbers *48* through *78*) by the Albina Engineering and Machine Works.

Production was slow for the first three months (June, July, August), when only 12 ships were commissioned. Beginning in September, between 20 and 23 were commissioned each month through December. Averages for January, February, and March 1945 were 10 ships per month with production ending in March. The total production for the nine-month period averaged out to one new LCS every other day!

Endnotes

[1] The best single source for information about the LCS(L) ship and its history is Raymond A. Baumler's *Ten Thousand Men and One Hundred Thirty "Mighty Midget" Ships—The USS LCS(L) in World War II* (Rockville, Md, 1991), to which I am indebted for information in this chapter.

[2] *History of United States Naval Operations in World War II*, (Boston: Little Brown, 1953), Vol. 8, 295.

[3] Ibid., Vol. 2, 271-272.

[4] Annapolis: Naval Institute Press, 1944.

[5] Ibid., 269.

[6] In practice only 35 of the 130 ships had three director-controlled twin 40mm guns. A larger number, 65, had, along with two director-controlled twins, a single 40mm, not director-controlled, on the bow. Thirty ships, primarily the ones that served in the Philippines and Borneo, had a 3-inch 50 gun on the bow.

Chapter 2

The Crews and the Training

In the months while the LCSs were being built from mid-1944 to early 1945, most of the men who would man them were being trained in centers and institutions throughout the United States. Others who would join the initial LCS crews were officers and enlisted men serving on ships and bases in the fleet and the amphibious forces. A number of the new LCS captains had served as LCI captains.

Men who would serve as officers on the 130 ships came from different sources. Older (25-35) college graduates, many with experience in the world, would come out of indoctrination schools (such as the one at the University of Arizona) to serve on LCSs as captains and executive officers and in other officer positions. Somewhat younger officers (20-24) who would serve in all officer positions came out of college and university Navy Reserve Officer Training programs (such as the one at the University of North Carolina). The majority of the officers who would serve as engineer, communications, and gunnery officers, and as first lieutenants (heads of deck departments) as well as captains and executive officers, would come directly out of four-month programs in midshipmen's schools. These schools were located at Plattsburg, New York, and such universities as Columbia, Cornell, and Notre Dame.

A number of these men had been in one of two Navy college programs: V-7, which allowed them to finish college before attending midshipmen's school, or V-12, which provided them with college courses in a Navy-oriented program (a curious combination of college and a somewhat refined version of boot camp) before attending midshipmen's school. A number of men attending midshipmen's schools came directly from the enlisted ranks of the fleet.

One important source of engineer officers, in addition to those coming out of midshipmen's schools, were former chief machinist's mates and motor machinist's mates who had been commissioned ensigns. These 'mustangs' were invaluable members of LCS crews.

Another source of officers, specifically for LCS captains, was probably unique in the amphibious forces and possibly in the Navy as well. While they were finishing their final year, June 1944 Naval Academy graduates were offered instant command of an LCS and a spot promotion from ensign to lieutenant by the Navy Bureau of Personnel. Fifteen academy men took the Navy up on this offer and became skippers of LCSs.

My training and education to become a naval reserve officer followed the pattern of the majority of the men who would serve as officers on the LCSs. After completing two years of college, I went on active duty in the Navy V-12 program at the University of Richmond as an apprentice seaman trainee. We did not wear boots, but much of our training was similar to that in the large boot camps providing basic training for enlisted men. We were also college students, however, living in a pleasant atmosphere on a beautiful college campus.

We were formed into platoons and companies, had frequent assemblies for receiving orders and for lectures on conduct and leadership, marched everywhere we went on the campus, singing and counting cadence much of the time, had calisthenics every morning and frequent physical fitness tests, ran through obstacle courses, and had white-glove inspections at least one a week. We were housed in two college dormitories, four of us to a double room, and our fellow V-12ers were from all over the United States. I was from nearby Maryland but two of my roommates were from Iowa and North Dakota.

On top of this busy schedule we took a full load of college courses—as I recall, five at a time—taught by University faculty members. Anyone who failed one or more courses was 'bilged out' and became a seaman in the enlisted ranks. Those of us who were prospective deck officers were, with some exceptions, allowed some choice in the courses we took. The duration of our stay depended on how much college we had had previously. I found the V-12 program worthwhile. We lived according to a set routine and we learned to follow orders, and on occasion, to give them. We also received additional college education which the Navy obviously wanted its reserve officers to have, even in wartime.

After two semesters in the Richmond V-12 program I was sent to the New York Naval Reserve Midshipman's School at Columbia University. There I spent the first month in a preliminary approval program and three months in midshipmen's school. The term '90-Day Wonder' is applied, often derisively, to graduates of this program and other programs like it. I have, however, always taken at least a little pride in being pointed out as such a 'Wonder'. After all, the great majority of naval officers in World War II were 'Wonders' and they served their country well. One very distinctive advantage of the midshipmen's school program, at least at Columbia, was the presence as trainees of a number of petty officers from the fleet. These young men had no resentment whatsoever toward those of us who had not yet seen combat action, and we V-12 college kids benefitted immeasurably from just listening to and being around these young 'Old Salts'.

In the school everyone took courses in naval administration, navigation, seamanship, gunnery, and recognition training, which were all generally well taught, but not always with our practical application of the material in mind. This was true of naval administration, navigation, and gunnery. Damage control and recognition training (of ships and aircraft, friendly and enemy) did deal clearly with application. Seamanship, which touched on a multitude of areas, was generally usefully informative, but some lessons were quaintly traditional and old fashioned (we practiced tying dozens of knots that we could never possibly use).

In one of our seamanship classes our officer instructor informed us that the CIC (Combat Information Center) was in a particular place in a battleship. One of our classmates, a former fleet man, disagreed. The instructor then said that he was right because he saw the CIC in that place when he had luncheon on the *Texas*. From then on that instructor was known by members of our class as 'Luncheon on the *Texas*'.

The strict military routine that we 'middies' were required to follow was useful as far as instilling discipline was concerned. Our company, in which all of us in it did everything together— eat, take classes, etc.—marched by the hour it seemed, on and off 116th Street in front the statue of Alma Mater sitting benignly in front of Low Library. As a company we performed commendably in weekly reviews. For watch training purposes, the school authorities pretended that our dormitory, Johnson Hall, that had been used as a girls' dorm before the Navy took it over, was a ship and that the entrance lobby on the ground floor was the quarterdeck. Here stood the sometimes very tense Midshipman Officer of the Deck with his messenger and other attendants of the watch. On the fifteen or so floors (decks) above, Junior officers of the Deck, Quartermasters, and other watch standers were stationed.

All of this was good basic training for us midshipmen. Every midshipman was at one time an OOD, a JOOD, a messenger, etc., for at least one watch and sometimes several. But the end purpose of it seemed to be to train us to be very efficient and conscientious juniors officers on a large ship. At times it seemed that ancient naval tradition ruled the day: even the language of the Eight o'Clock (PM) report by the OOD to Captain John K. Richards, Commanding Officer of the School, was quaintly archaic: "Sir, it is eight o'clock, the galley fires are out and the prisoners are secured in the brig." If he accepted the report, the captain would respond, "Very well, make it so." Occasionally, however, the good captain would inject a shot of reality into the situation and put that OOD on report if the stoves in the kitchen were not turned off.

As part of the program, midshipmen did get to go out on the East River and Long Island Sound on yard patrol boats, known as Yippes (YPs), where the potential for learning something about the operation of a small combatant ship existed. When my classes went out, however, there was no supervision or instruction of any kind and we all enjoyed the boat ride, but learned little or nothing.

In spite of these weak spots in the program, I thought that my midshipman training was worthwhile. I was impressed by the caliber of the young men in the program, the college kids as well as the men from the fleet. I did think, however, that a few of the college kids were somewhat too immature to be naval officers.

The majority of the enlisted men who would man the LCSs were young (17-20), and a large number were new to the Navy and to the wider world as well. Many of them came directly from boot training at the large naval training centers at Great Lakes, Illinois, Sampson, New York, and Bainbridge, Maryland. A number of men came from the numerous Navy specialists schools—radio schools at Bedford Springs, Pennsylvania, and Camp Bradford, Virginia; signal schools at the University of Chicago, Illinois; quartermaster school at San Diego, California; and gunner's mates schools at Farragut, Idaho, and Newport, Rhode Island.

Sailors from the fleet were an important source of enlisted men—primarily from the amphibious forces, with rates ranging from third class petty officer to chief. A number of these men had three or more years of service.

Approximately half of the initial 65 enlisted men in each LCS crew were rated as third class petty officers and above. The remainder were seaman and firemen, a number of whom would earn at least one promotion while on the ship. There were 15 different ratings for petty officers to be filled: boatswain's mate and coxswain; gunner's mate and fire controlman; quartermaster, signalman, radioman, radar man, and radio technician; motor machinist's mate and electrician's mate; ship's cook and steward's mate; pharmacist's mate; and storekeeper.

Although ships were not allotted a yeoman, a number of ships had them to do the heavy amount of paper work required. On my ship and a number of others, pharmacist's mates served as yeomen. Usually if a ship had a chief petty officer, he was either a boatswain or a motor machinist.

In assigning men to ships' crews, some attempt was made to provide every ship with at least a few men who had already served at sea so that the crew would not be made up entirely of landlubbers. On my ship the 'few' was a very few—not over 3 at most out of a crew of 71. Although most of the men were young, a number of men were in their upper 20s, 30s, and even mid-40s—perhaps as many as 15 to 20 in most crews. These men had a generally stabilizing effect on the younger, and sometimes more exuberant, crew members. On my ship these older men were worth their weight in gold. They made good sailors on a small, crowded ship.

The officers and men in the crews were from literally all over the United States; they included Catholics, Protestants, Hispanics, and others. The only group of American citizens that was officially limited in number on the ship was the Afro-American. Because segregation was still in effect at the beginning of the war, only one Afro-American was assigned, as a steward's mate, to each ship.

A survey of the geographical background of my ship's crew reveals interesting demographics: of the ship's six officers, one was from New England (Massachusetts), one from the Mid-Atlantic area (Maryland), two from the Midwest (Minnesota and Iowa), and two from the Far West (California and Washington). Of the 65 men, 26 were from the South (this is perhaps a little high; other crews would be higher in other areas), 8 from New England, 10 from the Northeast (New York, Pennsylvania, New Jersey), 16 from the Midwest, and 5 from the Far West (California).

One advantage that individual officers and men had when they joined the ships' crews was that most of them had trained and lived with men from other parts of the country for at least one basic period (basic boot training); a number had done so twice (in boot camp and at specialists schools); many officers trained twice, in the V-12 program (which took place in colleges and universities throughout the United States) and in midshipmen's school.

This meant that most of the 71 crew members had acquired a degree of tolerance toward their fellows that allowed them to work and live together in 1,430 square feet of living space in a highly crowded sea-going gunboat. This did not guarantee perfect harmony on every ship, but it probably helped establish a workable life style in cramped quarters.

Officers and men were assigned to prospective ships' crews soon after arrival for duty at the base at Solomons, Maryland. Five of the 6 ship's officers and 41 of the enlisted men were assigned first and immediately began training both individually and as a crew. After a few weeks these prospective crew members were joined by their gunnery officer and 24 men who had been undergoing six weeks of intensive gunnery training at Fort Pierce, Florida. The 6 officers and 65 men trained together as a crew for the rest of their time at Solomons.

Except for the LCS gunnery crews, who came from very primitive living and working conditions at Fort Pierce, practically everyone reporting for duty at Solomons experienced a distinct culture shock that took him from the usually well organized and amply supported traditional Navy and placed him abruptly in the very earthy real world of the amphibs.

As a brand new ensign who had just completed midshipmen's school at Columbia University and received his commission in the Cathedral of Saint John the Divine, I went from the refined and somewhat artificial world of midshipmen's school to the muddy and noisy Solomons base. My first officer's quarters was an upper bunk in a very noisy large barracks room that quartered at least 60 other new ensigns. A number of these new officers and 'gentlemen by an act of Congress' were celebrating their freedom from 24-hour surveillance by being as raucous and noisy as possible.

My first on-base liberty the next Sunday afternoon found me drinking beer and swatting away flies and mosquitoes in the steamy, sultry atmosphere of the Solomons officers' picnic ground. While making the best of this 'recreation', I was surprised by a Lieutenant Commander (an almost godlike figure in a new ensign's eyes) who came running into our loose group of relaxing officers exclaiming that he had solved his problem with his crew.

The officer then pointed to an LCVP out in the bay in which one enlisted man was beating and bloodying another one with his fists, evidently with official sanction and blessing. After having listened at Columbia to lectures on naval justice and the rights of the accused to a fair and well-conducted courts martial trial, I could hardly believe what I was seeing and hearing.

John Rooney, LCS *82* radioman, shared his reaction on reporting to Solomons, and summed up the Solomons experience: "Solomons sat at the mouth of the Patuxent River along Chesapeake Bay's western shore—sultry, mosquito ridden, and swampy in summer—a sort of down-home Guadalcanal without the Japs in the palm trees. It was a world removed from the country-club life I had enjoyed at naval radio school for six months at the old Bedford resort hotel: delicious meals in a grand dining room, beds made for us daily, no watch details, tennis courts, swimming pools, and regular liberty in town.

"Solomons jolted me right into the saltwater Navy and back into the war. All day long we were on the move. We ran over obstacle courses, swung hand-over-hand on overhead ladders, climbed over 20-foot cargo nets, learned how to handle small arms, fought gasoline, oil, and electrical fires, swam under burning oil slicks, and Lord knows what I've mercifully forgotten.

"It had been a rough grind, but necessary for most of us, and it didn't hurt anybody who had just been sitting on his can for six months sorting out dits and dahs. We came away from Solomons tougher and smarter then when we went in—better able to man a ship, handle trouble and survive."[1]

If living and working conditions were primitive to the hundreds of trainees at Solomons, they were even worse for the ships' gunnery crews training at Fort Pierce. There the men lived in tents in a jungle-like world—more like Guadalcanal than even Solomons. They worked in sand that constantly filled their shoes. A number of them wore sandboots, and were surprised to discover that sandboots were not part of the uniform at Solomons. They fought mosquitoes and spiders and sandflies in their hair. At one point men from one LCS crew were mustered out to dig trenches to let salt water into the nearby ponds to kill the swarming insects.

In spite of these unpleasant conditions, the physical indoctrination and the gunnery training the crews received were intensive and useful. The prospective gunners gained confidence and the ability to work as teams. The instruction was thorough and frighteningly realistic. Richard Lewis, our ship's gunnery officer, reported: "At the beginning of a class on booby traps, fuses, and firing mechanisms, a description of typical booby traps was given and we were warned never to pick one up or get close to investigate such an object. They were usually small mechanisms made in curious shapes.

"The lesson went on for another 45 minutes, covering the other subjects. Then came a break, so we could go out of the raised wooden cabin in which the class was held and lounge around for a few minutes before the next class. As I walked back along the side of the building, just under the edge I saw what looked like a plastic object almost in the shape of a manikin, so I stooped to pick it up. As I did so, I suddenly realized there was something strange, and instantly threw it under the house as I picked it up.

"Sure enough, about the time it hit the ground, it exploded, briskly, but not very powerfully—perhaps enough to blow open a hand or burn a face. During the class they had been planted; by the end of the class we'd more or less forgotten. No one had warned us that it would be done! It was a very instructive trap; and was truly a booby. Thank God, in preparing them, a delay factor had been built into the detonation."[2]

Gunnery training for LCS crews was not limited to the intensive six-week program at Fort Pierce. It also took place in the lower Chesapeake Bay on the

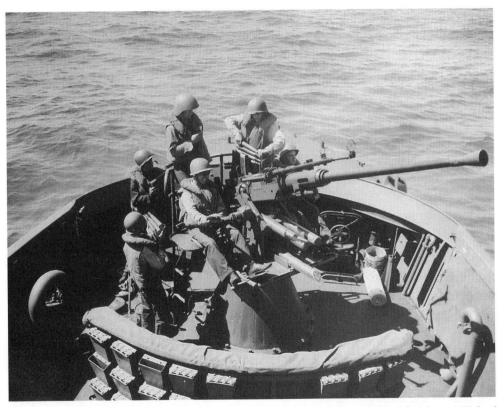

The single 40mm gun manned by its six-man crew and ready to fire. Half of the ships (65) had this gun on the bow. Thirty-five ships had a twin 40mm bow gun and 30 ships had a 3"50 gun on the bow. Courtesy of Charles Thomas.

The twin 40mm gun with its seven-man crew at the ready. One of these guns was located just forward of the pilot house, and the other was centered on the open after-deck or fantail. Courtesy of Charles Thomas

old battleship *Wyoming*, which provided firing training using shipboard guns of all calibers. It took place as well at the extensive gunnery training facilities at Solomons and off Little Creek, Virginia, on brief LCI training cruises out of Solomons.

On one of these cruises I was one of a group of LCS officer trainees who, as eye-witnesses to a near accident, learned more about the care needed in handling deck towing equipment than they could ever learn from a how-to-do-it demonstration. Richard Lewis, *85* gunnery officer, tells how close he came to being the accident victim: "Several of the LCI crew now stood on the fantail at the rear of the stern well-deck ready to cast the target sled into the water, and a group of us trainee officers were gathered a little further back by the anchor windless.

"A line had been led out to the sled, with extra loose coils on deck near the stern, and the rest of the line had been passed over the windless in two turns, and a larger pile of the rope lay coiled on deck next to the windless, where we were standing. When the target sled was tossed overboard, a somewhat bulky and surprisingly heavy assemblage, the nearby coil started paying out fast, and we were in danger of losing the target.

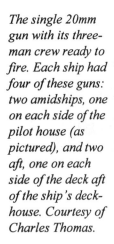

The single 20mm gun with its three-man crew ready to fire. Each ship had four of these guns: two amidships, one on each side of the pilot house (as pictured), and two aft, one on each side of the deck aft of the ship's deck-house. Courtesy of Charles Thomas.

"I leapt forward, tried for a second to pull on the rope, but also for a second got my leg ensnared by the snaking rope and instantly shook it free, let go, and stepped back, and I was pulled back by my fellow trainees. Had I not the good luck to be instantly freed of the ensnaring rope, it would have whirled me twice around the windless hub and pulled me up against the relatively small fairing guide; my head would have been smashed several times against steel, and my leg might have been ripped from my torso.

"Instead of skimming, the leading edge of the sled had partially submerged, thus creating tremendous resistance against the pulling power of the ship, all concentrated on the rope. I soon realized how fortunate I had been, and how naive my good intentions were in the face of my lack of experience in dealing with that kind of situation."[3]

Later in the training program at Solomons LCS gunnery crews fired guns on the training LCIs making firing runs on Bloodsworth Island across the bay. A few crews were lucky enough to participate in firing runs on one of the few training LCSs at the base. Because there were so few of them, these ships were objects of tremendous curiosity. Gunnery crews who made firing runs on a training LCS learned how to launch the ship's 4.5-inch rockets as well as to fire the guns.

Although nothing seemed out of the ordinary to those of us present at the time, a meeting I attended one afternoon at the Solomons base turned out to be a special occasion. It was during one of those frequent times when individual officers and men assigned to prospective crews were being introduced to their shipmates. This occasion was special because several of the fifteen June 1944 Naval Academy graduates, who had chosen to be LCS captains, were being introduced to the officers and men assigned to their crews.

Before the introductions were made, and while the Academy captains and the other officers (almost all naval reservists) were still standing in two separate groups, I heard one of the Academy captains began to complain vociferously to his fellows and to the world at large about the officers they would have to go to sea with. He disliked the very idea of serving with the officers assigned to the crews and he resented the fact that he had to do so.

After this singular outburst, to which no one either assented or dissented, introductions were made, officers and men got acquainted with their designated shipmates, and the Naval Academy captains took charge of their prospective crews. At the time I felt lucky that I would not have the complaining Academy officer as my captain. As will be demonstrated in the chapters that follow, however, this combination of Annapolis skippers and reservist crews for 15 ships worked out very well. Several of these ships earned citations, including the ship skippered by the officer who had condemned the officers present most strenuously.

Training appropriate for LCS crew members as individuals and as crews at Solomons was extensive. Areas in which the officers and men were trained included, in addition to gunnery, fighting fires of all kinds and operating firefighting equipment; damage control (trainees not able to control leaking in a mock-up ship's compartment might well find water rising over their heads); aircraft recognition, first aid, radio voice procedure, navigation, diesel engine maintenance; operation of fog generators, electrical generators, fresh water distillers, the gyro compass, refrigeration equipment; radar training, seamanship for amphibious vessels, and anchor windless operation.

The base at Solomons had been training LCT and LCI crews (including British LCI crews) for two years before the arrival of LCS trainees in the summer of 1944. As a result, Solomons was well equipped to train LCS crews. LCS crews were required, however, to participate in one exercise that was a carryover from LCI training. This was the practice beaching of their ship to discharge troops in a landing operation—an action LCSs would not be required to do.

Even so, LCS captains and crew members practiced the beaching of LCIs at Virginia Beach and learned the hard way always to let go the stern anchor on the way into the beach, or have your ship hard stuck or even high and dry on the shore. In the long run, LCS captains and crews probably did learn something useful about shiphandling and anchoring from this exercise.

Near the end of the program at Solomons, LCS crews were taken on an 'ocean cruise' in an LCI around the Del-Mar-Va Peninsula. They sailed down the Chesapeake Bay from Solomons, out through the Virginia capes into the Atlantic Ocean, up along the Virginia, Maryland, and Delaware coasts (approximately 150 miles taking 12 hours or more), into the Chesapeake and Delaware Canal, where they would spend the night, and then down the bay back to Solomons.

The LCI was usually filled to capacity with three LCS crews of approximately 213 men; conditions were crowded. Although the trainees were passengers and observers and not the ship's crew, they usually got more than a taste of what sailing on a relatively small amphibious ship in the open sea was like. This was particularly true on the northbound leg of cruises made in August and September, which every Eastern Shoreman knows is the northeaster season.

A number of LCS crew members learned very quickly how roughly LCIs rode while bucking a northeast wind and sea for 14 to 16 hours off the Del-Mar-Va coast. Eating supper aboard the first night out in the ocean was for most of the passengers a real challenge. When our *85* crew made its cruise, conditions were particularly stormy. At one point one of our seamen trainees, who was obviously frightened, said to me, "Sir, do you think she [the ship] will hold together?" With only limited success I tried to reassure him that there was no real danger, that LCSs were built to survive storms at sea, albeit in the most uncomfortable way possible.

John Rooney, *82* radioman, described his crew's experience on their first ocean cruise: "The little LCI pitched and rolled heavily. The crew went into a kind of self-preservation mode, and much of what we might have been learning about our shipboard duties was swept away by the storm. In the radioroom I tried copying some broadcast code from Norfolk, but the sturdy old Royal portable wouldn't space or carriage-return unless I pulled and pushed the carriage along, typing with the other hand, or held the machine nearly level against the wide rolls of the ship. We were all preoccupied holding our own against that angry sea.

"Many of the fledgling crew were miserably sick, some unable to function at all. The officers up in the conning tower, swinging in high, wide arcs, were filling the buckets passed to them. For most of us landlubbers it was a frightening introduction to sea life."[4]

On completion of their training, LCS crews were transported in Navy buses the relatively short distance from Solomons to Union Station in Washington. There they caught trains either to Boston, Massachusetts, or Portland, Oregon, where their ships were being built. The buses arrived at the station around six or seven in the evening; the departing trains left around midnight. Each captain and executive officer was challenged with his first big command decision—whether to grant liberty to the crew, many of whom had not had a real liberty in even a fairly large city for months.

Before the night was over every captain who granted liberty, and most did, wished he had not. Beginning around 11:40, a number of men came staggering back—singing, dancing, fighting, jumping on each other, hollering, throwing their hats in all directions, and generally being loud and obnoxious. Fortunately, not all of the liberty-goers were drunk. It just seemed that way.

What do you do with drunken sailors who have to be in assigned berths and seats on the lined-up train cars in less than an hour? Ships' officers and senior petty officers, who had not realized that they became shore patrolmen even before their ships were commissioned, turned to and herded and pushed and pulled the men into at least the right train, if not the right car, berth, or seat.

Ships' crews going to Boston to man LCSs built in nearby Neponset had a fairly short, direct trip on the train. In some instances, a few crew members reported to the shipyard three weeks ahead of the whole crew to serve on temporary duty connected with fitting out the ship before commissioning.

Although all crews going to Portland went by train, the circumstances of their trips varied considerably. The shortest trips took 4 days, the longest 8 and even 10. Some crews went on primitive troop trains; luckier ones had old Pullman cars with comfortable upper and lower berths. No crew or crews rated a train to themselves, and all crews traveled over at least two different railroads before reaching the West Coast.

In mid-October of 1944, our crew traveled with one other crew in five old Pullman cars from Washington to Memphis on the Southern Railroad, from Memphis to Kansas City on the Frisco Lines, and from Kansas City to Portland on the Union Pacific. At one point, the five cars were part of a train carrying hundreds of German war prisoners.

Our crew and the other LCS crews who rode the Union Pacific line, along with thousands (millions? We had 13 million people in uniform in that war) of service personnel from across the country, have a warm spot in their hearts for the kind ladies of North Platte, Nebraska, who provided the hordes of service travelers with buffet dinners and cakes and even birthday cakes for those with birthdays.

Some crew members on the trains made a special effort to speak and wave to relatives and friends in their home towns as their trains went through. "We went through my home town, Lenoir City, Tennessee, and that engineer had no idea of stoppin' for me, or even slowin' down. He was pourin' on the coal. Some of the guys was holdin' my feet as I hung out of the train window. I saw my uncle tendin' his garden beside the railroad tracks, and I hollered at him, and he hollered back and waved a turnip at me, and I saw two other fellows I had worked with. That was a good trip to Oregon—a lot of card playin', a lot of partyin' goin' on all the way, and people comin' out to wave at us as we came by."[5]

Soon after arriving at Boston and Portland, crew members began the job of outfitting and stocking their ships, equipping them in preparation for commissioning.

Endnotes

[1] John Rooney, *Mighty Midget—U.S.S. LCS 82* (Phoenixville, Pa.,1990), 3, 7.

[2] Richard Lewis, "Booby Trap."

[3] Richard Lewis, "The Target Sled."

[4] *Mighty Midget*, 6.

[5] Curtis Williams, LCS *82* seaman, *Mighty Midget*, 9.

Chapter 3

Commissioned Naval Vessels
Underway as before

Although the designation was completely meaningless once the LCSs left the country for duty in the war zone, LCSs were either East Coast Ships or West Coast Ships.

East Coast ships were the 47 ships built in Neponset, Massachusetts, near Boston by the designer of the first LCS, George Lawley and Sons. After commissioning, these ships first went to the Amphibious Training Base, Solomons, and to Little Creek for shakedown and training with ships' crews, and then to Norfolk for availability for repairs and maintenance. From there they began their journey to the Pacific Ocean through the Panama Canal via Key West.

Once in the Pacific, most of them went up the coast of Mexico to San Diego for further training with other LCSs. A small number of earlier ships, Flotilla One LCSs that would serve in the Philippines and Borneo, bypassed San Diego and Hawaii and went west and south into the South Pacific Ocean.

West Coast Ships were built in Portland, Oregon, by two shipbuilders, Commercial Iron Works, which built 52 of the ships, and Albina Machinery, which built 31. After these ships were commissioned, they went down the Columbia River and south down the California coast to San Diego. There they underwent a shakedown of the ship and the crew, went into availability for necessary painting and repairs, and trained extensively as ships' crews with other ships.

Movement of ships' crews into Boston and Portland and onto their assigned ships generally went smoothly, as the building went on apace. In a few instances, several crew members went ahead of the whole crew to assist with the ship's outfitting while it was being built. Earl Blanton, *118* gunner, who worked ahead on his ship's outfitting, shared his feelings about his new ship: "The workmen (at the Lawley yard in Neponset, Massachusetts) that built her said she went together the easiest of any of them yet. You know they build them in sections and they said every seam matched and went together without any trouble at all. That's good luck to start with.

"I stood on her deck today when she went down [the shipways] in the rain and snow, but I didn't even notice it for some reason or the other and I don't know how to explain it, but I just felt good and content. She is my ship and I am proud to be able to say so."[1]

While getting the ships ready for commissioning, enlisted men from the crews lived in the Fargo Building (which had earlier been a home to French and English sailors) and other places in Boston, and in the Naval Receiving Barracks in Portland. Officers lived in hotels and in rooms in private homes in both cities. While our ship was built in Portland, our gunnery officer and I lived first in a hotel downtown, the Saint Anne's I believe (I remember thinking it strange for a hotel to be named after a saint), and then in a private home in Council Crest, an attractive neighborhood appropriately named because the trolley cars that served it and climbed to its crest had to be operated by cables. They were not as quaint, however, as the ones in San Francisco.

Occasionally crews intended for one ship were forced to take another. "Ours was the *62* and, after six weeks of fitting her out for commissioning, we ran over a log in the river in our trial run—bent the shaft. Another crew got the *62*, we were transferred to *63* and started over with refitting."[2] When our crew was assembled earlier at Solomons, our ship was to be the *81*, but when we arrived in Portland, our activity was delayed by a polio epidemic at the Naval Receiving Barracks. Because of this, another crew got *81*, and the ship we outfitted and commissioned was *85*.

Although most of the crews spent several weeks in Boston and Portland, the pace at which the crew had to work to outfit their new ship varied according to how soon the ship was built. Some crews found their work cut out for them the day they arrived. They would have two weeks or less to get their ship ready to commission and to provision it and load it with ammunition, fuel, and water after the ceremony. With this tight schedule they probably had several busy 18-hour days. Members of other crews suddenly found that they had some free time to enjoy life in a pleasant liberty town.

Crew members who needed particular training were sent off during the outfitting period. Along with other first lieutenants and damage control officers,

I was assigned to a week's training at a firefighting school in Seattle. Training at this school was realistic, to say the least. For our final test before graduating we trainees went into an engine room mock-up to put out an oil and gasoline fire burning in the bilge at our feet. We could not retreat, even if we wanted to, because our instructor had locked us in. All that we had to fight the fire was a fire hose. At Seattle I stayed in the seedy old Frye Hotel downtown which was serving as a BOQ (Bachelor Officers Quarters). I was appalled to find that at least a third of the hotel was occupied by habitually drunken naval officers who roamed the halls and gave the place a nightmare atmosphere.

When crew members did not need specialized training, they were utilized, at least part-time, in different ways. Some of the men in Boston served as prison guards and on shore patrol. In Portland they served as shore patrolmen and worked on ammunition loading details. In both cities they served on work details of various kinds.

All the crews, even those hard-pressed, found some time to appreciate the two cities of Boston and Portland as their 'home liberty ports'. "Some of the boys were whooping it up since it would be the last Boston liberty, and Boston was a great liberty town. (Strangers were always buying you drinks, and to get a

Portland hospitality: a West Coast ship's crew enjoys a combination Christmas and commissioning party given by the Portland Sons of Norway.

ride, you simply stood by the roadside and you would be picked up in minutes. A sailor could have as many dates as he wished.)"[3]

"The weather was cold and damp in Portland; however the town was not dreary at all. People were cheery, vibrant, and excited, and the entire population was alive with a high morale. We were in this city planning the final touches on our mighty midget—LCS *64*. Portland, the city of roses, should be called the city of love and hospitality. I remember the White Center (hospitality center for servicemen) downtown where one could get a shave, a shower, a warm meal, and even a lovely date all in the same afternoon. One could be merely walking down the street and be asked to come to someone's house for dinner. I shall never forget the charm and the warmth of the beautiful people of Portland, Oregon."[4]

Somehow (maybe it was arranged by the USO or the Red Cross), on Thanksgiving Day of 1944 every service person in Portland had dinner in a private home. I remember our dinner host telling another officer and myself that he was a World War I veteran and had, in the 1930s, been one of the Bonus marchers who went all the way from Portland to demonstrate in Washington. He said that he certainly hoped that when we came home, the government would treat us better than it treated World War I veterans.

The simple and brief ceremony marking each ship's commissioning usually took place on a day when the crew could not have been busier provisioning and moving into its new home. To some crew members the commissioning ceremony was an inspiration, providing a sense of achievement and fulfillment. To others it was a letdown, a sort of anti-climax after all the work and preparation.

In both Boston and Portland, entire ship's crews were mustered out in dress blues with the captain and commissioning officer facing forward in the waist of the ship (just aft of the deck house), many of the crew members behind and around them. Facing the captain and commissioning officer were the five officers of the ship. Up above on the small flag deck were the rest of the crew.

The commissioning officer ordered the captain to read his orders and assume command. After this the captain ordered the executive officer, as the first Officer of the Deck, to set the watch. Then the signalman hoisted the commissioning pennant and the ensign. The ship with its crew of over 70 officers and men then began its official life. Unofficially, but beginning at this moment, all present crew members became 'plank owners' of their ships, a title that would last a lifetime.

All hands saluting the flag as a another LCS becomes a commissioned ship.

At some of the commissionings guests were present—often the wives and friends of crew members. When the LCS *45* was commissioned, Benjamin Dagwell, an Episcopal bishop, was one of the guests; his presence was considered a good omen, a silent blessing for a ship that would see a lot of action and come through it unscathed.

A different omen was in evidence when LCS *35* was commissioned: "As he began to hoist the flag, signalman Roche suddenly jerked it down when he realized the ensign was upside down! Recovering quickly, Roche ran up the flag correctly as everyone held their salutes. I don't recall much being said about what could have been a bad omen for our uncertain near future."[5] Inasmuch as *35* also came through unscathed after extensive action (although her superstructure was damaged at Iwo Jima), there was evidently no need for worry.

Proud new "plank owners" look over their ship that will be their "world" for the next 15 to 18 months.

After being commissioned, provisioned, fueled, loaded with ammunition and whatever else necessary, and tested thoroughly for last-minute problems, East Coast Ships proceeded from Boston to the Solomons/Little Creek/Norfolk area in the mid and lower Chesapeake Bay for shakedown, training, and availability.

Because a number of ships were going down the East Coast during the northeaster season, some of the ships encountered storms and had to put into sheltered waters at such places as New Bedford, Massachusetts, and the Chesapeake and Delaware Canal south of Wilmington. For many of the sailors aboard these southbound ships, this was their second taste of ocean travel on a flat-bottomed ship of LCI/LCS size. Their first had been the Solomons' ocean voyage around the Del-Mar-Va peninsula. The odds were that at least one of these two trips was rough, and the new LCS sailors were forced to find their sea legs, whether willingly or not.

Earl Blanton, gunner on the East Coast Ship *118* that spent six days completing its shakedown at Solomons, tells us what his crew did: "Two Navy lieutenants moved aboard as shakedown observers during the time. We fired all the guns and rockets. One day while anchored, the crew shot small arms off the fantail. We made three beaching runs, blasting away with 20s, 40s, and rockets. Then we shot at aerial targets, including sleeves and a remote-controlled plane which, to everyone's amazement, we shot down.

"For damage control we practiced going to general quarters, fire, collision, and abandon ship drills. For seamanship, we ran in columns, stood formations, practiced mooring, towing, refueling at sea, beaching, pulling ships off the beach, man overboard drills, and zigzag courses. To test our engines, we went out in the Chesapeake Bay and did speed runs over a measured mile. We would anchor at least once each day and sometimes twice. We also fired up the smoke generator and practiced laying smoke screens."[6]

After being declared 'ready' by the Navy shakedown observers, LCS *118* went through the degaussing process (neutralizing electrically the ship's magnetism to prevent detonation of magnetic mines). Then the ship moved to the Norfolk Naval Base where it was painted with a camouflage pattern, and necessary corrections and repairs were made. East Coast Ships spent differing time periods in the Solomons/Little Creek/Norfolk area, depending on their training and maintenance needs. LCS *111* and *118* spent approximately two weeks there; *14* stayed for almost a month.

While going through shakedown and maintenance availability in the Chesapeake Bay area, LCS *111* had an experience that few, if any other, LCSs ever had or reported having. While making a turn in the Bay, *111* lay completely over on her side, and then, while partially submerged, righted herself. Chuck Rhoades, *111* conning officer at the time, explains what happened:

> On a very windy, stormy day I had relieved the bridge for lunch on our way to have our ship degaussed. Mr. Culp, the captain, had left orders that upon reaching a bearing on a landmark, the ship was to make about a 90-degree turn to a new course.
>
> Since I was capable of sighting the landmark, I advised the helmsman to come left to a new ship's heading. Well, as coincidences occur, the helmsman was new, the rudder was over accomplished (30 vs 5 degrees) and the ship healed over in a trough, had its bottom 'into the sea'. The

ship started 'over' so I moved to the high side of the bridge and grabbed hold of the armor ring, around the perimeter, and the ship laid on its side.

My body was fully suspended with the mast edge at the water. I was wondering if we would 'right' ourselves, and, when we did, if I would be catapulted off the ship's bridge into the boiling sea. Well, we did right ourselves. The ship became upright while submerged to about four feet of water over the main deck; this water flowed over all sides of the ship as we came up above the water line.

I could hear the skipper calling over the voice tube. He didn't ask if I were there, but 'What in the hell is going on up there?' Returning [to the officers' quarters] below I found much disarray, namely the wardroom butter stuck on the bulkhead [wall], the desk drawers in the closets, and the mattresses piled on the deck. There were no casualties, only the thought 'and we haven't even gone 'way out' to sea yet.'[7]

After finishing shakedown and availability in the Solomons/Little Creek/ Norfolk area, East Coast Ships proceeded down the east coast around the Florida peninsula to Key West for a short stopover. From there they went south and west through the Panama Canal to the Pacific Ocean. A few of the earlier ships then went west and south to the Admiralty Islands/New Guinea area to join the invasion forces.

Most of the ships, however, turned north to go up the long coasts of Central America and Mexico to San Diego to join LCSs in training there. Since the long Norfolk-to-San Diego trip took roughly 27 underway days, East Coast Ship crews had a good idea of what crossing the wide Pacific Ocean would be like.

Crews stopping over at Key West found it to be a sort of end-of-the-world place with an abundance of bars and frequent brawls between crews from different ships. Some of the crew members who went ashore found the shore patrolmen there to be the harshest, most brutal, and unbending to be found anywhere.

Some of the ships going up the Central American and Mexican coasts found it necessary to put into a port to replenish their fresh water supply. One ship, LCS *14,* stopped at Manzanello, Mexico, and the crew was given liberty. "Manzanello seemed like it was out of this world. I don't recall seeing a car of any sort. The thing that got to me was the crippled beggars on the streets. I had seen poor people before but never anything like this.

"Raw meat hung from hooks and flies were crawling all over it. I watched the men making jewelry from silver and pots from copper, all by hand. Their work was beautiful. With very few tools the men formed beautiful lace earrings, bracelets and necklaces. The interior of the stores in the square were all tile and it was really beautiful workmanship."[8]

On its way to San Diego, LCS *118* put into Corinto, Nicaragua, apparently for fresh water, and to allow LCS *117*, traveling with her, to make repairs. This stopover turned out to be quite an adventure for the *118* crew.

At Corinto we moored to a dock alongside the town. Some locals were on the dock watching the ship. One guy must have been a guard, because he was armed with an old fashioned six-shooter and he had crossed bandoliers of ammo. He looked like Poncho Villa!

A fellow gunner and I started up the motors of the aft 40mm twin gun, switched it to fully automatic control and put on quite a show; swinging the gun around and up and down apparently without anyone operating it—like magic. The locals were very impressed, to say the least.

The town is really small. All the streets are ankle deep in dust and everyone goes barefooted. In town, transportation is on foot, horseback, and oxen carts with big wooden wheels. However, I did see one car and a truck. They have one narrow-gauge railroad also. One other thing about the town. They have plenty of bars. The village has mountains on one side and the jungle on the other. We were the first ship in six weeks and our welcome was like in the movies.

To his profound regret, the *118* captain split the crew into two sections letting one half ashore at a time. The first half had to be back by around 1100 or 1200 hours. They were drunk. The second half had to be aboard just prior to sailing, and they came aboard drunk-drunk!

After much effort, we finally rounded up all the crew and the captain put to sea. LCS *117* had the same problem. The town was too good and the liberty too short! Farewell and fond memories. When the ship got underway, so many guys were drunk we could hardly stand watch for falling asleep.[9]

Off the coast of Central America, LCS *118* crew members spotted 15 big sea turtles. They killed one and the cook made stew—enough to give every member of the crew a bowl. As they went north off the Baja, California, coast, they spotted thousands of porpoises, tuna, sharks, and seals.

At the same time East Coast Ships were moving north up the Baja California, coast to San Diego, West Coast Ships were coming down the California coast from Portland. Ships from both coasts trained together at the naval base; individual LCS crews soon discovered that their ships belonged to groups (of 12 ships) and flotillas (of 36 ships), and, in some instances, to divisions (of 6 ships, half of a group). From then on they would be working with other LCSs most of the time under the administrative command of division, group, and flotilla commanders.

Immediately before and after their commissioning, crews in Portland had pretty much the same things to do as the Boston crews did—provisioning, fueling, loading ammunition, checking for last-minute problems. More than likely, other problems worried the officers: Is the entire crew berthed satisfactorily? Is the ammunition stowed safely? Is the assignment of non-rated men to ship's departments satisfactory to all concerned?

Sometimes the assignment problems tended to solve themselves with a little help from the men and the ship's officers. Here is an instance where just that happened:

> The day following the commissioning, Whitten (a coxswain in the deck division) brusquely motions me to follow him to the pilot house, where he points to the engine order telegraph. "Thomas, get busy, take all the paint off, right down to the deck. Captain wants to see his face in that brass underneath the paint!"

> The engine order telegraph, used to ring signals to the engine room, is covered with what must be six coats of thick gray paint. Several signalmen and quartermasters lounge idly in the pilot house and watch my work.

> "You guys have got it made," I proclaim.

> "Like hell we have," one murmurs, "signalmen and quartermasters have to work too close to the damn officers to suit me," Billy G. Palmer, a non-rated signalman, responds.

> "Damn officers make me nervous, they are always asking me what they're saying, right in the middle of me trying to read a signal. If I had my way, I'd a whole lot rather just be a seaman in the deck division. I'd swap places with you in a minute, if they'd let me."

> After being assured that Palmer is serious, we go at once to the officer in charge of the deck division, Ensign Kline.

"It's Okay by me. Either way I get a seaman, but we'll have to talk to Mr. Sterrett. If he and the captain agree, I'll approve it."

Ensign Sterrett, the communications officer, muses that he doesn't know about that. While he prefers having someone who really likes communications in his division, it doesn't seem such a good idea to give up a trained man for one who does not know the first thing about signaling. After questioning Palmer briefly, Sterrett suddenly turns to me demanding, "Thomas, can you spell?"

"Yes, pretty good."

"Well, spell opportunity!"

"O-P-P-O-R-T-U-N-I-T-Y!"

Sterrett laughingly says if the Captain approves, he will give me a try on condition that I learn signals well enough to stand a watch alone within sixty days. Captain Huff promptly approves the change in duty, and I become a member of the communications division.[10]

As soon as they were ready for sea, West Coast LCSs departed Portland and moved down the Columbia River to Astoria, where they entered the Pacific Ocean and turned south down the long California coast to San Diego. On the Columbia River leg of their journey, the ships were under the control of a pilot, who was used to, and could reckon with, heavy thick fog, dangerous floating logs, and fishermen netfishing in the middle of the river channel.

Off Astoria, at the river's mouth, each LCS captain was on his own to cross the Columbia bar, where the huge ground swells of the Pacific came rolling in. Even in fair weather crossing the bar was a rough experience; it gave West Coast sailors their second initiation (after their Solomons trip) into ocean travel on an LCI/LCS class ship.

At sundown, just before we [LCS 35 crew members] reached the Pacific, the Columbia broadened and took several giant bends. About ten or twelve of us were clustered at the bow expectantly looking ahead. We could smell the ocean and each time we rounded a bend we expected to see it. At last, there was the Pacific before us. As we crossed the Columbia bar and entered the Pacific, the bow of the ship began to rise and fall as she met the big ground swells. We laughed from good spirits as we felt the movement of the ship and the brisk wind in our faces.

"Boy, we're seadogs now!"

"Thought they said it was rough on the ocean!"

"This ain't bad at all!"

"Hell, this baby rides good!"

Suddenly, one of the group turned his head away from the wind and vomited. His vomitus, caught by the wind, swept up and away in the late afternoon air. Within minutes, most of us were seasick. There may have been a few hearty souls on board, but most were incapacitated. Somehow the ship stayed on course and the night passed.[11]

"From Astoria we [the captain of LCS 82] were on our own. I remember with a gulp in the throat watching a companion LCS crossing the Columbia River bar (really big waves at the bar) and heeling to starboard at what looked like 60 degrees—enough to capsize her right there. Well, she came back upright, and out on the ocean we sailed."[12]

"When we [crew member, LCS 82] went out across the bar at the mouth of the Columbia River, our poor little ship would bang and shudder like it was going to break in two. It was built pretty good though because it was able to go through virtually the same when we came back [after the war] to Seattle after all the rough treatment in between."[13]

LCS sailors had a lot of faith in their ships! They had to have. When my ship began crossing the Columbia bar, it was evening and still light; by the time it was dark, the ship was rolling and pitching violently and every crew member, including the captain and myself, was sick. Within minutes the deck in the forward sleeping compartment (that would be known later as our 'roller coaster' compartment) was covered with vomit. It was a moment of great challenge for me, a seasick first lieutenant in charge of cleanliness on the ship. After a few difficult moments I recruited a half-willing volunteer helper and somehow the two of us cleaned the compartment deck as it heaved up and down under us. It was an initiation that I will never forget; fortunately, it never happened again.

On their way down the coast West Coast Ship crews were set back briefly by their initial bout with seasickness, but most of the crews recovered quickly and exercised at drills in preparation for meeting shakedown requirements at San Diego. In effect, they made their southbound journey into a shakedown cruise. On their way south, those crew members who lived on the coast pointed out their hometowns to shipmates. Hundreds of graceful porpoises and dolphins, as well as large whales on their way to Baja, California, provided welcome entertainment along the way.

LCSs from both coasts began arriving at the San Diego base in October of 1944. For the first two months their numbers were relatively small—4 in October and 12 in November. There were, however, 15 in December, and 32 in January 1945, and activity at the base accelerated. LCSs continued to arrive in February (13 ships) and in March (16), and through April and May, when 30 ships reported to the base. Altogether over 120 of the 130 LCS ships underwent training, availability, and shakedowns at San Diego.

At San Diego the LCS crews trained and exercised both as individual ships and in groups. They had extensive gunnery practice, both anti-aircraft and beach bombardment using rockets as well as guns. Ships went out from San Diego in groups for days at a time to the San Clemente and San Nicholas Island areas where they would steam in formation, exercise at tactical maneuvers, practice their gunnery, and hold shipboard drills. Steaming in formation and exercising at tactical maneuvers were often directed by group and flotilla commanders.

It was during one of these training periods off San Diego that an unfortunate accident occurred. LCS *127* ran aground on the rocks of San Nicholas Island so hard that it was completely out of water. The hull was so seriously damaged that the ship had to be scrapped.

Usually early in their time at the base, West Coast Ship crews demonstrated that their ships were ready for sea by successfully completing a series of drills and tests for shakedown inspection. West Coast Ships were also given availability for maintenance and needed repairs. East Coast Ship crews participated in all the training programs mentioned above. Since ships from Boston had proved that they were ready for sea while at Solomons, they were exempted from this at San Diego. They were, however, given availability for maintenance and repairs if needed. The length of time that ships from both coasts stayed at San Diego varied from as little as 15 days to as long as 2 months.

To expedite services to LCS crews and to provide programs to acquaint crews with their new ships, LCS flotilla commanders established themselves in the Base's Ship Training Groups for appropriate periods of time. Flotilla One Commander Rae E. Arison and his staff supervised Flot One ship programs from August 27 to October 20, when Captain Arison departed for duty in the Philippines. Flotilla Three Commander T. C. Aylward and staff directed Flot

Three ship programs at the base from October 14 to December 1, when Captain Aylward departed San Diego to begin preparations for the Iwo Jima operation.

Flotilla Four Commander Neill Phillips and staff supervised Flot Four ships from December 24 to March 11, when Commander Phillips moved to Hawaii to conduct training programs for LCSs there. From late March through mid-May, Flotilla Five Commander, Captain J. M. McIsaac, oversaw Flot Five ships training at the base.

While the naval facilities at Solomons, Little Creek, Norfolk, and San Diego provided testing and approval for ships' readiness for sea and for their maintenance and repair needs, the major emphasis at all the bases except Norfolk was on training. In fact, training was going on all the time. The ships' crews exercising frequently at shipboard drills to improve their readiness for sea was self-training at its best.

While the ships were exercising in groups of 12 or more at tactical maneuvers off San Diego, their crews were undergoing training at its most intensive. In these exercises the LCSs were literally drilled by the OTC (Officer in Tactical Command), usually a flotilla or group commander, in a way very similar to what a drill instructor or platoon leader does to drill his men on a drill field.

Using flaghoists that are raised and dropped simultaneously by all ships as command signals, the OTC ordered the ships to take formation at prescribed distances apart and to proceed at speeds and on courses he prescribed and to make a series of turn movements and flanking movements of different kinds, always maintaining their same relative positions with each other.

During these exercises, ships' signalmen worked frantically operating their signal lights and constantly changing flaghoists (even the quartermasters pitched in to help), captains rapidly received and executed orders and commands, conning officers struggled to keep the ships in the formation from running into each other, helmsmen, on constant alert, executed crucial turns smartly, and motor macs in the engine room responded sharply to bells from the busy engine room telegraph. As a conning officer (actually as OOD underway) I found it frustrating that if one or two of the ships were off course just a degree or two, ships in our immediate vicinity would come dangerously close to colliding with each other, and all I could do about it, because I had no authority to change course and speed, was to keep warning (and pestering) our captain.

At the time I was not certain why we were doing these demanding exercises. Here we were using old fashioned visual signals in the broad daylight, moving in all directions, and using up a lot of ocean in the process. I could not imagine using tactics and maneuvers like these in a real naval battle. After all, we were amphibious gunboats built to support invasions, not destroyers or cruisers planning to fight the Battle of Jutland (major naval battle in World War I) all over again.

What we were doing could not be honestly called battle tactics; instead they were training tactics and maneuvers in which ship crews learned to execute orders, to maintain stations on other ships at relatively high speeds (for LCSs), and to use the ships' turning and course-and-speed changing abilities as effectively as possible. Although it might have seemed that way to a friendly pilot flying over us, we were not simply 'marching our ships' all over the ocean just for the fun of it. And it did not hurt our egos one bit to be training our ships to be men of war on maneuvers while we were really amphibious gunboats in disguise.

Of the approximately 10,000 crew members in all of the LCS training programs, the individuals whose performance was most thoroughly scrutinized were the ships' captains and executive officers. Their abilities and inabilities were constantly being judged and evaluated. Evidently most of them did well and passed all their tests, since only three captains, along with one executive officer, were relieved of their commands in September and October.

On one occasion at the San Diego base two LCSs took emergency action that, for the first time in their training programs, was not a drill. On the evening of January 29 LCSs *116* and *118* helped to put out a large harbor fire at Berth #1 near where they were moored. The fire, which was probably caused by spilled fuel, was completely out of control when the LCS crews began fighting it. This action was the first of a number of occasions on which LCS crews would fight and extinguish dangerous fires.

Large numbers of LCS officers and men took full advantage of the liberty opportunities offered in San Diego and the surrounding areas while their ships were at the base. Probably the greatest attraction in the immediate area was the famous San Diego Zoo, which was ahead of its time with its open, natural living spaces for its animals and its park-like environment.

Hollywood was a very popular attraction. LCS sailors enjoyed seeing the movie studios, eating at famous restaurants, and having 'Breakfast at Sardi's'. I had to be satisfied with having lunch there, but I did get a good look at the large spread of pictures of Hollywood celebrities. Some sailors succeeded in meeting

Three 118 *crew members "get into character" to enjoy their liberty in Tijuana, Mexico. Courtesy of Earl Blanton.*

a movie star and getting an autograph or two. Los Angeles offered big-city attractions that many sailors found appealing.

The most enticing liberty town for large numbers of men was Tijuana, just across the border in Mexico. It offered the chance to visit a 'foreign country', to enjoy open gambling and easy women, and to purchase beautiful Mexican silver ornaments and jewelry and leatherwork. A number of sailors, many of them like myself from relatively sober, semi-puritanical Protestant communities back in the States (at the time in my Maryland home town there were no open bars, and Sunday movies had only recently been allowed), were sometimes shocked to discover bars and taverns with elaborate and sometimes garish furniture and large paintings of saints and Madonnas with Child looking down benignly on the noisy drinkers, gamblers, and prostitutes below. Even though we were only just a few miles across the border, we were 'innocents abroad' in a foreign country.

It was on their way to enjoy their first liberty in San Diego in late November that a group of men from LCS *14* had a very sobering experience—one that, although the men did not realize it at the time, was prophetic. "I don't think we will ever forget our first liberty in San Diego. As we walked to the main gate (of the naval base) we had to pass the ships that were coming back from the Pacific war zone. As we passed the drydocks we could see the destroyers and small aircraft carriers all smashed to hell with holes in their sides—holes big enough to drive a truck through.

"You might say we were stunned at the sight. If the Japanese were doing this to the bigger ships, what would happen to a ship our size if it were hit by a suicide plane? We were told by the men who were on these damaged ships that when you shot a suicide plane down, it just doesn't hit the water and sink. Most of the time the plane will hit the water and glance off it. The plane, or pieces of the downed plane, often would hit the ships at the water line and blow a hole in the side. Lighter parts of the plane would sometimes land on the ship, killing or injuring a lot of men topside."[14]

The following April these men, along with the rest of their LCS *14* crew, found themselves at Okinawa on radar picket patrol face-to-face with hundreds of the same lethal Japanese suicide planes that had attacked and damaged the ships they had seen at San Diego. The *14* crew, along with scores of other LCS crews at Okinawa, learned that what they had been told at San Diego was true, that the suicide planes, or parts of the planes kept coming at them even after their gunners had fired hundreds of shells directly into them. These planes were man-directed lethal weapons, almost impossible to destroy by conventional means.

During the three-month campaign at Okinawa LCS crews on radar picket patrol faced these planes and shot down scores of them. After the campaign, the LCSs were sent to the Philippines for rest and recreation and to prepare for the invasion of Japan. In the Philippines, the LCSs joined fleet ships, also enjoying R and R, at San Pedro Bay off Tacloban and between the islands of Leyte and Samar—the very spot where, in the previous October and November, some of the damaged ships the *14* crew had seen at San Diego had been attacked and severely crippled by suicide planes.

Endnotes

[1] Earl Blanton, *Boston to Jacksonville (41,000 Miles by Sea)*(Seaford, Va., 1991), 10.

[2] Bill Topping, *63* officer, "I Remember___," a series of reminiscences, n.d.

[3] Blanton, *Boston to Jacksonville*, 12.

[4] Gordon H. Wiram, *64* officer, "Bits of History," 1990.

[5] Charles Thomas, *35* signalman, "A Bad Omen?" n.d.

[6] Blanton, *Boston to Jacksonville*, 16.

[7] Chuck and Peggy Rhoades, letter to author, August 13, 1993.

[8] Frank Korany, *14* motor machinist's mate, *LCSL 14—One of the Mighty Midgets*, n.d., 28.

[9] Blanton, *Boston to Jacksonville*, 24-25.

[10] Charles Thomas, *35* signalman, *Dolly Five* (Chester, Va., 1995), 72-73.

[11] Thomas, "Crossing the Bar," n.d.

[12] *Mighty Midget—USS LCS 82*, 27.

[13] Ibid., 27-28.

[14] Korany, *LCSL 14—One of the Mighty Midgets*, 30-31.

Chapter 4

Moving Westward to the War

In October of 1944 LCSs began their long movement westward out of the San Diego Base, where they had trained, to Pearl Harbor and then on to the war zones across the wide Pacific Ocean. The first four ships to depart were LCSs *26, 27, 48,* and *49*—Flotilla One ships that would go on to participate in the Philippines and Borneo campaigns. Rae Arison, LCS Flotilla One Commander, was in LCS *48*.

At approximately the same time four other Flot One ships, LCSs *7-10*, from the East Coast, were bypassing San Diego and Hawaii and moving west and south across the Pacific Ocean to join their four sister ships from San Diego in the Philippines war zone.

In November, five Flot One ships, LCSs *28-30, 41,* and *50,* began their westward movement, and in December, LCSs *42, 43,* and *46* followed. In January, the eight remaining flotilla ships, LCSs *44, 45, 47, 58-60, 79,* and *80,* departed from the base. Differing from the other three LCS flotillas, Flotilla One, with its 24 ships in two groups of 12 each, was never brought to the standard flotilla strength of 36 ships in three groups. Why this happened is uncertain. Perhaps 36 ships were simply not needed in the Philippines and Borneo campaigns. Another unanswered question: Why was there never an LCS Flotilla Two?

Flotilla Three ships began moving out from San Diego in November, one month after Flot One ships. These ships were under Captain T. C. Aylward, Flotilla Three Commander, in LCS *36*. The seven ships that left San Diego in November were LCSs *31-33, 35, 36, 51,* and *52.* In December five more ships, LCSs *53-57,* followed. These two units, totaling 12 ships together, were a group in Flotilla Three—Group Seven, which served with each other first at Iwo Jima and then at Okinawa.

Also departing in December were seven other Flot Three ships, LCSs *23, 24, 34, 37, 38, 109,* and *110.* In January an entire group, Group Eight of the Flotilla, made up of LCSs *11* through *22,* and one other ship, *25,* departed San

---

Diego. In February and March five ships, LCSs *39, 40, 111-113*, made up the last installment of the flotilla's westward movement to the first major stop, Pearl Harbor.

Flotilla Four ships, under Commander Neill Phillips, LCS Flotilla Four Commander, began departing San Diego in January. The ships leaving were LCSs *61, 81-83, 88, 114-116, 118*, and *119*. Nine ships left in February—*62-65, 84-87*, and *91*. In March 14 ships departed—*66-69, 90, 92-95*, and *120-124*.

During April and May, 30 Flotilla Five ships departed San Diego under Captain J. M. McIsaac, LCS Flotilla Five Commander, in LCS *106*. They were LCSs *Two-Four* (which served as training ships for the first several months and then joined their sister ships fighting at Okinawa), *70-78, 96-108, 125, 126, 129*, and *130*.

The morale of most of the outbound crews was upbeat. They had had enough training, more than some of them thought they ever needed, and they were ready to move on. Because all of them had been to sea before, many of them twice, they worried less about getting seasick than before. Also because they had lived and worked and trained as crews, they were now shipmates, and they had a sense of allegiance to their ships and to each other. This gave them confidence that they lacked before and a guardedly optimistic outlook even though they knew they were going into battle.

In each flotilla organization there were, along with the flotilla commander, two or three group commanders of 12 flotilla ships. Some of these commanders accompanied their particular groups on their westward movement. Those who did not would join their ships in an advanced area later. Both the flotilla and group commanders had staffs of officers and men to help them with administration and to provide needed services to the ships and their crews.

After they arrived in the advanced areas, flotilla and group commanders were issued LCIs that had been adapted to flagship purposes and designated LC(FF) for themselves and their staffs. In the meantime the commanders used individual LCSs as their flagships, which made for crowded quarters on the affected ships, but was satisfactory otherwise.

The ultimate goal for ships in Flotillas Three, Four, and Five was to serve in the battle for Okinawa. Forty-two ships from Flotillas Three and Four participated in the massive Okinawa invasion, and over 80 LCS from all three flotillas served in combat action there. Altogether well over 100 of the 130 LCSs served at Okinawa in one capacity or another.

An LCS underway in just a moderate sea. Courtesy of Earl Blanton.

DEAR MOM & DAD:

WELL WE'IVE FINALLY ARRIVED AT OUR DESTINATION AFTER TWO WEEKS AT SEA. WHEN WE APPROACHED THE ISLAND WE MARVELLED AT ITS PLUSH GREEN APPEARANCE AND WE CAME FACE TO FACE WITH THAT FAMOUS VOLCANO THAT OCCASSIONALY ERUPTS. AS WE SAILED INTO THE HARBOR WE WERE IN AWE OF THE MANY DIFFERENT TYPES OF NAVY SHIPS THAT WERE COMING & GOING & THAT WERE AT ANCHOR ___ ALL HUGE COMPARED TO US.!! BEING AN AMPHIB SHIP AND VERY SMALL WE WERE INSTRUCTED TO GO TO THE LESS GLAMOROUS PART OF THE HARBOR AND UP INTO TULLE REEDED MUDDY CREEKS FOR OUR ANCHORAGE. OF COURSE THIS WAS WAY OUT OF THE BIG CITY OF HONOLULU AREA. NEVERTHELESS WE LOVED THE TALL PALM TREES SWAYING IN THE BREEZE. WE WERE ANCHORED OFF HUGE SUGAR CANE FIELDS ON ONE SIDE AND A PINEAPPLE FIELD ON THE OTHER. THE WEATHER IS BBEAUTIFUL ___ ALWAYS SUNNY AND HOT. WE GET RAINED ON ONCE A DAY EVEN WITH THE SUN SHINING. ONE DAY I WENT INTO TOWN TO SEE THAT FAMOUS BEACH CALLED WAIKIKI. IT WAS BEAUTIFUL ___ THE SAND WAS CLEAN AND WHITE ; THE WATER WAS SO CLEAR YOU COULD SEE TO THE BOTTOM OF THE BAY. THAT EVENING I WENT TO THE ROYAL HAWAIIAN HOTEL , WHICH IS NOW A NAVY HOTEL , AND HAD DINNER AND THEY HAD A SHOW WITH DANCING HULA GIRLS ___ GRASS SKIRTS AND ALL ___ WOW!!! WE WON'T BE HERE LONG. SAY "HI" TO EVERYBODY.

I LOVE YOU BOTH

gil

Censored mail: what 45 signalman Gil Nadeau wrote to his parents and the letter his parents received. Courtesy of Gil Nadeau.

DEAR MOM & DAD:

WELL WE'VE ████████████ OUR ████████
████████████ AT ████. WHEN WE ████████ THE ████
WE ████████ AT ITS ████████████████ AND WE
CAME FACE TO FACE WITH ████████████████████
OCCASSIONALY ████. AS WE ████ THE ████ WE
WERE IN ████ THE ████████████ OF ████████
THAT WERE ████████ & ████ & THAT ████████████ ----
ALL ████████████ TO US!! BEING ████████ AND
VERY ████ WE WERE ████████████████ TO THE ████
████████████ OF THE ████████ AND UP INTO ████
████████████ FOR ████████. OF COURSE THIS WAS
████████ OF THE ████████ OF ████████████████
NEVERTHELESS WE LOVED THE ████████████████ IN
THE ████. WE ████████████ OFF ████████████
████ ON ONE SIDE AND ████████████ ON THE OTHER.
THE WEATHER IS ████████ --- ALWAYS ████████. WE GET
████████████████████ EVEN WITH THE ████████
ONE DAY I WENT INTO TOWN TO SEE ████████████
CALLED ████████, IT WAS ████████ --- THE ████ WAS
████████ AND ████████; THE ████████ SO ████ YOU COULD SEA
TO THE ████████████████. THAT EVENING I WENT TO THE
████████████████, WHICH IS ████████████, AND
HAD DINNER AND ████████████████████████
████████ --- ████████ AND ALL --- WOW!! WE ████████
████████ LONG. SAY "HI" TO EVERYBODY.

I LOVE YOU BOTH

gil

One very important change in the crews' lives on leaving the continental United States was that all their mail had to be censored. This job fell to the ship's officers who soon became adept at applying black ink profusely or cutting out enough words with scissors to make the precious letters back home look like sieves. Most of the men conformed to the rules and avoided giving any potentially dangerous information. A few persisted in keeping the censors alert by seeing how much they could get away with. And there were always a few 'code users' who forced the censors into becoming amateur detectives.

As the ships left the continental United States and their former home liberty ports of Boston and Portland and their training base at San Diego, the men began to look upon their ships as self-contained worlds, albeit tiny, crowded and limited in many ways. Crew members sought recreation where they could find it on the overcrowded ship—card playing, reading, letter writing to an extent never done before (the strong urge to communicate with the world they left behind was in no way deterred by the threat of censorship), firing small arms off the ship's fantail (they were not aware that they might well be training to fight off suicide boats or even suicide swimmers in the war zones or to demolish floating mines on the high seas after the war). Some crews held divine services, usually, but not always, conducted by the officers. Some crews celebrated holidays and special occasions—crossing the Equator, crossing the International Dateline, Thanksgiving, Christmas, ship's anniversaries. Some crews sponsored basketball, softball, and volleyball teams that played in tournaments; other crews published newsletters, with drawings by crew members, and yearbooks, and accounts of their service. One crew built a gymnasium in Korea for all service men in the area, and another crew took over watch duties of a group of Marines so they could go home for Christmas.

To the individual LCS crews the journey to Pearl Harbor was a sort of third initiation into open-sea travel on an LCI/LCS class ship. And this third instance differed enough from the first to make it a challenge. In their first initiation at Solomons, LCS crews were passengers and had little or no control over their circumstance. The more formidable their seasickness, the more helpless they were.

In their second introduction, steaming up and down the coasts of North and Central America, they were 'masters of their fate', so to speak. They could always put into a port if the seas got unpleasantly rough or if they had an urgent need. In their sustained westward journey across the Pacific, they had no safety valve. They were completely on their own for the first time.

But how completely crews were on their own depended, to a great extent, on how many other ships were traveling with them and what kinds of ships they were. The great majority of LCSs traveled, most of the time, with other LCSs, usually with at least four or more, sometimes with up to 35. They occasionly traveled in medium and large convoys with other ships, frequently amphibious vessels—LCIs, LSMs, and LSTs, and, in special convoys, LCTs. Even though ships sometimes had little or no contact traveling together in formation, LCS crews appreciated having other ships with them more than they realized.

Almost by accident at least, one ship, LCS *Nine*, made the 8,700 mile journey from the Panama Canal to the Admiralty Islands alone. Frank Muth, LCS *Nine* crew member, explained: "Now when we left Panama, we were to head north to San Diego, but the hurricanes on the east coast put our timing way behind. So our flotilla left without us. We sailed across the Pacific Ocean by ourselves. We missed out on all the maneuvers they had (for our Flotilla One ships) on the west coast. We had to practice different shipboard drills by ourselves.

"We built a raft out of boards from different boxes that we had supplies in. We used it for practice for all our guns. We would also throw a milk can overboard for practicing man overboard drills, for which we used the ship's dinghy. [During one drill] the current took the dinghy a little ways from the ship and one of the men in the dinghy signaled excitedly to the ship. They were surrounded by a whole school of sharks, hundreds of them. It made the hair on your neck stand up to see all those sharks. We next sailed to the Galapagos Islands off Ecuador, but we couldn't get supplies of any kind there, just fuel for the ship."[1]

From Galapagos the *Nine* took a 'South Pacific' tour route to Bora Bora in the Society Islands, which are located 18 degrees south of the Equator, and include the famous Tahiti Island. At Bora Bora they were able to get fuel but still no food and other supplies. They did have liberty at Bora Bora, which is located inside a large volcanic crater whose center is a deep clear-water lake. They sailed on to Espiritus Santos in the New Hebrides Islands and from there to Manus in the Admiralties, where they joined other Flotilla One ships.[2]

One constant worry for LCS crews moving westward was the threat of collision. With each passing day while moving west, captains, conning officers, and helmsmen, as well as motor machinists and firemen answering engine room bells, sharpened and improved their skills and abilities so that station-keeping in formation and ship handling in harbors were less difficult than at first.

In spite of this, accidents and collisions happened. In early December LCS *43* collided with the *53* while they were traveling in formation from San Diego to Pearl Harbor. No one was hurt, but *43* suffered a hole in its bow, and *53,* a big dent in her port side.

Wes Clark, *43* crew member, described his crew's reaction to the collision and explained why and how it happened: "The collision in mid-ocean was a real introduction to sea life to a bunch of kids that had never been to sea. The helmsman became a bit confused that dark night. We were in a convoy that I believe to be about 40 ships. He was visually steering by simply following the ship ahead. He lost sight of his target and was given 'five degrees left rudder'—he gave it 'five right.' This was followed by 'ten' and finally by 'hard left.' Each command was followed in reverse. 'Full back' failed to stop us in time and the *43* pierced the hull of the *53* in the crew's quarters area. There was no damage that could not be repaired."[3]

In March LCS *21* collided with an LST off the island of Mog Mog, a favorite fleet liberty spot near Ulithi. W. H. Stanley, *21* crew member, tells us what happened: "The next day we pulled up close to an LST to take on fuel. The sea was choppy and our ship's bow was going up and down. The current swept us too close to the LST's stern. The bow of our ship went down, and when it came up, our bow's point punched a big hole in the LST's stern. Some crew members were sleeping back there, and one man took his pillow case and waved it out the hole (We surrender!)."[4]

But other LCSs and other amphibious vessels were not always what LCS captains and conning officers had to watch out for. While escorting several ammunition-laden LSTs between Pearl Harbor and Eniwetok, LCS *120* was detached to investigate a radar contact which appeared to be moving at the same speed on the same course as the LST convoy. "We [*120* captain] were baffled when we got close to the contact, whose profile was like no other ship the crew had ever seen." Moreover, the ship seemed to be evading contact. When the *120* got close enough to challenge by signal light, they discovered that the ship was a U.S. Army buoy tender—certainly the last kind of ship one would expect to encounter moving to the war zone in the middle of the Pacific Ocean.[5]

My ship, along with several other LCSs, had a dangerous encounter with a menacing phantom ship as Richard Lewis, our executive officer, tells us:

At night, while en route to Hawaii, we (a group of eight LCSs in double column formation) saw a sizeable ship approaching from the rear at high speed in relation to our rather slow 10 or 11 knots. As we watched it closing on us, we became increasingly alarmed, for it was on a collision course with our formation.

By the time it was a half a mile from us and coming up fast, we in the conning tower were all on sharp lookout, some with binoculars, trying to spot this marauder. Suddenly there it was, looming up out of the dark one-quarter of a mile away, going at full speed. Under wartime sailing rules, we were not allowed to break radio silence.

They were headed right through our formation, cutting across it at a slight angle. Was there no way we could signal them of our dangerous location? Yes! Perhaps! There was a preplanned signal of lights, changed for each day, sent up for identification if called for. By turning a small crank, lights in proper configuration along the mast would briefly light up with each turn of the crank—perhaps they'd see it!

At intervals of a few seconds I gave one turn of the crank. By now they were only a few hundred yards from us. They couldn't see the signal! Didn't they have their radar on? The huge bulk of the ship bore down upon us—its speed was frightening—at least twice our own; it must have been a converted liner used as a command ship or transport. The top of our mast was only half way up to their deck.

It was against the rules to break formation, but as they bore down upon us, at the 'last minute' I broke formation and veered the ship away from them. As they passed by, we could hear the power of the thrusting propellers churning the waters, and we could feel the large waves cast by the passage of the ship. The rest of the whole formation also scattered like chicks before an angry hen, and we all spent considerable time pulling our ships back into the semblance of a proper formation again.

During all this time all that we ships had in common was a radar image of a threatening intruder and the scattering and reforming of our formation. Not one word was exchanged by radio. That's how it had to be. We also never heard anything more about it in Hawaii, although we did file a complaint.[6]

Several of the westward-bound ships encountered albatrosses on the way. Soon after LCS *14* left San Diego an albatross started following, but was unable to land in the ship's yardarm because of the sea swells. But it did land on a broom held up by a crew member. Crew members captured the bird, but released it after one of them explained what happened in Coleridge's famous poem, "The Rime of the Ancient Mariner."[7]

An albatross accompanied the LCS *82* on its way from Majuro to Eniwetok: "Sea birds found us and followed us for a while. A great albatross swung down on the restless wind, hung above a yardarm, measuring our speed, flicking a wing this way, that way, riding ripples in the breeze. He did not alight on the ship. For days he floated above us, effortless, beautiful, master of his vast and lonely domain. At mealtimes he swooped down to pick at garbage in the wake, and at night he slept on the sea, catching us again next morning. One morning he was gone. We watched for him."[8]

LCS *124* crew members were convinced that an albatross accompanying them between Panama and San Diego brought good fortune: "Our pharmacist's mate said 'That's an albatross and his following us makes us a charmed ship. We will have nothing but good luck and soon the cook will make home made bread and bake pies and we will come out of all danger unscathed.

"We had been having trouble with our water distiller and suddenly it was easy to fix. The cook baked some bread and later baked some pies. At Okinawa a kamikaze dove at us and was promptly shot out of the sky by an F4U Corsair right on his tail. On radar picket duty we suddenly found ourselves among some mines [in time to evade hitting them]. We invaded Ie Shima and were never fired on. One night on radar picket it was pitch black and a kamikaze came so close to our yardarm we thought we were goners. And so it went—the albatross had done a good job."[9]

LCS sailors looked forward to their first major stopover, Hawaii and Pearl Harbor, with great anticipation, and with a certain awe. Marvin Bertoch, *121* executive officer, recalled that "A paralyzed silence fell over everyone. Pearl Harbor! this was the place. We passed the submarine nets, and saw Hickam Field and its charred planes not yet completely cleared away. Black ashes that recalled a black day. My sudden flaring animosity wavered between hatred for the Japs and infuriation at the criminal carelessness and stupidity of Americans in high places at Pearl and in Washington who were caught asleep at their watch."[10]

The first LCSs to arrive at Pearl Harbor, the Flot One ships that left San Diego in October, were objects of great curiosity, particularly among Navy personnel. "What Navy are you from?" "Are you amphibious?" "What kind of gunboat are you?"

The Pearl Harbor base was a busy and crowded place. LCSs were berthed in West Lock, the berthing area farthest from the liberty area and Honolulu. Going from West Lock to the fleet landing took at least one hour and two boat rides; there was no liberty at night.

Even so, the weather was ideal most of the time and 'Liberty Hounds' crowded the streets of Honolulu, which some described as a city of souvenir shops and sailors, a city crawling with servicemen of all branches. There were bars, tatoo parlors (that tried the nerve of some LCS sailors, not unlike girls getting their ears pierced), a large USO (very convenient to thousands of servicemen), a Royal Palace, which served as a background for photos of LCS crews, and handsome churches.

In one of these, a large Congregational church, probably built by descendants of the New England puritans who converted the natives (as James Mitchener described in *Hawaii*), I witnessed a curious thing happening. Because of the mild weather, all doors were open and all windows lacked screens. During the Sunday morning sermon a large bird flew into the nave, perched on the keystone over the chancel and started chirping rather loudly, just as the preacher was quoting this line, "Why hast thou disquieted me?"

Depending on the time the ships were allowed to stay at the Pearl Harbor base, which varied for LCSs from eight days to several weeks or longer, crew members could attend schools; ships could load provisions and fuel and water, obtain engine parts, and have equipment fitted. A number of LCSs had their 50-caliber machine guns installed in Hawaii, not necessarily at naval installations. My ship got its four 50-caliber machine guns from an Army base in Hawaii. They seemed to have a surplus of these guns that were so essential to LCSs in the Philippines, Borneo, and Okinawa. Ships could be painted, and in cases of real emergency, repairs were not impossible, although LCSs were not high priority for such. Lucky crew members purchased movie projectors, record players, and sports equipment.

One real advantage of being berthed out in the 'boonies', so to speak, was that crew members could take walks and even all-day hikes and see and feel the rugged countryside, usually with a vast blue seascape as a backdrop. We could walk through sugar cane and pineapple fields for the first time in our lives. We could get at least some feel for the unique structure of the larger Pacific islands, which are plateaus and the tops of mountains, thousands of feet high above the ocean bottom. Later on, farther west, we would see, and even walk on, edges of submerged craters, which are the atolls—very high mountains in the sea.

Incidentally, I am certain that, like myself, very few of the LCS sailors had any idea of how deep the Pacific was in the areas where we sailed. The vastness of the water world under our ship's shallow flat bottoms would, had we known, have staggered our imaginations.

A few days before they were scheduled to leave Pearl Harbor, the *118* crew was surprised to see workmen place a huge combination money safe on their ship's fantail and lash it to the deck. Along with the safe, they received as passengers an ensign paymaster and three storekeepers. The crew was then informed that since the Navy always paid in cash, their ship would be the flotilla's cash carrier from which literally hundreds of crew members would be paid. Since the safe was too large to go below deck, it had to be carried topside and lashed down so it wouldn't go overboard.[11]

So even though LCS flotilla and group commanders in the advanced areas had several LC(FF)s at their disposal, they found it necessary to transport their cash in a large safe lashed to the deck of one of the ships—a safe too large to fit into any of the ships so that it had to be treated like a freight shipment. This arrangement served its purpose well, however, and is a good example of how the amphibious forces could, and did, improvise effectively when the need arose.

LCSs moving out of Pearl Harbor had four destinations—the Philippines, Iwo Jima, Borneo, and Okinawa. The first ships out were Flotilla One ships going in January to join the invasion forces in the Filipino island of Luzon. The first group of these ships to leave followed a southerly route, first to Funafuti in the Ellice Islands, and from there to the Russell Islands in the Solomons. From there they went to Hollandia, New Guinea, where for most of December training classes and practices for LCSs and other invasion support vessels were held.

During December eight ships joined the original group at Hollandia. In early January, two of these ships were assigned to a guerilla supply unit that would operate independently. In late February a group of three Flot One ships joined the ships serving in the Luzon area. In early March the remaining Flot One ships, which had been pressed into duty escorting LCTs from Pearl to Eniwetok, joined the Flot One ships to serve with them in the invasions of Borneo.

The first Flot Three ships to move out of Pearl Harbor were the 12 ships of Flot Three's Group Seven which proceeded to Eniwetok and then to Saipan to prepare for the Iwo Jima campaign. From Saipan they moved on to Iwo Jima where the campaign began on February 19.

Flot Three Group Eight ships left Pearl, and, like the Flot One ships, took a southerly route to Florida Island in the Solomons for preparation for the Okinawa campaign. Some of them went by way of Funafuti. From the Solomons they proceeded to Okinawa via Ulithi for the April 1 invasion. Several LCSs from Flot Three Group Nine escorted an LCT flotilla from Pearl to Eniwetok and went from there to Leyte and on to Okinawa. Other Group Nine ships went directly to Saipan via Eniwetok and then on to Okinawa.

Among the first Flotilla Four ships to leave Pearl Harbor were nine ships that served in the Okinawa invasion with Flot Three ships. These ships went to Okinawa via Eniwetok and Saipan, where they prepared for the invasion. Two groups of Flot Four ships escorted LCT flotillas from Pearl to Guam, taking over 35 days. My ship was an LCT group flagship in the second group; our crossing took 41 days. Consequently we didn't arrive at Okinawa until mid-April, after the invasion.

Flotilla Four ships continued arriving at Okinawa through May. Except for a few ships that arrived at Okinawa from Ulithi, the Flot Four ships traveled to Okinawa via Eniwetok, Guam, and Saipan, with some of them stopping over at Majuro. This same general travel route was followed by Flotilla Five ships which arrived at Okinawa during May, June, and July.

During February and March, a number of LCSs served as escorts for the hundreds of LCTs moving, under their own power, from Pearl westward, primarily to the Guam area. Previously these extremely useful 120-foot-long LCTs that carried troops, supplies, small vehicles, as well as tanks, had been transported in sections on freighters and 'papoose-fashion' on the decks of LSTs. These facilities evidently were no longer available. On at least six occasions LCSs escorted LCTs to advanced areas where they were sorely needed.

Outgoing LCT convoys were usually made up of one LCT flotilla (36 ships), five to nine LCSs, and a variable number of other ships—such as LCIs and LSMs—and at least one anti-submarine (ASW) ship such as a submarine chaser or destroyer escort. One feature of the convoys that varied the least was the convoy speed—4.5 to 6 knots depending on the sea and the winds. Because we had the sea and the winds with us most of the time, our LCT convoy averaged just under 6 knots for the Pearl to Guam trip.

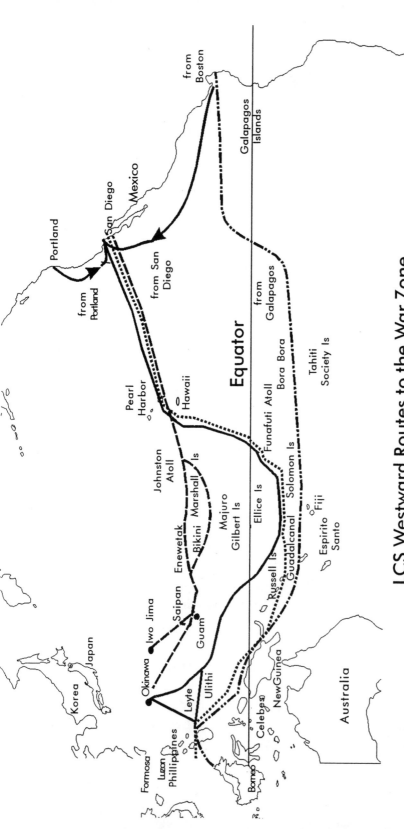

LCS Westward Routes to the War Zone

Most Flotilla One ships followed southern routes,

▬▬▬ from San Diego via Pearl Harbor, the Ellice Islands, the Russell Islands and New Guinea to their destinations in the Philippines and Borneo.

•••••• Some Flot One ships (from Boston), also destined for the Philippines and Borneo, bypassed both San Diego and Pearl Harbor, sailing below the Equator all the way from west of Galapagos to New Guinea.

━•━•━ Some Flot Three ships followed a southerly route via the Solomon Islands and Ulithi.

━━━ Some Flot Three ships and all Flot Four and Five ships moved west from Pearl Harbor to Okinawa with possible stopovers at Johnston Island and or Leyte to their destination Okinawa.

━ ━ ━ Other Flot Three ships and all Flot Four and Five ships moved west from Pearl Harbor to Okinawa with possible stopovers at Johnston Island and Majuro Atoll, definite stopovers at Einewtok and Saipan, and a final stopover at Guam or Ulithi.

Moving out ahead of the other Flot Three and Four ships, Flot Three Group Seven ships turned north at Saipan to fight at Iwo Jima and then go on to Okinawa via Saipan.

While this speed was tediously slow for the LCSs, who had to use only two of their eight engines to maintain it, it was a real challenge for the LCTs that were not designed for ocean voyages. They had an endurance of only 700 miles at 7 knots and a maximum speed of only 8 knots. Because a number of LCTs had seen considerable service, their engines and steering equipment were not in the best of shape. Consequently they did suffer engine breakdowns as well as rudder jams and other problems; their small crews of one officer/chief petty officer and 11 men were sometimes hard-put to maintain station and keep them moving forward at even 5 to 6 knots. Yet through efforts sometimes close to heroic, LCT crews moved their vessels over thousands of miles to advanced areas where they were most useful.

In February there were three convoys, two out of Pearl (one to Eniwetok and one to Guam), and one out of Biak, New Guinea, to Leyte. In March there were three more convoys, all out of Pearl—two early in the month (one to Guam and one, made up of about 100 LCTs, to Eniwetok), and the third later in March to Leyte. The convoys going the farthest—from Pearl to Guam—took from 35 to 42 days, usually with at least three welcome stopovers.

In a typical convoy the LCTs were spread out—six columns across and six ships deep, with LCSs and other ships at the flanks and to the rear, and the ASW ship(s) darting and almost dancing from side to side at the head of the convoy. In this formation the convoy moved at a turtle's pace for days into weeks toward the war zones.

With a slight stretch of the imagination, the slowly moving spectacle could be pictured as 36 covered wagons (some of the LCTs had canvas awnings) with armed riders guarding each side and the rear and a scout leading the way at the front. But this covered wagon train, rolling across the prairie of the Great Pacific, did not stop at night and form a circle for protection. It kept moving west night and day, and its riders continued to pray for good weather (which, miraculously, most of the convoys enjoyed the whole long time). The LCSs were the armed guards 'riding shotgun' and on constant alert for an attack.

In reality this formation was used so that the three LCT group commanders at the rear could supervise their charges in front of them with their loud bullhorns, and could come to their aid when necessary. In the convoy from Pearl to Guam in which my ship participated, we served as an LCT group flagship. Our 'flag' was the group commander, who had with him a small staff to help him supervise and give aid to the 12 LCTs moving in three columns ahead of us. Curiously, during the long endless days the LCTs in our convoy seldom needed aid. Night was a different story. LCTs would sometimes 'fall out' of formation, and we and the other LCS group flagships spent part of our mornings rounding up our charges.

When LCTs broke down or their rudders jammed, they required towing. At this point, we discovered the hard way our ships' shortcomings as salvage and towing vessels. Getting the LCS's anchor cable (the strongest cable we had) over to the men on the bow of the bobbing LCT on a pitch-dark night turned out to be more challenging than the LCS crews had imagined. Even more discouraging was the towline parting three minutes after the start of the towing. In spite of these setbacks, and sometimes after two or three unsuccessful attempts and occasionally with the help of fleet tugboats, LCSs in our convoy were able to provide the towing necessary to get the LCTs to their destination.

Although the nights were sometimes nightmarish, the long days were pleasantly monotonous; those of us in the LCS crews, many of whom were 17-to 19-year-old boys, found ourselves living in a world that seemed to be standing still, a world that forced us to call on our own resources to find meaningful things to do. Here we were going into battle, but in a world and at a pace we never imagined.

By way of compensation, we were as close to nature and as acutely aware of nature as we would probably ever be again. Some of us put out lines from our ships and caught strange and exotic fish. We were frequently entertained by hundreds of graceful and engaging porpoises and dolphins over the side and off in the distance. We saw dramatic sunrises and sunsets. At night we were startled by the brilliant planets and constellations of stars spread across an unbroken sky. Almost every morning we threw overboard flying fish that had landed on the deck during the night. One crew member suggested that maybe the fish had mistaken us for an aircraft carrier. We were living on and with the vastness of the sea in an experience of a lifetime.

Richard Lewis, our ship's executive officer, shared an experience he had at Majuro when our convoy stopped there:

Along the route of the long slow voyage from Hawaii to the islands of Tinian, Saipan, and Guam, our little convoy of 36 LCTs, 8 LCSs, and 2 destroyer escorts, also made a brief stop at Majuro Atoll. We had the commander of a group of LCTs on board, Lieutenant Stan Osman, and that relieved the monotony of the voyage (41 days in all—the longest single good weather period of the war in the Pacific—therefore the convoy of light and slow LCTs on the high seas). He taught us to play cribbage, and that was a new game to several of us.

As we landed in the gloaming of sunset at beautiful, tropical Majuro, we docked at a T-shaped pier made of floating pontoons. It was a quiet evening when we went ashore later. At the Officer's Club, we drank, talked with those from other ships in our group, and made friends with the men stationed at the Atoll.

When it came time to go home, the wind had come up, there were occasional light showers, and, of course, it was dark due to the cloud cover—and most of us had had a few drinks. Stan Osman was pretty jovial as I helped him along the pier; I wanted to look out for him. It was just about totally dark, and the pier's pontoons were booming noisily as they bobbed about and banged into each other in the watery chop.

Official certification signed by both Neptunus Rex and Davey Jones that an LCS sailor has crossed the Equator and has been initiated into the "solemn mysteries of the Ancient Order of the Deep." Courtesy of Robert Amick.

As we worked our way forward, Stan said, 'Do you see it, Dick?' and I reassured him, 'Yeah, I see it!' but I didn't know what he meant. The next moment, I was in the water. A gap had opened up (which I didn't see) where two of the pier pontoons had swung apart. Just as I came up, there was a loud boom when the two pontoons banged together—fortunately I was in the opening watery space between the pontoon's corners, so when they banged together, I was not decapitated. Of course, I realized my buddies would be concerned, so down in my dark watery hole I called out, 'I am topside!'—meaning my head was out of the water and I was safe. When they heard this, they were, on the one hand, greatly relieved, but on the other hand, the words I had said, in contrast to being out of sight, in a dark hole, submerged in the water, beneath steel pier flanges, were such a caricature of the reality, that my friends burst out laughing in the rain before jerking me up out of the water by my arms when the pontoons swung open.[12]

Some LCS crews crossing the Equator on southerly routes to their destinations held King Neptune ceremonies, or, more appropriately, Shellback Initiations, to celebrate the crossing. For these occasions, the Shellbacks (sailors who had already crossed the Equator) prepared all sorts of impossible things for the initiates to do. All the answers that initiates gave to questions from Neptune's court were wrong, even when they were right, as several initiates reported. Officer initiates got the same treatment as the men.

Initiates were lucky to escape without getting a haircut (either a Mohawk or a bare stripe front to back), or a beating, or having their body painted. Not all the ceremonies, however, were as wearing on the initiates. For his initiation on a Flot One ship, an officer was required to stand 'iceberg watch' on the ship's bow in long winter underwear and souwester boots. Ships that took the occasion seriously flew the Jolly Roger, informing the world that they were pirates (of the Gilbert and Sullivan variety). At least one ship's crew took the Order of the Golden Dragon ceremony seriously on crossing the International Date Line which all ships crossed in both directions. Initiates at that ceremony got their heads shaved.

In late February, while they were in the Solomons Islands, LCS *14* crew members did what a number of their sister ships' crews would do later in a number of places. They helped to put out a fire on a large cargo ship, the SS *Henry M. Stephens*, which was carrying aviation fuel. The *14* crew's presence at the fire was crucial because when the LCS pulled alongside the cargo ship, only the ship's captain and two crew members were fighting the intensely hot fire three decks down. The rest of the ship's crew were crowded on the ship's fantail seemingly waiting for word to abandon ship.

The only access to the fire was a ladder in a vertical tube, through which the ship's captain and five men (a fresh five each time) from the LCS *14* crew would take turns going down for as long as they could stand it. The fire was so intense that when water hit it at one point, great volumes of steam and smoke filled the compartment and choked the firefighters.

It took a crucial action to finally extinguish the fire. The LCS *14* crew rigged a Handy Billy portable fire pump so water could be put on the fire from another direction. In addition to discovering how difficult intensely hot fires below decks can be, the *14* crew witnessed a valiant captain in action, going down again and again into the hot inferno to show fresh groups of firefighters what to do.[13]

Maintaining shipboard discipline over relatively long periods at sea could be a vexing problem for captains and executive officers. It was much easier to punish offenders while the ship was in port; they could be restricted to the ship, be given extra duty, be confined to the ship's brig or to a brig on the shore. Complicating the problem was the LCS's lack of an official brig—a place to confine and punish offenders. Some ships converted magazines and other storage places into brigs, usually on a temporary basis. But there were problems with these. Space in them was limited, particularly for two men, and ventilation was inadequate.

One perennial problem with confining men on bread and water in the brig was that crew members would slip food to them on the sly. Also this temporary brig was not a suitable place for anyone to be while the ship was underway. Crew members had to be free to deal with the sometimes violent rolling and pitching of the ship.

Occasionally ships' captains, out of frustration, perhaps, would devise punishments for their crew that their executive officers would have real difficulty enforcing. This happened on my ship, as Dick Lewis, who was acting executive officer at the time explained:

> We had left Guam behind, now we were really heading into the war zone.
> The weather had been nasty for several days. A few of the crew were
> sullen and somewhat 'rebellious'. So the captain singled out one of them
> and decided on an unusual punishment. Then he ordered me, temporary

executive officer at the time, to order the man to do what the punishment consisted of.

The waves were still running heavy, but not so bad as before. When the small snub-nosed bow (of the ship) dipped down after a wave, the water would come just about up to the level of the deck, sometimes just sloshing across it, before the bow would begin to come up again before the next wave, and the weather was lousy. The swing of the bow up and down was considerable and lively. Near the rear of the bow surface was a solid steel bollard with a small flat top for attaching ropes to when tying up.

I had to order one of our quartermasters to go up on the bow and sit on that bollard for one hour, where he was totally exposed to the by-no-means clearly predictable seas. He was in danger of being swept overboard. Against all my feeling of decency, I had to carry out the order, possibly risking the life of a man against my will.

This heightened the already existing tensions on the ship to a high degree. I sure didn't want to get thrown overboard in those seas. For some days I wore a pistol on my belt just 'in case', and felt very insecure in regard to the crew, and filled with outrage and resentment toward the captain.[14]

As their ships moved closer to their assigned battle areas, crew members speculated on and questioned what was in store for them. Their thoughts and anxieties were somewhat along these lines: Will the Iwo Jima invasion be as bad as they say it will be? Will we meet heavy opposition going into Okinawa? Will the Japanese put up a strong defense in the Philippines invasions?

How long will we bombard the beaches? Will we be using our guns against enemy planes after the invasion(s)? Since our primary purpose is to support landing troops in invasions and to bombard the beaches, what will we be doing after the invasion(s)? Will we encounter suicide planes? Suicide boats? (Crew members were probably not even aware of the existence of suicide swimmers at that time.) Will we have to fight fire and serve as salvage ships, and who will we serve? After Iwo Jima, the Philippines, Borneo, Okinawa, will we invade Japan?

Flotilla One ships moving into Luzon and into the southern and central Philippines later knew they would be involved in invasions, but how many and how large? They were aware of suicide boats, but knew little or nothing about their number or their menace. They did not know that they would be protecting minesweepers and underwater demolition teams before the invasions, or shooting their guns (even their small arms) at floating mines. Unless the ships going into

Borneo had served in the Philippines, they would not know either about these pre-invasion imperatives.

Group Seven ships (of Flotilla Three) invading Iwo Jima were certain the invasion would be dangerous. They would be assaulting the beaches with all the artillery they could muster—thousands of shells and rockets. But they probably did not anticipate firing continuously for 48 hours and making 10 to 13 rocket bombardments of the beaches in those first two days. Nor could they foresee supporting troops ashore with their guns and rockets, and as part of spotting teams, directing fire from the larger ships to targets on the beach.

Crews of Flotillas Three, Four, and Five going into Okinawa knew they would be part of a large invasion, but what else might they be doing? Would they be used for small-scale invasions of nearby hostile islands? Certainly their firefighting ability would be used. And their anti-aircraft firing ability, but how, where, when?

They did not know that they would serve on anti-suicide boat patrols or on radar picket patrol 50 miles out at sea—they had no idea what radar picket patrol was. They did not know that they would be shooting down kamikaze planes and keeping larger ships afloat, pumping out their flooded compartments and providing them with damage control.

They did not know that they would be taking care of hundreds of wounded men from the damaged and sunken radar picket ships, that they would rescue over 2,600 men from the waters and the sinking and damaged ships on the picket stations.

Endnotes

[1] Frank Muth, Untitled autobiographical narrative, n.d., 4-5.

[2] Ibid., 5.

[3] Wes Clark, letter to author, n.d.

[4] Stanley, "Kamikaze—The Battle for Okinawa," 1988, 9.

[5] Frederick H. Lamartin, *120* captain, letter to author, September 9, 1996.

[6] Lewis, "Near Miss," n.d.

[7] Korany, *LCSL 14—One of the Mighty Midgets,* n.d., 36.

[8] *Mighty Midget—USS LCS 82,* 64.

[9] R. L. Stone, *124* crew member, letter to Richard Rhame, Dec. 28, 1989.

[10] *The Little Ships* (Salt Lake City, Utah, 1989), 54.

[11] Blanton, *Boston to Jacksonville,* 40.

[12] Lewis, "Majuro Pontoons," n.d.

[13] Korany, 42-43.

[14] Lewis, "Wet Seat," n.d.

Chapter 5

Retaking and Liberating the Philippines[1]

The first LCSs to arrive in the advanced area, *26, 27, 48,* and *49,* reached Hollandia, New Guinea, in December of 1944. These ships, under Captain Rae E. Arison, Commander, LCS Flotilla One, in LCS *48,* along with others that were to join them shortly, became part of the Seventh Fleet's VIIth Amphibious Corps early in January 1945 at a crucial point in the campaign to retake and liberate the Philippine Islands. In the previous fall the Navy had won the important Battle of Leyte Gulf; by the end of 1944, US forces had retaken important areas on the strategic island of Leyte.

In December they captured Mindoro Island just below the island of Luzon, and on January 9 they invaded Luzon itself at Lingayen, spearheading a move to cut off the Bataan Peninsula from the rest of Luzon and retake the strategic Corregidor Island as well as the capital city of Manila. One of their primary objectives in taking Manila was to free the survivors of the hundreds of American prisoners held there by the Japanese since 1942. After this, US forces would go on to retake and liberate areas in the central and southern parts (primarily the Visayas and Mindanao) of the extensive Philippine Archipelago.

Accompanying Captain Arison on his arrival in Hollandia and the Philippines was his Flotilla One staff which he organized at San Diego in September and utilized thereafter. Officer positions on his staff included an operations and gunnery officer, a material officer, a communications officer, and three communication watch officers, who also served as staff secretary, flotilla personnel officer, and radio material officer. Under the supervision of the communications officer the three watch officers maintained a 24-hour radio and visual signal watch for flotilla ships throughout the Philippines and Borneo campaigns.

Enlisted positions, several of which were filled by chief petty officers, included a number of radiomen, radio technicians, and at least one radar man; three signalmen and a quartermaster; two yeomen and two storekeepers; one motor machinist's mate and one electrician's mate; and two steward's mates.

Captain Rae Arison, USN, Commander, Flotilla One. Courtesy of Robert Amick.

Some of the staff's duties, in addition to maintaining a communications watch, were to support all flotilla operations and handle personnel matters (there were between 1,750 and 1,800 officers and men serving in Flotilla One). To the fullest extent of their facilities, the staff provided individual ship's crews with help for their repair and maintenance problems.

Arriving with his staff in the Philippines early in January was Lieutenant Commander Willard F. Hunt, Commander of Group One (12 ships) of Flotilla One on LCS *30*. All of the ships in his group (except *Nine* and *Ten* as pointed out below) participated in the Philippines campaign, and several of them went on to serve later at Borneo. On March 3 Lieutenant Maynes C. Fitzgerald, Commander of Group 2, the other Flot One group, arrived on LCS *42* with his staff. A number of his 12 ships served at both the Philippines and Borneo, and those of his ships arriving later served at Borneo.

These two group staffs each had an operations officer, a material and engineering officer, and a communications officer. They did not maintain a 24-

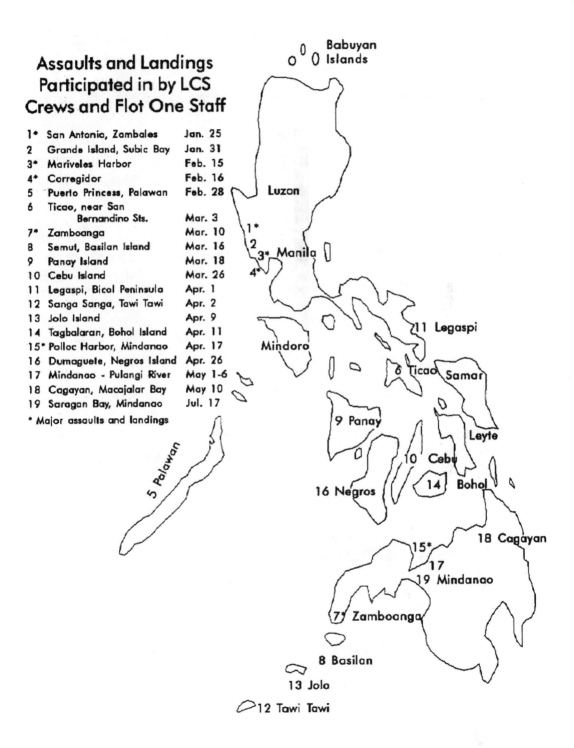

Assaults and Landings Participated in by LCS Crews and Flot One Staff

1*	San Antonio, Zambales	Jan. 25
2	Grande Island, Subic Bay	Jan. 31
3*	Mariveles Harbor	Feb. 15
4*	Corregidor	Feb. 16
5	Puerto Princess, Palawan	Feb. 28
6	Ticao, near San Bernandino Sts.	Mar. 3
7*	Zamboanga	Mar. 10
8	Semut, Basilan Island	Mar. 16
9	Panay Island	Mar. 18
10	Cebu Island	Mar. 26
11	Legaspi, Bicol Peninsula	Apr. 1
12	Sanga Sanga, Tawi Tawi	Apr. 2
13	Jolo Island	Apr. 9
14	Tagbalaran, Bohol Island	Apr. 11
15*	Polloc Harbor, Mindanao	Apr. 17
16	Dumaguete, Negros Island	Apr. 26
17	Mindanao - Pulangi River	May 1-6
18	Cagayan, Macajalar Bay	May 10
19	Saragan Bay, Mindanao	Jul. 17

* Major assaults and landings

hour watch like the flot staff, but they included two very essential officers not found on the flot staff—a medical officer and a supply and disbursing officer. Consequently, these group staffs had fewer enlisted positions in communications and navigation areas but had at least three storekeepers and a comparable number of pharmacist's mates.

On January 1 Captain Arison became the Commander of Close Support in the VIIth Amphibious Corps, in charge of an LCI(R) group, an LCI(G) group, three LCI(D)s, three LCI(M)s, as well as all the LCSs in the area. As of January 1st, seven more LCSs—*7, 9, 10, 28-30,* and *50,* joined the four ships that arrived in December. Not all of these, however, were utilized immediately as part of the Close Support Group. Two of them, in fact, *Nine* and *Ten,* became primary fire support ships in a small guerrilla supply task group that would for the next six months support guerrilla operations over a large part of the Philippines. (These operations are described in Chapter 6. The Liberators—Task Group 70.4)

On January 25, Captain Arison, on LCS *48,* was in the advance echelon of Task Group 78.3, Amphibious Group IX, under Admiral Strubble, on the way to amphibious landings in central Luzon. LCSs in the force were *7, 8, 26, 27, 48,* and *49.* The group's first encounter with the enemy was surprisingly noncombative. While the LCSs were leading the first assault waves into the beach off San Antonio village in Zambales Province and preparing to provide them fire support, the attack group discovered an American flag flying among a crowd of friendly natives. Thirty thousand Sixth Army troops were landed in the midst of hundreds of cheering Filipinos.

Here is an on-the-spot account by one LCS crew member from the gun deck of the *26:*

> *We head right in toward the coast,*
> *Each ship a blur, just like a ghost.*
> *Each crew's alert, all guns are manned,*
> *We must surprise, just as planned.*
> *Mine Sweeps go in to sweep for mines,*
> *We now await signals or signs.*
> *Scouts have landed and signal out,*
> *"Friendly natives, no Japs about."*
> *A six mile beach we are to seize,*
> *A stretch of sand, then miles of trees.*
> *We head straight in, then wheel to port,*
> *There's not a shot, not one retort.*

Small craft are next, they come in groups,
Wave after wave, jammed with troops.
They hit the beach, troops make a rush,
Across the sand to gain the brush.
Just then a mob bursts from the town,
Waving and shouting they run on down
To meet the troops and welcome them,
A thousand souls no power could stem.
Two flags were borne by standard bearers,
The one is ours, the other theirs.
I never thought that I would see
Folks so starved for liberty.
It is a sight I'll ne'er forget,
It thrilled me so I feel it yet.[2]

On January 31 the LCSs led an assault group into Subic Bay past large guns on Grande Island, which might have been manned, but fortunately were not. The LCSs proceeded on toward Olongapo, but did not open fire because enemy troops were seen retreating. That night the LCSs were assigned to remain in Subic Bay as a naval defense unit.

At this time the XIV Army Corps was moving to capture and retake Manila and release American prisoners held since 1942.[3] LCSs conducted a reconnaissance on February 1 of the beaches and inlets in the Subic Bay area, where they found a deserted Japanese boat repair base for suicide ('Shinyo') boats. Used as weapons by the Japanese, these 20-foot boats were manned by a volunteer driver who aimed his boat at a US ship so that the 500-pound TNT charge in the bow would detonate on impact and cause severe damage. This boat repair base was later destroyed completely by Filipino guerrilla forces.

Two days before the assault on Corregidor on February 16, two LCSs, *26* and *27*, participated for the first time in escorting and protecting minesweepers and in mine demolition duty. LCSs would pursue this activity both in harbors and on the high seas throughout the rest of the war and for months afterward in distant waters around China, Korea, Japan, and Formosa. Around Corregidor and Mariveles Peninsula the LCSs escorted minesweepers, provided anti-aircraft and anti-shore fire protection when needed, and destroyed by gunfire and even small arms all mines cut and released.[4] Some LCS crews later became very adept at this highly dangerous and important work, described in the pages that follow.

While working with minesweepers in the Corregidor/Mariveles area, crewmen on *26* witnessed one sweeper's sinking after being hit by a mine and two destroyers limping away after taking hits. In this operation *26* demolished 30 mines; *27* demolished 29 in the two days. On February 15, 6 LCSs, *7, 8, 26, 27, 48,* and *49,* as part of Task Unit 78.37, supported landings in Mariveles Harbor, where they bombarded beaches with their rockets and met only minor opposition. In the operation LCS *48* towed and protected LSM *169*, hit by a mine, and rescued 12 of its crew who had been hurled into the bay by a large explosion.

On the evening of February 15, after the assault on Mariveles Harbor, five of six LCSs, *7, 8, 26, 27,* and *49,* were anchored across the harbor entrance as a screen against suicide boats to protect three beached LSTs and LSM *169*, hit earlier by a mine. Beginning at approximately 0300 on February 16, the anchored LCSs were attacked by a number of suicide boats. Three of them, *7, 26,* and *49,* were sunk; *27* was so severely damaged that it was forced to beach. The *27* had destroyed five enemy boats during the attack, but was mortally damaged when the sixth exploded close by. Only the *Eight* and *48,* the flagship, were unscathed and thus able to participate in the major assault on Corregidor a few hours later on the same morning.

Here is a vivid eye-witness account of the tragic event by Richard Rhame, who at the time was serving on *48* as communications staff officer for Flotilla One:

> As the sun set over the hills ringing Mariveles, the six LCSs assumed their assigned positions 500 yards from each other across the mouth of Mariveles Bay. The narrow confines of the Bay precluded the usual post-invasion LCS off-shore moving protective picket formation. They were ideally situated to experience the panorama of the combined firepower focusing in on Corregidor by the big ships out at sea and the planes overhead, blasting 'The Rock' in preparation for the following day's landings. The mighty guns of the Seventh Fleet pumped ear-splitting round-after-round from their muzzles, hurling their deadly messengers directly onto 'The Rock'. The planes drenched the tadpole-shaped island's crags with napalm bombs, exploding into molten cascades of volcanic fire—both beautiful and awesome—flowing down the rugged cliffs.
>
> Suddenly the stillness of the early morning was shattered by a blinding flash! Simultaneously, multiple explosions erupted all along the line of

stationary LCS(L)s. The morning sky was aglow with deadly pyrotechnics: bursting shells, fiery streaks of ricocheting tracers piercing the darkness from all directions. Burning oil transformed Mariveles Bay into a blazing sea of flames!

The LCS(L)s in their exposed positions had come under a surprise attack by Japanese suicide boats ('skunks'), sallying forth from their hidden sea-caves on Corregidor—each heavily packed with deadly explosives designed to detonate upon collision with its selected target.

The staccato firing from the 50-caliber machine guns from the LCS(L)s echoed amidst the din of the battle. The larger guns could not be angled down sufficiently to be effective against the surface-level invaders. Voice messages from the ships of the fleet outside the harbor flooded the Communications Center of LCS *48*. The larger fleet vessels at sea were not positioned to offer assistance; a destroyer, firing illumination shells over the harbor in its efforts to be helpful, was ordered by Captain Arison to cease such activity as it was being used by the attackers to zero in on their targets with great accuracy.[5]

Ensign D. C. Demeter described what was happening on the *Seven*: "By the time our radar operators interpreted the signal, there wasn't much time for shooting. Not even time to man all guns. When I regained consciousness (after the blinding explosion) the conn [bridge] was a mass of wreckage. The entire port side and superstructure was ablaze. Our rockets were going off and ammunition was exploding all around. Men were lying about the decks with burns and broken bones. The ship was sinking."[6]

Lieutenant(j.g.) Charles Trezona, on *49*, recalled his ship's last moments:

We had no warning of the attack. The ship was hit twice in a minute and a half and didn't have a chance. At 0300 something whizzed out of the darkness, holed into the after end of the ship, and our port side shot into flames. None of us had ever seen anything like it before. The low-slung pointed boat just disintegrated against the side of the ship. We had organized a party to fight the fire caused by the first ramming, when something struck us forward on the starboard side and the ship heaved. I was thrown into the water.

Some of our rafts and gas drums floated by in the wreckage. The officers were swimming about rounding up groups of men and assigning the badly hurt to rafts. It was one of the coolest performances I've ever seen and all

---

hands deserve the credit. The skipper was seriously injured himself, but gave his lifebelt to one of the weaker men and held another in his arms for two hours while clinging to a drum.

One of the wounded men had a lifebelt and couldn't inflate it. Though part of my upper teeth had been knocked out in the explosion, somehow I managed to blow his belt up; I still don't know where the necessary air came from.[7]

The most vivid and expressive account of this tragic event and the feelings it generated was given by W. M. (Marty) Kingwell, crew member and survivor of the *26:*

> *Tonight we're placed at Harbor's mouth,*
> *Five ships in line from north to south.*
> *I'm standing watch, t'ween three and four,*
> *There comes a flash, an awful roar.*
> *We stand in awe, we hear men scream,*
> *It seems unreal as if a dream.*
> *Another flash, they've hit one more,*
> *It lights us up, the flames now soar.*
> *We look in vain, we cannot see,*
> *What caused all this, what can it be?*
> *I see them now, just two grey shapes,*
> *They're coming fast, I see their wakes.*
> *Torpedo-like boats, Suicides,*
> *A crazy Jap in each one rides.*
> *The one hits near, we feel the thud,*
> *It don't explode, it is a dud.*
> *It was God's will, I'm satisfied,*
> *He interfered or I'd have died.*
> *Toward the bow, the other hit,*
> *A blinding flash the sky is lit.*
> *Our ship's in flames, men run about,*
> *Trapped men now scream, others shout.*
> *I turn to leave, a blow I feel,*
> *My forehead stings, it makes me reel.*
> *I keep my feet, I gain the rail,*
> *I can't give up, I must not fail.*
> *I hit the sea, I head for shore.*

Some mates are near, there's three or four,
We swim awhile, then turn to gaze,
The ship now sinks, the sea's ablaze
From burning oil, which soon burns out,
Once more it's dark, men swim about.
Jap snipers fire from off Bataan,
I'm glad it's dark, three hours til dawn.
They say at dawn the trees bore fruit,
Jap bodies hung, quite limp and mute.
I reach the shore, I utter thanks,
Then stagger up the rocky banks.
At dawn they come to rescue us,
We're cold and grim, there's little fuss.[8]

An account from Lieutenant Risley P. Lawrence, captain of the severely damaged *27*: "After the first explosion we heard and saw the *49* come under attack and sink. Shortly we came under attack by small boats coming at us amidships on both sides. Our guns, now fully manned, sank the two coming in and strangely they did not explode. It was then that the *26*, anchored just forward of us, came under attack and sank, just as the *7* and *49* had done. The *27* then became the focal point of the attack and she was able to sink three additional boats before the attack ceased. One of these boats did blow up close aboard our port side causing two deaths and several injuries and much damage to our vessel."[9]

Don Profitt, crew member on the undamaged *Eight*, described the rescue effort: "While the men of the *Seven* and the *27* struggled to control their fires, our ship and the *48* searched for survivors. At the same time, we sure tried to keep a sharp eye out for more skunks. After we picked up as many survivors as we could find in the darkness and confusion, a few more were transferred from the P.T. boats that had come out to help us."[10]

Earlier during this action, *Eight* reported sighting a midget submarine firing into the harbor area. It disappeared, however, before action could be taken against it.

Casualties suffered in the action included the complete loss of the *Seven*, *26*, and *49*, and the beaching and putting out of action of the *27*. Two officers and 60 men were killed and a number wounded.[11] Of the original six-ship unit, only *Eight* and *48* remained to support the invasion and assault on Corregidor the next day.

LCS Eight *and* 48 *(from which the picture was taken) bombarding the beach in support of the Corregidor invasion on February 16. Courtesy of US Navy.*

Richard Rhame concluded a detailed account of the loss of the ships and the men at Mariveles Bay with words that echo the feelings of all LCS sailors everywhere, even today: "Left behind beneath the blue-grey waters of Mariveles Bay were those 62 brave men who had given their lives in the best tradition of the Navy. Their sacrifices will live forever in the hearts and minds of their mates."[12]

After the rescue of survivors, Captain Arison established a screen made up of *Eight* and *48* for the protection of LST *666* (serving as a hospital ship) and LSM *169*, both of which had LCS survivors aboard.

Evidently the suicide boats' attack on the LCSs could have been more devastating than it was; all the boats dispatched by the Japanese failed to reach the screening ships according to Japanese records. The Japanese officer in charge sent out approximately 30 boats on February 15 to attack the anchored landing craft. A number, however, lost their way or were stalled and swamped so that only about a dozen got to the harbor. The wonder is that the Japanese did not send more suicide boats in the beginning.[13]

Early in the morning of February 16, a very few hours after the suicide boat attack, the amphibious/parachute assault and landing on Corregidor took place. At first there was slight opposition from the Japanese on the island; the feeling was that the heavy and extended bombardment by air and ship had taken its toll, but then heavy fire from Caballo Island opened up on the landing boats. "Every boat making the beach was hit, one boat in the third wave was hit 40 times by enemy fire."[14] Japanese in tunnels and caves put up a fanatical resistance; casualties among the thousands of paratroopers dropping on the island were so high that the third wave, scheduled to drop the next day, was flown to Subic Bay to be taken in by boat.

The part played in the assault and landing by the two remaining LCSs, *Eight* and *48*, was detailed by Richard Rhame, staff officer for Flotilla One:

The two LCSs participated in the assault with four LCI(R)s. All hands were in a highly nervous condition after the previous night's events, but this served, it seemed, to increase the fury of their attack rather than to decrease it. As was customary, the Close Support Craft preceded the assault craft toward the beach. After passing inside of Caballo Island, Japanese coast defense guns and artillery on that island opened fire on us from the rear, and mortar, three-inch, and machine-gun fire were coming from the left flank and machine-gun fire from ahead.

When we are about 600 yards from the beach, a line of controlled mines was exploded and the Support Craft were tossed clear of the water but not otherwise damaged. The rocket barrage had been fired and as three of the LCI(R)s had been hit by enemy shell fire, the LCI(R)s were directed to retire and the two LCSs took over the work of rendering close support to the troops ashore. Enemy fire was coming from caves on the left flank of the beach so these were taken under three-inch and 40mm fire and the enemy silenced by blocking the cave entrances with fallen soil. A shoreline reconnaissance was then made of the entire southeastern arm of the island. Destroyer and cruiser fire had silenced Caballo Island. No further fire came from that area.

Army troops reported mortar fire from ravines on the eastern slopes of the main island. The LCSs closed to the beaches in that area and subjected the ravines to concentrated rocket barrage. Japanese mortar fire ceased. A close reconnaissance of the lower slopes of the south and east side of the main island gave evidence of enemy troops located in well camouflaged strong points. These positions were strafed with 40mm and 20mm fire. The day's action was so fast that it was necessary to retire several times in order to allow the 40mm cooling systems to cool off. The assault lasted until 1800.[15]

Eight and *48* participated in landings on Corregidor the next day (February 17); on the following day, *48* (with Captain Arison in command) supported Army reconnaissance patrol along the Bataan coast and discovered evidence of enemy evacuation.

In late February Commander Flotilla One acquired a flagship LCI(L) *778*; on February 24 the new flagship, *Eight,* and *48* began working with the minesweepers in Manila Bay and on February 27 in the San Bernardino Straits. The three ships provided gunfire support and served as a mine demolition unit. At 1350 on February 24, *Eight* destroyed a Japanese barge containing six or seven Japanese. On the afternoon of February 25 the *48* spotted, at different times, two life rafts containing Japanese military. As they approached the first raft with five men aboard, the Japanese set off grenades or booby traps which wounded eleven LCS *48* crew members, forcing *48* to shoot the Japanese. In the second instance, *48* shot the four Japanese military on a raft as soon as they were in range.

During February, while the US Army was continuing its attack on Manila and bombarding the Walled City, Japanese soldiers attempting to escape to Bataan took to the waters off Manila and subjected the new flotilla flagship (LCI(L) *778*) to attack. Here is Richard Rhame's description of this unusual conflict: "The waters off the northern section of the city were crowded with Japanese soldiers floating on bamboo rafts, using bamboo logs to support individuals and, in a few cases, in small boats. The Japanese in the water were fanatics and LCI(L) *778* was subjected to a concentrated attack by swimming Japanese. Several hand grenades were thrown at the ship. One Jap blew himself up under the bow and another blew himself up alongside. The ship was tossed in several directions but no damage was sustained. Small-arms fire and machine-gun fire were brought to bear on the swimmers and no further trouble was encountered. One Japanese soldier was captured by LCI(L) *778* and sent back to Subic Bay."[16]

On February 28, LCSs *28-30* and *50*, working under Commander D. H. Day, VII Amphibious Corps, participated in the assault and invasion of Palawan island in the central Philippines. Joe Rhoads, engineering officer on *50*, described the part played by the LCSs: "We escorted the first waves of troops toward the beach banging away with our 3-inch 50 and twin 40s until we were within rocket range. We then put our rockets on the beach, SWISH, SWISH, SWISH! The early morning jitters and fears were gone. We had done it and now were 'Seasoned Veterans.' Later that afternoon the LCSs escorted a smaller task force to a small island, just off Palawan."[17]

Taking Palawan brought US air forces 150 miles closer to Indochina. Although the invasion was unopposed because the Japanese had gone into the hills, there was a real sense of danger that everyone was aware of, as *28* crew member Fred Bors reported: "When we invaded Puerto Princessa, Palawan, our ship was assigned close support to the Army. The first night our anchorage was close to an island at the mouth of a river. There were reports of suicide swimmers and boats in the area. We were most vulnerable at night when the tide was running out. Every log and bush that floated out was cause for concern. We knew that our 20mm's wouldn't depress low enough if we were attacked at that close range, so our only defense was hand weapons. We didn't get much rest until the island was secured."[18]

Bors went on to report that his ship acquired 50-caliber machine guns as soon as they possibly could. Many LCSs moving to advanced areas, to Okinawa as well as the Philippines, followed suit when their crews realized the elevation limitations of the 20mm and 40mm guns.

The LCSs that fought in the Corregidor campaign and those campaigns immediately previous to it joined hundreds of other naval vessels in bringing about an event of tremendous symbolic significance—the return of General MacArthur on March 3 to Corregidor, which he had been forced to leave on March 12, 1942, almost three years before.

On March 3 LCSs *Eight* and *48* and LSM *316* participated in the US troop landing at Ticao near the San Bernardino Strait. At what turned out to be another friendly invasion, landing and assault vessels were guided into the beach by cheering natives.

Two days later *Eight*, along with an LSM, engaged briefly in actions similar to those of LCSs *Nine* and *Ten* and two LCIs from February to June—providing transportation and logistical support for Filipino guerrilla troops, of which there were many thousands in the Philippines. On March 5, the *Eight* transported five wounded guerrilla troops from Bulon Cove, Luzon, to San Fernando. The next day the two ships carried guerrilla troops from Samar to Leyte. Later in the Philippines campaign, LCS *80* supported the guerrilla movement by transporting an Army colonel to a Filipino unit upriver in eastern Mindanao. This mission required the use of the ship's dinghy to row several miles through heavy jungle-like forest, and return to deliver the officer to Davao.[19]

In the meantime Captain Arison, Flotilla One, reported on March 3 to Rear Admiral Royal (Task Group 78.1) in Mindoro for training for landings at Zamboanga in Mindanao on March 10. The Close Fire Support Unit assigned to this operation, which Captain Arison commanded, consisted of LCSs *28-30, 41-43,* and *50*, along with LCI(R)s, (M)s, and (G)s. Beginning on March 6 the LCSs supported the minesweeping unit clearing the area of mines. LCSs protecting sweepers were under fire part of the time on March 8 and 9; they knocked out a 6-inch gun emplacement as well as a number of pillboxes and machine gun nests on the beach.[20] On March 9 the LCSs provided close-in cover fire for a hydrographic unit working near the beach.

The assault and landing on Zamboanga took place on March 10 as planned. Here is a brief eye-witness account by Charles Doddridge on the *43*: "8 March— We were supporting the minesweeps. Today B25s came over and really gave the place a pasting. I don't see how anyone could live through it. No enemy action was received today. 9 March—Went in a little closer today but no fire from beach yet. Maybe there are no Japs there. 10 March—Really went in close today. 150 yards to be exact. All hell broke loose, too! One shell hit about 10 yards off our port bow. Everyone was scared but staying on station. We really gave them some shots back. The invasion at Zamboanga, Mindanao, had begun."[21]

Just what the LCSs did in the invasion is described by L. E. Guilott, serving on *41*: "On the day of the invasion we lined up about 40 yards apart and headed for the beach that was designated in the Operations Orders (which he describes as comparable to the Dallas Yellow Pages in size) as the place to hit. We started pushing buttons to shoot ten rockets at exactly 1100 yards. As soon as those ten left the ship in a hell of a noise, we pushed the next button, and so on, until all hundred rockets were gone."[22]

Enemy opposition to the landing was primarily mortar fire which hit one LST and damaged two LCIs. The *28* was fired on by mortars but was not hit.

After the landing, the support ships moved out to the flanks to seek enemy strong points, brought them under fire, and silenced them. The LCSs strafed the beach most of the day. The next day they provided fire power support for US Army troops moving toward Zamboanga Town and toward Calderon Point. That night they patrolled the beachhead.

As a result of faulty intelligence reports, a support unit made up of LCSs *41, 42,* and *43* and LCI(M)s and (R)s fired on the village of Semut on Basilan Island on March 16 before realizing that the people on the beach were Moros natives and not Japanese. 'Cease Fire' was called immediately after natives sent out a Moros canoe to warn off the invaders, but by then 20 natives and been killed and 54 wounded badly. A medical officer, pharmacists' mates, and medical supplies from the three LCSs were sent ashore and an operating room was established. Surgical work went on through the night; serious cases were transferred to hospital in Zamboanga. Richard Rhame described the reactions of the natives: "The attitude of the Moros was interesting. They had suffered at the hands of the Japanese and they took for granted the fact that in our attempts to clear Basilan of Japanese it was probable that some natives would suffer. They were very appreciative of aid given them, and the Iman (ruler) of Sag Jag visited Commander LCS(L) Flotilla One and thanked him for the efforts of the US Navy in helping the people who had been injured."[23]

In the last half of March, landings were conducted on three of the islands in the Southern Visayas section of the Philippines—Panay, Negros; Occidental; and Cebu. LCSs participated in landings on the first and third islands. On March 15, LCS *30* served in the support group in a landing on the south coast of Panay Island, 12 miles west of Iloilo. This was a friendly landing in which all gunfire

---

Bombarding the beach at Legaspi Bay on Easter morning, April 1, 1945. Courtesy of Robert Amick.

was cancelled because natives could be seen on the beaches. In the Cebu landing with TG 78.2 on March 26, however, the enemy provided serious opposition including land mines and barriers on the beach. LCSs *28-30* and *50* participated in this assault and landing near Talisan, which was about four miles west of Cebu City. For the three days before the invasion, LCSs performed an important service for the first time—covering and protecting a Navy Underwater Demolition Team that worked to clear enemy barriers to the landings.

While protecting a UDT, the crew of the *50* witnessed an unfortunate accident. Joe Rhoads, engineer officer, reported: "We were able to observe pre-invasion bombing runs by the Air Force. Even saw one of the bombers drop his bombs on one of our bombers returning from his second run. Two of the crew members were able to bail out with chutes. One was strafed by Jap bullets on the way down and probably was lost in the action. The other landed offshore and was picked up by a Kingfisher aircraft spotter plane."[24]

LCSs would do this dangerous and worthwhile work of covering UDTs again before they left the Philippine/Borneo area. Curiously, while working in the Cebu invasion operation, one LCS crew did not discover that it had been fired on until after the action. On March 27, *28* patrolled off Caiut Island firing at suspicious areas on the shore, but discovered no enemy presence. After securing, the crew found that they had been hit by a 37mm round that struck a cable reel on the deck, but did not go off.[25]

Soon after the Cebu landing in the Visayas, a strategic landing was made on April 1 at Legaspi on the lower tip of the Bicol Peninsula in the very southeastern part of Luzon. The *Eight* and *48* participated in this landing and worked with two small LCVP minesweepers in the inner Legaspi harbor. They drew fire from the beach; *Eight* had seams in her starboard side opened (fortunately not dangerously so) by near misses as close as 50 feet. The ships returned fire and silenced every enemy battery before shelling and strafing the beach. Afterward they were assigned to work with minesweepers in the important San Bernardino Straits area between the Bicol Peninsula and northern Samar.[26]

The assault and landing at Legaspi was the last amphibious movement by the VIIth Amphibious Corps on Luzon. From April 7 to 22 *Eight* and *48* escorted convoys to Iloilo on Panay, to Cebu, and to Leyte.

While the Bicol Peninsula in Southern Luzon was being secured, assaults and landings were made on two islands some distance southwest of Zamboanga and within 30 miles of the large island of Borneo, the next major objective of the campaign. LCSs *41* and *42* participated in the liberation of Sanga Sanga Island in the Tawi Tawi group on April 2 and of the nearby Jolo island one week later. The two LCSs worked with minesweepers during the Sanga assault; one sweeper was lost during this operation.

While working with these minesweepers, L. E. Guillot, *41* gunnery officer, discovered something very curious about the attitude of native villagers concerning mining their waters. Guillot described the incident: "After one of the sweepers that the *41* and *42* were working with was hit and sunk, the sweeping stopped. When we finally did start sweeping again, I noticed we were going around in the same circle. This lasted the rest of the day, and I figured the lead minesweeper had turned chicken and didn't want to get out of a line that had already been swept. It turned out to be even more interesting than that. The Moros who had moved back into their village had asked whoever was in charge of the operation to leave the mines where they were and they (the Moros) would chop the mines from their moorings and save the Navy some time and possibly some lives. What they really wanted was the dynamite that was inside the mines. They actually cut the cables, very carefully dragged the mines up on the beach and disarmed them with a monkey wrench. They used the explosives on schools of fish. I am sure they lost a few men, but I'll bet they got a lot of fish!"[27]

During April the liberation of the southern Visayas was completed by assaults and landings on April 11 at Tagbalaran on the island of Bohol on April 11 and on April 26 near the town of Dumaguete on the coast of Southern Negros. LCSs *29* and *30*, working with LCI(R) *225*, participated in these assaults and landings.

On April 17 major landings took place in the Polloc Harbor area on the western coast of southern Mindanao. Participating in these assaults and landings under the direction of Captain Arison were *28, 29*, and *50*, which supported the Malagang/Parang area landings, and *43*, which supported the landing at Illana Bay. The objective in these operations was to give the landed US troops the opportunity to cut off and gain control of the southern quarter of Mindanao by moving across the width of the island to Davao Gulf on the eastern side. Because the only cross-country road eastward for the first part of the troop movement was very primitive, it was decided to use the Mindanao-Pulangi River for the transportation, supply, and support of the troops moving inland.

This was the genesis of the Mindanao River Campaign, which, while it involved no LCSs directly, provided a real challenge in river seamanship for the LCS Flotilla Commander Arison and his communications officer, Lieutenant(j.g.) Rhame.

To provide adequate firepower support for the troops moving eastward in small amphibious craft on the river, three PGMs and two LCI(G)s were dispatched on April 19 to accompany the troops to Fort Pikit and Kababan some 35 miles upriver. These ships made slow progress on the river but served their purpose well, astonishing Japanese defenders along the shore and causing them to flee. When the ships reached their goal and started to return, however, they discovered that the tide had turned and they were marooned. Captain Arison and his communications officer, Richard Rhame, were ordered to go upriver on May 1 to free the stranded ships. Here is Rhame's eyewitness account:

> We reached our destination after a two-day voyage aboard an LCM and then we studied the plight of the mud-bound 'dread-noughts' to determine the best course of action to undertake. An initial rescue attempt—securing a line from the LCM to a PGM for a tugging tactic—resulted in failure. It was noted that the river tended to rise several inches in the early morning before dropping in depth about midday. I positioned myself in a spread eagle position in the bow of the versatile, shallow-draft LCM and, as it tacked from bank to riverbank to take soundings, calling out the depths—

'by the mark etc.' using my now-forgotten nautical terminology previously learned from the *Blue Jacket's Manual*.

When the deepest channel through the shoals was discovered, that information was relayed to 'The Commodore' aboard a PGM astern who gave orders to secure lines, again, to the PGMs which, when successfully extricated, tied onto the LCI(G)s and simply dragged them across the mud shoals.

The tactic was a success. After five days 'up the river-stuck in the mud,' the 'river-rats' made it back to Polloc harbor, slightly crippled with bent screws. This incident was just one of the many instances of undaunted ingenuity in the face of fathomless obstacles successfully accomplished by the crews of the 'little ships'![28]

LCSs serving in the Philippines did not participate in assaults and landings on Samar because that island had been secured early in January 1945. LCS crew members did, however, go ashore there, and one of them, Raymond J. Ross, electrician's mate on *60*, reported what he saw:

On Samar the background of mountains is beautiful, foliage grows everywhere. As you approach the shore you can smell the dusky tropical scent. The Navy recreation buildings were framed in wood cut from the pithy or fibrous coconut log. The roof was made by natives from a wide blade grass or leaf folded and bound with a thong in a naval manner. The true tropical atmosphere, as seen in the movies, was supplied by the split bamboo stakes driven into the ground which in turn served as a support for the horizontal members, making a neat and serviceable fence. At one of the buildings two attractive girls, wearing a combination of Army shirts, Navy dungarees, and mattress cover headgear, were busily occupied pounding nails out of 2 x 4s brought in by a truck from somewhere. The natives here are of the melting pot heritage—Japanese, Chinese, Malayan, Polynesian, Spanish, Mexican.

Later I had an opportunity to look inside a native hut. There was no furniture except a table made of split logs. There were no real beds. They were of palm leaves on the floor. The inhabitants looked healthy enough in spite of it. The natives here have a whiskey made of coconut milk that is a barn burner. Up on the hillside was the man of the family working in the field with a water oxen (caribou). He was plowing slowly and laboriously with a hand-fashioned wood plow with a metal piece fashioned for the bottom. I met a small boy carrying a bag of sweet potatoes down the road. He stopped and gave me a sweet potato to examine with a shy smile. 'Hi Joe.' I gave it back to him. He smiled and went on his way.[29]

In late April while the Philippines campaign was winding down, most of the LCSs in the area were preparing for the Borneo campaign; a number would take part in the first major landing at Tarakan Island off Borneo on May 1. Captain Arison, however, remained with his Flotilla One staff and a number of his close support ships, primarily LCI(G)s, in the Philippines until late May.

On May 11 Captain Arison became Senior Officer Present Afloat and Commander of the Gulf Naval Defense Group at Taloma Bay, Davao Gulf, on the southeast side of Mindanao. On May 12 Captain Arison with a group of PGMs and LCI(G)s shelled enemy positions on Samal Island and joined with PT boats in driving enemy troops from the eastern shore of Davao Gulf. LCI(G)s under his command, in conjunction with PT boats, conducted a reconnaissance of Japanese motor suicide boats and large torpedo boats in the Davao Gulf. Their strafing of the mangrove areas in the vicinity of Piso Point led to the destruction of a large Japanese torpedo boat base. This action was credited with saving the Taloma Davao area from serious suicide-boat attacks in the future.

Captain Arison's support group, made up of LC(FF) *778,* LCI(G)s, a PC, DE *346,* and DD *371,* participated in a number of strikes against enemy concentrations in the area, including an assault on St. Augustine Point in early June, causing the Japanese there to surrender.

During May, June, and July landings and assaults against enemy installations in Mindanao took place but far less frequently than before. On May 10 LCSs *42, 79,* and *80* participated, as part of Amphibious group IX, in an assault and landing at Cagayan in Macajalar Bay in northern Mindanao. In early June allied forces cleared out Japanese outposts at Luayon, the entrance to Davao Gulf, Balut Island, and Saragan Island. On July 17 LCS *79* and *80* took part in the landing and assault at Sarangam Bay in Mindanao, the very last amphibious landing in the Philippines Archipelago in World War II.

Endnotes

[1] Primary sources for this chapter: Richard Rhame, Staff Communications Officer, "War History, Commander LCS(L) Flotilla One," Nov. 20, 1945; Samuel Eliot Morison, *History of U.S. Naval Operations in World War II,* Vol. XIII, *The Liberation of the Philippines* (Boston: Little Brown, 1959), Parts II and III, 123-251: factual information from individual ship histories, action reports, personal accounts.

[2] W. M. (Marty) Kingwell, "World War II Navy Experiences in Verse." Kingwell served as a gunner on LCS *26*.

[3] This release occurred on February 3 and 4 when the US Army liberated American prisoners from the famous Santo Tomas camp in Manila.

[4] In this operation off Corregidor, approximately 100 mines were destroyed.

[5] From "Mariveles Bay—15 February 1945," in US LCS(L) *1-130* Assn. Newsletter, Jan. 1988, 4-5.

[6] Walter Karig et al, *Battle Report—Victory in the Pacific* (New York: Rinehart & Co., Inc., 1949), 238.

[7] "How Suicide Boats Sank US Vessels," AP News article, June 1945, in USS LCS(L) *1-130* Assn. Newsletter, May, 1988, 5.

[8] "World War II Navy Experiences in Verse."

[9] "The Night of February 16, 1945," in USS LCS(L) *1-130* Assn. Newsletter, Spring-Summer 1989, 10.

[10] "A Night to Remember," USS LCS(L) *1-130* Assn. Newsletter, Spring 1989, 14.

[11] The names of those men killed in this operation appear in the Appendix.

[12] "Mariveles Bay—15 February 1945."

[13] James H. and William M. Belote, *Corregidor, The Saga of a Fortress* (New York: Harper and Row, 1967), 211-12.

[14] Morison, 204; attributed to Wm. F. Heavy, *Down Ramp,* Washington, 1947, 154.

[15] "War History," 4.

[16] Ibid.

[17] "The Birth and Life of our Ship, USS LCS(L) (3) *50,* 3.

[18] "Ditty Bag," USS LCS (L) *1-130* Assn. Newsletter, Winter 1989, 7.

[19] Ray Suggs, "A Thumb Nail Sketch of the History of USS LCS *80,* 34.

[20] Charles J. Lausberg, Log—LCS(L) *42,* March 8th entry.

[21] USS LCS(L) *1-130* Assn. Newsletter, Winter 1989, 6.

[22] L. E. Guilott, *How Did We Ever Win the War?* n.d., 40-41.

[23] "War History," 5.

[24] "The Birth and Life of our Ship, USS LCS *50,*" 3.

[25] Letter to author from Kenneth R. Krayer, June 18, 1993.

[26] "LCS(L) *Eight* Ship's History," 4.

[27] Guilott, 50-51.

[28] "This is the Way it Was," LCS(L) *1-130* Assn. Newsletter, Fall 1988, 7.

[29] Diary of Raymond J. Ross, LCS(L) *60,* 3-4. Used with permission.

The Missions of Task Group 70.41

From February 1 to May 30, 1945 Task Group 70.41 provided arms, food, clothing and other supplies to guerrilla troops in 53 places in central and south Philippines: 30 places in Mindanao (as indicated on the map), 1 place on Burias, 2 places on Cebu, 9 places on Negros, 5 on Masbate, 6 on Bohol, and 1 on Samar, and 1 place on Camiguin. The Task Group bombarded the beach and landed troops in a number of places.

From June 1 to August 1, the Group harassed and annihilated pockets of Japanese troops in 29 places in the Luzon area; 24 places on Luzon, where they bombarded the beaches and landed troops several times, 2 places on the Polillio Islands, 2 places on the Babuyan Islands, and along the north coast of Luzon from Aparri to Cape Engame.

Babuyan Islands 2

Cape Engane 1

Aparri

Luzon 24

Manila

Polillio Is. 2

Mindoro

Burias Is. 1

Masbate Is. 5

Samar 1

Palawan

Panay

Cebu 2

Leyte

Negros 9

Bohol 6

Camiguin Is.1

Mindanao 30

Zamboanga

Basilan

Jolo

Chapter 6

The Liberators: Task Group 70.4[1]

From February through July of 1945, when Seventh Fleet Amphibious Forces were assaulting beaches and landing troops throughout the Philippines and Borneo, a tiny amphibious task group was supplying the thousands of guerrilla forces in the Philippines with food, clothing and arms, assaulting and destroying Japanese garrisons in numerous waterfront villages, and landing and supporting guerrilla troops in areas known to contain concentrations of Japanese.

This Task Group, number 70.4, known simply as 'Guerrilla Supply,' was one of the smallest amphibious forces operating in the remote areas of the Philippines. It was made up of two LCSs, *Nine* and *Ten*, and two LCIs, initially *361* and *363*. The two LCIs provided the supply and troop-carrying capability for the group, and all four ships used their guns and rockets to destroy enemy installations and to support the landings of thousands of guerrilla troops. At the time the Task Group was established in early February, LCSs *Nine* and *Ten* were more or less detached from the main body of LCSs serving under Commander LCS(L) Flotilla One. Earlier the *Nine* and *Ten* had raided Japanese positions on the north coast of New Guinea and had served on picket duty to protect two ammunition ships that had been attacked by a suicide boat off Hollandia, New Guinea.

Guerrilla troops that the Task Group was supporting were under the command of Colonel Wendell Fertig, who had been an American mining engineer before the war. There were thousands of these troops in the Philippines—25,000 on Mindanao alone. During 1944 and up until February 1945, logistics for these guerrilla forces had been handled by Seventh Fleet submarines.

Lieutenant Albert Eldridge, captain of the *Ten*, was appointed commander of the Task Group. Eldridge, who had served as captain of an LCI in the Southwest Pacific before assuming command of the *Ten*, had recently been vice commodore of a large convoy of merchant ships, tankers, and amphibious ships traveling from Hollandia, New Guinea, to Leyte with an escort of three destroyers.

As the paragraphs that follow will demonstrate, the officers and men of this tiny task group became, in many respects, true liberators of the Philippines, serving from February 4 to June 6, 1945, on 13 missions to over 50 places in the islands of Samar, Cebu, Negros, Masbate, and Bohol in the central Visaya section of the Philippines and on the large important southern island of Mindanao. In June and July they went on two more extended missions over 500 miles north to 29 places on the east coast of Luzon from the Polillo Islands in the south coast area to the Fuga and Babuyan Islands north of Luzon itself.

Because the task group was constantly engaged in providing villages and troops with supplies and arms, and on occasion moving troops from place to place for assaults and amphibious landings, most of the missions involved extensive circuitous travel to a number of places, frequently moving by night and remaining under cover during the day to catch the enemy by surprise and to avoid detection by Japanese aircraft. The task group used Tacloban in Leyte as its headquarters and logistics base for its first 13 missions.

The first mission began on February 4 with the departure of the task group (with the two LCIs loaded with guns, ammunition, medical supplies, and clothes for the guerrillas) to the village of Mambajao on Camiguin, a small island strategically located off the north coast of Mindanao. On their arrival at this island village the task group crew members became aware that in the eyes of the natives they were heroes and liberators.

Here is how Eldridge described his Task Group's heart-warming reception: It was shortly after dawn that we stood off the pier. Through the glasses we could see many people on it and many more streaming down to greet us. We broke formation, allowing the LCIs which were going to discharge cargo to tie up first. As the *361* approached the pier there was not a sound to be heard. She slid silently toward the piles, then reversed her screws to make her landing.

"Over two!" came the command from her conn.

"Over two!" from the deck. The ballshaped weight preceded a gracefully arching heaving line though the air toward the assembled group ashore. When it was about in mid-passage, it seemed to be the awaited signal. A low murmur went through the crowd—ragged, motley, thin, tense people. One started to clap, two, ten. A shout, a cheer; the whole pier came alive with joyful yells and cries and whistles.[2]

The crew of LCS 10, flagship of the tiny force of "Liberators of the Philippines." This crew called their ship "The Mighty Ten." Courtesy of US Navy.

There were shouts of "Liberators!" "V for Victory!" and the like. The natives came down from their hiding places in the hills and shouted, and even cried, for joy. They had little to offer, but what little they had, they were very willing to share with Americans who had at last returned. During his stay the Jap made sure to leave his trademark: all of the main buildings were leveled to the ground, the natives were left nothing for clothing, what there was for food was either eaten or destroyed. And so the natives came to greet the Americans after about three long years; they came barefooted, they came with little clothing on (and what little they had on was torn and patched beyond recognition), they came with diseases that ranged from dysentery to tuberculosis, they came undernourished and suffering with beriberi; but they all came with smiling faces and prayers of thanks to the Lord above. They had nothing to complain about anymore—the Americans had returned to redeem them!!! and they were happy, with the happiness that quite easily provokes tears.[3]

That many of the natives were hungry was confirmed by this LCS *Nine* crew member's eyewitness account: "When the natives were allowed to come aboard the ship to look around, many of them brought bowls and cans which they would fill with their bare hands from the G.I cans into which we had scraped our leftovers. Our G.I cans were completely cleared out by them. For lunch at noon each of us ate only a mouthful and scraped the rest into their cans and bowls. They were surely grateful for this."[4]

"With great pride they took us around what remained of their little town showing us the large church, giving us drinks of their spring water which they claimed to be the best in the islands. All day men from TG 70.4 were the honored guests of Camaguin Island. Dinners and dances were held. We sang 'God Bless the Philippines' and 'God Bless America' intermittently, each to the same tune with the same emotional gusto."[5]

Richard Kreider, *Ten* quartermaster, further described the natives' hospitality: "The natives insisted that we come upstairs and play the piano and sing. They sang 'St. Louis Blues,' 'Dinah,' and 'Ferry Boat Serenade,' and some hillbilly music for us. For about an hour they fed us and entertained us with songs."[6]

The next day when the task group sailed into Iligan, a village on Mindanao, and unloaded their cargo, this was their reception: "It was really a sight. There was a large crowd and a brass band there to meet us. I was up on the bridge and when they played 'My Country, Tis of Thee' and 'Anchors Aweigh' I had a very empty feeling down in my stomach and I could feel a small tear run down my cheek."[7]

Important community leaders in the area walked long distances to greet their 'liberators'. "None other than the governor of Lanao Province and the Director of the Filipino Boy Scouts for Mindanao and the Sulu Archipelago came aboard to welcome us. They had walked 30 miles to extend their greeting."[8]

Even though the task group was warmly received by the natives, the LCS crews had to keep gun watches all day because the Japanese were only 20 miles away in all directions and had an air strip only 40 miles off.

According to Kreider, life there on Mindanao at the time was extremely primitive and "very picturesque with water buffalo drawing huge carts with large round wooden wheels, as in Biblical days."[9] Yet the hospitality of these people to the Navy crewmen knew no bounds, and that evening the natives held a dance in the task group's honor with the pier decorated with palms and reeds and, much to the crew's amazement, with local girls jitterbugging with the sailors.

The next day the task group fired their guns and rockets in anger for the first time. Here is Task Group Commander Eldridge's account: "It was on Mission 1 that most of the men were initiated into battle. It wasn't a great battle; it was more of an amphibious assault and the results were more than gratifying. The place: Talisayan, Mindanao. The time: 1453 to 1620, February 6, 1945."[10]

"Our hearts were in our mouths though when the *Nine*'s 'overs' missed her intended target and burst on the slopes in front of us; we were all tense when we skirted 50 yards offshore to look for targets; but we won our spurs by crippling barge traffic in the area when their fuel [supply] was destroyed."[11]

"The results: many crew members experiencing a shakiness of the knees, chattering of teeth, and learning to recite their prayers again—hundreds of barrels of enemy gasoline and oil blown to the high heavens and about 600 Japs making their supreme sacrifice for the Mikado. Yes, the LCSs of the Task Group had shown that their rockets and 3", 50-cal, 40mms, and 20mms could cripple the enemy enough to make them worth their while."[12] And an immediate result was Fleet Admiral Thomas Kincaid's congratulations to the Task Group and permission for them to choose where to make future runs.

The task group's second mission involved delivering ammunition to Sibonga on Cebu Island only 22 miles from Japanese-held Cebu City. In this instance and in most of the instances that followed, the task group ships were the first allied surface ships to land in the area since the Japanese occupation in 1942. Evidently very few ships of any kind had landed in Sibonga for some time, since the Filipino ship pilot guiding the Task Group did not even recognize Sibonga as the Task Group was approaching the pier. In Sibonga the hospitable natives held a banquet for the ships' officers and served breakfast and held dances for the crew.

For Mission 3 the task group went to the island of Negros west of Cebu in the western Visayas. While working with guerrilla forces in the surrounding areas, the force bombarded the towns of Dumaguette and Sibulan on February 17. They destroyed their objectives—the power plant and radio station—in Dumaguette with their rockets, and they strafed all the buildings where Japanese were known to be. They next bombarded the smaller town of Sibulan which held a garrison of a hundred Japanese. By doing this they allowed the guerrilla forces in the area to take Sibulan so they could outflank the Japanese at Dumaguette.

Because of their successes in these engagements, the four-ship task group soon became known to the Japanese as "The Devils in the Philippines."[13] The supplies that the task group carried into Negros for the guerrilla forces were sorely needed because the guerrillas were down to 25 rounds of ammunition per man. Also the group was able to bring more supplies more frequently than the fleet submarines had done in the past. Not only were the task group ships the first allied surface forces to land at Negros since the occupation, their assault was the first one made on the island.

The Task Group's fourth mission took them to Claver in Mindanao on February 23 to land supplies for guerrilla troops. A guest on this mission was Colonel Wendell W. Fertig, commander of all the guerrilla forces in the Philippines. At this time LCS *Ten* crewmen met Major Bob Spielman who was taken prisoner at the fall of Bataan and imprisoned at Donao with others. He escaped and was working with the guerrilla troops under Colonel Fertig. Task Group crewmen also met an American Army first lieutenant who had been in that part of Mindanao since the beginning of the war in 1942. He had been separated from his division and had attempted to escape to Australia in a small boat, but the boat capsized and sank offshore, and there he was, three years later, leading the guerrillas into battle.[14]

The first major event on the task group's fifth mission was bombarding the beach at San Carlos on Negros Island on March 1. Task Group Commander Eldridge described this engagement: "We held reveille for the Nips in San Carlos. We used our new toy, an 80mm trench mortar mounted on our bow, effectively for the first time. We plopped some white phosphorous into the Sugar Central [warehouse] ruins (on the beach) and it brought the Nips out on the double. They thought it was gas. The Filipinos had a field day picking off the runners."[15]

"In the meantime the *Nine* had taken a few rounds from a Jap gun installed near the inshore end of the pier. Immediately she gave it her full attention. That was followed by general silence. To make it a perfect day, gunners on the *Ten* scored a bullseye on a barge tied to the pier."[16]

The procedure used by the Task Group in most of their ten troop landings has been described for us in a brief history of the *Nine*: "The procedure was to land one force under cover of darkness to take up positions in a perimeter about the Japanese positions. At dawn shell fire and rocket fire were used to drive the enemy out of their holes (they invariably withdrew from the area being shelled) and a landing party was put ashore on the beach. The operation was timed so that the Japanese would strike the perimeter just as the beach party moved into the positions they had vacated. Then the Japs were caught in the middle. The process never failed, and Japanese casualties were very high. The process was made possible by the excellent intelligence supplied by the guerrillas."[17]

On March 3rd, two days after the San Carlos bombardment, the task group undertook its first guerrilla troop landing at Masbate Island south of Cebu and Leyte. While this landing was a success, the problems and complications that the Task Group encountered were formidable. These were best described by the Task Group Commander:

> On this run we had two substitute LCIs while the originals, the *361* and *363*, were being repaired. The *704* and the *1074* were new at the beaching game in the Philippines and spent some 36 hours, collectively, perched on mud banks when the skippers plowed in too enthusiastically. Before we got to the target areas, part of the guerrillas were put ashore south of the town of Dimasalang. As we swung through the straits at the mouth of the harbor, we received a radio message not to fire on the beach because the Japs were already on their way elsewhere. Nonetheless we continued on with all hands at GQ. That entrance was one of the most spooky of the lot. Quiet bay, quiet jungle, quiet ships. Close to the opposite shore we drew without a sound anywhere to be heard. We lay to—no firing on us. If they're there, this is their chance—still quiet, might be friendly Filipinos in the village by now; lie to until the LCIs get here.

The news which came with the other two ships (LCIs) was that on report of a stray Filipino, all troops had remained aboard for a free ride instead of splitting up for a two-direction attack and one group having to walk the distance. As the four ships were moored together for a pow-wow, U.S. Corsairs were spotted overhead. We tried to contact them by radio as previously arranged to tell them not to strafe and bomb because of the info received that the targets had disappeared. No sense in shooting up the town needlessly. No radio contact. Down the planes dove with guns talking, bombs putting exclamation points to their sentences. The little devils set fire to a good part of the place. As we moved up the bay to put the troops ashore, WHAM, a roar and concussion swept out of the town to meet us. The planes had done well. Ammo dump. By golly, if they didn't take their ammo, they planned to come back. No Filipinos in that town. The light spraying we were going to give the place just in case some had remained behind was turned into a full barrage. Rockets, white phosphorous from the mortar, forties and twenties pounded designated areas. The three-inch No. 1 gun picked off specialties. Ashore the troops advanced, taking the town in about a half hour.

Among the captured souvenirs were flags galore, rifles, swords, etc. The prizes were the ammo, food, and 70mm pack howitzer whose chamber was neatly stuffed with a round of unfired ammo. All they had to do was to pull the lanyard for at least one shot before taking to the hills, but evidently they weren't interested. How droll that could have been. But then one shot from them would have given their position away, and shortly they would have had much company in the form of explosive shells marked for them. Maybe they were smart after all.[18]

On their return to Tacloban after their mission, the Task Group flew all of the Japanese flags they had captured in celebration of their victory at Dimasalang. Usually the guerrilla troops were competent soldiers ashore, but occasionally groups with very little training would have difficulties, as a crew member on the *Nine* pointed out: "When the LCIs brought in troops to a village we had been shelling, they pulled alongside a concrete dock so the troops could step onto the shore. But the troops wouldn't move. An American officer had to walk up and down the dock to show them nobody would shoot at them. After they got past the dock into the jungle, somebody fired a shot and all hell broke loose. They started to fire in every direction. It's a wonder they didn't shoot each other."[19]

The major event of the task groups' next mission was a second bombarding on March 10 of Dumaguette on Negros Island, which they had bombarded on February 17. In addition to firing on the town, they blew up several beached enemy barges and fired on a nearby Japanese air strip. On this mission, LCS *Ten* rescued seven natives from a boat that had been swamped in a sudden storm in open water. After the Dumaguette bombardment, LCS *Nine* and the LCIs went to put cargo ashore in Jagna in Bohol. As the crewmen went ashore among large crowds of natives covering the pier, a leading Filipino said to Lieutenant Donovan Ellis, captain of the *Nine*: "Sir, if these people dared, they would fall down and kiss the feet of the Americans who have come back."[20]

On Mission 7 (March 15-21) the Task Group first went to Bohol Island between Cebu, Leyte, and Mindanao. At Loay, the first stop in Bohol, the natives greeted the liberators with a large enthusiastic crowd and brass band at the dock. The task group next bombarded two places in Bohol/Baclayan and Manga, and shot up several enemy boats being built on the beach. While supporting the guerrilla troops ashore off Manga, the task group was firing on a town hidden by jungle and hills. With the help of native Filipinos and a chart, the task group was able to hit its target and provide solid support. They next went up to Mindanao where on March 20 they bombarded Talisayan for the second time and landed 380 troops they had picked up at Lagonglong. From this action they captured two trucks, two steel barges, a radio station, ammunition, rifles, and the complete plans for the defense of Mindanao. As Task Group Commander Eldridge described it: "To hurry the mopping up operations, the task group returned to Talisayan and finished the job with another bombardment and then sent in the guerrillas to take over."[21]

Mission 8 involved bombarding and landing guerrilla troops at Masbate City on Masbate Island just below the southern tip of Luzon. Here is Lieutenant Eldridge's report: "Before dawn the LCS *Nine* as lead ship (her skipper had won the toss for the position farthest inside the bay) nosed through the narrow entrance into the harbor. Our bow was about 1,200 yards behind her stern. Two red tracers split the distance in two when the guard on shore realized he had visitors. Inside the harbor we took position before the town proper and blasted targets on schedule. The LCIs had mortars for the first time. They filled the bay with 60mm bursts. The *Nine* with her No. 2 twin forty did a precise decapitation of the machine gun pits on the military crest of the hill overlooking the harbor."[22]

This intensive bombardment of the city lasted for at least two and a half hours, causing, as crew member Frank Muth reports, "the *Nine*'s 3" 50 gun barrel to turn blue and its forward twin 40mm to get so hot that the water hose broke loose."[23] After the bombardment the *Nine* used a boat to move wounded Filipinos to the rear for treatment. *Nine* crewmen also carried a wounded guerrilla to safety under fire, an action for which they were later decorated.

During this engagement the *Nine* ran over a reef, fouling her screws and leaving her high and dry as the tide receded. When the *Ten* came to her aid and was standing by, both were taken under fire by enemy forces on the beach. This sniper fire persisted throughout the night as the *Ten* attempted to secure a tow line to the *Nine*. Later two crewmen on the *Ten*, William A. Powers and Woodrow W. Pack, would be awarded Bronze Star medals for their valiant efforts to secure the tow line. The next morning after the rising of the tide, the *Ten* towed her sister ship back to their base at Tacloban.

Even though the task group had to overcome these difficulties in the action at Masbate City, the operation was a great success in that it placed strategic

The "Liberators," Task Group 70.4, at half strength with two ships, embarking and disembarking Filipino guerrilla troops at one of the scores of places they served in the Philippines. Courtesy of National Archives 80-G-31883.

Masbate Island securely in the hands of the Filipino forces. This achievement was all the more remarkable because, as Task Group Commander Eldridge pointed out, "Masbate City was so located that higher naval and army authorities had planned to stage an invasion with DDs, DEs, LSTs and LSMs and were amazed when they learned that two little LCSs and two more LCIs with but a handful of guerrillas had captured it all by themselves. Not only were they amazed but for a long time they wouldn't believe it to be true."[24]

In their ninth mission (April 4-9) the task group visited seven different places on Mindanao doing some of the same things done on previous missions: delivering arms and supplies, picking up and discharging guerrilla troops, and bombarding Japanese garrisons. On this mission they were also looking to intercept Japanese barges reportedly off Iligan, Mindanao, but these failed to appear. The two places that the task group did bombard and shell on this mission would be assaulted again by them later.

On April 9 the task group attacked the Japanese installation at Buenavista, to assault and annihilate it later on Mission 11. Also on April 9 the task group bombarded and shelled Nasipit, to attack it again and to land troops there on Mission 10. Concerning this April 9th bombardment, Filipino observers, who were not aware of the task groups's existence, sent out this radio message:"TWO AMERICAN LIGHT CRUISERS SHELLED NASIPIT FOR ONE HOUR UP TO 1900 NASIPIT STILL BURNING."[25] During this 9th mission the *Ten* hit a reef which damaged its skegs and fouled its screws, forcing it into drydock on April 10.

At the beginning of Mission 10 (April 4-19) LCI *361*, which had been working along with *363* in the task group for eight missions, had engine trouble and was replaced by *429*. The major event of Mission 10 was the bombarding and landing of guerrilla troops on April 18 to destroy the Japanese troops at Nasipit.

During this landing guerrilla troops captured a large supply of ammunition including 5-inch shells, which indicated that Nasipit must have been an ammunition supply depot for larger Japanese ships and submarines.

When the Task Group was back in Leyte after the second Nasipit landing, the *Ten* carried two Japanese prisoners ashore for the Eighth Army headquarters. The crew witnessed the prisoners amazement at seeing a DUWK (amphibious truck) metamorphose from being a boat to being a four-wheeled truck when it reached the beach. The Japanese were so flabbergasted at seeing the wheels appear, seemingly out of nowhere, that they almost fell overboard.

Mission 11 took the task group to 11 different places, most of them in Mindanao. As in previous missions the first stop was the village of Mambajao on Camiguin Island on the way to Mindanao from Tacloban. In this village, as in the also frequently visited Iligan on Mindanao, task group crewmen became acquainted with the natives. On this mission at least one crewman discovered the joys of eating a native dish—shredded meat in coconut milk. His hosts were amazed that he had never tasted this before.[26]

When the task group arrived at Iligan, they were greeted again as liberators with a brass band and a huge crowd on the dock. The more serious business of the mission was the bombarding and shelling of Japanese garrisons in four places, one for the second time. The first of these was Tagaloan, where LCSs worked with PT boats. The second was Cagayan where they strafed the beach. The third was Butuan, after which they transported guerrilla troops to Nasipit, where they had bombarded and landed troops on the previous mission. The last bombardment was at Buenavista, which they had bombarded on Mission 9.

At Buenavista the task group accidently bombarded the wrong hill, but, fortunately, there were no casualties. It was late the same night while the task group was underway from Buenavista to Guiuas on Samar that they encountered hundreds of lights low on the water off the northern tip of Mindanao. They thought they were approaching land but discovered that what they saw were at least 200 native *barcas* [canoes] out on the water, each with one or two torches.

While in Tacloban between missions, crewmen on the *Ten* discovered an amazingly yellow oriental dog that was the mascot of an LCI crew there. "It was not just the common variety; it was as bright a yellow as those chicks are dyed at Easter time. It had some black markings on its head, no tail, and whiskers like a cat. It was just a pup but it was the natural color. They had washed him many times and even the hairs in his ears were yellow."[27]

Missions 12 and 13 (May 4-22) involved no bombardments and troop landings, but they served a real purpose, as Task Group Commander Eldridge pointed out: "Missions 12 and 13 were rather quiet in a sense of the word, but on the other hand Iligan and Gingoog were repeatedly visited and the guerrillas there as well as at Villanueva, Biutuan, Balingasaag, Tago, and Tandag received their supply of guns and ammunition when needed."[28]

At Gingoog the task group sailors attended a formal fiesta in the village market: "The place was all decorated with palm leaves, roses, sweet peas, etc. It was very beautiful. The girls had exceptionally nice formals. They were quite a contrast to the Navy men in dungarees. We paid three to five pesos to dance. It was all for the civilian hospital fund. The music was good and I danced a couple of times. There were about a dozen boxes belonging to girls there that were auctioned off—very similar to a box social back home, only they introduced the boy and the girl before the bidding started. Some of the boxes sold for as high as 85 pesos."[29]

On May 8 the task group received a letter of commendation from Colonel Wendell Fertig for all they had achieved up to that time. The letter, which went to the Commander of the Seventh Fleet and Commander-in-Chief, Southwest Pacific Army Forces, expressed appreciation to the tiny naval amphibious force for providing excellent support for U.S. land forces.

For its last two missions, the 14th and 15th, the task group was redesignated from 'Guerrilla Supply Mission' to 'Special Mission', and it no longer served a supply purpose but continued to harass Japanese troops as its primary mission. For Mission 14 (June 2-23) the task group went over 500 miles from Tacloban to the northernmost island of Luzon. Using Infanta on Luzon as its headquarters, the task group made stops at 25 places (11 of them different) on the eastern side, as well as on the northeast coast and even on two islands east and directly north of Luzon. They were seeking out Japanese garrisons and installations to harass and destroy as well as opportunities to provide support for guerrilla troops against the Japanese.

On June 10 they bombarded the village of Dillongan and landed guerrilla troops from Anderson's Battalion [guerrilla] to annihilate the Japanese there. On June 20 "at Fuga Island, just north of Luzon, the task group made an attempt, with American Alamo Scouts, to rescue American pilots captured by the Japanese. During the first phase of this operation Alamo Scouts were landed in the middle of the night uncomfortably close to the enemy headquarters. The operation was terminated when on the following night the Scouts returned with the news that the pilots were tied, bayoneted, and burned at a ceremony for the entertainment of the Japanese."[30]

The next day (June 21) the task group bombarded Japanese shore installations along the northern coast of Luzon from Aparri to Cape Engame.

The task group's 15th and final mission (July 4-31) was one of their most active and productive. LCSs *Nine* and *Ten*, working this time with LCIs *364* and *432*, circulated through areas in Luzon calling at 18 places, 9 of them different. Their mission's purpose was the same as that in Mission 14. They bombarded and landed guerrilla troops in four different places and landed Philippine Army troops in one other. In the early part of this mission they landed Sixth Army scout teams at different locations to locate enemy installations.

During the period before the bombardments began, however, several crew members ventured inland from Casiguran Sound to trace a water stream's source up into mountain country, which they found to be really rough and beautiful. Here is an eyewitness account of the natives there: "They hunt with bows and arrows. They are mean looking too. The arrows have six inch steel points. There were also some fuzzy wuzzies there. The kind that wear nothing but a G-string and their hair stands out from their head."[31]

The Group's first bombarding and landing of guerrilla troops on its final mission took place at Palanan Bay on July 12. On the beach at Palanan the Task Group found the remains of a Japanese Zero shot down earlier by a U.S. plane. On sending a party up in the hills to see the bombardment's effect, the Task Group discovered that a rocket from the *Nine* had destroyed a Japanese log-reinforced outpost.

After the Palanan landing, Lieutenant Eldridge and two other officers from the *Ten* had an adventure that almost got them in trouble. They took a trip up a local river in a small motor boat. On their return the officers were stranded when the tide went out. Because no boats from below could get up to them, they were forced to use native log dugout canoes for the trip down. These delicately balanced canoes drew only four inches but they were scraping bottom much of the time. When the party reached the shore of Palanan Bay, it was dark and they were forced to paddle with a pole and a palm frond out to their ship in a small collapsible Japanese boat. When they got in the vicinity of their ship the executive officer had No. 2 gun trained on them.[32]

Later when a party from the ship was exploring a mountain near Palanan, they met natives who spoke neither English nor the local Filipino dialect. Yet in the midst of these people was a boy who spoke excellent English. They never found out why this was true.[33]

On July 21 the Task Group landed Philippine Army troops in Japanese-held territory at Tuno Creek. Two days later the group bombarded the beach and landed guerrilla troops at Magnac River. The Task Group commander's firing orders for this operation, which appear below, give a good idea of the parts played by the four Task Group ships in this bombardment and in earlier similar ones:

"Upon reaching the first target area, the LCIs will commence strafing and lobbing mortar shells. Firing at almost flat trajectory with knee mortars will help clear any log positions (if there are any). At the main target area, the *Nine* will sink the rockets north of the river and not more than 200 yards inland. The *Ten* in the meantime will cover any likely area not being covered by either of the other firing units. The *Nine* will follow rockets with standard bombardment. The hill indicated on the map as 'M G' in the main target area can be a target for either or both LCSs, but there must be no 'overs'."[34]

The troop landing in this operation was part of an attempt to capture alive Japanese Naval Captain Nakayoma, commander of Japanese forces in Eastern Luzon, for naval intelligence purposes. Although the captain was killed trying to escape, the task group did obtain his diary "which gave information on jet propulsion, Jap intelligence concerning our fleet and task force composition, Filipino political leaders and collaborators."[35]

The Task Group bombarded Masanga River and landed guerrilla troops there on July 26. Three days later the group bombarded and landed troops at Laguin Bayan, their last action in their active 15 missions in the Philippines.

In the performance of their missions the Task Group served continuously for six months (February 2 to August 1) with only a few days between missions for logistics. Altogether they went on 15 missions over hundreds of miles to scores of different places covering large areas of the Philippine Archipelago. They bombarded and shelled over 20 places held by the Japanese; they landed troops at 10 places; they destroyed thousands of Japanese soldiers, their garrisons as well as their fuel dumps, ammunition supplies, suicide boats, and their equipment.

After the Philippine campaign was over, Admiral Thomas Kincaid, Commander Seventh Fleet, awarded the Legion of Merit medal to Lieutenant Albert C. Eldridge, captain of the *Ten* and Commander of Task Group 70.4, and the Bronze Star Medal to Lieutenant Donovan Ellis, captain of the *Nine*. In presenting these awards, the admiral was saying in effect, 'Well Done' to the tiny but potent force of 'Liberators' of the Philippines.

Endnotes

[1] Primary sources for this chapter are two writings by Lieutenant Albert C. Eldridge, captain of LCS *Ten* and commander of Task Group 70.4: "The Story of the Cruise," unpublished booklet, n.d., listed hereafter as 'Story,' and "LCS(L)(3) 10 Ship's History," December 23, 1945, listed hereafter as 'History'; factual information about missions from "LCS(L)(3) *10*—Duty in the Philippines—Missions 1-15," a typed report.

[2] Eldridge, Story, 5-6.

[3] Eldridge, History, 12.

[4] Frank Muth, untitled account of his naval service, 6.

[5] Eldridge, Story, 6.

[6] Richard C. Kreider, "Log of LCS(L)(3) *10*, 20 Oct. 1944-12, Dec. 1945, diary, 9-10.

[7] Kreider, 13.

[8] Eldridge, Story, 6.

[9] Kreider, 16.

[10] Eldridge, History, 13.

[11] Eldridge, Story, 7.

[12] Eldridge, History, 13.

[13] Karig et al. *Battle Report—Victory in the Pacific*, 261.

[14] Kreider, 31.

[15] Eldridge, Story, 8.

[16] Ibid., Story, 6.

[17] History of USS LCS(L)(3) *Nine*, 2.

[18] Eldridge, Story 8-9.

[19] Muth, 8.

[20] Eldridge, Story, 9.

[21] Ibid., Story, 10.

[22] Ibid.

[23] Muth, 8.

[24] Eldridge, History, 13.

[25] Eldridge, Story, 12.

[26] Kreider, 79-80.

[27] Ibid., 86.

[28] Eldridge, History,14.

[29] Kreider, 99-101.

[30] Eldridge, History, 15.

[31] Kreider, 108.

[32] Eldridge, Story, 16.

[33] Ibid., 17.

[34] From Commander Task Group 70.4, Operation Janfu, Bambanan River, General Plan.

[35] Eldridge, Story, 17.

Chapter 7

Supporting the Aussies in the Borneo Campaign[1]

In late April and early May of 1945 while the Philippines campaign was all but over, the campaign to retake Borneo got underway. The first major assault and landing was to be on May 1st at Tarakan, an oil-rich island on the eastern coast of Dutch-ruled Borneo. This attack and landing was designated Operation Foo-Foo. There were to be two other major landings at Brunei Bay and Balikpapan, and three subsidiary landings at Sadau Island, Mempalol, and Miri Lutong, in which elements of the Seventh Fleet provided naval forces for landing large numbers of Australian troops, as well as some Dutch officials, in the retaking of Dutch and British Borneo. The Japanese had held Tarakan since January 1942.

The Tarakan Attack Group (TG 78.1) under Rear Admiral F. B. Royal held rehearsals for the landing on April 19-24 at Morotai Island, west of New Guinea. Admiral R. S. Berkey's close fire support unit of the attack group, which included the several LCSs mentioned below, left Subic Bay, Luzon, on April 24 and arrived off Tarakan on the 27th.

While traveling to the Tarakan area, LCSs *28* and *43* encountered five rafts with Japanese survivors on the open sea. The ship's officers attempted to get the survivors to surrender; instead, however, the survivors fired small arms at the ships and were quickly dispatched. On April 27 and again on the 29th the *44* fired on Tarakan beach.

Beginning on April 27, the *8, 28, 43, 44, 48,* and *60* protected the minesweepers off Tarakan and served as a mine demolition unit. The area had been heavily mined earlier by the Dutch, the Japanese, the Australians and British, and the U.S. Air Force. In addition the Dutch had planted hundreds of anti-landing posts. The *50* worked with and protected an Aussie underwater demolition team. On the 30th the *Eight* supported the landing of Aussie troops and artillery at Sadau Island nearby and worked with harbor minesweepers and obstacle demolition engineers at Tarakan.

Borneo Campaign

Major Invasions

Tarakan   May 1
Brunei   Jun. 10
Balikapapan Jul. 1

Minor Invasions

Sadau Island Jun. 12
Mempahol   Jun. 19
Miri Lutong   Jun. 20

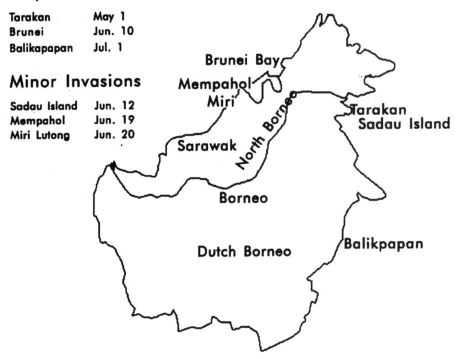

The allied assault force of approximately 18,000 was made up primarily of Australian troops, but included a U.S. Navy shore party, about 500 men of the U.S. Army, and 400 Dutch (including civilian government officers). Supporting the invasion of Tarakan on May 1st were the *8, 28, 43, 44, 48,* and *50*. While protecting the right flank of the advancing landing craft, the *44* spotted and destroyed what must have been a Japanese ammunition ship from the size of the explosion. Karig reports that in this engagement "the shore batteries were knocked out and silenced before they could reload by APD *Cofer* and two heavily gunned LCSs."[2]

On May 2nd a concealed enemy shore battery at Cape Djoeata fired on the working minesweepers (YMSs), hitting two of them and sinking one. LCS *44*, on her own initiative, rescued the crew of the sinking YMS *481* being strafed in

---

the water by the Japanese. The *44* went in between the men in the water and the Japs on the beach and opened up with all guns, driving the Japs into hiding. The badly wounded survivors were treated by the *44*'s pharmacist's mate. For this well executed rescue, the ship's crew received a commendation from the commander of the destroyer division in charge of the operation. At the same time that the *44* was rescuing the YMS *481* crew, LCS *28* escorted one of the two damaged YMSs to alongside the cruiser USS *Boise.* Later on the same day, the *28* resumed protecting the minesweepers from shore fire. Earlier in the day the *Eight* destroyed a suicide boat.

While serving in the Tarakan operation the *43* crew managed to play a basketball game against an LST crew on May 9. The LST team had been beaten only once. The *43* crew made it 'twice' by just one point!

From May 10 to 12, several LCSs, including *8, 28, 43* and *44*, attempted to pull LSTs off the beach at Tarakan, a job they were ill equipped for because of their shallow draft and lightness (approximately 380 tons for the LCS as opposed

LCS 50 moving into Tarakan, Dutch Borneo, for a rocket bombardment and broadside shelling of the beach in the invasion on May 1. Courtesy of Ray Baumler.

to 2,500 for the LST). Kenneth Krayer, *28* crew member, gave an eyewitness account: "When we made the landing at Tarakan it was made at high tide for the day, and the month. So we ended up with LSTs hung up on the beach so bad we couldn't get them off. Some of the LCSs got on each side of the LSTs using themselves as tugs, and attempted to get them off. But all we succeeded in doing was chewing up our screws. Shaft vibration was terrible."[3]

However, the *Eight* and *43* did succeed in retracting one LST on May 11, but both damaged their screws so severely in attempting other retractions on May 12 and 13 that they, along with the *28*, had to be towed to Morotai by the same fleet tugs that pulled all but one of the LSTs off the beach.

One of the greatest dangers to these LCSs working in the Borneo area at this time was getting caught in a minefield and striking a mine. Evidently, however, ships could brush against certain mines any number of times without lethal effects, as this account by Gil Nadeau, *45* signalman, demonstrated:

> On our first night on our way to participate in the Brunei, Borneo, invasion we were informed that we had inadvertently sailed into a Japanese minefield and were in it—like right now!! When the announcement was made, I and another shipmate were seated on the 'trough' [the community

LCSs shell targets ashore after making their rocket runs in the invasion at Brunei Bay. Courtesy of Ray Baumler.

toilet] in the head. My shipmate was a lean, lanky guy wearing nothing but sea-bees shoes, undershorts, and well-worn, ragged dungarees, which at that time were both down at his shoe tops. Suddenly we heard a loud metallic thump/clanging coming from under the ship towards the bow. My shipmate got real startled, cursed and said, 'Shorty, do you think that's what I think it is??' I replied, 'Cripes Yes!!! Sounds like we just run over a mine!!' Just about that time, the metallic bump and scraping and clanking happened again about midships near where we were sitting. This time my shipmate cursed, jumped straight up so fast he left his shoes, shorts, and dungarees right there on the deck where his feet were and flew out of the head and headed aft. Seeing this happen—jumping out of shoes, shorts and dungarees like a Mack Sennet cartoon—and heading aft bare naked, I laughed so hard and so much I couldn't have run even if I had wanted too!! A minute or so later the banging, scraping, clanging sound came again—aft. We had definitely run over a mine!!! A couple of minutes later my shipmate returned—nothing on, excited, and visibly shaken. He took one look at me still seated on 'the trough' and began yelling, 'Geez Shorty!! Don't you know we ran into a mine?? How come you're still here?? You a dummy or something?? Weren't you scared?? Cripes!!' Still laughing like hell, I answered, 'Yeah I know it was a mine. No, I'm no dummy. You are for running aft where the mine hit again. And hell yes, I was scared—that's why I just sat where I was!' I was still laughing, he hopped back into his clothes and shoes, cussed me out again, and stormed out raving!![4]

The second major assault and landing in the Borneo campaign was to be conducted by Task Group 78.1 on June 10 in the Brunei Bay area on the western side of the large island in British North Borneo. LCSs and other support ships practiced for five days at Morotai for this operation.

On the way to Brunei Bay from the practice area at Morotai, the amphibious force ran into heavy weather. An excerpt from the diary of 60 crew member tells us what was going on. "The morning brought still heavy seas and left one minesweeper behind who had run aground in the dark. An LCI proceeded to pull her off. I am getting salty now—heavy seas and I am not seasick. If I can hold out until night, I'll be O.K.

"Tony Damato, Doc Murlin and myself put on rain gear and stood on the gun deck. The gun tub on the bow would dip under water and spray us on the gun deck. The bow would then be heaved high in the air and the flat bottom of the craft would smack another swell, causing the whole ship to quiver as the screws came out of the water at the stern. This was pretty good sport until the lashings broke on provisions stored under No. 1 gun platform. They were being washed overboard, so we took off our shoes and went down to gather them up and lash them down once more."[5]

The Brunei Bay operation involved simultaneous landings at three different points as far apart as 18 miles. This large area of approach required extensive minesweeping, hydrographic survey work, and reconnaissance, with much of it to be done in restricted waters before the landing date. On June 7 three days before the invasion, the *45* helped in the marking of the three separate landing beaches.

For this operation Captain Arison, Commander Flotilla One, was the Officer in Tactical Command of the advance echelon unit made up of close-fire support ships (including eight LCSs), minesweeping units, underwater demolition teams, beach reconnaissance units, and the hydrographic party. Evidently the arrival of this large unit on June 7 in Brunei Bay deceived the Japanese forces on shore. Here is what Richard Rhame, staff officer, reported: "On the day of our arrival in the area, it was observed that numerous fires had been started ashore. The size of the advance echelon, though composed almost entirely of ships under two hundred feet in length, had apparently given the enemy the impression that the actual assault was underway; the Japs offered no opposition to the early operations but retired inland."[6]

As in the Tarakan operation, one of the most serious problems was the huge number of mines in the bay area. On June 7 and 8, LCSs *42, 45-47, 58-60* provided protection for the minesweepers and served as a mine demolition unit. In this operation approximately 1,000 mines were destroyed.

Raymond Ross, crewman on the *60*, recorded what was going on on his ship on June 7: "Morning saw us in the South China Sea off the northwest coast of Borneo. No 2 engine is miraculously repaired and is ready for operation. During the night, 4 cruisers and 12 destroyers teamed up with us. The sea was rough all night, nearly rolling me out of the rack at times. With the tension taking hold too, I didn't sleep well.

"The mine sweeps were working all day and we went right along with them quite close to the beach. An LCI exploded one mine that I knew of up near the beach. PBMs and PBYs [Navy patrol aircraft] patrolled with us all day on the alert for subs and mines. B-24s flew over and bombed and strafed the beach we are to take. No shell fire from the beach as yet. If there are installations, they are holding fire in order not to betray their positions. Tomorrow morning we tow the demolition squad in to blow up obstructions to clear the beachhead while we shell Labuan just outside Victoria Bay."[7]

On June 9 the *46* shelled Brooketon to protect a hydrographic ship working in a narrow channel. LCSs also provided protection for beach reconnaissance operations during the June 7-10 preinvasion period. In the minesweeping operation, the *Salute* (AM *294*) was severely damaged by a mine. Using their salvage equipment, LCSs *42* and *48* kept the *Salute* afloat for four hours, but because her damage was too severe to allow for towing, she was sunk by friendly fire.

Just what the LCSs and the accompanying LCIs were doing at this time was described by Ross: "We started for the beach along with minesweepers over water which LCS *60* traveled time after time yesterday. To my chagrin the sweeps picked up eight contact mines. A little farther on they picked up more. LCIs proceeded to detonate them with rifle fire. When they went off, water and black smoke blew sky high. The *58, 59* and *60* and two LCIs proceeded to within 1,500 yards of the beach when someone shouted, 'There she comes,' and the beach literally blew up in front of us. We were now broadside to the beach and shells were dropping ahead of us about 400 yards to starboard. The first terrific blast was from U.S. B-24s, two waves of six, dropping demolition bombs. The cruisers were far behind us getting the range on the beach. We received the order to open fire and strafe the beach. Concentrating first on the shoreline, then working back inland, Johnson and I put several rounds and concentrated on a building about a 1,000 yards inland. We started a fire and then the whole sky was filled with trees, stone, mud, and wood with flares and black smoke going in every direction. We had hit an ammunition dump. The boys said it was the best show of the day. Wave after wave of B-24s and Australian Beanfighters [dive bombers] bombed the same area we were strafing."[8]

On June 9 an accident occurred involving the Underwater Demolition Team that the *60* was protecting and working with. Here is an eyewitness account: "Presently, the demolition squad moved in as we moved up to 500 yards of the shore, giving cover to the demo squad. The squad jumped overboard and started immediately to explore the ocean floor for booby traps and mines while we fired on the beach over their heads. Presently two beanfighters swooped low and unleashed their bomb load while the swimmers were about fifty yards from the beach. The bombs missed the target and fell in the water among the demo squad. A column of water rose like Niagara in reverse. No demo squad could be seen. Soon heads began to bob around. The Higgins boats went in and picked up the men. One man suffered shock from concussion, and another boy named Stevens from Delaware could not be found. Most likely he was the object of a direct hit. We retired from the area very hungry and thirsty after six hours of General Quarters. Net result—channel cleared of mines. One ammunition dump blown up. Beach reported clear of land mines by Demo Squad. Beach thoroughly strafed and bombed."[9]

Actually both Aussie and U.S. UDTs in the Brunei Bay operation had more than their share of hazards without being bombed by 'friendly aircraft'. In addition to the large number of mines and the extensive underwater barriers, there were many very poisonous coral snakes (unattended bites produced death in eight minutes) as well as sharks and crocodiles to contend with.

The LCSs actions with the sweepers before the invasion were commended by the ships' Group Commander, Lieutenant Commander Maynes C. Fitzgerald, who wrote to the ships under his command: "Your action does not merit my congratulations alone. The publicity men aboard the *42* have been on 12 other invasions in this area including Lingeyan. Their opinion is that they have never seen anything to compare with your march with the minesweepers down the whole length of the beach with the ever-present possibility of being blown out of the water coolly ignored. The commander of the sweeper unit reported that he has never swept a beach with more confidence in his safety after the first few minutes of the action showed what you could do. The FLAG itself issued a WELL DONE; short of individual awards, that is the Navy's highest praise."[10]

The landings of large numbers of Australian troops in the Brunei Bay area took place as scheduled on June 10. LCSs *58-60* supported the Brown Beach landing on Labuan Island, which was nearly 20 miles from the other two landings. During the Brown Beach landing, the *58*, which had UDT #4 aboard, destroyed two suicide boats and shot down a church steeple that had been used as a watch tower by the Japanese. LCSs *42* and *47* supported the landing on Green Beach one mile east of Brunei Bluff, and LCSs *45* and *46* supported the White Beach landing on Maura Island.

Two runs, a preliminary one and one for the landing, were made on Brown Beach, and a single landing was made on Green. Because of the geography of White Beach, support craft were required to make unusual and somewhat

"LCS 44 Daze": These cartoons depicting life on LCS44 appeared in a booklet published in 1945 by the ship's crew. They were drawn by 44 gunner James C. Downey. Courtesy Nisi Dionis.

complicated approaches. Ross on the *60* supporting the Labuan Island landing reported on the LCSs in the invasion: "At 0810 we made the first run at the beach. During the night, the Aussies and supply ships arrived. A Jap plane came over and dropped one bomb on the troop ships but missed. We went into the beach with several LCSs and LCIs. Strafed the beach at a 1,000 yards and set off 120 rockets. The beach exploded and smoke hung so thick you couldn't see it. Turning broadside we strafed the beach and came back out. The Aussies in amphibian tanks fell in behind us.

"We prepared and went into the beach again. Meanwhile, cruisers and destroyers were firing over our heads. There would be a crack and a whistling swish overhead and then an explosion as the shell hit the beach.

"We were firing as we came into range and at 1,000 yards planted another 120 rockets on the beach. By now, the jungle was removed. The guns fired until the Aussies passed us. We were now within 300 yards of the beach. We waved as their tanks passed and watched the Aussies go onto the beach without a casualty. Within an hour LSMs and LSTS were on the beach unloading ammunition, trucks, and supplies."[11]

During a crucial moment in the rocket firing operation at Maura Island, the LCS *46* crew had a serious problem. After the 90-degree turn was made and the 'fire rockets' order was given, nothing happened. The rockets would not fire. The crew felt that they should rid themselves of these armed rockets as soon as possible. So, much to the chagrin of the ships still moving in, the ship stopped in position while the crew carefully threw the rockets overboard with just five minutes to spare before the troops hit the beach.[12]

At 1700 on invasion day LCS support craft supported troop movement west of Victoria Town, and at 1804 the Commander of Task Unit 78.13 sent the *47* to sink three mines swept by LCVPs in the Brunei Bluff area. Following the invasion the *46* was assigned to night patrol duty; the *60* stayed on night picket duty off the beach until June 17.

Although this action lacked the strong symbolic significance of the Corregidor landing in March, General Douglas MacArthur landed on Borneo on June 10 at Labuan Island with other high ranking officers. He proclaimed that "The execution of the Brunei Bay operation had been flawless—a splendid performance."[13]

Because the Brunei Bay area had been so heavily mined (it was reportedly the second largest minefield in the Pacific theater), LCSs continued to work with the minesweepers as mine demolition units after the invasion. On June 12 LCSs *42* and *45-47* reported to USS *Phillip* (DD *498*) to cover minesweeping in the Miri-Lutong area. As of June 13 the *42* had detonated 80 of the 338 mines destroyed by that time. From June 17 to 19 the *42, 45, 46, 58*, and *60* formed a mine demolition unit off Miri and were credited with destroying a large number of mines. As of the 29th, the *42* had a total of 100 mines to her credit; the total destroyed in the area was approximately 380. On June 14 the *60* worked with the Hydrographic Department's crew as they charted a ship route along Brunei Bay.

After the major Brunei landings on June 10, vessels from Captain Arison's Close Support Unit participated in subsidiary landings in the vicinity. On June 19 Captain Arison was the Attack Unit Commander for a landing at Mempahol. On June 20 the *45, 46, 58*, and *60* participated in an invasion of Miri Lutong in the Province of Sarawak, where 1,800 Australian troops were landed. In this operation *58* came and protected an Aussie UDT as they worked before the invasion. As late as June 21 the *60* was detonating mines in the large minefield off Miri.

At this time Australian Army forces recovered survivors of the 225 allied prisoners held by the Japanese in Borneo for three years. Here is the June 23 diary entry by Ross describing the event: "U.S. news commentator announced that of 225 allied prisoners taken three years ago (mostly Australian) by the Japanese, the Aussies took the remaining 16 survivors of the original 225 brought to Borneo to work in the oil refineries. They had no medical attention for three years, were starved to skin and bones with unsightly ulcers and afflicted with BeriBeri. It took Aussie medical officers 24 hours to treat the 16 men."[14]

The third and last major invasion of the Borneo campaign was set for July 1st at Balikpapan on the east coast of Dutch Borneo some distance below Tarakan. This invasion was to be the final major amphibious operation of World War II and involved the taking of a strategic and important area that had been in Japanese hands since 1942.

As in the Brunei Bay area, the water off Balikpapan was heavily mined; minesweeping operations began on June 15. LCSs in the area were first assigned to mine demolition detail with sweepers in the area. While on this duty, the gunnery officer on *41* reported seeing four minesweepers blown up. In one instance the whole stern of a YMS was blown off. After the invasion, *50* served on a river in the area with a YMS that was sunk by a mine. The next day the *50* went up the river to rescue to missing YMS crewmen who had spent the night ashore hiding from the Japanese.

Shortly after this, the bulk of the LCSs in the area were assigned to provide close support to the UDTs working to clear the harbor of barriers and obstacles. Supporting the UDTs from June 21 to 28 and again on June 30 were the *8, 28, 29, 43, 44, 48*, and *50*. The LCSs were under fire in mined waters for much of this service; *Eight* was hit by three 75mm shells on June 28, with five crew members wounded.

Kenneth Krayer gave details:

LCSs continued the beach bombardment along with additional support from the destroyers. But at 1015 enemy gun emplacements started shelling the support ships. We [*28*] were the ship immediately to the east of LCS *Eight*, and she was about 300 yards off our port quarter. I was the sight-setter on the aft 40mm Mark 51 director so I watched it all happen.

I wasn't exactly sure what was happening as the *Eight* got underway at flank speed and passed us on our starboard side. She was trailing her stern anchor behind like a surf board. She got underway so fast that her anchor was still out. I remember banging the pointer-trainer on the shoulder and tell him to "LOOK!" It really looked crazy.

I then got the word over my headphones that she'd just taken 3 hits from a 75mm. We thought she was sinking as she immediately started to take a heavy list. We later found out that her crew was shifting ballast to get a hole out of the water.

We were later told that she took one hit in the conn which hit the jettison bag and one of the men got shrapnel in his legs. So they immediately moved him to the signal [flagbag] area and they took a hit there. We were told it knocked a box out from under a man on watch and lodged in a fuel tank and never went off. They took the shell topside and threw it overboard.[15]

LCS(L) *Eight*'s ship history accounts for the movement of one of the three shells: The shell went through its conning tower and into its electric room where a crew member put the live shell in a can and threw it overboard. For this action he received the Silver Star, five of his shipmates received Purple Hearts, and the captain received the Bronze Star.[16]

In the same action LCS *41* was hit four times with slight damage, and LCS *44* was attacked by suicide planes, one of which crashed in the water just 200 yards from the ship.

The UDTs' good work and the LCSs' valiant support of them at Balikpapan has been described in some detail by Samuel Eliot Morison: "The underwater demolition teams turned in a fine performance. This work was simplified by a heavy blanket of gunfire support from cruisers and destroyers and close support of seven LCS(L) gunboats. On June 25 the gunboats took station 1,200 to 1,500 yards offshore and were taken under fire at once. They retaliated with heavy bombardment. [They] also received heavy fire at 800 to 1,000 yards. Withdrawal was made under heavy fire. On June 27 the gunboats were continually under fire while the 'frogmen' were doing their work, but the UDTs were able to retire without a single casualty."[17]

Morison goes on to quote Lieutenant L. A. State's Action Report on the Balikpapan operation: "This job at Balikpapan was one of the bravest and best by the 'frogmen' during the entire war."[18]

On July 1st the landing of the 7th Division, I, Australian Corps (35,000 troops) took place at Balikpapan on a beach that had been well defended with many barriers and tank traps. Supporting the landing boats and bombarding the beach as part of TG 78.2 were LCSs *28-30, 41, 43, 44, 48,* and *50.*

During this action a destroyer working with the LCSs came to *41*'s rescue. L. E. Guillott, gunnery officer, explained what happened: "Just before the invasion while we were right up at the beach, a very big gun opened up on us. They must have shot six or eight shells at us from about a half mile away, but we couldn't seem to get the right range on them with our three-inch to put a stop to that business. We were at anchor since we were in a mine field, and two of their shells straddled up. This meant that they only had to shoot the next shell at half the correction between the previous two in order to score a hit. We asked for permission to move. The third shot never came because a destroyer came so fast to our aid that I thought they would drive themselves high and dry on the beach. That was the prettiest destroyer I ever saw."[19]

When the Australian soldiers waded ashore at Balikpapan, they were met by a very large sign that read: "Welcome to Borneo. United States Underwater Demolition Team No. 4." Whoever wrote that sign should have added right after 'Team No. 4' "and the LCSs that protected them under fire."[20]

Endnotes

[1] Richard Rhame, "War History, Commander LCS(L) Flotilla One," Nov. 20, 1945; Samuel Eliot Morison, *History of U.S. Naval Operations in World War II*, Vol. XIII, *The Liberation of the Philippines* (Boston: Little Brown, 1959), Part IV, 225-277; Commander Amphibious Group Six (TG 78.1), Report of Amphibious Attack on Brunei, Borneo, 14 June 1945. Factual information from individual ship histories, action reports, personal accounts.

[2] Karig, *Battle Report—Victory in the Pacific*, 266.

[3] Letter to author from Kenneth R. Krayer, June 18, 1993.

[4] From a letter to the author from Gil Nadeau, undated.

[5] Raymond J. Ross, LCS *60*, diary, 7. Used with permission.

[6] Rhame, "War History," 7.

[7] Ross, 8.

[8] Ibid.

[9] Ibid.

[10] Letter to the Officers and Men of LCS(L) Group 2 from Group Commander, undated.

[11] Ross, 8-9.

[12] Letter to author from W. M. Beckert, executive officer, *46*, January 17, 1990.

[13] Morison, 265.

[14] Ross, 10.

[15] Letter, Krayer.

[16] LCS(L) *8* Ship's History, 6.

[17] Morison, 271.

[18] Ibid.

[19] L. E. Guillott, "How Did We Ever Win the War?" unpublished book, 63.

[20] Guillott, 65.

Chapter 8

"Well done, little guy!"
LCS Actions at Iwo Jima[1]

Crewmen of the 12 LCSs off Hawaii and Tinian rehearsing in December and January for the Iwo Jima invasion on February 19, 1945, could not have been fully aware of the forces of man and nature that would be pitted against them at that tiny isolated volcanic island.

To defend their small, strategic island, which they knew U.S. forces wanted for an air base, the Japanese attempted to make Iwo into an impregnable fortress. They built a large number of pillboxes into the ground and on the sides of Mount Suribachi and into the cliffs north of the landing beach area. In addition, they placed machine guns and other artillery pieces in numerous caves and underground and wherever else they could be hidden on the island.

The pillboxes were so sturdily built and so thoroughly dug in that only point-blank shelling by large-caliber guns could knock them out. So that their 23,000 troops could operate underground much of the time, the Japanese excavated 5,000 meters of underground tunnels.

That the Japanese troops were making a 'last ditch stand' is evident from this statement by a member of Iwo Jima's commanding General Kuribayashi's staff: "The defense policy was that each man should think of his defense position as his graveyard, fight until the last, and give many damages to the enemy."[2]

In addition, Iwo's lack of a harbor and its exposure to the open sea on all sides meant that landing the troops and beaching the landing craft and unloading vehicles and supplies might be difficult under normal conditions, particularly for the smaller landing craft. If the sea and winds should rise, the landing could be infinitely more difficult.

LCS crewmen preparing for the invasion could, however, take some comfort in the fact the U.S. forces had been softening up the 'impregnable island' for several months. B-24s had begun bombing Iwo as early as the previous August, and there had been numerous air raids in the fall, as well as heavy ship and air bombardments in December and January.

For the first two weeks of February, U.S. forces bombed the island day and night. According to the historian Samuel Eliot Morison, "Probably no island in World War II received as much preliminary pounding as did Iwo Jima."[3]

One thing that LCS crewmen could not take comfort in was that the time and place of the invasion were generally known in mid-January in the Pearl Harbor and Honolulu areas. Evidently what was Top Secret information concerning a major operation had become common knowledge. As if to rub salt into the wound, just five days before D Day (February 19), Tokyo Rose radioed to the U.S. Fleet, "We know that you will be here on the 19th and we will be waiting for you."[4]

On January 22, after invasion rehearsals and practices off Hawaii, Group 7 of LCS Flotilla Three, under the command of Captain T. C. Aylward, departed Pearl Harbor on their way to Iwo via Eniwetok and Saipan. There, off nearby Tinian, they would participate in a final 'invasion dress rehearsal'. In Group 7 were the flotilla commander's flag ship, LC(FF) *988* and the 12 LCSs that would serve in the Iwo Jima campaign: *31-36* and *51-56*.

Although there was almost a month between this departure from Pearl and the group's arrival off Iwo on D Day, LCS crews were on the move much of the time: "It was a hustle after Pearl, with logistics stops at Eniwetok and Saipan, but stops in the briefest sense of the word. At Eniwetok it was long enough to let the flagship dog have puppies which were promptly named 'Ene', 'We', and 'Tok'. At Saipan it was long enough to practice a little without live bullets . . . but at any time of night or day the ship must be moved alongside big ships for supplies, water, fuel, and ammunition. At Saipan the anchor was on the ground once for five hours, but that was almost like a weekend in the country."[5]

The same crew member described the *35* crew's feelings as his ship left safe, secure Saipan for the invasion of dangerous, explosive, 'God knows what' Iwo Jima: "There is a sort of nervous electricity in the air and each of us has that feeling that he alone is going to be the target of every enemy on the island, an experience most men have before their first fire, I guess. The Jap has stuff on that island and we know it; how much he will give to the Navy is a question to which the answer lies seven days and 1,200 miles ahead."[6]

Throughout the night of February 18th, LCSs of Group 7 moved closer and closer to their appointed rendezvous point with the large amphibious landing

Amphibious exercises for landing craft and LCSs off Tinian near Saipan in preparation for the Iwo Jima invasion on February 19. Courtesy of National Archives 80-GK-2696.

force off Iwo Jima. Soon after midnight and through the hours until dawn on D Day, LCS crewmen could see lights flashing off in the distance: "We could see the glare and flash of the heavy naval bombardment. It was an eerie sight, because we couldn't hear the gunfire for several hours."[7] And as they got closer, they could see the cascading trajectories bombarding the island from all sides.

By dawn on D Day the LCSs had arrived at the rendezvous area and were preparing to line up for the first rocket run to the beach. Crew members on *36* were having a traditional steak and egg breakfast. All hands on all the LCSs were at general quarters preparing themselves for battle.

Here is what was happening on *35*: "All hands cover their faces with anti-flash compound, giving the impression of a group of Zombies manning the vessel. Slate grey it is, and there it remained until two days later when the first free washing could be accomplished in quiet. Each officer wears a pistol, and men not stationed on ship's guns man the 50-caliber machine guns. Each man wears also a life jacket, helmet, whistle, flashlight, and dog tag just in case."[8]

During the Iwo Jima operation Captain T. G. Aylward, Commander LCS Flotilla Three, served as Commander Gunboat Support Group operating under Commander Amphibious Forces, Pacific Fleet. The commander and his staff on LC(FF) *988* coordinated close in-shore fire support of the LCSs with the Marines and assisted in salvage operations. In immediate command of the 12 LCSs was Lieutenant Commander Frank Stone, Commander LCS Group 7, and his staff on LCS *31*.

Two naval historians have noted the presence of LCS(L)s in the Iwo Jima campaign. Walter Karig calls them "new combination gunboats and rocket ships—rocket bristling gunboats—leading wave after wave of assault craft in the invasion."[9] S.E. Morison is more explicit: "It was now time for the newest type of boat, the Landing Craft Support, to do its stuff. Twelve of these 160-foot craft, each capable of firing a salvo of 120 4.5-inch rockets and bristling with 40mm and 20mm and 50-caliber machine guns as well, were present."[10]

H hour for February 19, D Day for the Iwo invasion, was set at 0900 hours.

At 0640 while the large landing force off Iwo was beginning to take the shape it would have during the invasion, the large fleet ships continued to bombard the island from all sides with literally thousands of projectiles ranging from 5 to 16 inches in diameter.

As the LCSs passed through the big ships bombarding the beach to take formation for their initial run, Captain Thomas Aylward, Commander of LCS Flotilla 3, broke a night-long visual and radio silence with this 'All Ships' message: "No matter how good looking a girl is, there is an even money bet she has a pimple on her bottom!"[11]

Frank Osterland, *33* officer, described the scene: "The twelve LCSs had formed up several thousand yards offshore from the island, while the bulk of the transports and support ships in the invasion force were lying to farther offshore. The rumbling roar of high-velocity projectiles passing through the air high over our station was unending. Finally with the approach of daylight, the thunder of bombardment came to a halt. The island in the distance was a smoking mass in the early morning light. Black sand beaches were pitted with craters; the rocky hillsides appeared to be devastated."[12]

After the bombardment, while the LCSs were readying themselves for their first rocket run, the LCS crews learned that the 12 LCI(G) gunboats in the landing force would not run alongside them because they had been severely damaged on

February 17 while leading four underwater demolition teams into the beach over roughly the same area the LCSs would go.

The LCI(G)s came under intense fire from shore batteries with a number of men killed and wounded and all participating ships put out of action. All the LCI(G) crews performed courageously in this operation, continuing their leading and protecting of the UD teams until absolutely forced to stop. It is believed that the Japanese fired on them because they thought they were leading the invasion itself. Fortunately, in the process, the Japanese revealed the locations of their major defense guns for the first time. This allowed the heavy naval artillery to target and destroy at least some of the guns, thereby reducing casualties to landing troops on D Day.

Even though most of the LCI(G)s at Iwo were put out of action on February 17, the flotilla of small support craft in the invasion force was a formidable 42 ships. In addition to the 12 LCSs, there were 3 LCI(G)s, 18 LCI(M)s (mortars), and

Several of the 12 LCSs that served in the Iwo Jima campaign can be seen serving as guides to the waves of assault boats in this famous picture of the Iwo invasion. Courtesy of U.S. Navy.

9 LCI(R)s (rockets). The LCI(M)s were praised later by the Marines for their effective firepower against the enemy throughout the campaign.

At 0738 the 12 LCSs began their first run to the beach, firing their guns at one mile from the beach and bombarding the beach with massive barrages of over 1,400 rockets at one half mile. After firing their rockets, the LCSs turned and ran parallel to the beach, firing all possible guns on the beach at every available target.

Lieutenant Joseph Sansone, *36* captain, described the effects of the rocket barrage: "At this point the gunboats let out with a beautiful barrage of rockets. I think that the children would have delighted in seeing the sight. They look like a lot of sky rockets set up on the Fourth of July, only these little missives when they hit the beach shook the island and even the water extending from the island. If the devils in hell didn't feel that blast, they must have been in a complete state of numbness."[13]

For this run and for subsequent runs and actions in the Iwo campaign, LCS *33*, on the left flank, and *56* on the right of their designated beaches, were equipped with expert staff radar teams and state-of-the-art radar equipment to ensure accuracy in navigation and coordination of timing. Actually there were three teams, made up of one officer and one radarman each, the third of which was on the Flotilla Commander's flagship.[14]

In addition to providing heavy gunfire and rocket support, the LCSs served as guides to the waves of troops landing on seven adjacent beaches designated by colors. Two LCSs served as guides at the ends of each beach area. At this time the weather was good and the sea relatively calm.

During their first rocket run to the beach, LCS *33* was hit by a mortar shell which did slight damage to the ship and injured five crewmen. LCS *51* was hit by an enemy anti-tank gun from the beach and set on fire; *51*'s damage control party, however, put out the fire so fast that the captain, who was busy maintaining position, did not know about it until it was over. While firing on the beach, *32* destroyed a small Japanese ammunition dump and killed a small group of troops.

On their second run, the LCSs led the first wave of three Marine divisions to land at 0900 (H hour). Lieutenant Kenneth Huff, *35* captain, has described the scene: "Directly astern of you are hundreds of small craft crammed with Marines. The roar from those boats sounds like a thousand planes in the air. Now 'H hour' is here, and this time you go in with the division slowly, just ahead of those small craft firing and offering protection. It seems to take an hour to get 900

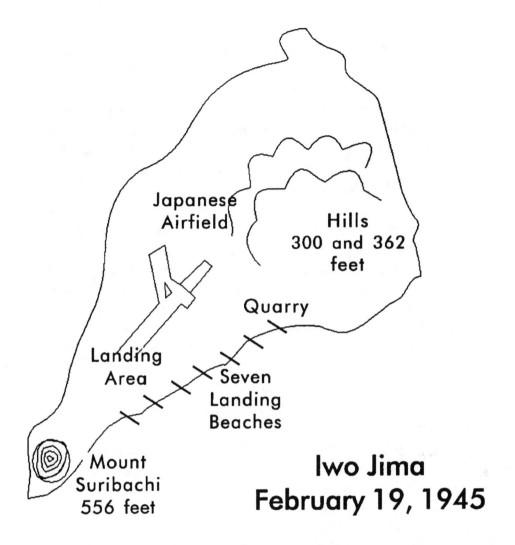

Japanese
Airfield

Hills
300 and 362
feet

Quarry

Landing
Area

Seven
Landing
Beaches

Mount
Suribachi
556 feet

**Iwo Jima
February 19, 1945**

yards off the beach, and it occurs to you what a fine slow target you are, especially since every Jap is looking right at your ship and in particular right at you. Again it is 'rockets away', and then the first waves of small stuff pass you. There they got a boat, but the wave has hit the beach and is digging like moles. Now you turn away and stand by at the flanks about a thousand yards from the beach, firing at the caves which pimple the island. Now and then you spot a burst of smoke from enemy fire, and you blast away. Usually the burst will reappear when you stop because they are really dug in."[15]

On this same second run, LCS *32* encountered mortar and machine gun fire from the beach. Some of the mortars landed within 100 yards of the ship, and

---

shrapnel hit the ship but caused no damage. When reaching within 200 yards of the beach, *53* fired into caves, pillboxes, and mortar positions, setting a cave and small fuel dump on fire.

LCS *53* reported that fire from the beach was light except for an occasional 1,000-pound rocket overshooting the island and sending up a high geyser nearby. Near the completion of the second run, *36* wiped out a machine gun nest on the beach. Immediately after the run all LCSs not serving as guides moved slowly along the beach, rapidly firing all possible guns at caves and targets of opportunity.

"The LCS(L) guide ships halted their advance several hundred yards offshore, while the amtracks [landing vehicle tractors] covered the remaining distance on their own. The guide ships remained in position all that first day to identify beach landing zones and to maintain a line of departure for following waves of incoming landing craft. First on the beach were the Marine shock troops in their amtracks, then hundreds of troops and vehicle-laden LCVPs and LCMs, followed by LCIs. As soon as the beachhead had been established by our troops, the heavier LCTs, LSMs, and LSTs brought in the heavy duty guns, tanks, and other equipment."[16]

Marine troops began the actual landing at H hour, 0900, as scheduled, and by 0944 the larger LSMs carrying tanks, had beached. There were difficulties, however, at different places on the landing beaches.

The initial amtracks (LVTS) could not climb the first terrace at the beach, which rose to 15 feet in places. Their troops were forced to climb the volcanic ash and cinder terrace, which reduced their important initial run to a walk. Many amtracks, as well as landing craft that followed, were stranded at the beach, causing congestion that worsened as the day progressed.

At the same time the Japanese greatly intensified their firepower, and the landing Marines were hit with withering shell and mortar fire. Much of this fire came from numerous underground gun emplacements with only a narrow slit for the barrel showing above ground.

Unfortunately, just these small parts showing above ground made these emplacements impossible for support ships and aircraft to spot and knock out. Only the advancing troops could destroy such positions with their grenades, flame-throwers, and other equipment. Fire support ships present, however, were able to provide useful support to the troops in a number of ways.

About 1100 on D Day the wind shifted and the sea rose, causing even more difficulties at the landing beaches. Loaded LCVPs and LCMs were swamped and flooded, and many were broached and hit by mortar fire. The beaches were so littered by nightfall that landing anything was almost impossible.

This bad weather and heavy seas on the first day and intensifying conditions on the second day were to test the ship handling and seamanship abilities of LCS crews assigned to salvage duty as they had never been tested before.

In spite of these difficult conditions, approximately 30,000 Marines were landed the first day. Some troop units were able to advance only slowly by inches, and others by rapid strides, but most of the units moved ahead, even though they suffered 2,420 casualties. By 1035 a small party of Marines worked their way across the narrowest part of the island to the western side, and by 1500 on D Day, the courageous Marines had succeeded in cutting off Mount Suribachi from all other Japanese defenses on the island.

"Our ship's close-in position provided a vantage point from which to observe the fierce hand-to-hand combat between Marines and the enemy. We saw tank-to-tank confrontations, the flare of flame throwers, the burst of exploding missiles, and the slow advance of Marines against their entrenched foe. It was a sight never to be forgotten."[17]

Because there was limited space on Iwo Jima for artillery emplacements and because getting artillery ashore was difficult, the naval gunfire support ships present provided primary artillery for the campaign, and supported the troops ashore in every way possible. As providers of close-in gunfire support, the LCSs took every advantage of their capabilities, such as their ability to work in shallow water and to beach to support the troops.

Each Marine battalion ashore had a shore fire control party in communication with the LCSs. These parties would call the LCSs to fire (known as 'call fire') on enemy troops opposing the advancing Marines, to destroy particular targets ashore, to fire continuously for 24 to 48 hours at crucial targets ashore, and to provide harassing fire to keep the enemy guns out of action throughout the night. In addition LCSs, under the direction of the Flotilla and Group Commanders, fired guns and rockets. Also individual LCSs fired their guns and even their rockets selectively at apparent targets ashore and made extra rocket runs on D Day.

Although LCSs could fire into caves and destroy such exposed targets as tanks, ammunition dumps, machine gun posts, and enemy troops, they lacked the firepower to knock out the numerous heavily reinforced pillboxes that the Japanese had embedded over much of the island.

The heavy ships, which were capable of destroying the pillboxes with their 5- to 16-inch projectiles, were some distance out in the ocean, some as far as ten miles. Because of this, they had difficulty focusing on particular targets ashore. On the other hand, LCSs could operate within 50 yards of the beach and provide excellent observation for shore gunfire. In fact Marines ashore involved in gunnery support claimed that LCSs close ashore could spot targets more readily than could the forces ashore.

Almost immediately after the second rocket run on D Day, while the troops were landing in force, LCSs became key members of gunnery support teams with the larger ships. LCS *51* became a Shore Fire Observation ship. Expert Marine spotters were put on *51*, and on other LCSs to serve as the 'eyes' for the larger ships out in the ocean.

The spotter in touch with the ships by radio would sight a target into which the LCSs would fire their tracers. Then the large ships would fire their projectiles into the tracers. "A few seconds after the spotter phoned the info, you could hear the 16-inch projectiles whistle overhead and explode at the target. We all prayed 'Hail Marys' that none would fall short."[18]

Sometimes the LCSs would move in close to the shore to draw the enemy's fire and then locate the fire's source with the same results mentioned above. LCS *51*, with Marine Lieutenant J. J. Sweeny aboard, became the 'eyes' for the cruiser *Vicksburg*, which was thus able to annihilate spotted targets within seconds after the spotting.

This method of spotting was first used at Iwo Jima in the morning of D Day to knock out enemy gun emplacements at the old quarry on the northern extreme of the beach landing area. This was a major achievement because these guns had been firing down directly on the landing troops and slaughtering then by the hundreds. Throughout the campaign LCSs worked with each other and with larger ships, even battleships, using this effective team approach.

After the second rocket run, LCS crews demonstrated ingenuity in providing support for the landing troops and the troops already ashore. Beginning at 1005 LCS *32* fired its rockets and its guns selectively at apparent targets on shore. For instance, after launching a salvo of 10 rockets above Green Beach one, it fired its guns at an apparent mortar emplacement. It next fired at enemy personnel in a cave and at a mortar emplacement on Mount Suribachi.

Its next target was a pillbox just south of Green Beach. It first fired at this and then fired two salvos of eight rockets each at the same target. It then fired one rocket at an enemy dugout south of Green Beach, and from 1631 to 1750, its target was enemy personnel in the same area. In this action, *32* demonstrated that LCSs could fire a small number of their rockets as readily and as accurately as mortar shells could be fired. At 1920 LCS *32* moved out to one of the transport areas to serve on a counter measures patrol throughout the night.

On the next day *32* fired at apparent targets on the beach and delivered 'call fire'. Her targets were enemy personnel and enemy positions on the beach. Throughout the night she served on counter-measures patrol duty again.[19]

All LCSs at Iwo provided extensive fire support, bombarding the beach and supporting the troops ashore during the first days of the campaign. LCS *34* made 12 rocket runs to the beach during the first two days and fired at various targets on the shore between the runs. LCS *35* fired on the beach continuously for 48 hours and made two rocket runs beyond the initial two on the first day. At night *35*, along with *34, 36,* and *51,* provided harassing fire. During the next day *35* delivered 'call fire' with *34* and *36,* and fired on two anti-aircraft emplacements on orders from Commander Flotilla Three.

The night-time harassing fire had one primary objective, as this personal account revealed: "Night falls and the flare shells start to come over, giving light enough to keep the Japs from doing anything rash. You settle down to a routine. Fire on shore and go out for ten minutes; and so on and so on, varied only by rocket runs. Keep the Jap down is the object. Keep him down so we can keep the beachhead until daylight. After a century, daylight and rain come. The wind is picking up and the seas with it. Wonder how the men on the beach are doing? Here and there is a tough spot. Once in a while a group of Japs is seen and you blast away. Your sister ship just went in and actually scraped the beach up north while she shot a load of rockets. That was a beautiful job. It took a lot of guts."[20]

The LCS crews got no sleep during their first two days and nights at Iwo. The *35* crew was not able to enjoy even the relative stability of being at anchor until the night of February 24, over five days after D Day.

LCS *36*, the venturesome 'sister ship' referred to above, made eight rocket runs the first day—runs which came closer and closer to the beach each time—according to one crew member, "close enough to spit." From 0900 to 1120 *36* delivered call fire and fired on targets of opportunity. Working with *51* and four destroyers, *36* helped to wipe out an enemy position and fired on an enemy tank in a gully ashore.[21]

The exact nature of the shore target was sometimes not discovered until after it had been fired on according to this report from *36* crew member Morris Shuldenrein: "I was looking at the cliff, not too far distant from the beach, maybe 200-300 feet or so, not even 100 yards. I saw something. I didn't know what the hell it was, you know, with binoculars, near the top of the cliff, too. So I told the Officer of the Deck there, I thought I saw something. He says, 'All right, take it under fire.' We fired a couple of rounds in there, and all of a sudden there was some kind of WHOMP, some kind of WHOMP, and this big ball of flame went up there, and everybody on the ship started to cheer and well. You thought we had dropped a bomb on Tokyo. I imagine we hit some gasoline or something like that."[22]

LCSs bombarding enemy-held positions at the base of Mt. Suribachi at Iwo Jima. Courtesy of National Archives 80-G-307186.

The stress on the LCS crews and on the officers, in particular, during these firing operations was intense, as the *36* captain has told us: "Between maneuvering the ship in such a position to keep her out of hailing distance from the shells of the bigger naval vessels and reloading our rocket launchers for more runs, and answering our radio messages, which directed our call fire on the beach, all hands on board had a job. All day long we pounded what we thought to be the toughest spot on the island." When *36* captain learned later from sources in the States that the Marine troop commander, General H. M. Smith, called that particular spot 'Hell's Half Acre', he commented, "All I can say is that he should have left off the Half Acre."[23]

The news coverage of the Iwo Jima invasion to people in the states was fairly extensive and reached them in a relatively short time. Evidently movie theater newsreels throughout the country showed LCSs in the Iwo operation soon after the invasion. Virgil Thill, *52* crew member, writes that the wife of one of his shipmates saw her husband's ship on a theater newsreel and started screaming. The theater manager rushed in to settle her down and was kind enough to show her the newsreel again after the movie.[24]

The intensity of *35*'s and *36*'s firing during just their first two days at Iwo Jima can be realized from these lists of ammunition expended:

	35	*36*
Rockets fired	350	860
40mm	12,000	9,841
20mm	3,500	8,704
50 cal.	4,500	
Totals	20,350	19,405

On the second night *36* along with *32-35* were assigned to provide harassing fire into Mount Suribachi. Here is *36* crew member Morris Shuldenrein's report:

The Japanese had big guns apparently in this mount[ain], they had 'em on railroad tracks, behind heavy steel doors. What they do is open these steel doors and slide this gun out and fire a couple of rounds at the poor Marines who were on the beach, and then go back in. They were virtually impregnable. I don't see how the hell you could get in there, you know. And these guys laid on the beach for two days and two nights, on top of the volcanic ash that the beach consisted of, and their vehicles were being mired by the ash, and you'd see these mortars arching in on them, from the hills they had them zeroed in and, bang, you'd see them goin' all night long, and these guys were really gettin' clobbered. And, they couldn't get up there and get the airfield that they wanted to get, past the ridge there. Well, this went on like that for two days. Our ship was assigned to fire one 40mm round a minute, all night long, at Suribachi, as harassment fire, to try and keep these guys from opening the doors. All night long our ship fired these rounds at Suribachi.[25]

In addition to the extensive firing done by *32* and *34-36*, every other LCS at Iwo provided gunfire support for the troops ashore during the first week, and, in some instances, throughout the campaign. LCSs *52, 55,* and *56* spent part of the first two days providing close-in fire support. LCS *31*, Group 7 flagship with Lieutenant Commander Frank Stone aboard, had a Marine gunfire team aboard much of the time and attacked small tanks, moving groups of enemy troops and machine gun nests on shore, going in time after time as close as possible without touching bottom in order to make their gunfire as telling as possible. Every day that they fired, *31* would use up their entire allotment of ammunition and every night they would replenish their stock.

When *31* was asked to provide cover for troops several times just beyond the brow of a hill, they would steam out far enough to get the right range, and then dump a salvo over the hill. During the campaign, LCS *31* was found also to be most effective for close photographic reconnaissance and was used for this purpose.

Laurence McKenna, *31* gunnery officer, explained the tactics his ship used to deal with deceptive targets ashore: "An observation plane was droning over nice and low. I happened to be watching the particular batch of bush that suddenly moved aside, clearing an anti-aircraft battery to take the plane under fire, knocking it down with a single burst. Within 30 seconds the camouflage was back in place. I had the spot marked and we had it wiped out in 60 seconds."[26]

Concerning the amount of ammunition fired by the LCSs at Iwo, McKenna makes this claim: "Because Lieutenant Commander Frank Stone (LCS Group 7 Commander aboard *31*) was so eager to be a part of the action, it is safe to say that of the total ammunition fired by Group 7 (all 12 LCSs), *31* fired 25 per cent."[27]

LCS *33*, early in the campaign, worked with teams of LCSs assigned to fire on Mount Suribachi, the volcanic mountain at the southern end of the island that one crewman described as a very large pillbox, which actually diminished in size as the terrific bombardment took its toll in the first few days.[28]

After the landings LCS *34* delivered call fire to support the troops ashore with *51* and other LCSs. According to the *51* captain, "This was nerve-wracking work, since all this activity [of firing ashore and directing large ships where to fire] was going on just a few yards ahead of our own lines, but it was very effective."[29]

LCS crews sometimes tried different strategies when firing their rockets and shells into the shore, but occasionally what they were trying to do backfired: "We moved in close to try to lob the rockets over the cliff and behind, assuming the rocket flight was parabolic. Whether we did any damage wasn't evident. Shortly thereafter the enemy tumbled to the scheme and lobbed some heavy stuff at us, so we left."[30]

Other LCSs were active in supporting troops ashore, in addition to those mentioned above. LCS *54* served as the 'eyes' for cruisers and battleships directing their essential heavy fire to demolish enemy gun emplacements. LCSs *55* and *56* continued to provide close-in fire support at various crucial places on the island. The *53*, which had during the runs fired at caves, pillboxes, mortars, and mortar emplacements on Mount Suribachi and set afire a cave and fuel dump, worked extensively with spotters directing fire for the large ships. In fact the Marine Corps spotters later in the campaign praised the high effectiveness of *53*'s support firing.

On one occasion in the very early hours of February 21, 10 of the 12 LCSs were providing harassing fire to the western side of Mount Suribachi at the same time. They soon discovered that they were firing over each other and creating a dangerous situation. They found it much safer and more expeditious for two or three ships to take turns firing while the remaining ships stood by out in the ocean.

A member of the *52* crew, storekeeper Charles Cullens, spoke for all crew members of the dozen LCSs providing fire support at Iwo when he reported: "The hardest part of all was not getting enough sleep. We were on watch four hours on and four off, with General Quarters for firing, aircraft watch, and smoke duty thrown in. We got to where we paid no more attention to shell fire than we would a fly. We didn't even bother, when a big shell went over from one of our battle wagons, to look up and see where it landed. We could even sleep while our own guns were firing, with thousands of Japs a few hundred yards away and Japs and American Marines fighting and dying."[31]

Evidently some LCS crews were quite eager and even competitive about firing into the beach and beyond in the first week of the campaign, as a *35* crew member has pointed out: "I remember *51* and *33* being the most aggressive. Those nuts would go practically on land to do their shooting."[32]

With each passing day, LCS crews became more adept at firing on targets ashore. This excerpt from LCS *53*'s history demonstrates this and describes an event of tremendous importance in the long and deadly battle against Japan: "On February 23, we were requested to lay an intensive 30-minute barrage into the western slopes of Mount Suribachi. The guns were set on automatic fire and the gunners had a field day. Marine shore batteries, other LCSs, and destroyers added to the merciless bombardment. Upon being secured, we lay about 150 yards off the extinct volcano awaiting further orders. An hour later our Marines had overrun the last Jap positions on the 'rock' and we witnessed one of the most thrilling moments in the history of the war: the raising of the American flag over Mount Suribachi. We were very proud of our fighting Marines."[33]

Practically all LCS gunfire at Iwo Jima was directed at targets ashore. It is possible that LCSs could have provided a considerable amount of anti-aircraft defense firepower if they had been given the opportunity. LCSs not engaged in fire support, salvage duty or firefighting, or other assignments were frequently required to provide smoke coverage for the larger ships during air raids.

During these raids LCSs were not allowed to fire unless individual ships were attacked. If the LCSs could have fired at the raiding planes, they might well have reduced the effects of the air raids considerably. As they later demonstrated conclusively at Okinawa, they could produce a formidable amount of effective antiaircraft firepower for their size, and they were highly maneuverable under air attack.[34]

Barely two hours after the troops started landing at 0900 on D Day, it seemed that the forces of nature began conspiring to create real hazards for small ships and landing craft as well as for the troops landing at Iwo. Before noon the weather began to worsen and the seas to rise, making landings at the beaches precarious. The bad weather continued the second day, bringing with it rain, cold air, and heavy seas, and damaging surf on the landing beaches.

LCSs supporting troops ashore found the high seas causing real damage to their superstructures and to their hulls while they obtained sorely needed ammunition from other ships at sea. Ships firing more or less continuously for 24 and 48 hours needed to replenish ammunition three, four, and five times for each 24-hour period. And unfortunately for the LCSs, loading required that ships stay tied up alongside each other while crew members carefully transferred the ammunition by hand.

At least three LCSs were damaged while taking on ammunition from other ships. The *33*'s superstructure took a real beating: "We were ordered alongside the battleship *Texas* to replenish our ammo supplies. *Texas* was considerably higher and more ruggedly constructed than *33*. Wind and waves combined to smash us unmercifully against the larger vessel, causing considerable damage to our superstructure."[35]

LCS *53* suffered damage to her sides every time she took ammunition from battleships. There were, however, happy moments when the battleship's crew gave the exhausted *53* crew ice cream, and *53* gave them first-hand accounts of the battle action on the shore. Here was an instance, perhaps a rare one, where a small, flatbottomed amphibious gunboat was able to provide a large capital ship first-hand accounts of the battle they were both engaged in.

LCS *35* was damaged taking ammunition from LCS *33*, and later, in very rough seas, she was forced to stop taking ammunition from *56*, after suffering the following damage: three of the ship's docking hawsers were broken, two gun tubs were damaged, stanchions were bent and recognition lights were knocked out, her radar antenna was damaged, fourteen frames (ribs of the hull) were cracked in the midship area, 16 frames were stressed in other areas of the ship's hull (these 30 frames represent almost a third of *35*'s 101 frames).

Later, even while the ships were in the lee of Mount Suribachi, *35* was forced by rough seas to separate from *56* again while taking ammunition. The *35* was damaged again on February 20 taking ammunition from *Salt Lake City* and later while taking supplies from APA *119*.[36]

Beginning on D Day morning, as many LCSs as could be spared from providing supporting gunfire were assigned to salvage duty, clearing the congested landing beaches of broached and sunken landing craft and debris. Problems that began with the initial landing amtracks not being able to surmount the steep beach terraces multiplied in rapid order as the weather worsened around 1100, making it very difficult for LCVPs and LCMs to land their troops. Because of the heavy surf these boats could not hold themselves on the beach. At the same time the heavy surf broke over their sterns and the backwash flooded them.

Many were broached and sunk and a number were hit by mortar fire. Conditions at the landing beaches were so bad for the first two days that 160 landing craft were damaged beyond repair. At times even the larger LSMs and LCTs had difficulties landing troops and supplies. Large pontoon causeways and landing docks, dropped by the LSTs and put out for landings, were turned over and washed up on the beach or drifted out to sea. From the morning of the first day the beaches were strewn with overturned tanks, as well as pontoons, LVTS, DUKWS, and other small craft. And this congestion got worse as more boats and craft ran into trouble during the second day when the weather became even more foul.

LCS crews assigned to salvage duty realized, as soon as they saw the chaos at the beaches, that their ship handling and seamanship abilities would be tested beyond anything any one had ever dreamed of back at the stateside training. And their problems were not limited to the forces of nature that seemed to be conspiring against them at every turn.

Although some LCSs had recently had fore and aft towing pads installed on them, LCSs were by no means equipped and suited for salvage work and towing in particular. A brief comparison with tug boats will demonstrate LCSs' unsuitability. Tugboats are relatively short, and moderately wide of beam, with much of the hull under water, with powerful engines and large deep single screws well under the stern. LCSs were long (158 feet) and narrow (23 feet) and light (390 tons) with less than 6 feet of maximum draft fore and aft, with standard size screws just a very few feet below the water line and with engines not abundantly powerful.

LCSs also lacked proper towing equipment and were forced to tow with their 4-inch and 8-inch docking hawsers and 7/8-inch anchor cable, which they discovered were inadequate for most salvage jobs. And because they were long and narrow, LCSs were in grave danger of being accidentally beached or broaching themselves in the strong tides and high pounding surf at the landing beaches.

To maintain necessary control and do salvage work in the pounding surf, LCS crews used different methods of approach to the beach. Some let go their stern anchor some distance out while moving into the beach. Then they would take the swamped and broached vessels in tow using their stern anchor, as well as their engines when possible, to withdraw from the beach. They would tow the vessels out to sea and sink them. This method worked for some ships (both *33*

Chapter 8

and *36* found it useful at times). Much of the time, however, the beach was so very crowded that making a clean run into it was not possible.

LCS *35* crew tried two approaches: (1) they paralleled the beach and had a small boat take anchor cable to the disabled vessels on the shore. This method proved impractical since the LCS could not be controlled when pulling. (2) They nosed their ship onto the beach, dropping the anchor on the way in, or not, depending on beach and water conditions. This method was basically successful; however they broke all their hawsers and cables trying to pull boats badly stuck in the sand.[37]

In spite of these difficulties LCS crews used their ingenuity to help in the clearing of stranded craft from the beaches and beach front, to round up and tow crippled landing craft and stray pontoons and landing docks, and do whatever else they could do to keep the beaches clear. On D Day, LCS *31* helped to tow a broached LCVP out of the way, and after touching the shore with its bow, put out a fire on the beach using hoses connected to its stationary bow plugs.

During the first four days (February 19-22), LCS *51* cleared the beaches of debris and dragged disabled craft and wreckage off to sink them in deep water. The *51* also recovered (by taking them in tow) stray Rhino barges (pontoons propelled by large outboard motors) that had drifted out to sea, sometimes for long distances. "The weather was foul most of the time and turning beam on to the waves (turning the ship's side into heavy surf and 10-15 foot waves) after each transit [to and from the beach] was thrilling to say the least."[38]

On February 20, a strong current running parallel to the beach made landings difficult, and only the larger LSMs were able to land troops and supplies. By 0930 the beach was clogged, even though underwater demolition teams had cleared it early that morning. The next day, *35* began salvage duty at the beach and was removing one disabled tank from the shore when its tow line broke. The *35* later went out patrolling beyond the transport area, searching for landing craft that had gone adrift.

On that same morning (February 21) LCS *36* reported at 0740 for salvage duty. Two hours later the ship was ordered to extinguish an ammunition dump fire on Beach Blue One, an assignment which other LCSs had been reluctant to take. Here is *36* captain Lieutenant Joe Sansone: "It seems that everyone was pawning the job off on some other as the damaged dump was a mass of flames, of burning tanks and exploding ammunition. Shells bursting all over the place. The fire was bad enough, but when I discovered that it was an ammunition dump,

. . . my heart accelerated quite a bit and the job of doing it with the fewest casualties to my personnel was a problem . . . even before we got to the burning dump [that same morning] we had a hot reception when we passed Suribachi Mountain."[39]

The ammo dump fire was at the water's edge in an area heavily congested with broached and wrecked landing craft and debris of different kinds, including the bodies of Marines killed in the landing action there. The surf was high and the sea was rough, and to reach the fire, the *36* captain had to place his 23-foot-wide ship in a slot only 35 feet wide between a sunken Japanese landing craft and a wrecked allied landing craft. The burning dump had sustained heavy Japanese mortar fire; two Marines had been killed in tanks there.

On the ship's first approach, the pressure on the fire hoses was inadequate to reach the fire. The *36* crew then transferred a Johnson P500 pump with hose connections to an LCVP, but the small boat crew could not find personnel willing to man the equipment. The captain then made a second run, which as he reported "was perfect . . . the best beaching ever made and [we] ran the ship right up into the fire."[40] At the time of the beaching, the ship was protected from enemy fire by the intensive action of our own aircraft.

Even before the ship was fully beached, some members of the fire-fighting party jumped into the water off the ship's bow, not waiting for ladders or lines to lower them down with the fire hoses. "As soon as we hit the beach, I jumped over the bow and sank into the volcanic ash over my knees. Other firefighters followed me. The skipper started backing down off the beach, and all the men were being pulled off the beach by the undertow, plus the pull of the ship's engines in reverse. I hollered to the skipper to get the ship back on the beach. I grabbed Cris Psoma's hand; he in turn grabbed someone else, and soon I was pulling all of them onto the volcanic ash, or we might have ended up in the screws. We then proceeded to put out the ammunition dump fire while standing on live mortar shells, heads, arms, legs of some of the guys (Marines) that were blown apart."[41]

Another firefighter tells what he saw after the fire was out. "Right by the dump was this tank that had been hit, and there was this beautiful kid lying across the top of the tank, dead. Big, blond kid, probably a six-footer, tear your guts out; and lying on the ground was another kid covered by a poncho, and down at the water's edge, kids were all lined up on stretchers to take them out to the hospital ship, and one kid says 'Let me get to hell outta here'; they were all moaning and all . . ... In retrospect, when you really looked at it, it really hurts . . .."[42]

With the tanks at the dump continuously burning and shells exploding in all directions, it took the firefighters two hours to put out the fire.

While the firefighters were hard at work, *36*'s chief motor machinist's mate, Michael Satota, and his helper, Bill Veldman, were demonstrating more than a little Yankee ingenuity. The *36*'s engine injectors (the diesel engine's equivalent of spark plugs) on its eight diesel engines (six-cylinders each) were in need of replacement, and the chief had gotten the captain's permission to see what he could get from the engines of the wrecked landing craft littering the beach.

Fortunately for the chief and for the *36* crew, the smaller landing craft were equipped with the same diesel engines as the LCSs (only fewer of them—just one in the LCVP, two in the LCM, and three in the LCT) and the same injectors! Just before the fire was completely out, the chief and his helper reported aboard, dripping wet but beaming, with 30 good injectors, enough to keep *36*'s diesels throbbing for many a nautical mile.[43]

As if some fatal force had miraculously been kept at bay, just after *36* pulled off the beach, a large enemy shell demolished the area where they had been fighting the fire.

The *36*'s mission was completely successful. Not only was the dangerous ammo dump fire put out, fires in five tanks were extinguished and one burning crane was salvaged. Most important of all, beach Blue One could be used for landings again, and, almost immediately, a wave of amphibious craft moved in to land troops at that point.

LCS *36* suffered no casualties, although her crew was utterly exhausted. She did suffer slight damage to her hull in the form of several holes in the boatswain's locker, from bumping against a derelict tank while beached. The ship's damage control party, however, plugged up the holes and pumped out the damaged locker.[44] Immediately after putting out the ammunition dump fire, the exhausted *36* crew began salvage duty with equal determination but with less immediate success. This result confirms what was said above about LCS's unsuitability as a salvage towboat. The *36* captain, who had a few hours earlier made what he called a perfect approach to the ammo dump fire, had difficulty maneuvering his long narrow ship in very restricted quarters and keeping it from beaching itself while pulling a submerged DUKW off Yellow Beach.

The *36* crew continued salvage duty throughout the night of February 21, even though they snapped their hawsers and anchor cable towing submerged DUKWs and tanks and attempting to pull broached LCVPs from the beach. The crew was determined to do a good job in spite of encountering difficulties at every turn. They took an abandoned DUKW in tow, then lost it when a hawser snapped, then retrieved it, but lost it again when two hawsers broke. They went 18 miles south of Iwo Jima attempting to save the DUKW. At 1330 the next day (February 22), they lost a partially submerged LCM after towing it first with a hawser then with anchor cable, both of which snapped.

The *34* crew ran into difficulty doing salvage work on February 22. The hawser they used to tow an LVT parted and fouled their port screw. The *34*'s executive officer dove under the ship and cut the hawser adrift. The LVT rammed into *34*'s stern, however, and knocked its anchor into the sea. On February 23 they lost an abandoned LCVP because the only place they could attach their towing cable was to the boat's ramp. The strain on the cable forced the ramp open and the LCVP sank in a rough sea.

In the afternoon, *36* helped ARS *114* take a drifting pontoon in tow. That evening the crew retrieved an LCM and towed it for over three hours, but its bow ramp accidentally became lowered and it filled with water and sank. Like her sister ships, LCS *36* was valiantly doing whatever salvage work she could possibly do. She was partially successful in keeping the landing beaches clear of obstacles, even though she had difficulty retrieving boats and craft because of inadequate towing equipment. LCS *36* suffered some damages from her salvage duties. These included damage to her engines, to her hull (including a hole in the stern), to her life raft, gun tub, yard arm, and mast.[45]

Other LCSs had better luck with their towing, although there were problems at times. On February 21, LCS *32* successfully towed a large pontoon deck to its destination. Two days later, *51* was sent out to look for a landing dock section from an LST. This turned out to be a nightmarish expedition because it took place at night in rain, thick fog, and a rough sea. The *51* found the section 10 to 15 miles south of Iwo and had trouble getting it in tow, taking over 12 hours to tow it to Iwo at one to two knots. While *51* was in the vicinity of wrecked craft on the landing beaches, her motor machinists collected diesel engine injectors from the wrecked engines, as *36*'s motor macs had done earlier during the ammo dump fire on February 21.[46] On February 23, LCS *34* salvaged an LCVP and returned it under its own power to PA *208*.

On February 22, LCS *35* searched for and offered assistance to small craft that had drifted out to sea. After standing by two drifting Rhino pontoons while their portable engines were being repaired, the *35* crew escorted them into Iwo. The next day, *35* took a pontoon barge in tow and towed it in and around the anchorage at Iwo Jima for 24 hours, until they found some ship able to relieve them of it.[47] Also on February 22, LCS *34* rescued seven Marines from a disabled LVT and delivered them to the beach.

On that night fire-fighting parties from LCSs *53* and *54* fought and put out an ammunition dump fire on the beach. The *53* firefighting party was made up of two officers and nine men, who, with the *54* party, fought the fire for over an hour and a half.

The firefighters encountered difficulties, yet discovered that one apparent hardship was really a boon in disguise:

> Huge swells necessitated the constant use of our engines to keep the bow of our ship on the beach. Wrecked equipment littered the area and our bow grated dangerously on a submerged tank. The fire burned fiercely. Its intense heat could be felt back to our fantail, which was about a 100 yards distant from the fire. Like a volcano, it erupted sporadically due to the exploding shells, and showered the ship with bits of hot casings.

> Japanese from the bluffs on the right flank directed a continuous mortar bombardment at the ship in the attempt to impede our efforts. However, their aim was bad and most of their shells fell far short of the mark. The few near misses caused no casualties. Hot shells cast out of the fire landed among the firefighters. They threw this live ammunition down the embankment into the water. Several exploded after being tossed aside.

> The deep loose volcanic sand impeded their progress and made the handling of the fire hoses a laborious job. However, the sand proved to be a boon. Just as the last glow of the fire was being put out, a Jap bomber glided in at mast height and dropped a stick of four bombs scarcely 75 yards from the scene. The bombs burrowed deeply and exploded harmlessly, showering the area with sand. Gunners at battle stations were ordered not to fire, for although the bomber's proximity made it an easy target, it continued across our lines, and had it been knocked down, it would have crashed into our Marines dug in on the slopes, causing casualties. Physically exhausted from handling hoses with 200 pounds pressure, the fire-fighting party had to be hoisted aboard.[48]

The eleven members of the *53* fire-fighting party and the five members of the *54* party were later awarded Bronze Star medals for their meritorious service of putting out the ammunition dump fire on February 22.

The new challenges LCS crews at Iwo were encountering have been cast in personal terms by an officer on *54*: "Iwo Jima was our first experience of real war. It was a fast learning experience for all of us. Looking back is more frightening than the actual time we were there. As I recall, most of us had about 15 to 20 hours of sleep during the first week of action. All of our little ships had many assignments."

He listed three of them, and then mentioned a special one: clearing the landing beaches, patrol duty around the island while providing supporting fire for troops ashore, and serving as an observation ship for gunfire from the larger ships. "A few days after the invasion we received a message late at night that the ammo dump had been hit during the air raid and we were ordered to beach and extinguish the fire—another hair-raising experience."[49]

Just a few days into the campaign, two LCSs at Iwo went so far as to take captured Japanese soldiers on their ships and send them ashore to convince their fellows that theirs was a lost cause. One day *56* put her bow on Orange Beach and its crew captured a Japanese soldier and sent him ashore to discourage his fellows.

At approximately the same time, the *31* crew "put a captured Japanese officer on the beach so he could go and tell his friends that the cause was lost. Two nights later another LCS picked him up on the other side of the island. They said that after he went ashore and ducked into a cave, he did not have to surface again but went across the island through tunnels."[50]

One evening after *53* had taken on ammunition, her crew answered an SOS call from six and a half miles at sea. They discovered that the LCVP in distress was lost, and the nine wounded Marines aboard had spent over four hours trying to locate a hospital ship. Since the only hospital ship in the area had left, *53* took the Marines aboard in spite of a rough sea and an air raid in progress. The *53*'s Group Medical Officer treated them, and the next day the wounded were transferred to the USS *Solace*.[51]

On February 23, unloading operations at the landing beaches were shifted from the east to the west side of the island to avoid the cluttered wrecks on the beach. However, because of continued bad weather, unloading conditions were no better than before. Pontoons were broached and ordinary landing craft were unusable because of the steep beach gradients. LCSs were assigned to salvage duty on the west side. While doing duty there, LCS *35* crew was annoyed by shells and bullets coming from ships on the east side and falling on and around them.

After February 25, unloading conditions at the beaches improved considerably with a change in the weather. Also because of the persistent and dogged determination of LCSs and a number of other craft doing salvage work since D Day, the clutter of wrecks and stranded craft on the east side beaches was cleared away. Beginning on March 3, both the eastern and western beaches were used for unloading, as wind and surf conditions dictated.

On February 26, six of the 12 LCSs of Group 7, the *51* and *32-36* departed Iwo Jima with their Flotilla Three Commander, Captain Thomas Aylward, in command.

That their commander was aware of what the LCS crews had been through and proud of what they had achieved at Iwo Jima is evident in his message to all LCS crews at Iwo dated February 25: "I take a great deal of pride in the way each of you contributed toward the success of the operation. Every ship in our flotilla [of 36 ships] has a big job cut out for it, that is, of meeting the standards of seamanship, precision, and the devotion to duty set by the officers and men of your 12 ships in the past week's work. I congratulate you all and look forward to working with you again in the big jobs to come."[52]

What the LCS crews were doing at Iwo was also appreciated by the crews of other ships, as this account by a *36* crew member demonstrates: "One day when we had had no hot meals because the galley was secured for fear of fire, and the guys were a little grimy, we went alongside the cruiser USS *Salt Lake City* for ammunition. The Captain of *Salt Lake* got on his bullhorn and he addressed our Captain: 'Tare, Victor, George. Well done, little guy! Anything we can do for you?' Our captain said, 'Could you give us some ice cream?' He says 'You bet!' And he gave us some ice cream. And we got our ammunition."[53]

The six remaining LCSs of Group 7—*31, 52-56* —continued their varied duties at Iwo until March 8. They provided smoke coverage for the larger ships during air raids, they did whatever salvage work remained, they patrolled the shores of the island and delivered call fire at selected targets, they provided close-in fire support (from ranges of 150 to 500 yards) for the advancing troops, and they worked with spotters of targets from the larger ships.

Their primary duty for the period was a combination of the last three duties. The first instance occurred on February 28 when, as the Marine divisions moved northward, "LCSs assigned to work with the naval gunfire spotters peppered caves and ravines along the west coast with 40 mm guns. Experience showed that observers on LCSs could distinguish positions of friendly troops near the coast as well, or better, than anyone ashore; and support vessels were given more and more initiatives to fire on targets of opportunity. Observer teams were placed aboard these support craft and for the next eight days, these teams cruised up and down the coast directing fire against enemy installations and reported enemy activities."[54]

On March 2 a group of gunboats, including LCSs, worked with destroyers, coming "close in along the eastern bulge of the island to place well directed fire up rocky draws that led down to the sea." Two days later a destroyer and a gunboat [LCS] worked all day along the coast in the Hill 382 area locating and engaging targets in the cliffs and draws."[55]

On March 6, one battleship and two cruisers fired 8- and 14-inch shells in support of an attack. "These same ships, plus three destroyers and two LCSs, working in direct support of the Fifth Marine Division, provided call fire throughout the day."[56]

As early as February 27, light aircraft began using one of the airfields that Marines had taken on Iwo. On March 3, the first twin engine plane was received on No. 1 airfield. The next day the LCS *54* crew witnessed a moment of triumph for the United States and allied forces in the Pacific war: the first landing (of many to follow) of a B-29 bomber on an Iwo airstrip.

The cost in men killed and wounded had been high in the extreme, but the goal of US forces had been achieved—to provide a base for B-29s and other large bombers delivering bombs to the Japanese homeland to bring the war to an early and victorious end.

In his description of the Iwo Jima invasion, Morison tells us that the newest gunboat, the LCS, did its stuff by leading the landing assault waves, launching its rockets, and firing all its guns at the beach.[57] This is what the LCS crews rehearsed for earlier off Saipan and Tinian. And, of course, they knew that this was what they would do.

Curiously, as this chapter has illustrated, it was what the LCS crews didn't know they would be doing at Iwo Jima that they did so well.

The integral part played by the LCSs and other gunboats in the important and successful naval support gunfire system at Iwo has been acknowledged: "Once troops were ashore, naval gunfire performed the usual scheduled and call fire missions by day, and conducted harassing and counterbattery firing at night to the satisfaction of the Marines. The cooperation of these vessels, from the largest battleships to the small specialized gunboats, was excellent. Supporting ships and craft were quick to observe enemy activity and take it under fire after first checking with units ashore to determine that the shelling would not endanger friendly troops."[58]

Even today, fifty years later, the importance of gunboats to the naval support gunfire system at Iwo Jima is recognized in an authoritative treatment of the amphibious assault on the island: "in all other respects, from casualty handling to fire-support coordination, the Navy-Marine team functioned smoothly at Iwo Jima. During the four-day fight for Suribachi, U.S. destroyers moved in close to the volcano at night, bathing its cave-socked sloped with searchlights and blasting anything that moved. Rocket gunboats added great shock and devastation to suspected enemy concentration points.

"The Suribachi flag-raising signaled the end of a chapter, but hardly the end of the battle. Ahead lay a full month of additional fighting, combat as savage and relentless as the Marines had ever known. The ships, gunboats, and attack aircraft accompanied the infantry with fire every agonizing yard northward. Each infantry battalion included its own naval element—surgeons, corpsmen, chaplains—plus an attached naval gunfire control party and an air liaison party. . . . The fact that the amphibious task force stood by and delivered combat support throughout much of this protracted assault reflects how thoroughly the fleet had isolated the objective."[59]

On March 8, the day on which the six remaining LCSs departed Iwo, Rear Admiral Harry W. Hill, Commander of Task Force 53 directing the Iwo operation, sent this message to LCSs *31* and *52-56*: "You Lobsters [LCSs] have done a splendid job. Your ready cooperation to accomplish a multitude of odd jobs has been particularly appreciated. Igloo [Headquarters Landing Forces] reports your fire support has been most valuable. Well done and good luck."[60]

Endnotes

[1] Primary sources for factual information: Samuel Eliot Morison, *History of U.S. Naval Operations in World War II*, Vol. 14 (Boston: Little Brown, 1960), 3-75; individual ship histories, personal accounts, and action reports. The title is from Shuldenrein transcription "n. 53 below."

[2] "Explanation of Japanese Defense Plans and Battle of Iwo Jima," by Major Y. Horie, quoted in Karig, *Battle Report—Victory in the Pacific*, 289.

[3] Morison, 12-13.

[4] "Ship's History USS LCS(L) *35*", 2.

[5] Excerpts from letters written at the time, whole series dated March 12, 1945; submitted by Kenneth Huff, captain LCS *35*. Hereafter called "Letters excerpts, LCS *35*."

[6] Letters excerpts, LCS *35*.

[7] Ibid.

[8] Ibid.

[9] Karig, 302, 303.

[10] Morison, 37.

[11] "Synopsis, LCS *35* Deck Logs—Iwo Jima Operation," prepared with comments by Charles Thomas, *35* signalman. Quote is addition by Thomas to 04-08 entry for February 19, 1945.

[12] "Dolly Three," typed manuscript, 3. (Used with permission.)

[13] "Describes Naval Attack in Invasion of Iwo Jima," in *Daily News*, Lebanon, PA, March 10, 1945.

[14] Frank Osterland, letter to author, Nov. 4, 1993.

[15] Letters excerpts, LCS *35*.

[16] Osterland, "Dolly Three," 5.

[17] Ibid.

[18] Herm Siri, letter to author, November 17, 1993.

[19] "History of USS LCS(L) *32*," III-V.

[20] Letters excerpts, LCS *35*.

[21] Action Report, USS LCS 36's participation in invasion of Iwo Jima, Enclosure A 2, 2/19-2/26/45.

[22] Transcription of Morris Shuldenrein's oral statement about his service on LCS *36*, transcribed by John Rooney, September 8, 1992, 8.

[23] Joseph Sansone, "Describes Naval Attack in Invasion of Iwo Jima."

[24] Virgil Thill, letter to author, February 6, 1993.

[25] Shuldenrein transcription, 6.

[26] Laurence McKenna, letter to author, n.d., 6.

[27] Ibid.

[28] Letter from Charles Cullens to his folks, written soon after the event, sent to author, December 27, 1993.

[29] Chickering, "World War II," 30.

[30] J. Gebhardt, "A Brief Account of the Travels of the USS LCS(L) 51," 1-2.

[31] Letter from Charles Cullens.

[32] "Synopsis, Deck Logs LCS *35*," comment on 04-08, February 20, 1945, entry.

[33] "History of USS LCS(L) *53*," 3.

[34] A recommendation of this effort appears in the LCS(L) *32*, history/action report, v.

[35] "Dolly Three," 6.

[36] "Synopsis, Deck Logs LCS *35*," entries for 1600-2000, February 20, and 0800-1200 and 1200-1600, February 23, 1945.

[37] Entry for February 20, Direct transcript of LCS *35*'s War Diary.

[38] J. Gebhardt, "Brief Account of Travels of LCS *51*," 2.

[39] "Describes Naval Attack at Iwo Jima."

[40] Ibid.

[41] Raymond E. Quimette, account of actions on LCS *36* in World War II, 2.

[42] Shuldenrein, transcription, 7.

[43] Same as n. 38.

[44] Action Report, LCS *36*, Enclosure A for 21 Feb.

[45] Action Report, LCS(L) *36*, entries for Feb. 21, 22, 23, 1945.

[46] Chickering, *51* captain, letter to author August 13, 1994.

[47] Synopsis of Deck Logs LCS *35*, entries for 04-08 and 08-12, Feb. 22, and 16-20, Feb. 23, 1945.

[48] "History of LCS *53*," 2.

[49] Herm Siri, letter to author, Nov. 17, 1993.

[50] McKenna, letter to author, Jan. 31, 1994.

[51] "History of LCS *53*," 2-3.

[52] Radio message to Lobsters (LCSs) from Com FLOT 3, Ref. #250045.

[53] Shuldenrein, transcription, 7.

[54] Whitman S. Bartley, *Iwo Jima; Amphibious Epic,* U.S. Marine Corps Historical Branch (1954), 129-30.

[55] Bartley, 164 and 166.

[56] Bartley, 143.

[57] Morison, 37.

[58] Bartley, 203.

[59] By 'gunboats' here is meant the 3 LCI(G)s, the 27 LCI(R)s and LCI(M)s as well as the 12 LCSs. "Iwo Jima—Amphibious Pinnacle," by Col. Joseph H. Alexander, USMC, *Naval Institute Proceedings*, Feb., 1995, 32.

[60] Radio message to Lobsters(LCSs) from Commander Task Force 53, Ref. #081417/K55.

Captain Theodore C. Aylward, USN, Commander LCS Flotilla Three. Courtesy of National Archives 80-GK-2692.

Chapter 9

New Challenges for the LCSs at Okinawa[1]

Officers and men on the 42 LCSs in the massive invasion of Okinawa knew the importance of the capture of that strategic island to the allied cause. They were aware that Okinawa was just 350 miles from Japan itself and part of the long chain of Ryukyu islands that extended to the larger homeland islands of the Empire. They were also aware that Okinawa would probably be the last major battle before the invasion of Japan itself, and would probably be difficult, more difficult even than Iwo Jima.

The 42 LCSs participating in the Okinawa invasion and in the dangerous encounters with enemy kamikaze planes and boats and swimmers that followed included 33 ships from Flotilla Three: *11-22, 24, 31-40, 51-57, 109-111,* and 9 ships from Flotilla Four: *62, 64, 84, 87, 114-116, 118,* and *119.* Twelve of these ships that served previously at Iwo Jima were *31-36, 51-56.* During the month of April 11 LCSs arrived at Okinawa: Two Flot Three ships, *25* arriving on the 16th and *23* on the 26th; and nine from Flot Four: *61, 81, 82,* and *83* arriving on the 16th, and *63, 85, 86, 88,* and *117* arriving the next day. Throughout May and even in June and July, scores of LCSs from Flotillas Three, Four, and Five would join their sister ships in the battle for Okinawa.

Because they had only just recently served in the difficult Iwo Jima campaign, crew members of 12 of the 42 ships had some feeling for what might be in store for them at Okinawa. Not eager for another harsh and difficult invasion, the crews were nevertheless more assured, having been seasoned under fire. The captain of LCS *36* commented: "Just how does one feel when he knows he's headed for a little action and that the results may not be favorable to him and his shipmates? Being veterans of the toughest one yet—Iwo Jima, we wish it [Okinawa] was all over with. The tension before this landing is not at all great and no noticeable fear is present with all hands aboard. They all know their jobs, have been briefed on the targets, and on the various duties of each department. One just says, 'Let's go and get it over with, the quicker, the better.'"[2]

The most hardened veterans of Iwo would be surprised at what the LCSs were asked to do at Okinawa. It would be a whole new world of challenges that would test the crews' mettle in unforgettable ways.

The campaign to take Okinawa would be long and hard. The intense and bitter fighting of our Marine and Army troops ashore against the stubborn Japanese defenders would go on for nearly three long months—through April and May and most of June. The Japanese would send thousands of planes, many of them kamikaze (suicide) planes, from Japan and Formosa over the Okinawa area throughout April, May, and June, and in July and August after Japanese ground resistance ended in June.

Their sole purpose would be to destroy all our forces—our troops ashore, our transport and supply ships in the anchorage, our large combatant ships off the coast providing heavy artillery for troops ashore, and our ships serving in the protective ring of radar picket stations around Okinawa. The Japanese would send out from hidden places in the area suicide boats and even suicide swimmers and divers (human torpedoes) to destroy our ships and our troops aboard them. Japanese artillery ashore would attempt to destroy our troops ashore, our planes in the air, and our ships in the harbors and anchorages.

LCSs would serve wherever and whenever they were needed throughout the campaign: on anti-aircraft and anti-suicide boat and swimmer patrols in the bays and anchorages at Okinawa and outlying island areas, on salvage and firefighting duty on the beach or out at sea, in supporting invasions of hostile islands around Okinawa, in supporting troops ashore with rocket and gunfire, in providing smoke screens for anchored ships, and in serving with other ships on the radar picket stations on the important outer protective ring around the Okinawa area.

The onset of the invasion (L Day) was scheduled for April 1—April Fool's Day.

Some of the LCSs bound for Okinawa encountered rough weather and heavy seas. The *35* reported green seas over the bow on the way, and *54* encountered 30-foot swells that made it very difficult for the relatively small flat-bottomed gunboats to keep station on each other in formation. The *20* reported very rough seas out of Ulithi causing the convoy of LSTs she was escorting to Okinawa to lose one LST as well as an LCT and two pontoon barges that were swept overboard. The *18* reported that on one LST a man lost his life trying to make the side-attached pontoons fast.

Iheya
Shima

East China Sea

Ie Shima

Kouri Shima

Motobu
Peninsula

Nago Wan

Aguni Shima

Naval Artillery Force
(from 4/8)

Yontan
Airfield

Kimmu
Wan

Hagushi

Kadena
Airfield

Pacific
Ocean

Anchorage
Landing
Beaches

Kerama Retto

Zamami
Shima

Maye Shima

Shuri

Nakagusuku Wan
(laterBuckner Bay)

Naha
Yonabaru

Tokashiki Jima

Decoy
Landing
Area

Okinawa
And
Surrounding
Islands

Like LCSs on their way to the Iwo invasion, ships' crews moving toward Okinawa early in the morning of April 1st could see eerie lightning-like light flashes as early as 2200 the night before. Capital ships in large numbers were bombarding and softening the beaches of Okinawa for L Day, which was, more seriously and symbolically, Easter Sunday.

The landing force the LCSs joined very early on L Day was the largest such force ever gathered in the Asiatic Pacific campaign. The force included more than 1,457 ships, exclusive of all types of personnel landing craft, but including 318 combatant vessels, battleships, cruisers, destroyers, patrol craft, tenders, landing ships, and support ships and craft of all sorts, as well as scores of attack transports and cargo transports. Farther out at sea, but in instantaneous communication with this force, were numerous aircraft carriers with hundreds of aircraft ready to challenge the large number of Japanese aircraft expected to appear at any time.

Aboard the huge landing force of ships and craft were over 548,000 Soldiers, Sailors, and Marines, including 182,000 combat-ready troops. The first wave of troops to be landed at 0830 was made up of 20,000 troops, over twice the size of the first wave at Normandy. Eight days later on April 9th 160,000 troops were landed.

Admiral Richmond Kelley Turner, commander of the expeditionary force for Okinawa, had wisely chosen to take over the major islands of Kerama Retto, a group of small islands southwest of Okinawa, before invading the main island. U.S. forces discovered and destroyed 390 suicide boats at Kerama. These boats, with large explosives in their bows, were poised for action against U.S. forces invading the Okinawa mainland. Even though there were still numerous suicide boats at Okinawa, the destruction of the 390 boats reduced considerably the impact of these raids. Similar raids had sunk three LCSs and severely damaged a fourth one on February 16th in the Corregidor campaign in the Philippines.

LCSs in the Okinawa invasion served under the overall command of Captain Theodore Aylward, Commander of LCS Flotilla Three on LC(FF) *988*, who was Commander of the Gunboat Support Flotilla for the expeditionary force under Admiral Turner, Commander Task Force 57. Captain Aylward had 200 landing craft and ships under his command, including LCI(G)s, LCI(R)s, and LCI(M)s, as well as LCSs.

Accompanying Captain Aylward was his Flotilla Three staff which he organized in San Diego in October and utilized in the Iwo Jima campaign. Officer positions on his staff included an operations officer, a gunnery officer, a material officer, a radar officer, a personnel officer, a communications officer, and four communications watch officers with parallel duties such as staff secretary and radio material officer. This staff maintained a 24-hour radio and visual signal watch for all LCSs at Okinawa, as it did at Iwo Jima.

Enlisted staff positions included thirteen radiomen, four signalmen, one quartermaster, two radar men, and three radio technicians; three storekeepers and three yoemen; one motor machinist's mate and one electrician's mate; and one ship's cook and two steward's mates. In addition to maintaining a communications watch, the staff's duties included supporting and directing all flotilla operations, handling flotilla personnel matters (a full LCS flotilla was made up of over 2,500 officers and men), supervising gunnery activities on flotilla ships, and dealing with logistics problems for flotilla ships at Okinawa. Although they lacked the facilities to act as a tender for the LCSs, the staff provided LCS crews with help for their repair and maintenance problems.

LCSs in the invasion worked under the immediate commands of their assigned Group commanders in Flotilla Three, and the nine LCSs of Flotilla Four were under the immediate command of Lieutenant Commander Clifford Montgomery, Commander Group 11 of Flotilla Four. After L Day, all LCSs at Okinawa served under the overall command of Captain Aylward.

Group commanders of the three Flotilla groups serving at Okinawa were Lieutenant Commander Frank Stone, Commander of Group Seven made up of the twelve ships that participated in the Iwo Jima campaign; Lieutenant Commander Edwin C. Thomas, Commander of Group Eight; and Lieutenant B. A. Thirkield, Commander of Group Nine. Early in the Okinawa campaign group commanders were furnished LC(FF)s as their flagships. Group Seven Commander Stone, initially having LCS *36* and then *31* as his flagships, was assigned *LC(FF) 484;* Group Eight Commander Thomas, initially on LCS *12,* was assigned *LC(FF) 485;* and Group Nine Commander Thirkield, initially on *24,* was given *LC(FF) 536.* Flotilia Four Group 11 Commander Montgomery, initially on *84,* was assigned to *LC(FF) 367.*

Flotilla Four ships continued to arrive at Okinawa through April and May. On April 16 Lieutenant Commander B. D. Voegelin, Commander of Flotilla Four's Group 12, arrived at Okinawa on *66,* and was later assigned *LC(FF) 789.* Early in May Captain Neill Phillips, Flotilla Four Commander on *LC(FF) 1082* arrived at Okinawa along with Lieutenant Commander Joseph Dodson, Commander of Group 10, the third group Of Flotilla Four ships.

On their respective staffs these six group commanders of Flotillas Three and Four each had an operations officer, a material and engineering officer, and a communications officer. In addition they had two officers very essential to the well being of the over 850 officers and men in each of their groups—a medical officer and a supply and disbursing officer. Each group staff's enlisted positions included at least 3 storekeepers and 3 pharmacist's mates. Like the flotilla staffs, the group staffs did everything they could do to assist the individual ship crews with their problems.

The landings at Okinawa differed somewhat from those at Iwo Jima. There were simultaneous landings at two different locations at Okinawa, only one landing at Iwo. The main landing was on eight color-designated beaches over a wide two-mile frontage on the western side of the island in the vicinity of Hagushi. In fact, as they moved in on L Day, the landing forces moved directly over what was to become the major anchorage area at Okinawa.

LCSs getting into position for the Okinawa invasion. Note small size of LCSs compared to the battleship on the right. Any two of the LCSs could fit in tandem on the BB's fantail. Courtesy of US Navy.

The second landing was a decoy landing on the southeastern tip of Okinawa at Sakibaru-Saki in the vicinity of Nakagusuku Wan. In these two landings, 42 LCSs, over three times the number at Iwo, participated in just one primary run to the beach with H Hour at 0830. Some ships in the decoy landing, however, did make two runs.

In the main landing two ships, *12* and *20*, served as division commanders leading their sister ships in the initial assault. The *20* directed its column to Blue Beach. Leading its assault waves into Red Beach was *22*. Just before the main action started, a torpedo from a Japanese plane passed just 50 yards off *19*, giving the crew an early alert.

LCSs *24, 37, 38, 40,* and *57* in the leading assault wave into Brown Beach began firing on the beach at 0805. During this run, *37* was briefly aground on one of the many reefs in the area. Another ship leading assault waves into Brown Beach was *36*, which was later assigned to guide duty off that beach for several days. Supporting the Tenth Army's landing at Purple One was *34*. LCSs *18* and *19* served as control ships for the first two waves, remaining near the shore and then joining their divisions for further assignment.

The *32's* actions supporting the landings on Purple Beach One can be considered as generally typical for LCSs in the main landings. The *32* arrived at 0759 at the line of departure and at 0800 commenced its run to the beach on a prescribed course at four knots. At 0822, when 1,200 yards from the beach, *32* opened fire with all its automatic weapons. At 0827 the *32* fired a salvo of 42 rockets, and at 0832 a salvo of 112. At 0845 after the fifth assault wave passed abeam, *32* retired from the beach using the left flank of the formation. LCS *35* launched its first salvo of rockets while 900 yards from the beach and its second while only 700 yards.

On all of the LCSs moving to the beach in both invasions, crew members could see and hear large shells from the capital ships, some as large as 16 inches in diameter, whizzing overhead. The *21* crew felt the strong vibrations from thousands of rockets being launched. Men on *11* watched a seaplane from a cruiser downed unintentionally by fire from another U.S. plane.

Differing sharply from the landings at Iwo, there was no opposition to troops landing at the designated beaches. There was, however, some slight opposition from the beach to the LCSs leading the assault waves. LCS *14*, firing rockets and shells into Orange Beach, encountered mortar fire from the shore, and an LSM to its starboard took a hit. LCS *35* reported that a few mortar shells fell in

With her crew at general quarters, an LCS moves in to protect troops in the boats during the invasion and to bombard the beach at Okinawa. Courtesy of Ray Baumler.

their general area. LCS *20*, leading its column into Blue Beach, had six of its men injured by a mortar explosion just 20 feet from the ship. At approximately the same time, a gunner on the *21* was injured when his 50-caliber gun exploded.

Also participating in those important main landings in the Hagushi area were nine other LCSs: *13, 15-17, 39, 62, 64, 109*, and *110*. These ships were supporting the landings and assaults by doing basically what *32* was doing.

LCSs participating in the decoy landing on the southeast tip of Okinawa included *22, 31, 51-54, 56,* as well as *84, 87, 111, 114-116, 118,* and *119.* These ships shelled and bombarded the beach with their rockets as did their sister ships in the main landing. During the bombardment, *111* set a house afire on the beach. Also *111,* which served as flag of Task Unit 52.29.7 in the decoy landing, made a diversionary feint at landing on Green Able One and Green Able Two, two of the Hagushi beaches.

LCSs guiding the assault boat waves at the decoy landing had the benefit of three radar teams (an officer and enlisted man on each team) located on flotilla flagship *33* and on *56,* on the two outboard flanks of the assault boat waves. These experts used the ship's radar as well as their own radar equipment to maintain exact positions at precise times for guiding LCSs in their runs to the beach. These same three teams had performed similar services on the same three ships at Iwo.[3]

There was little or no opposition from the Japanese on the beach to the decoy landing. There were, however, kamikaze attacks on individual ships in the landing force.

At 0549 on L Day, while the decoy landing force was positioning itself for the landing run, a kamikaze crashed into LST *884* which was carrying a landing party of 300 Marines and a large amount of ammunition and gasoline. The *884* caught fire immediately. Violent explosions of the ammunition continued relentlessly for several hours. The *884's* crew was unable to control the raging fire because its pumping equipment was not operational. The captain ordered 'abandon ship'.

At 0700 the *115, 116, 118,* and *119* were ordered to render all possible aid to the severely stricken LST which had fires out of control topside and below decks. When they arrived at the scene, there were many men in the water. The fleet rescue tugboat (ATR *80*) and the *Van Valkenburgh* (DD *656*), standing off the LST's side, were throwing water from hoses, but they were reluctant to go directly alongside to reach the fire because of the dangerously heavy sea swells. LCSs *115* and *118* encountered problems with the swells, but tied up alongside *884* and proceeded to get the topside fire under control in a half hour. In the meantime, *Van Valkenburgh,* LST *678,* LST *838,* and ATR *80* picked up the men in the water, and *116* and *119* joined *115* and *118* alongside the LST.

Realizing that boarding parties were absolutely necessary to fight the *884's* below-deck fires, *118* sent a boarding party aboard at 0723, followed by men

---

from the other LCSs and from *Van Valkenburgh* with all possible fire-fighting equipment. These teams fought the serious fires below deck in spite of the dangers of ammunition exploding in every direction around them.

Around noon all fires were out, but *884* was listing from the massive amount of water pumped into her to fight the fire. Beginning at 1225, LCSs *115, 118,* and *119* began pumping thousands of gallons of water out of the LST.

Rescuers also buried the dead from *884* while firefighters continued their job. Earl Blanton, *118* gunner, described the scene: "There were seven bodies aboard. All burned pretty bad, but the LST skipper came back and guessed the dead to be around 25. The seven were wrapped in blankets, weighted and buried at sea without much ceremony. There just wasn't time for any. When we slid them over the side and I watched them go sinking down in the clear water, I thought of their folks back home—we regret to inform you—your son, husband—killed in action—buried at sea—Easter Sunday. I guess this is hard on our folks too."[4]

That evening LCS *56* came alongside the stricken LST and fed its weary crew. These men hoped the worse was over, but later that night armed Japanese swimmers fired at the LST and attempted to board her. These swimmers killed one crewman and wounded another who was raising the ship's embarkation net in an attempt to repel them.

Fortunately casualties on the LCSs were limited. During the action, one officer on *115* and two men on *118* were injured. The hull of *118*, however, was seriously damaged: "The sea was pounding our ship against the LST the whole time we were alongside and now we are a pitiful sight. Our port side is battered in. Approximately a dozen frames [structural ribs of the hull] and several overheads [ceilings] are broken and some more [are] twisted. The decks are buckled in several places. We have several small holes above the water line. Topside the life-lines were torn away and a 20mm [gun] tub support damaged. The [gun] mount was sprained—the gun cannot properly be trained [turned]. Forward the side above the main deck is leaning over at about 30 degrees. We will take a lot of repairing and we will never be the same again."[5]

After the action the LCSs received several messages. One from *Van Valkenburgh* (DD *656*) to *118* read: "You people have done a splendid job. Let me congratulate you." Another read "Good work and good luck in the future." The *118* captain said that he was proud of his crew because "in spite of the many risks involved, you have saved a ship and much important cargo."[6]

Early on L Day off the decoy beaches the troop transport *Hinsdale* was struck by either a torpedo or a kamikaze plane and set on fire and her engine rooms flooded. Shortly after this LCS *51* went to her aid. "My ship went alongside the stricken transport, fought fires, then pumped furiously as the casualties were removed. From my bridge, it was a scene from Hell, to look at the gaping hole in her side, and to see their crew frantically dragging out dead and wounded soldiers. This went on all night long."[7]

At 2050 on the night of April 1st, *32* was directed to *Alpine* (APA *92*) for salvage duty. A kamikaze plane had crashed into an open hatch causing a serious fire in the holds 2 and 3. The *32* moved alongside, put over five hoses through a huge hole in the APA's hull, and pumped an estimated 260,000 gallons of water into the ship before the fire was brought under control. Forty members of the *32* crew were required to handle hoses and operate pumps. By 2300 the *32* had *Alpine*'s fire well under control.

Differing from the landings at Iwo Jima during which the landing troops were killed and wounded in large numbers, the Okinawa landings were unopposed and the thousands of Marines and Tenth Army troops were allowed to land and move inland at their own pace. In fact the Marines moved rapidly all the way up to the base of Motobu Peninsula at the northern end of the island where they encountered their first real resistance on April 9.

The Tenth Army took over the two airfields, Kadena and Yonton, just north of the landing beaches and moved south toward Yonabaru airfield, Shuri, and Naha, where they met stiff resistance on April 9. From that time on the Marines were fighting to take over Motobu Peninsula in the north and the Tenth Army was fighting to take major positions in the south.

On April 8 Admiral Richmond Kelly Turner, head of the expeditionary force, ordered a Naval force of combatant vessels to support the Tenth Army with heavy nighttime artillery fire using spotting planes to point out enemy targets on the ground and star shells for illumination. Anchored some distance off the Hagushi anchorage and made up of 5 battleships, 5 cruisers, and 17 destroyers, this force hurled thousands of shells ranging from 5- to 16-inch night after night into the Japanese troops opposing the Tenth Army in the south.

After the massive landings on April 1, the outer protective ring of radar picket stations was put in place around the greater Okinawa area, including Kerama Retto and several of the outlying islands. Sixteen stations were established to provide warnings of incoming planes, many of which were kamikazes.

Destroyers, destroyer escorts, LCSs, LSMs, LSM(R)s, and other patrol craft were assigned to these stations. LCSs began serving on this duty on April 1 and continued to serve in large numbers throughout the campaign. The actions of LCSs on picket patrol duty will be described further on in this chapter after some of their other duties have been told.

LCSs were assigned to various duties in different areas in and around Okinawa. On April 1st and 2nd, *24* and *57* were assigned to make smoke screens to hide the larger ships from incoming hostile aircraft. This duty, which practically every LCS at Okinawa would be doing sooner or later, sometimes for days at a time, involved making large clouds of smoke with the ship's fog generator on the fantail (stern) of the ship. During the three-month campaign, as many as 25 LCSs at a time would be making smoke to protect the capital ships in Hagushi anchorage and in other harbor areas including Kerama Retto.

Beginning on April 2, *34* and *35* served as salvage boats for the next ten to twelve days, keeping the harbors clear of debris and towing abandoned and stranded small boats. These same two ships did at Okinawa what they became so adept at doing earlier at Iwo Jima—firing on shore targets of opportunity, primarily at enemy troops, sometimes firing over the heads of our advancing troops and into caves and enemy gun emplacements.

On April 5th, *24, 37, 39,* and *40,* working with *Cassin Young* (DD *793*), fired for two hours on targets ashore, and on April 10th, working under the direction of the 77th Infantry Division, *21* sailed close to shore to draw fire from the enemy and then to fire both rockets and guns at the newly revealed enemy emplacements.

Beginning April 1st, LCSs were assigned to patrol duties of different kinds, working either individually or with other ships. The first day, *18* began anti-aircraft patrol duty in the harbor and *20* began anti-aircraft patrol off Zampa Misaka, a centrally located point of land on Okinawa's western side, whose radio call, 'Point Bolo', was used to indicate distances and directions to the various radar picket stations around the island. Both *54* and *55* served on anti-suicide boat patrol in the harbor and coastal areas by day and by night, depending on need. Early on April 2, *18* assisted in destroying a kamikaze plane attacking ships in the harbor.

On April 4th, LCSs *18-22* were assigned to anti-aircraft and anti-suicide boat patrol in Kerama Retto. During the April 2-5 period, *37* did this same duty. On the 2nd, *21* was assigned to guard the submarine net at Kerama Retto, and on the 7th, *18* assumed harbor entrance patrol duty at the Kerama south gate. While serving there, *18* shot down an enemy plane.

The Navy's name for suicide boat was 'fly', and anti-suicide boat patrol duty, on which almost all LCSs at Okinawa served, was called 'Flycatcher operations'. Suicide boats were a menace at Okinawa, and there were a number of them there in spite of the earlier destruction of 390 of them at Kerama Retto. The boats were similar to the ones in the Philippines. They were manned by one person and usually carried a very heavy bomb in the bow, which produced a tremendous explosion as it struck one of our ships. Their Japanese name was 'shinyo' but to U.S. Navy men they were 'skunks'.

LCSs usually worked with other ships and under orders during the first and second weeks at Okinawa, but in emergency situations, took action alone. Early in the campaign, *31* provided close-in support for units doing reconnaissance in different areas. While patrolling on a radar picket station on April 5th, *115* made radar contact with a Japanese submarine at 8,000 yards. After visual confirmation, *115* made a run, attempting to ram the submarine, but when *115* was within 1400 yards, the sub submerged. *Hudson* (DD *475*) nearby then carried out a depth charge attack which the presence of a huge oil slick for the next few days indicated was a success.

On April 5th, an LCI(G) and 6 LCSs (probably *12-14, 31, 36* and *37* or *52*) formed a 'flycatcher unit' to provide a screen against suicide boat attack for two destroyer transports (APDs), the *Scribner* and the *Kinzer*, which were carrying a Marine Corps reconnaissance battalion that was landing on Tsugen Jima on the east side of Okinawa off Nakagusuku Wan.

Also on April 5th, *84* destroyed a radio station along with its antenna and a concrete blockhouse on the tip of the strategically located island of Yoron Jima. The Japanese had been using this station to direct their aircraft into the picket station areas around Okinawa.

Thanks to the determination and persistence of her captain, *57* rescued a downed Marine pilot who crashed near Iheya Shima on April 10. For hours after the organized search had been called off, *57* kept searching into the night until its crew saw a single light in the water. "Sometime during the wee hours of the morning, I heard the quiet noise of an engine. I waved my one-cell flashlight, and suddenly I heard the wonderful sound of 'Ahoy!' My God, that was a beautiful word! I was taken aboard the *57*."[8]

The pilot, Second Lieutenant Charles Coppedge, USMC, stayed aboard *57* through April 12, when the ship was severely attacked by eight planes. But Lieutenant Coppedge was not simply an idle passenger. Among other things, he manned a 50-caliber gun and poured shell after shell into the attacking kamikazes.

On April 10, LCS *21* captured a Korean and found a place where a large number of skunks were hidden and fired on it. In the next 19 days, *21* took 40 Japanese prisoners and destroyed 14 skunks and an army camp. On April 12, LCS *11* escorted, and towed part of the way, a damaged PBM aircraft to Kerama Rhetto.

On April 7, while *13* was returning to Okinawa from picket patrol duty, crew members were absolutely awestruck on encountering, almost head-on it seemed, the huge U.S. naval fleet that was moving out from Okinawa to challenge and destroy the approaching smaller Japanese fleet, which included *Yamato*, the largest and most heavily armed battleship in the world at the time.

Early on April 10th, crews of *116* and *118* discovered how aggressive suicide boats and suicide swimmers could be. At 0425, while the two ships were moored alongside AKA *67* (USS *Starr*), Japanese in a skunk threw two bombs at the decks of the AKA. The first bomb missed the deck and blew up alongside the cargo ship in the water. The second landed on the deck but did not go off. The skunk disappeared before gunners on the ships could spot it; however two Japanese suicide swimmers were discovered hiding underneath the large amount of debris floating around the ships. They were quickly dispatched. No damage resulted from the bomb explosion.

From April 8 to 12, *55* was on skunk patrol and on the lookout for enemy attempts to lay mines in newly swept areas in Nakogasion Bay at Okinawa. For the next two days, *55* served in the outer anti-aircraft screen area (the next protective ring in from the picket stations) by day and provided smoke screens at night. From the 16th until the end of April, *55* was on skunk patrol off the northeast tip of Okinawa. At one point she escorted a number of LCVPs carrying Marines through the patrol area, providing them protection against enemy fire.

On April 19, LCS *55*, with the help of sharp-eyed Corsair pilots, located and picked up a Marine adrift in a Japanese canoe. On April 6 and 7, LCS *54* provided coverage for Underwater Demolition Teams leaving the islands of Tsuken Shima and Ichi Hanare. From April 8 to 11, *54* patrolled in Nakagusuku Wan, searching for enemy attempts to lay mines. For the next two weeks, *54*

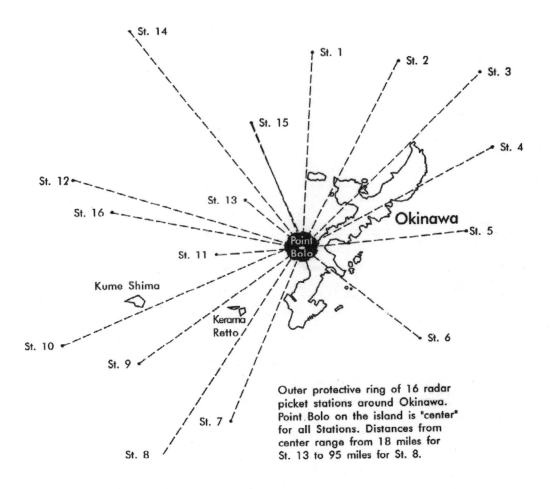

St. 14

St. 1

St. 2

St. 3

St. 15

St. 4

St. 12

St. 13

St. 16

Okinawa

St. 5

Point Bolo

St. 11

Kume Shima

Kerama Retto

St. 10

St. 6

St. 9

Outer protective ring of 16 radar picket stations around Okinawa. Point Bolo on the island is "center" for all Stations. Distances from center range from 18 miles for St. 13 to 95 miles for St. 8.

St. 7

St. 8

The 16 radar picket stations around Okinawa.

served on anti-aircraft screen duty and provided smoke screens for battleships and for transports.

The most dangerous assignment given to LCSs, as their crews discovered almost immediately, was duty on the radar picket stations on the outer protective ring surrounding Okinawa. There were 16 of these stations[9] on which one or two (just one in the beginning!) destroyers, destroyer escorts, or comparable ships patrolled back and forth over a large assigned area. Using their state-of-the-art radar, the ships in the ring provided earliest warnings to U.S. forces of approaching enemy aircraft.

Duty on these stations was lonely—some of the stations were as far as 95 miles out at sea and 15-20 miles from each other. Furthermore this duty was fraught with anxiety since no one knew when and in what numbers the Japanese aircraft would come. One thing everyone did know was that many of the planes would be kamikazes—suicide planes that were not only terrifying and vicious weapons in themselves but sometimes carried and hurled huge bombs and deadly torpedoes.

Beginning on April 1st, LCSs, as well as LSMs and LSM(R)s, and occasionally other patrol type ships were assigned to provide anti-aircraft support for the larger destroyer-type ships serving on the 16 stations, some of them since March 26. Of this support by the smaller ships, S. E. Morison has said, "They added punch to the anti-aircraft fire and proved a present and courageous help in time of trouble."[10]

Further praise from a naval historian commends the LCSs and LSMs on the ways they would accomplish their tasks in spite of limitations:

Both (LCSs and LSMs) were ordered up to the radar picket line to provide additional heavy machine support for the destroyers, and also to provide a nearby rescue ship when the radar picket absorbed a kamikaze. Both the large amphibious ships and the smaller amphibious craft, which had to fight back at this death-dealing weapon, had the minimum in sophisticated gun controls which were needed to blow the kamikaze to smithereens before it came aboard. Despite this, they went about their multitude of tasks with enough equanimity to accomplish them effectively.[11]

Just looking at comparative sizes and capabilities of LCSs and destroyers, it does not seem likely that the relatively small, flat-bottomed LCS (average displacement 350 tons and overall length 158 feet) with no air search radar and only the crudest surface radar and limited fighter direction equipment for its main 40mm battery, could provide any kind of support to destroyers of five times the size (average displacement 1850 tons) and over twice the length (360) and with sophisticated radar and fighter direction equipment for its 5-inch guns and batteries of 40s and 20s, as well as over twice the speed (35 knots to the LCSs' 15-16).

Yet the little LCSs provided the strongest possible kinds of support to the DDs and DEs, firing and shooting down and outmaneuvering enemy planes, diverting them from the DDs, fighting and putting out fires on DDs, supplying electricity and water pressure, helping to keep them afloat, caring for their wounded, and rescuing thousands of their men in the water and on the sinking and stricken ships. While not as fast as the DDs, LCSs were highly maneuverable under aircraft attack and had great firepower for their size.

Evidently the officer in charge of the destroyer on the picket station that LCS *114* reported to for its first radar picket duty was somewhat startled to see such a small ship so far out at sea on its own: "During the evening of the second of April 1945, a destroyer on patrol duty some fifty miles northeast of the newly established beachhead on Okinawa blinked a challenge to a little ship on the gray horizon. On receiving the proper reply the destroyer flashed the following message:

'WHAT ARE YOU DOING OUT HERE?'

'RADAR PICKET SUPPORT ASSIGNED THIS AREA' blinked the little ship, not much worried by the note of derision in the question. There was a pause as the destroyer drew closer to investigate. Her light flashed out again.

'WHAT KIND OF SHIP?' There was a brief wait.

'LANDING CRAFT SUPPORT', the little ship replied . . ."[12]

One serious problem for all ships serving on radar picket patrol was the Japanese pilots' use of everything at their disposal to jam the U.S. radar and achieve a surprise attack. Their planes would drop 'window' (aluminum foil) to make it hard for our ships' radars to pick up moving targets. Japanese planes would fly overhead just above the ships' gun ranges to attract attention, while at the same time other planes would come in from another direction at high speeds and so close to the water that our radar could not detect them. Pilots would take advantage of the clouds and sun to cover and hide them as they approached a station. Pilots would also fly at twilight or shortly afterwards when they were very hard to see.

For these reasons the destroyer-type vessels were not always immediately aware of incoming planes and could not always send warnings to the supporting ships. One evening on *54* the ship's cook rushed to his 20mm gun and started shooting at a plane skimming the waterline and heading directly for *54*. This man was evidently the first man topside to see this plane. In this attack the plane coming in was just the first of five planes attacking ships on the station. All five planes were shot down without doing any damage.[13]

Even though the first of ten massive air raids on Okinawa from Japan and Formosa did not occur until April 6, LCSs serving on radar picket patrol the first week of April were subjected to severe air raid attacks from the beginning. Reports from different LCSs ran like this at the time: "frequent air raids," "almost constant air raids," "many bogies [Japanese aircraft] both day and night," "we are at general quarters [full battle ready condition] most of the time."

Between April 1st and 10th, 21 LCSs were assigned to duty on radar picket patrol. This sounds like a relatively high number—actually one-half of all the LCSs at Okinawa at the time. All these ships, however, were not assigned to the 16 picket stations at once on April 1st, but over a period of ten days. On the first day, LCSs *51, 84,* and *87* were assigned to stations. On April 2nd, 7 ships were assigned: *11, 62, 111, 114, 115, 118,* and *119.*

By April 6th, LCSs *14, 24, 37, 56,* and *64* were on stations, and by the 7th, *13, 32, 33, 38,* and *116* were also serving. Also on the 7th, LCS *11* and *13* which

Radar picket patrol ships shoot down one Japanese suicide plane. Note the black clouds of flak (exploding shells) in the sky. US Navy photo courtesy of Earl Blanton.

had been assigned to Station 12 were called back because a Japanese naval force, including the large battleship *Yamato,* was approaching that area. Neither of these ships was reassigned to picket duty until April 12th. On April 9th, LCS *36* was serving on Station 4.

In the first ten days of April these picket stations were undermanned, with the ships highly exposed to hordes of incoming kamikaze planes. An LCS going on picket duty then might either serve alone or with just one other LCS and with one destroyer type vessel. The destroyer(s) served as one unit, patrolling over a wide area on the station. The support ships worked, under the Officer in Tactical Command (OTC) on the destroyer(s), as a separate unit at a prescribed distance from the DDs, moving over a smaller area at a slower speed.

To each picket station was assigned a group of fighter planes, the Combat Air Patrol (CAP), which would drive enemy planes off and shoot them down. The CAP, which initially operated only in the daytime, was extremely helpful, effective, and frequently even daring and ingenious in dealing with the enemy planes. And they would also perform magnificently when sorely outnumbered and limited in what they could do. During the first ten days of April, they were outnumbered much of the time.

While providing support to destroyers out on the far-flung picket stations during the April 1-6 period, three LCSs were credited with shooting down enemy planes. On April 3rd, LCS *62* shot down one enemy bomber and was credited with assisting in one other. The force manning *62's* station was credited with downing 6 planes altogether. LCS *111* downed one plane on its station and on April 5, the *115* splashed a Japanese Betty, a medium-sized bomber than often carried large bombs and Baka bombs [manned bomb gliders]. In 'picket station lingo', this aircraft was 'Big Butt Betty'.

What picket duty for the LCS crews on those lonely, exposed stations was really like has been detailed by someone who was there. Lieutenant H. D. Chickering, captain of LCS *51,* which served continuously on different radar picket stations from April 2nd for 14 days, recalled:

> The raids seemed ceaseless, our guns were always manned and the gunners literally slept at them. As captain, I seldom left the bridge. Food was coffee, hard boiled eggs and occasionally sandwiches. Sanitary facilities were a bucket, once in a while I caught a catnap in my seat. For a week we fired on, or reported, dozens of raids, and lost count very quickly. The radio reported continuous fighting, hits and sinkings on all stations.

Looking back over thirty years, it is very difficult to pinpoint the welter of emotions and memories of that nightmare picket duty. I clearly remember worrying about my crew. They were so young and the situation looked so hopelessly grim. The Japanese planes didn't even attempt to engage our planes. Their mission was to kill ships, and the ring of picket stations seemed to infuriate them. The gunboats and destroyers caught flaming hell.

Radio Tokyo kept up a barrage of broadcasts, addressed to the ships on the picket stations. 'Tokyo Rose' called us by name and number, taunting us and gloating each time someone was hit by a suicide plane. This propaganda backfired for them, since our men reacted with ever-growing hatred. When 'Rose' singled out "You poor guys on LCS *51*, get ready to die!" the crew cursed and screamed their rage—and waited.

Whenever planes came close enough we took them under fire, and our air cover planes [CAP] just murdered them during daylight hours. [At all times] our Marine pilots flew right into the thickest anti-aircraft fire in selfless and desperate determination to stop the raids. The nights were uniquely horrifying, since we could not see the raiders clearly, except on radar, while they could see us very well. We dared not fire until we were absolutely sure we were under direct attack, since the kamikazes would otherwise fly right into us, following our stream of tracers.

The strain became almost intolerable. We were gaunt and filthy, red-eyed and stinking. The ship was a mess, with empty shell casings everywhere. My face was pocked with particles of burned gunpowder, since our Oerlikon anti-aircraft gun was fired as close as three yards from my battle station. We prayed for bad weather, which was about the only thing that slowed down the stream of Japanese planes.[14]

Welcomed light moments helped the intense, unbearable strain for the picket line ships' crews. According to Hanson Baldwin writing at the time: "Only that saving American trait, a sense of humor, keeps some [picket ship crew members] from the brink of horror. On one picket station a tiny gunboat [LCS], its crew fed up with close brushes with death, rigs up a huge sign with a pointing arrow: To Jap Pilot. This way to Task Force 58!"[15]

The first large air raid by 355 Japanese planes from Kyushu took place April 6. This raid, involving kamikaze planes as well as conventional fighters, bombers, and torpedo planes, focused on the outer radar picket patrol ring and on Stations #1 and 2 in particular.

Patrolling Station #1 on April 6 before the raid began were one destroyer, *Bush* (DD *529*), and *64*. Gordon Wiram, *64* officer, described the station's initial encounter with the kamikazes: "The planes launched their attack on our ship and the *Bush. Bush* took the first blow—a direct hit by one of the kamikaze planes. *Bush* appeared to be dead in the water. We steamed toward *Bush* with the intent to go alongside to rescue some of the crew. About the time we made a close approach, Japanese planes started making another attack toward both our ships. We immediately backed away. At least two more planes careened into the *Bush*."[16] *Colhoun* (DD *301*) came to the *Bush*'s aid from another picket station and immediately took several hits by the kamikazes.

Wiram described the attack on his ship at the time: "One plane came the closest and almost had our number. The captain kept maneuvering our ship full right then full left rudder at top speed. At the last moment when I knew the aircraft would collide with our ship, I curled up into the tightest ball possible and laid on the deck thinking that the worst was about to happen. There was a strong thud. The ship shook like a strong earthquake! The plane had exploded and the ship was covered with small pieces of aluminum, wadded like paper. One piece of shrapnel had hit me and bruised me on the back. The plane did not hit the ship, but smashed into the water so close that water splashed over the stern and spilt over a huge gash in the ship's side. Our damage control teams made immediate repairs which kept us afloat. Pumps kept the water from flooding the after part of the ship."[17]

In this encounter, *64* shot down two of the attacking planes. As a result of being attacked five times by kamikazes in 15 minutes, *Colhoun* was severely damaged and in need of aid herself. Late in the afternoon of April 6, *Cassin Young* (DD *793*) and *84* and *87* came in very rough weather to the aid of *Bush* and *Colhoun. Young* was prevented from going alongside *Colhoun* because of the heavy roll of the sea, but "after a harrowing half hour" *84* went alongside from 2015 to 2110, even though it took a severe pounding by the DD's heavy roll. The *84* took 226 crew members from *Colhoun* (including 78 wounded, 7 seriously). The *87* also went alongside taking off the balance of Colhoun's crew (approximately 36). The *87*'s boatswain's mate cut the *87*'s lines to *Colhoun* as she settled lower and started to sink. The sinking *Colhoun* was then destroyed and sunk by the *Cassin Young.*

In the meantime, *Bush* had sunk and two more LCSs joined the rescue party, *24* and *37*. Along with *64*, these two ships picked up *Bush* survivors from the water. The *37* picked up 2 survivors and 2 bodies, *24* rescued 42 (6 of then badly wounded) and *64* rescued 95 (20 of them wounded). The injured survivors were treated by Lieutenant(j. g.) James Dattilo, Medical Corps, LCS Group 11 medical officer. The ships on the station shot down all 12 of the attacking planes, including the two shot down by *64*.

Wiram described *64's* operations as a night-time rescue ship seeking as many *Bush* survivors as possible: "We steamed ever so carefully into the area where *Bush* and *Colhoun* had gone down. Slowly we moved through the water while calling with our bull horns. After cautiously maneuvering, we began to hear voices, then suddenly small lights flickering in the water all around us. The area was soon filled with lights like little stars in the sea. Slowly but surely, the survivors started to board our ship with many of our hands pulling them out of the water. I remember walking one very talkative and relieved survivor through the darkness of our ship to the mess hall tables serving as hospital beds. I assumed that he didn't need much medical treatment but when the doctor cut off his bloody dungarees, we could see a 10-inch gash in his left thigh. The worst case had been burned from head to toe in the *Bush*'s engine room. He was bandaged like a mummy—only his eyes and mouth were visible."[18]

In this overall rescue operation, in which *Cassin Young*, as well as *24, 37, 64, 84*, and *87* participated, a total of 295 of the *Colhoun* crew were rescued, 252 of them by LCSs, and after a long night of searching, 246 of the *Bush*'s crew, 151 by LCSs.

During this first air raid on April 6th, many ships on radar picket patrol were attacked and seven destroyers were damaged. The only ships sunk, however, were *Bush* and *Colhoun*. Although the next massive raid was not to come until April 12, the attacks on the radar picket stations went on incessantly.

On the day after the raid, *33* reported for duty on Station #1 to witness the ugly aftermath of the raid. The *33* crew found the waters littered with debris and oil slicks and the dead body of a Jap pilot floating in his parachute. The next day *33* picked up a downed Japanese aircraft and its dead pilot in the immediate area. Two days later on April 10 the *33* was attacked, but repelled the plane, although a section of its wing crashed on the ship.

On April 9th the *36* was seriously attacked on Station 4 where *Sterett* (DD 407), accompanied by *24, 36,* and *114,* was also attacked by five kamikazes and damaged with several men wounded but no one killed. Morris Shuldenrien, *36* fire controlman was there: "We could see three [enemy] planes coming in—one peels off and heads for the can [destroyer]—he was splashed [shot down] fifty yards from the destroyer. The next one peeled off and hit the destroyer amidship. The third one comes after us from the stern; the aft twin firing at him forced him too high, but he came in high, and his wing hit the radar ball (antenna) on top of the mast right over my head and over the conn.

"He was strafing and I ducked, fortunately, and right where my head had been was a bullet; funny thing was, he didn't wound anybody in the aft part of the ship, but from the conn forward, the director pointer [operator] was slightly injured, and on the forward, single 40[mm gun] mount, four or five guys were wounded, at least one seriously. The plane just went over the [forward] gun and bounced on the foc'sle [the inboard edge of the bow], and went into the drink. And everybody, in my place [the conn area], we were covered with red paint from his meatball [red symbol on wing of Jap plane] and aluminum pieces, and gasoline was on the gun deck."[19]

Raymond Quimette, *36* fireman recalls, "The rear twin 40[mm gun on the *36*] shot out the enemy plane's engine and sprayed gasoline all over the *36*. The left wing [of the plane that went over us] was in my gun tub. I put three magazines of 20mm ammunition into the next plane coming in and my ammo loader said 'You got that one, Quimette.'" Quimette cites five men on the forward gun who were injured or wounded. One man, Wykowski, asked Quimette to help him hold the tail of the Jap plane that was teetering on the bow of the ship.[20]

Escorted by *24*, LCS *36* next went for repairs to the Navy's temporary repair base in Kerama Retto, which, because it harbored so many damaged ships, was also becoming known as the graveyard for ships at Okinawa. "And, geez, when we got there, we saw ships with holes in them you wouldn't believe. As big as they come, as big as a living room, or bigger. Imagine what the hell that must have done to the personnel there."[21] The *36* spent close to 30 days getting repairs at Kerama Retto.

On April 10th suicide planes attacked ships of the fleet, including *Missouri, Enterprize,* and *Kidd.* On this day LCS *14* shot down a kamikaze plane attempting to suicide into the hospital ship *Comfort.* At sunrise on April 10, *87* shot down a bomber that was attacking her on Station 1.

Beginning radar picket duty assignments on April 11 were *15* and *16*, which joined *24* to serve with *Brown* (DD *546*) on Station 7 until the 14th. Ships on this station were attacked but with no damage or casualties.

From April 12 on, LCSs that had been serving other purposes at Okinawa, *12, 17-22, 31, 34, 35, 39, 40, 52-55, 57, 109,* and *110,* were assigned to radar picket stations. At approximately that same time a greater number of destroyer-type vessels as well as LCSs, LSMs, LSM(R)s, and other patrol-type vessels were assigned to stations so that all 16 stations would have a minimum of two or more destroyer-type vessels and at least three, and possibly four, of the smaller support ships.

Also, from this time on, all LCSs at Okinawa followed this duty routine: ten days duty on radar picket patrol on one or more stations, as they were needed, followed by four days in the anchorage and harbor areas where the ships would obtain their logistic needs (food, fuel, ammunition, etc.) by day and go on flycatcher (anti-suicide boat) patrol or anti-aircraft patrol by evening and night.

When not serving on radar picket patrol or on skunk and anti-aircraft patrol, LCSs were performing a variety of duties and participating in the special missions described and enumerated earlier in this chapter.

During their stay at Okinawa, LCSs crews, as well as all ships' crews, were never entirely free from the possibility of suicide attack, no matter where they were, and they were never allowed any time for rest and recreation. In fact, for the hundred of thousands of Sailors, Soldiers, and Marines in the Okinawa campaign the terms 'rest and recreation' literally did not exist.

The second large air raid on Okinawa came roaring in on April 12, the day that President Roosevelt died. It brought with it approximately 380 Japanese planes, fighters and bombers, as well as those 'single purpose' kamikaze planes. While in this raid the planes did not concentrate as severely on Radar Picket Stations 1 and 2 as before, approximately 40 planes fiercely attacked Station 1 at 1340 and again at 1445 on April 12. Patrolling the station were *Purdy* (DD *734*) and *Cassin Young* (DD *793*) and *33, 57, 114,* and *115*. The attacking planes' tactics on this station illustrate very vividly for us the truth of Lieutenant. H. D. Chickering's statement (above) that the Japanese planes' "mission was to kill ships," not to engage our planes; "the ring of the picket stations [around Okinawa] seemed to infuriate them."[22] And, as we shall see, although the Japanese pilots went after the larger ships first, they were just as eager to kill the smaller support vessels. In this attack they succeeded in killing one LCS and seriously damaging another, but not without valiant fights by the LCS crews and the cost of at least 20 enemy aircraft.

In the first attack *Cassin Young* shot down two planes but the third crashed into the forward fireroom killing one man and wounding 59. *Cassin Young* left the station immediately for the main anchorage. *Purdy* was also attacked. In the second attack, *33* was attacked by several planes in rapid succession and severely damaged and sunk by one of them, with five men killed and twenty-nine wounded. The *57*, which was off to itself five miles from the other ships, was attacked by eight planes and hit by four of them with severe damage and two killed and eight wounded.

Also in the second attack *Purdy* was hit again and seriously damaged with thirteen killed and twenty-seven wounded. The *114* rescued ten men in the water from *Purdy*, as well as a Marine pilot. LCS *115*, which later rescued *33* crew in the water, was strafed by an enemy plane and suffered casualties. During the intense attacks *115* shot down two planes and was credited with two 'probables', and *114* shot down one plane and was credited with two 'assists'. Of the six ships initially serving on the station, only one, *114,* came out of the encounter unscathed.

The attack on *33* by a group of dive bombers was intensive and fatal. The captain maneuvered the ship in quick changes of speed and direction to confuse the pilots, and gunners shot down the first plane, which splashed off the ship's starboard quarter. Gunners then hit the second plane which fell into the sea after diving at the ship so closely that it sheered off *33's* radio antenna. One crew member remarked that he could have touched the plane's wheel by simply raising his hand. Just before a fourth plane crashed full force into *33's* starboard side in the vicinity of the conning tower, gunners shot down a third plane that strafed the ship, injuring several crew members. Although *33* paid a very high price, she was responsible for the destruction of four of the attacking planes.

Lieutenant(j.g.) Frank Osterland, a staff radar officer with Amphibious Forces Pacific serving on *33,* saw what happened when the plane violently struck the ship's side. "There was a terrific crash and gasoline was sprayed over the ship. Fire immediately engulfed much of the superstructure. Many of the crew topside were temporarily rendered unconscious by the concussion (several were thrown overboard). The captain was thrown violently against the conning tower and suffered a broken vertebra. The mortally wounded ship began to list in the water and go out of control. Below decks [Osterland was in the radio/radar room] in what could very quickly become a steel coffin, we were deafened by gunfire and tossed about by the wildly maneuvering ship. Then came a terrific crash when the plane struck, and suddenly, for me, there was only darkness, stillness, and emptiness."[23]

John Murray, Jr., *33* quartermaster, describes what happened to officers and men in the conning tower: "all were knocked unconscious—I was on top. When I came to, the others were all regaining consciousness. We were all on fire. I beat out the flames on signalman Sam Laflin's back and we helped each other."[24]

In addition to engulfing fires throughout the ship, ammunition stored below was blowing holes up through the steel decking. One man, thrown overboard by the violent impact, was struck by the same gun that he had just been firing, which had been torn lose from the deck.

Men still on the ship were jumping into the water and escaping from the ship in every way possible. Two men escaped by swimming out into the ocean through a hole made in the hull by the crash. Since the ship was out of control turning sharply in circles with engines full ahead and rudder at hard right, men jumping in the water were being run over by the ship and were in danger of the ship's whirling propellers.

Acts of heroism on *33* that day were commonplace: the captain directed operations, though in excruciating pain with a broken vertebra; Boatswain John Nicely, who later died of his own wounds, put a shipmate who had lost both legs in a life raft and lowered it over the side; Lieutenant(j.g.) Frank Osterland applied tourniquets and rendered first aid to the wounded men on the rafts and in the water. At one point a destroyer almost ran down one group of men. For nearly an hour, the *33* crew, with numerous seriously wounded among them, remained in the cold water. Then came a 'Marvelous Sight;' the *115*, which had been under fire, picked up 69 members of the crew (the entire crew except for a missing officer and a man who were presumed drowned) as well as a Japanese pilot who informed everyone in earshot of his acquaintance with San Francisco and the University of California. His information was not appreciated and he was quickly dispatched by the *33* crew.

One of the wounded *33* crew members, L. D. Gramling, had also been wounded in the invasion of Iwo Jima. Although greatly relieved at being rescued from the water, fireman Carp Yushhevick was saddened by what he saw: 'On the ship that picked us up—at the stern was Electrician's Mate 1c Gertz, covered with canvas—screws got him."[25]

If anything, the kamikazes' attack on *57*, going on at the same time as the *33* attack, was even worse. Eight planes, two waves of four each, had *57* entirely to themselves since she was alone and five miles from the other ships. The ship's gunners kept firing away as they watched the first plane to attack them get larger in their sights. But it veered off at the last minute and splashed just 50 yards off the port side. One *57* crew member was wounded by 30-caliber fire from the plane.

The two waves of four planes next approached, and *57* gunners took the first wave under fire. As in the case of *33*, the *57* captain maneuvered his ship to best advantage throughout the series of attacks. One gun crew, however, found their hands tied at a very crucial time. Lieutenant H. W. Smith (the captain) explained:

> The ship swung around to allow the stern guns to bear on the first attacker. A second plane peeled off and headed for the ship from dead ahead, this one not six feet off the water. Suddenly the forward main gun stopped firing. The plane had come in so low that the gun's safety cams allowed it to depress no further. It never fired again—the plane was repeatedly hit by the smaller guns. But it did not stop. It kept coming and coming, until the noise was deafening."

The plane kept coming until it hit the *57*'s forward gun tub and something exploded.

> A white wave of heat swept over the forward part of the ship and pieces of plane, aluminum, bullets, iron and enemy flesh pelted down on all sides. But that was all. It had just been a glancing blow." And the plane splashed 25 yards from the ship in the water. At this point, another *57* crewman was wounded by fire from the plane. But then, still another plane came "skimming the water like a huge dragon fly, spitting bullets it came. It wasn't stopped until it was ten feet from the ship, heading straight for the gun that finally hit its bomb and exploded it with a blinding flash. Smoke began to envelope the stern of the ship as gasoline fires broke out everywhere. A gaping hole opened up to the sea in the side of the ship. The barrels of the remaining main gun looked like pretzels.[26]

The damage from this plane crash was extensive: the engine room was flooding; men were burned and wounded; all systems, pumps, and guns were out; fire was out of control and a magazine of ammo was threatened; the ship had a 10° list and four men were blown overboard.

And as if all of this was not punishment enough, a third plane hit *57*'s forward gun with a violent explosion, killing two men instantly, putting the only operating 40mm gun out of commission, flooding the forward living compartments, and causing the ship to take a heavy list to starboard. The ship was also well down in the water with only a few inches of freeboard (normally six feet or more) left.

The *57* then sent these messages: "Have been hit again. Possibly sinking. Request permission to try to make port." Permission to this request was granted.[27]

Throughout the *57*'s battle, Lieutenant Charles Coppedge, the rescued Corsair CAP pilot on board, was very active, not only manning a 50-caliber gun, but also helping to jettison weight when the ship was in danger of sinking, and boosting the morale of the crew. In fact, the great respect and admiration that the *57* crew had for Lieutenant Coppedge and the other CAP pilots, who supported the picket line ships so energetically, became mutual during the battle: "The LCS *57* crew was terrific. I can truly say they were all brave men, and I admired every one of them. I am unable to say enough about the brave crew members of the *57*. They deserve all the plaudits one could lavish on them. They were simply superb in action, and the U.S. Naval Service could not ask more from any man."[28]

On April 16, Lieutenant Coppedge, a Corsair pilot again, avenged the severe kamikaze attack on *57* by shooting down three enemy planes while supporting USS *Laffey*, serving with *51* and *116* on Station 1.

Later, when the attacks were over, on the night of April 12 on Station 1, only three (*57, 114,* and *115*) of the six original picket ships were left, and one of them was severely damaged but still afloat and under her own power. *Purdy* and *Cassin Young* had suffered major damages and had returned to the main anchorage, and LCS *33* was no more.

Because *57* was sorely crippled, the three ships took seven hours to get back to Okinawa. As the *57* captain has described: "Wearily they [the *57* crew] dropped anchor after midnight. The wounded had been transferred. Tired as they were, the crew stood a strict watch for the rest of the night. Even here there was danger. Every box, every floating object in the water might conceal an enemy swimmer, ready to plant an explosive charge on the hull or silently climb aboard and slit a throat."[29]

At the end of the long seven-hour journey to Okinawa, some of the *115* crew members were overwrought and in a state of shock from their harrowing experiences on the picket station. They had been under sustained aircraft fire for some time and had suffered casualties; they had seen a sister ship (*57*) severely damaged. More importantly, they had seen a sister ship (*33*) sink, and they had rescued survivors and cared for her wounded.

Even though *57* had been off to herself, approximately five miles from the other ships on Station 1 when attacked by the eight planes, she was able to provide continuous and accurate anti-aircraft fire and to destroy seven enemy planes. These planes had relentlessly strafed her, knocked a large hole (10 feet in diameter) in her hull at the waterline, killed and injured members of her crew, knocked out all of her vital systems and her 40mm guns, and set her on fire.

In addition to fighting enemy planes resolutely throughout the entire encounter, putting out her fires, and patching up the hole in her hull, repairing her vital systems, pumping out her flooded compartments, rescuing her missing, and caring for her dead and wounded, *57* was able to get back to the anchorage at Okinawa under her own power.

A large number of American ships were damaged and sunk during the second air raid of April 12 which hit both the radar picket lines and the transport and anchorage areas. LCSs were serving with several of these ships. Patrolling with *Stanley* (DD *478*) and *Lang* (DD *399*) on Station 2 was *32*. These ships were attacked by seven kamikaze bombers. During the encounter *32* fired on two enemy planes attacking *Stanley* and one plane crashed into the water. Most of the bombs dropped on the ships missed their targets, but a Baka bomb did hit *Stanley*.

The Baka bomb was a 20 by 16 1/2 foot manned glider carrying a high explosive charge in the bow and launched from a Japanese bomber (usually a Betty) to dive on ships at glide speeds of 400 to 500 knots. Fortunately, damage by this new secret weapon to the *Stanley* was limited, and *32* was not needed to provide aid.

Mannert L. Abele (DD *733*) on a picket station was sunk by a Baka bomb. The two supporting ships with *Abele* were LSM(R)s, and they evidently did a very good job of aiding *Abele* and rescuing her crew because the *Abele* captain said afterward that "the LSM's were worth their weight in gold as support vessels."[30] Fortunately the Baka bombs at the time were still in the experimental stage; only three of them hit our ships, and only *Abele* was sunk by them.

While serving on different picket stations, *12* and *13* shot down attacking planes. In fact hits from the *13*'s guns rendered a Japanese plane tail-less by literally chewing up its tail. LCS *37,* on duty on Station 3, rescued a U.S. pilot and a few hours later picked up a dead Japanese pilot still in his parachute. The *37* crew gave the dead flyer a sea burial. On April 15, LCS *40* and *119* each reported shooting down one enemy plane while under attack in the Station 2 area.

During the raids and even between them, enemy planes often penetrated the radar picket ring and attacked ships in the anchorage and harbor areas. While on salvage duty in the Hagushi area on April 12, LCS *35* had a stick of bombs dropped just a 150 yards from the ship. The crew was hit by shrapnel and a fire controlman suffered a minor wound.

On moonlit nights, ships in the anchorage and harbor areas were particularly vulnerable to air raids. LCS crew members often had to forego sleep and were required instead to make smoke to screen the larger ships. Lieutenant K. Huff, captain of *35*, recalls one moonlight raid:

This is the sixth one [air raid] today. Lord it keeps you up. No sleep again tonight—wish it would rain and hide that moon.

"Conn from radio, make smoke." There it [the fog generator on the fantail] goes, a loud cough like an old Ford, a shower of sparks, and then a gush of smoke like the pores of hell exuding. Now the ship, every rusty inch of it, crawls in smoke, a smoke which is made of oil, and an oil which gets on everything, and everything includes you.

"Bogie bearing 190 degrees distance ten mile." All guns stand alert— helmets go back on tired heads, guns swing around, and silence—nice moon but I wish it would rain.

"Conn front gun seven, plane engine heard." Oh, oh, he must be close. I hear it now. Diving too—damn that moon.

"Open fire when you see it." Listen to that engine. He must be coming right at us—he must be coming right at me. There go the guns. No, he is off to the right a bit. What a screech that engine makes—wonder who will get it—hope he misses the ships—gone. Wonder if he will come back? Look! There goes one across the moon, but he is ten miles [off] at least. Looks like that old picture of a witch riding over the full moon. Hey, [look over there], it's a plane falling, slowly spiraling down leisurely twisting and turning just like a flare—pretty sight. Down behind the hill and the dull red glow that marks the end.

Three hours now, and only an hour until dawn, and then there will be other work to do. If they could win by creating a nuisance, they would be in Frisco today or tonight or—damn nice looking moon—wish I could enjoy it more—never looked so big before.[31]

While many LCS crews at Okinawa got very tired of making smoke screens for larger ships, the alternatives to making smoke were sometimes fraught with danger. One such alternative was for all ships in the anchorage to throw up as much anti-aircraft fire as they possibly could. While this was going on during an air raid on April 15th, an LSM, serving next to *14*, had no less than 16 crew members injured by shells from 'friendly' ships.

Although the third raid of 165 planes on April 16th was not as heavy overall as earlier raids, the kamikaze pilots seemed more determined than ever to destroy every last one of our ships on the picket lines.

USS Laffey *and LCS 51, in the distance, under attack by Japanese kamikaze aircraft, April 16 on Station #1. Not visible here, LCS 116 was also under attack on the station. Painting by John Hamilton, courtesy US Navy Memorial Foundation.*

Early in the morning of the 16th, one of the most violent and intensive attacks on picket ships took place. At least 36 planes attacked the three ships on Station 1—*Laffey* (DD *724*) and LCS *51* and *116*. For the next 80 minutes, these planes coming from every direction made twenty-two separate attacks on *Laffey*, which was strafed by one plane, hit by six planes and four bombs, and near-missed by both a bomb and a seventh kamikaze, which landed very close to the ship. During the attack *Laffey* shot down eight more planes, making a total of fifteen planes she destroyed. In the process *Laffey* took terrible punishment with 31 killed and 72 wounded. But she stayed afloat to be towed off later.

As soon as the attack began, *Laffey* went to flank speed to try and dodge the planes, leaving the two LCSs behind. The *116*, several miles off from the DD, was attacked simultaneously by three kamikazes. Gunners drove off two of them, but the third crashed into *116*'s stern gun mount causing an explosion and fires and killing 17 and injuring 12 crew. While the crew was fighting the fires and caring for the wounded, two more planes attempted to hit the ship. Ship's gunners shot these down and the second crashed in the water just 100 yards from the ship. Answering a call for aid, LCS *32* came from Station 2 and went alongside to help care for the wounded.

While *116* was being attacked, *51* caught up with *Laffey* in an attempt to protect her. For a solid hour *51* was attacked by swarming planes. Ship's gunners shot down six of these, but one of them, a dive bomber, blew up just 50 feet away and drove its engine into the *51*'s waterline, and showered the ship with wreckage and bits and pieces of its pilot. When the station's CAP was able to drive off the still swarming planes, the damaged *51* went alongside the burning Laffey to put out her fires and to pick up men blown overboard from both of the ships.

The *51* then took *Laffey* in tow, but was soon relieved by a salvage tug. Intentionally listing heavily to keep her damaged side above water, *51* moved slowly on to the repair station at Kerama Retto. Fortunately, she had limited casualties—no men killed and only three wounded.

The *51*'s conduct throughout the attack was highly commendable. She opened fire immediately on the first three enemy planes to approach the concentration of ships. Throughout the duration of the extended attack, she provided a steady stream of anti-aircraft fire on the enemy planes and destroyed them by her accurate and intense fire. After destroying one of these planes, she fired on another diving at her, causing it to explode, inflicting damage on herself.

A kamikaze aircraft engine enters LCS 51's hull in an attack on April 16. The violence with which the kamikaze planes dove down on the target picket ships is evident here. Courtesy of Ray Baumler.

In spite of this, she went alongside *Laffey* to fight fires, rescue survivors, and help the stricken ship get to port.

Soon after the attack began on Station 1, the ships on Station 2 were ordered to go to the aid of *Laffey* and the two LCSs. These ships were *Bryant* (DD *665*) and *32* and *35*. While underway to Station 1, the *Bryant* was attacked. One attacking plane was driven off and shot down by gunners on *32*. The *32* fired on another plane diving into *Bryant* but this plane crashed into the DD. Gunfire from *35* caused another plane attacking *Bryant* to veer off. While *32* went on to Station 1 to provide aid to *116*, *35* picked up survivors from *Bryant* in the water. As the *35* captain has reported: "It was a bloody sight. Finally five living and three dead crewmen of *Bryant* were picked up. There were three other bodies without life jackets, and so they sunk from sight before we could get them. We proceeded to picket station #1 and transferred the living and the dead to DD *795*."[32]

At the same time that heavy attacks were taking place on Stations 1 and 2, four ships on Station 14 came under attack. These ships, working in two groups ten miles apart were *Pringle* (DD *477*) and *Hobson* (DMS *26*), and the support ships LSM(R) *191* and LCS *34*. Both groups were attacked at the same time. Gunners on *34* shot down two of the three planes attacking it and forced a third plane to veer off when the pilot saw all guns aimed at him.

Enemy planes managed to sink *Pringle*, and *34* rescued 87 of her survivors. Although damaged in the attack, *Hobson*, along with the LSM, rescued the remaining 171 of *Pringle* survivors.

While serving at the same time on nearby Station 12, *11* shot down an enemy plane and rescued a pilot who went down near them. The *11* was called to Station 14 to assist the damaged *Hobson* and to search for survivors of *Pringle*; however before they arrived on 14, *Hobson* had left and *11* was unable to locate any survivors.

High-level recognition for what the picket line ships were doing came on April 16 in this message by Vice Admiral Richmond Kelly Turner, Commander of the Joint Expeditionary Force for Okinawa: From CTF 51 to TF 51: "This dispatch is for the purpose of giving honor to the ships who are and have been on radar picket duty. DDs, DEs, LSMs, and LCSs, repeat LCSs, are all on this distant guard whose work is doing so much to help our troops make this operation a success. We are proud of the magnificent courage and effectiveness with which these vessels have discharged their difficult and hazardous tasks."

And even higher level recognition followed the next day in this message by Fleet Admiral Chester W. Nimitz: From CominCh Pacific Fleet to Task Force 51: "The Commander-in-Chief Pacific Fleet shares with the entire Navy the admiration expressed by Commander Task Force 51 for the valor and gallantry of the resolute ships on radar picket duty who are contributing so magnificently to the successes being achieved by the current campaign."

Later on April 24 General S. B. Buckner, Commanding General of the Tenth Army, confirmed what Admiral Turner said about picket ships helping our troops: "On behalf of all members of the Tenth Army, I desire to express appreciation of the splendid services rendered by crews of radar picket boats in contributing to the anti-aircraft protection of our forces. Without their skill in warning and guiding our planes, our forces would have suffered heavily in life and equipment. Although the bulk of enemy air attack was directed at them, resulting in their suffering serious casualties, they performed their hazardous duties with cheerful efficiency and displayed an heroic degree of courage. They are fulling deserving of the highest commendation."

On April 15 the *56* was ordered to go north around the island of Ie Shima to intercept Japanese suicide boats coming down from the north to oppose our force's planned invasion there the next morning. For LCSs to go around Ie Shima to intercept the skunks would have taken several hours. To avoid this, Lieutenant(j.g.) David Trice, staff radar officer serving on *56*, made detailed charts of the entire area. He describes the results: "Instead of going around Ie, we went through a very small channel between Okinawa and Ie. Fortunately the tide was high and we barely made it through the coral. We would never have made it without the charts. The Japs didn't suspect that crazy Americans would go through such a narrow channel, especially at night. Surprise, Surprise."[33]

The invasion of Ie Shima the next morning was a success, although the invading force faced bitter opposition for the next few days on the island. It was in this fighting that the beloved war correspondent Ernie Pyle was killed by a machine gun burst on April 18th.

April 16th, a crucial day for LCSs at Okinawa, was also the date of the arrival of five sister ships—*25, 61, 81, 82,* and *83*, the first LCSs to join their fellows since the initial 42 ships appeared for the invasion on April 1st, fifteen difficult days before.

These ships first arrived at Kerama Retto and their crews were rudely introduced to the harsh realities of the war even as they were arriving. Lieutenant(j.g.) Powell Pierpoint, *61* officer, describes his ship's arrival: "Our destination was Kerama Retto and our first indication that the laughs were over came as we steamed in. Without any warning, two enemy planes came out of a cloud and made a suicide run on one of our escorting destroyers. She got them both, but one of them almost got her, shrapnel and flying debris killing five men and wounding others aboard."[34]

Crew members on the arriving ships had difficulty believing what they saw around them, as *82* radioman John Rooney explained: "Kerama harbor was part anchorage and part junkyard. We stared in disbelief at the smashed and burned ships towed in from the battles around Okinawa—half sunk wrecks, heeled over, sitting lifeless in the quiet water. Proud beautiful ships days before suicide planes had decimated their crews and ended their fighting days. Kerama was a place of sadness and gloom, a floating graveyard."[35]

And while crew members were seeing and hardly believing what they saw around them, a blackened burned-out LCS was towed into the graveyard. Before the four ships moved into Okinawa the next day, LCS *61* gave her guns some exercise by firing at a shack on the beach.

At 0903 on April 17th, the *11* and the *118*, serving with DMS *23* (USS *Macomb*) on Station 3, fired on a plane that strafed *Macomb* and dropped a bomb on her. The plane escaped. In this same encounter, *Macomb* fired at a plane which sneaked in with little warning very low on the water, and very close abeam.

On the same day, April 17, LCSs *63*, *85*, *86*, *88,* and *117* joined their sister ships at Okinawa. However instead of entering the area by way of Kerama Retto and meeting war head on, as did the ships the day before, these ships came into the relatively quiet eastern bay of Kimmu Wan.

Although our captain may have been briefed and sworn to secrecy on the issue, just what was expected of our ship, the *85*, and the others in our group at Okinawa was unknown at this time by the rest of the officers and the crew. We were aware that the Japanese used both suicide boats and swimmers and that we had acquired 50-caliber machine guns to deal with them. We were aware that the Japanese were also using suicide planes (kamikazes), but we had no idea that the enemy air raids were so frequent, so massive, and so destructive, and that our ships and other landing ships were supporting destroyer-type ships against the kamikazes on distant picket stations. What our ship would be doing in the next few days at least was made clear when we were assigned to anti-suicide boat and anti-aircraft patrol and required frequently to make smoke in Kimmu Wan.

While we were on patrol the next afternoon, members of a small landing party from our ship were shocked when they participated in an incident that, with a few date changes, might have come right out of a story by Joseph Conrad. Richard Lewis, our executive officer, recalled: "As we patrolled the entrance to Kimmu Wan, our skipper spotted a green boat on a small sandy beach. The skipper ordered eight of us to make a landing party using our ship's small clapboard-style wherry, and off we went with two men rowing us ashore and us wondering whether any Japanese would appear and give us a 'hot reception'. When the skipper saw the huge bomb in the boat's bow, he ordered everyone to take cover behind nearby rocks. He then took a Springfield rifle, and shot at the boat's bow; nothing happened. He took a second shot; a thin wisp of smoke arose. He took a third shot—then a tremendous explosion! causing large pieces of rock to sail through the air. When the smoke cleared, we could see a huge crater where the boat had been and our boat had been blown 35 feet out into the water. Even so only one man was scratched by a rock fragment. Yet after that huge concussion, we were all shocked, shaky, and excited and emotionally overwhelmed. Someone retrieved our boat and we all piled in, and in a more subdued and thoughtful mood made our way back to the ship."[36]

Our crew's second 'encounter with the enemy' was utterly different from the boat experience, but it was highly memorable. While our ship was patrolling on a dark midnight the day after the boat incident, the radarman on watch reported a small object moving across the bay in our direction. Since we were still feeling the effects of the violent boat explosion and were aware of suicide boats in the area, everyone was apprehensive. Ensign Lewis has given this report:

All men were at their stations, including gunners at the extra 50-caliber machine guns specially mounted on the forward gunwales for firing at low targets approaching at high speed. All, of course, in total darkness. When we drifted to within 60 feet of the small unknown object, and it made no overt action, the tension was very great. Then the skipper had the powerful signal lights switched on. In the spot of light there was a small narrow dugout boat with an outrigger. In it were a grandfather, a grandmother, a daughter, and a baby grandchild in the mother's arms. The boat sat very low in the water.

At the sight of the boat so near, with Orientals in it, a speaker on one of the guns snapped and cried out, 'Kill the yellow bastards!' I immediately gave the order, 'Hold fire! Hold fire! Do not fire!' There we all sat, the tension slowly draining out of us, looking at those poor people fleeing for their lives under hazardous conditions and obviously impoverished.

They, on the other hand, had no idea that anyone was anywhere near them, and when the powerful searchlight burst down upon them from above, they were flabbergasted, filled with fear, and pleaded for their lives—finally sitting quiet and dejected in their boat as we stared down on them. To them we must have seemed huge and powerful, in the circumstances. After a couple of minutes we switched off our lights, returned to blackout restrictions, secured from general quarters, and proceeded with our routine patrol. Not a word had been exchanged between them and us as they slipped off into the darkness, continuing on their way.

The sight of the old grandparents, and the young mother and baby, left a strong and lasting impression in the souls of the men. They hadn't seen anything like that for a long time.[37]

Out on the picket stations LCS gunners used different anti-aircraft techniques and honed their marksmanship skills with each encounter. On at least one occasion, tense nerves made them too quick on the draw. On April 18, LCS *81, 111,* and *118* started firing at four approaching planes, before they were in range, to set up a barrier of flak (exploding shells in concentrated areas) against them. The barrier served its purpose—the approaching planes turned around. Two of the planes were then shot down by friendlies (either CAP or carrier-based planes). Almost immediately, two friendly planes zoomed across *118's* bow and the gunners, quick to respond, fired about a dozen rounds of 40mm at them. Fortunately, the planes took no hits, but the shells came close enough for one pilot to eject his auxiliary fuel tank.

Gunners relax while cleaning their 50-caliber machine guns. LCS gunners discovered that keeping all their guns clean was just as important as keeping their powder dry. Courtesy of Charles Thomas.

Suicide boats were aggressive in their attacks in the Okinawa area in late April. On April 20 the *84* was attacked by three of them. The *84* was patrolling in heavy smoke off Makimato Saki. Their 40mm gunners sank the first boat at 150 yards off their bow. While the second boat was coming in on *84's* port bow, the ship turned hard right at flank speed allowing all gunners to fire on and destroy the oncoming boat. Both boats exploded fairly close to *84*, which was uncomfortable but did no real damage. The *84* went after the third boat but could not find it in the smoke.

Toward the end of April, *37* was attacked and damaged by a charge dropped on its port side by a skunk. Details of this attack will come later.

On April 18th, the *86*, also a new arrival on April 17, destroyed a small Japanese barge in the Kimmu Wan area. Three days later, *86* supported the Marine-Army occupation of Taki Hanare. The landing force met no opposition in the landing, and, remarkably enough, the entire *86* crew was allowed to go ashore on the island. This 'liberty' for the *86* crew at Taki Hanare was highly exceptional, because even though some crew members got ashore very briefly, as did the *36* crew at Kerama Retto, the great majority of sailors at Okinawa did not set foot on land at all.

For most of the three- to four-month campaign, Navy men were simply not allowed ashore except under very special circumstances. When three men from my ship went ashore for just an hour or so, they were shot at by Japanese snipers. Later, in May, when LCS *90* crew members did go ashore, they were refused refreshments at the Red Cross tent even though they had just come in from picket duty. They were told that only servicemen serving on Okinawa could have refreshments.

On April 22 the *14* crew was surprised to find a Japanese mine hanging on their anchor as they hoisted it in. And whenever they tried to lower the anchor back down, the mine would start to float up under the ship. In the meantime the ship drifted very close to an ammunition ship whose crew was ready to jump overboard when they saw the mine. The *14* was then towed from the anchorage out to sea where a mine disposal crew directed an LCI(G) to break the mine loose from the anchor and sink it safely.[38]

On this same day (April 22), a second LCS was lost at Okinawa. Serving on Picket Line Station 14 at this time were *Van Valkenburgh* (DD *656*), *Wickes* (DD *572*), LSM(R) *195*, and the *15, 37*, and *83*. In the evening the six ships were attacked by 37 suicide planes. An enemy plane coming in out of the sun was taken under fire by *Wickes, 15,* and *83*. This same plane crashed into *15,* causing it to settle by the stern and sink within three-and-a-half minutes. *Van Valkenburgh*, LSM *195*, and *37* and *83* picked up survivors. All survivors were transferred to *Van Valkenburgh*.

The enemy plane hit *15's* port side and its bomb exploded, severely damaging the ship above and below the waterline in the critical engine room area. Gasoline from the plane exploded, spreading fire over half the ship. The ship then capsized and sank stern first with 15 killed and 11 wounded. *Fifteen* Radioman Harold J. Kaup has given us a first-hand account from his position in the radio room: "We lost all power in the radio room and it began filling with smoke; there were flames in the passageway outside the radio room. After opening the (only) porthole and looking out I saw people in the water and the deck below covered with water. Only Richard Slama and I were left in the room. I crawled out the porthole after Slama. When I stepped down on the deck the water was crotch deep. The [ship's] fantail was under water. The bow was clear of the water.

"I went over the side without a life preserver of any kind. Initially I clung to a 40mm ammo can. I was practically a nonswimmer and having a tough time at it. Finally someone helped me get to the wooden potato locker (from the ship) floating in the area. There were several of the wounded lying on the locker and a number of others clinging to its sides. The ship in the meantime with its bow in the air turned 180 degrees pivoting on its fantail and went down stern first. We were picked up shortly by other ships in the area."[39]

There is a story behind these two men's ready ability to escape from the radio room through the only porthole. Back in San Diego while off duty in the radio room one night Kaup challenged a ship's officer's claim that getting through the porthole was impossible with "Five bucks on the chart table says I can." Kaup forthwith removed his jumper and T-shirt, opened the porthole and to his total surprise with little difficulty proceeded to get through it.

After this, Kaup and Richard Slama practiced and perfected their ability to go out through the porthole, not necessarily to improve their exit technique but in the hope of making a few betting dollars in the future. Little did they know that they were practicing to save their lives one day while their ship was sinking at far-off Okinawa. Curiously, Kaup learned 42 years later at an LCS reunion that on hearing of Kaup's and Slama's success, other LCS crews conducted drills using the porthole to escape from the radio room.[40]

By April 22 the *51*, severely attacked and damaged on April 16 while serving with *Laffey*, had been repaired and was back on duty and about to participate in an experiment. Lieutenant H. D. Chickering, *51* captain, has detailed the plan: "The aim of the experiment was to provide 'extra protection against suicide raids'. The plan was for my ship to act as decoy, and a direct target for night-flying kamikazes [who] always dived at anything on fire or that showed lights.

"We rigged up a raft carrying oil drums with trash and gasoline soaked wood and rubbish, which we towed behind us. At dark we set the thing on fire. Then we waited until planes were attracted to our lure, and if we could see them, we took them under fire. The plan did not work as well as had been hoped. The pilots obviously saw that the bait was false, but they could also see us clearly. I think this particular job was the most terrifying of all [that his ship was assigned to at Okinawa]. We were absolutely sitting ducks in the flame-lit shadows. I was greatly relieved when the project was cancelled."[41]

A few days later on April 26 the crew of *20* witnessed the surrender of 35 Japanese soldiers on the southeast shore of Zamami Shima, one of the larger of the Kerama Retto islands, which we invaded on March 26. These Japanese defenders of Zamami had taken to the hills during the invasion, and after bitter resistance, had finally given up. Also on April 26, LCS *23* arrived to make eleven ships to join their sisters in April.

The fourth air raid on Okinawa by Japanese planes on April 27 and 28 was relatively light compared with previous raids. This raid involved a total of 115 planes; there were no intensified attacks comparable to those in earlier raids where LCSs were serving. From April 27 to 30, however, a number of LCSs were under attack while providing support for the larger ships. And other LCSs were serving on a variety of different assignments.

The extent to which, as well as the manner in which, LCSs were serving with other ships on picket stations the last days of April is evident in this April 29th dispatch by Admiral R. K. Turner, Commander of the Joint Expeditionary Force at Okinawa: To: *Bennion, Allen, Brown, Cowell, Daly, Hudson, J. W. Ditter, R. H. Smith, Twiggs, Wadsworth, Wickes, Van Valkenburgh, Bache, H. F. Bauer*; LCSs *23, 61, 81-83, 21, 31, 11, 87, 110, 52, 54, 109, 13, 16, 53, 62, 64*; LSM(R)s *194, 198, 189, 199, 195, 190, 192, 196*: MY HEARTY CONGRATULATIONS TO ALL PILOTS AND RADAR PICKET GROUPS CONCERNED IN YESTERDAY'S SUPERB DEFENCE OF OUR SURFACE FORCES IN THE OKINAWA AREA X WELL DONE.

On April 28, just six days after her crew rescued survivors from LCS *15*, which was sinking, *37* was damaged by a depth charge dropped on her port side by a suicide boat. At the time *37* was on anti-skunk patrol in Nakagusuku Wan on the eastern side of Okinawa. The *37* fired on the suicide boat, setting it afire and killing its crew. Although only three men of the crew were slightly injured, *37* suffered considerable damage to its hull from the depth charge. Her rudders were seriously damaged, her propellers were knocked out of alignment, her fire main was knocked out, and her engine room was flooded. While the ship's damage control party was doing salvage work, *37* was taken under tow at different times by *24* and *38* and escorted by *40*. She was towed to Kerama Retto for repairs.

During the last days of April, several LCSs were engaged in actions on the picket stations. On April 28, LCS *54, 82,* and *109* patrolling with *Harry F. Bauer* (DM *26*) and *Cowell* (DD *547*) came under attack. There was no damage or casualties. While off to itself from Station 1 on April 28, *61* gunners drove off an enemy plane that passed over the ship. Later that night *61* radarman A. H. Bleiter picked up a single plane closing in on the ship. Gunners on the forward 40mm gun took the plane under fire and set it on fire almost immediately. The plane fell within a 100 yards of the ship's port side. The *61* crew was full of confidence at this point. They had shot down their first 'bogey'.

While patrolling on another picket station on April 29, the crew of *87* had a somewhat similar experience. They were at their regular sunrise alert and had been at general quarters for only four minutes when an enemy plane attacked. Gunners shot the plane down before it got any closer than 1,000 yards from the ship. The day before, *19* assisted in shooting down an enemy plane just 200 yards off its bow. LCS *21*, serving on Station 1 during the last days of April, reported that enemy planes invariably attacked their station at sunrise and sunset.

Very early on April 30, LCS *18*, in a column with an LSM(R) and *52* and *110*, took a low-flying enemy plane under fire, but scored no hits as the plane continued on to the destroyers five miles off on the station. The destroyers opened fire with their five-inch guns, and the plane reversed its course and headed back toward the *18.*

Gunners on *18* opened fire while the plane was just 1,000 yards from the ship at 200 feet altitude. They set one of the plane's two engines afire and the plane winged over the ship just missing the mast. Gunners on the forward gun took the plane under fire; it crashed 2,000 yards off the ship's bow. Several minutes later the *18* crew heard and felt a large explosion, although there was no

---

damage and no casualties. The next day *110* picked up a Japanese pilot who had evidently fallen out of the attacking plane before it landed.

On a dark night in late April, LCS *83* took an enemy plane under fire while returning to Hagushi anchorage from picket duty. Even though Lieutenant J. M. Faddis, the captain, maneuvered the ship to bring all possible guns to bear on the plane and most guns were firing, *83* gunners were not sure they had scored a hit on it.

Then the captain saw a big splash in the water and thought it was the plane. But just a few seconds later the plane flew directly over the ship so close that it left tire marks on the radar antenna (according to the signalman the next day). A few minutes later, *83* heard and felt an explosion off the ship's port side.

The plane had launched a torpedo at *83* which either passed by or under the ship, but was set for a depth greater than the ship's shallow six-foot draft. This may have been the only instance when an LCS serving with the fleet on the high seas saw its flat bottom as an advantage. A life or death one!

Although the torpedo explosion did no damage and inflicted no injuries in its self-destruction at the end of its run, its explosion was very shocking to the ship's crew. "The ship traveled the rest of the way at top speed, all hands in suspense and praying that no other kamikaze would spy our foaming wake in the moonlight."[42]

Two LCSs participated in the rescues of U.S. pilots in the last days of April. On April 27, LCS *24,* while joining a task force at Nakagusuku Wan, witnessed the crash of a Kingfisher plane from the battleship *Tennessee.* They picked up the aviators in the water, took the crashed plane in tow, and delivered both pilots and plane to the battleship. Next day *11* rescued a Marine Corps pilot whose plane was shot down by an enemy plane. At this point *11* was becoming somewhat professional about rescuing U.S. pilots. They had rescued a Marine pilot earlier on April 16 and would rescue more before the campaign was over.

While on anti-aircraft patrol in Kimmu Wan, *111* provided a smoke screen for a command ship, the *Bowditch* (AGS 4), and LST *670.* On April 29 the *111* destroyed a Japanese Betty, the medium-sized bomber sometimes used to carry Baka bombs. While on anti-suicide boat patrol *86* destroyed a skunk on Maye Shima island in Kerama Retto.

On April 28 LCS *118* began patrol duty at 2055 in a target area of Nakagusuku Wan. At 0840 the next morning the ship moved to a new patrol

---

station inshore in the same bay. The *118's* gunners commenced firing at 1025 from 800 yards offshore on enemy emplacements and pillboxes on an island. At the same time the island was under bombardment from the larger ships, with shells ranging from 5 inches to 16 inches. "The shells were passing overhead and, boy, did they sound funny. They didn't exactly whistle, but sounded like someone frying bacon."[43]

The *118* resumed patrol and at 1145, U.S. aircraft, torpedo bombers, and Curtis hell divers started a napalm attack on a series of buildings, an orchard grove, and some private grass-roofed houses on the island. The planes drew enemy fire as they pulled up from the bombing run, and *118* poured 40mm fire into the area, being guided by the enemy tracer fire. Curiously, even though *118* was only 800 yards offshore, it didn't receive return fire. The *118* next fired several rounds of green incendiary ammunition into the roof of each of a number of houses, setting them afire. Gunners fired for 65 minutes, ceasing at 1750, since they had done all the damage that they could do. The *118* resumed patrol as the fire burned late into the night.

On April 30, LCS *114, 118,* and *119* went to Japanese-held Yonabaru Bay to search for aviators who had bailed out of a TBF (torpedo bomber) over a shore on the bay. The *118* and *119* provided cover for *114* which went in to within 500 yards of the bay head. On its way in, *114* destroyed a mine. The *114* found no evidence of the flyers and, while coming out of the inner bay, it came under mortar and machine gun fire from the beach. In response, *114* and *119* strafed machine gun emplacements on the beach and withdrew to ascertain the source of the mortar fire.

The *114* then bombarded the beach with her rockets and set fire to much of the town on the shore. She next fired at a cave thought to contain gun emplacements and at a house which blew up with a tremendous explosion that threw off a large cloud of black smoke. This led everyone to believe that the house was an ammunition dump. The *114* suffered only slight damage from the firing from the beach.

On the last day of April, *32* was providing anti-aircraft coverage for larger ships at Nago Wan. While on this duty, she was called to do what she and five other LCSs (*51, 115, 116, 118, 119*) did on their first day at Okinawa—put out a raging fire on a damaged larger ship. Early in the morning of April 30, LCS *32* went alongside SS *Hall Young,* which had taken a bomb from a kamikaze plane about six feet above the water line. *Hall Young* had a serious fire in two of her holds containing ammunition, gasoline, and automotive equipment. In the hold next to these were 5-inch rockets.

Using four hoses placed in the holes made by the crashing plane in the ship's hull, *32* poured streams of water and foam directly into the burning holds. Because *32*'s pumps and hoses were delivering 2,400 gallons of water and foam per minute, she pumped well over a 100,000 gallons into the freighter. The *32*'s fire party of forty men and three officers put out the fire in just over an hour. The *32* completed pumping out the *Young*'s hold two hours later.

In his commendation to Lieutenant J. M. Evans, *32* captain, Rear Admiral L. F. Reifsnider, Commander Task Group 51.2, said, "You and your crew demonstrated a commendable alertness, a keen sense of duty, and a courageous disregard of personal safety in fighting the potentially dangerous fire. This conduct is worthy of the best tradition of the service. Well Done!"[44] Ensign H. A. Beckstead, who was in charge of the fire party, also received a letter of commendation.

Endnotes

[1] Sources for factual information: S. E. Morison, *U.S. Naval Operations in WW II*, Vol. 14 (Boston: Little Brown, 1960), 140-250; War History of LCS(L) Flotilla Four; A Factual History of LCS(L) Flotilla Three; and individual ship histories, action reports, and personal accounts.

[2] Joseph Sansone, "Naval Action Traced in Series of Stories," *Lebanon Daily News*, May 5, 1945, Lebanon, PA.

[3] Frank Osterland, letter to author, Nov. 4, 1993.

[4] *Boston to Jacksonville*, 58.

[5] Ibid.

[6] Ibid.

[7] Howell D. Chickering, "World War II," 31.

[8] Charles Coppedge, letter written 12/12/90, submitted to Harry Smith, Captain of LCS 57.

[9] The number of these stations varied somewhat over the course of the campaign. At times in April, there were as many as 17 or 18. In May the number was reduced.

[10] Morison, 179.

[11] George C. Dyer, *The Amphibians Came to Conquer—The Story of Admiral Richard Kelly Turner* (Washington: Department of the Navy, 1972), Vol. 2, 1102.

[12] Charles Thompson, "War Cruise of the USS LCS *114*," 1.

[13] Herm Siri, Officer on LCS *54*, letter to author, Nov. 17, 1993.

[14] Chickering, 32-33.

[15] Hanson W. Baldwin, "The Greatest Sea-Air Battle in History," *New York Times Magazine*, March 26, 1950, 65.

[16] "Tidbits of History," 2.

[17] Ibid., 2-3.

[18] Ibid., 4.

[19] Transcription, 15.

[20] Raymond E. Quimette, account of actions on LCS *36* in World War II, 3.

[21] Transcription, 13.

[22] Chickering, 32.

[23] "Dolly Three," 10-11, used with permission.

[24] Untitled collection of accounts of LCS *33* crew members compiled by Roy Lambert, Jr., 1990; account by John Murray, Jr., 76.

[25] Ibid.; account by Carp Yushkevich, 50.

[26] H. W. Smith, "The Mighty Midget," 2-3.

[27] Ibid., 4.

[28] Coppedge, letter.

[29] Smith, "The Mighty Midget," 5.

[30] Morison, 224.

[31] "Air Raid, or How to Enjoy the Full Moon."

[32] LCS(L) *35*, Chronology 1944-45, by Lieutenant T.K. Huff, Captain.

[33] David Trice, letter to author, 9/5/91.

[34] "History of the War Cruise of LCS *61*," 3.

[35] Rooney, *Mighty Midget—USS LCS 82*, 84.

[36] "Okinawa Coral Dust," by Richard Lewis.

[37] "One Dark Night," by Richard Lewis.

[38] Eugene W. Scott, "Experiences of a Sailor in World War Two and the Korean War," 15.

[39] "Death of a Ship," 103.

[40] Harold J. Kaup, "Thank God for Portholes."

[41] Chickering, 32-33.

[42] The History of USS LCS(L) *83*, 2; and J. M. Faddis, letter to author, 6/20/94.

[43] Earl Blanton, same as n. 4, 80.

[44] USS LCS(L) *32* Ship's History, 1 Jan. 1946, Enclosure A, x.

Chapter 10

"A Present and Courageous Help"
LCSs at Okinawa, May - August[1]

During April while the picket ships making up the outer protective ring around Okinawa were being attacked by hordes of Japanese planes, bitter and intense fighting between Marine and Tenth Army troops and the Japanese forces ashore was going on. Marine troops, who moved north after landing, continued fighting for Motobu Peninsula and by May I had overrun and taken the entire northern part of the island. They then joined the Tenth Army that was fighting very stubborn Japanese forces in the south.

On May 4 the Japanese troops led a strong offensive against the Tenth Army. The Tenth Army and Marine troops turned back the offensive, however, and on May 27 the Tenth Army took the important city of Naha. Two days later the Marines captured the shell of Shuri Castle, a primary objective of our forces, in the south. By the end of May US troops were driving the Japanese into the south end of Okinawa.

At the beginning of May the naval artillery force of 27 combatant ships anchored off Hagushi that had been supporting the Tenth Army since April 8 was divided into two groups. One group continued firing from the original position off Hagushi, while the newly formed group fired from a new position off Nakagusuku Wan on the east side of the island. This new positioning allowed the two forces to shell the Japanese troops from different angles.

As seen from a ship in the Hagushi Anchorage or in Nakagusku Wan, the spectacle of these ships in the distance firing 5- to 16-inch shells several miles onto the shore about a mile or two inland from the ship was unforgettable, as was the whole panorama of night-time war at Okinawa that spread out before the viewer's eyes: shells of different sizes exploding on the ground, as many as 12 at a time lighting up the landscape so that you could at least make out the hills and valleys. Bright balls of light (star shells for illumination) gracefully floating or wiggling down, some from the distant ships and some from the opposing

---

troops on shore, some brilliant white and some a strong bright yellow, revealing to the anchorage ship observers only smoke and fire and a world of indistinguishable brown and black mass and swirl.

Up in the dark sky were as many as four planes afire plunging to earth or into the sea. Reaching up to more planes, inaudible from this distance, were streams of hundreds of tracer shells from anti-aircraft guns on ships or on the shore. There were flashes from bombs dropping from friendly and enemy planes on enemy targets ashore and on ships off Hagushi. Off in the distance there was an explosion at the waterline that could be seen but not heard—a skunk being exploded or an unlucky ship being rammed by one of them.

If an air raid was threatened or in progress, small ships and craft would be making billows of smoke. On at least two of them, their smoke generators would be on fire. Through the smoke could be seen the brightly lighted hospital ship (appropriately named Comfort) with its large red cross highly visible.

During the day and even at night, when ships passed the *Comfort* within a quarter of a mile or less, all binoculars were broken out in hopes of seeing the nurses. The enemy's failure, however, to honor the red cross was confirmed on April 28 when a kamikaze crashed into the ship, demolishing the operating rooms and killing 30 persons, including 21 soldiers and 6 Army nurses, and wounding 48, 31 of them soldiers and 10, patients.

LCSs on the picket lines were very active during the first four days of May. On May 2nd, LCSs *13, 16,* and *61*, patrolling on Station #7, met the USS *Sangamon* (CVE) and two destroyers coming out from Kerama Retto. As these three ships were maneuvering to positions close to each other, they were attacked, and two kamikazes went after the carrier. One was shot down by a destroyer but the second hit the carrier in its most vulnerable spot, the base of its island. The destroyers went to help the carrier, but *Sangamon*'s entire topside was afire, ammunition and bombs were exploding everywhere, and the *Sangamon* crew were pushing burning planes over the side. One of the destroyers, *Hudson*, was discouraged from going alongside the carrier when a burning plane landed on its fantail. Another burning plane narrowly missed hitting *61*.

In spite of these difficulties, however, the LCSs offered assistance, and just the appearance of these smaller ships coming to the aid of the carrier had a tremendous effect on the carrier's crew. As soon as they saw help on the way, men on the carrier stopped abandoning their ship and gave the new arrivals a hearty cheer.

The *13* was able to get alongside *Sangamon*, but had its mast knocked off and its radar put out of service by the carrier's overhanging superstructure. In spite of this, *13* was able to put its pharmacist's mate, Stanley Christensen, aboard *Sangamon* to help care for the wounded.

When *61* managed to get alongside with its fire hoses ready, the smoke on the carrier was so heavy that their fire party couldn't see enough even to direct their hoses. The *61*'s presence was important, however, even at this point and helped the *Sangamon*'s crew save their ship. "By this time the men on the Sangamon had gotten the terrific fires partially under control, the explosions were much less frequent, and we stood off to render any assistance she might ask for. The last job we did for her was to read and report her draft. The men of *Sangamon* did a truly magnificent job. When we first came up to her, no one would have bet a nickel on her chances of survival, but her crew stuck to her and with stubbornness and guts, saved their ship. It was a great and inspiring performance."[2] Although the *Sangamon* crew saved their ship, the cost was high: 6 dead, 24 missing, 79 wounded.

On Station #9, LCSs *89, 111*, and *117* were serving with *Macomb* (DMS 23) and *Bache* (DD *470*) on May 3rd, when *Macomb* was hit on the fantail by a kamikaze plane, causing a large explosion and fire. The *Macomb*'s damage control parties brought the fire under control without assistance. At the same time, a damaged U.S. plane landed 5,000 yards off *117's* starboard quarter, and *111* picked up the uninjured pilot. The *111* picked up a *Macomb* crew member's body and transferred it to *89,* which had rescued four of the *Macomb* crew. The LCSs were unable to fire at the attacking planes because the larger ships were in their line of fire.

On May 4, the USS *Sangamon* sent this message to LCSs *13, 16,* and *61*: "The Commanding Officer wishes to extend his thanks to all ships for their cooperation and assistance." USS *Hudson* (DD *475*) sent this dispatch: "The support ships of Roger Peter (radar picket) Seven are to be congratulated for a superb job last night. You were certainly responsible to a large degree in saving the carrier."

One reason for the high rate of activity on the picket lines in early May was the fifth raid on Okinawa by the kamikazes on May 3rd and 4th, made up of 125 planes. Although this was smaller than the first three raids (1st—355; 2nd—185; 3rd—165), the raiding planes' determination to eradicate the picket ships seemed greater than ever.

One station that was subjected to an intense and withering attack on May 3rd was #10 on which *Little* (DD *803*), *Aaron Ward* (DM *34*), LSM(R) *195*, and LCSs *14*, *25*, and *83* were serving. In this clear-weather afternoon encounter, the enemy planes first mounted a massive attack on the two destroyers, setting them on fire in just a few minutes. *Little* was stopped dead in the water and *Aaron Ward,* which seemed almost out of control, moved off from the *Little*. LCSs *14* and *25* followed *Ward* to give her aid, and *83* and the LSM moved toward *Little*.

Just how frightening these kamikaze attacks were, even to seasoned destroyermen, is expressed by *Little* gunner Frank Whall: "Having been in the Pacific for four years and earned six battle stars before these kamikaze attacks, I was so scared I couldn't speak. When one of the ammunition passers was standing, blank-faced, and doing nothing, I had to kick him in the ass and point to the ammunition. No matter what you had seen and been through before, kamikaze attacks were the ultimate terror!"[3]

Little, which had been seriously hit and damaged, was breaking in two and sinking. *Ward*, which had taken several hits by planes, was still firing some of its guns. The mass of attacking planes then made targets of all the ships on the station. A kamikaze attacked and crashed into LSM(R) *195*, setting it afire. Another kamikaze attacked *83* from very low in the water. This plane was shot down about 150 yards astern of *83* after it bounced on the water with its gun firing over the mast of *83*. Within minutes, the hundreds of rockets on the LSM exploded and blew up like the finale of a Fourth of July celebration, and the ship sank rapidly with the loss of 8 killed or missing and 16 wounded.

Still another plane attacked LCSs *14* and *25* but just missed crashing into *25,* although it took much of its mast, killing one man and wounding several others. The *14* also sustained damage and two of its men were wounded in the attack. The *83* was rescuing survivors when it was attacked. The plane barely missed *83's* bow and crashed into the sea among survivors. This plane was so low that Lieutenant Jim Faddis, *83* captain, saw the 'meat ball' on the top of its right wing. Two more planes attacked *Ward,* and one of them crashed into *Ward'*s bridge. This made a total of seven planes that had crashed into *Ward.*

At 1915 the *83*, along with DD *Bache* from Station #9, began picking up survivors from *Little,* lowering life rafts with *83* crew members on them to help men in the water get aboard. The *83* picked up 88 *Little* survivors from the water; two of them died of wounds in less than an hour.

Conditions on *Ward* were more than precarious—much of the ship was flooded, her decks were awash, and she was low in the water and possibly sinking; men were bailing out flooded compartments and fighting numerous fires and coping with exploding ammunition with the only thing they had to work with— buckets; some of the wounded, who were all over the ship, were being loaded into rafts and put in the water where, it was believed, they would be more comfortable. The crew was on the verge of abandoning their battered ship.

Suddenly the harassed *Ward* crew members heard above the noisy din *"Aaron Ward,* Ahoy, Ahoy, *Aaron Ward,"* as LCS *14* came alongside with fire hoses at the ready and damage control parties.[4] The *14* stayed alongside from 1930 to 2119, fighting fire, caring for the wounded, and pumping out *Ward*'s flooded compartments. Beginning at 1943, *14* picked up survivors in the water with their small boat.

At 2030 the *83* came alongside *Ward*'s starboard side to treat the wounded and to pass over fire hoses and a P500 (portable pump) to pump out water. With the two LCSs fighting them, *Ward*'s fires were soon put out. The *14* and *83* took the worst of *Ward*'s wounded crew aboard for treatment. At 2105, at the request of Commander W. H. Sanders, captain of the *Ward*, *83* moved to *Ward*'s port side so that *Ward* could jettison mines. The *83* continued to care for the wounded, passed another P500 pump to *Ward*, and supplied them with gasoline.

The two P500 pumps furnished to *Ward* by *83* allowed the *Ward* crewmen still aboard to pump out their flooded compartments at the rate of a thousand gallons a minute to keep their stricken ship afloat. While alongside *Ward*, *14* had to maneuver with its engines because *Ward*'s decks were too hot to secure lines. At 2242 the *83* went to where *Little* and the LSM went down to continue search and rescue of missing crew members.

Tony Greco, a crewman on *14*, participated in a unique rescue earlier that evening: "With the coming of night the attackers broke off, leaving LCS *14* with more than a 100 dead and wounded from the *Ward* on our fantail. While heading for the hospital ship at Naha to discharge the wounded and dead, I spotted a small flashing light in the water. A shipmate and I went over the side when we saw it was coming from a survivor not yet rescued. Lo and behold, when we reached him, he was a big black man holding up a wounded man in each of his arms! One of the men kept crying out for his little dog and we managed to get them all, including the little dog, back to our ship. I put one of the wounded men in our captain's bunk and held his hand as he took his last breath—he was so young. It hurt me so much."[5]

The large number of planes attacking all the station ships during the battle seemed to bring out close to superhuman strength and agility in the gunners facing these relentless manned missiles, most of which were armed with 500-pound bombs and torpedoes. Frank Korany, crewman on *14*, watched with admiration the two-man 20mm gun team on his ship: The team was "firing so many shells, the gunner had to change barrels. He changed barrels in what seemed like seconds and slammed the barrel into the water tube to cool. We had practiced the drill of changing barrels but this had to be a record. In what seemed like seconds, he was pumping out shells!"[6]

Throughout most of the night after the battle, LCSs *14, 25,* and *83* searched for survivors from *Ward, Little*, and the LSM. At around midnight *83* transferred dead and wounded survivors from the three ships to PCE *853*, where they received medical aid. The *83* resumed the search until 0835 the next morning. Altogether *14* picked up 156 of *Ward*'s survivors, 35 of whom were wounded. Five of them died on the way to Okinawa. The *83* took 11 badly wounded men from *Aaron Ward* and picked up a number of survivors in the water. Even though it was damaged and had sustained casualties, *25* picked up 66 survivors from *Little*. By midnight the searchers were joined by four destroyers, LSM *167*, PCE *555* and LCS *85*, all searching the Station #10 area but with little success. One of these ships, the *Bache*, located two dead bodies.

During the intense battle on May 3rd the ships on Station #10 shot down 25 planes, *83* accounting for 3 of them. The three LCSs cared for a large number of wounded men and picked up at least 310 survivors from the stricken ships. The *14* and *83* provided power and water pressure to *Ward* and helped substantially in extinguishing several fires on *Ward*. The *14* pumped huge quantities of water out of *Ward*.

These paragraphs from the *Ward*'s commanding officer to *83's* captain catalog well the contributions of *83,* as well as of *14* and *25*:

> The *Aaron Ward* was almost helpless at the time, without pressure on the fire mains, and all gasoline driven pumps out of commission, when, with great courage, presence of mind and excellent seamanship, you brought your ship alongside, and fought fires and removed the wounded. There was imminent danger of further attack and of our magazines exploding.

We feel that without your aid the number of casualties would have been much greater and that the saving of our ship was in very great measure due to your splendid cooperation.

The skill and courage displayed by you, your officers and crew, was in keeping with the highest traditions of the Naval Service.[7]

May 4th, the day after *Ward, Little* and LSM(R) *195* were severely attacked, was another bad day on the radar picket stations. On Station #12 both *Luce* (DD *522*) and LSM(R) *190* were sunk, serving with LCSs *81, 84,* and *118,* which rescued over 200 survivors from those two ships. At the same time on Station #1, nicknamed 'coffin corner', *Morrison* (DD *560*) and LSM(R) *194* were sunk, *Ingraham* (DD *694*) and LCS *31* were damaged, serving with LCSs *21* and *23,* which rescued over 200 survivors from *Morrison* and the LSM.

Station #12 was attacked by 19 planes on the morning of May 4th; two of the planes attacked *Luce* directly. The first crashed off the starboard side near the first stack and caused a fire over much of the ship. The second plane crashed into the hull near the engine room. Gunner Earl Blanton, on *118,* which had the attacking planes under fire, described the second crash: "There was a hell of an explosion and a big balloon of orange flame shot up at least 200 feet and a huge cloud of black smoke rolled up to at least 500 feet. You could only see her [*Luce*'s] bow out of the smoke and she was cutting around in a tight circle burning like everything."[8]

As a result of these two devastating crashes, 'Abandon ship' was ordered and *Luce* sank within minutes. This tragic action was particularly ironic because *Luce* was scheduled to leave for the States on that afternoon of May 4th. In the meantime, the enemy planes were swarming and attacking relentlessly, and the ships were taking them under fire, but all the ships could not continue firing because friendly CAP plans were also fighting them. Even so, when a Betty bomber started a suicide run on *118* from dead ahead and very close to the water, forward gunners exploded one engine and shot off part of the plane's wing before it crashed into the sea just a 100 yards from the ship. Two of the enemy planes hit the LSM(R) *190* and four missed her and crashed into the water nearby. The LSM was burning badly and it sank stern first. At about this time strong underwater explosions from the sinking *Luce* went off; they were so loud and strong that gunner Blanton, on *118,* thought his ship had been hit.

Although they were under fire, LCSs *81* and *118* went to the aid of *Luce,* and *84* went to help the LSM. In both instances the ships that they were going to help sank before their eyes. All three LCSs, still under fire, then began to rescue the many men in the water from the two sunken ships. Crewmen on *81* drove sharks away from survivors with small arms fire. At 0933, USS *Henry A. Wiley* (DM *29*) arrived in the area of the sinking and began rescuing survivors in the water.

Blanton describes the rescue work of *118*, picking up men from *Luce:* "There was a lot of heavy black oil all around and they were covered with it. The water was dotted with their heads. Some were waving their arms but none were crying out. There was a lot of wounded around. One fellow's whole face was gone—another had his arm gone but was still conscious. They were cut and torn and burned and broken and they were naked or their clothes hung on them in rags and they were all covered with black heavy oil except where the blood was running from their cuts and wounds. The ones that were not wounded helped their shipmates aboard. Most of them just sat down shaking like a leaf. They would look at you and their eyes seemed to say 'Thanks buddy'"[9]

The *118* picked up 114 men from *Luce*. The *81* rescued 47. The *84* rescued 53 men from the LSM. In each of these groups were a number of seriously wounded. The *118*'s rescue of 114 included 23 badly wounded. On all three LCSs these wounded survivors were treated in mess halls turned into emergency rooms by pharmacists' mates and their volunteer helpers. At this time PGM *Nine* brought medical supplies to the station from an APA at Hagushi. As soon as possible, the seriously wounded were transferred to larger ships with medical officers and hospital facilities, and to hospital ships.

At this stage in the battle for Okinawa, officers and men on the picket line ships were beginning to feel that the Japanese had a definite advantage. We were losing thousands of men and many valuable ships while the Japanese were paying with fewer numbers of men and less valuable planes. Yet, in spite of this, the men had the spirit and determination to fight on, to the very end if necessary.

In his personal log entry for May 4, 1945, Earl Blanton spoke for the picket line sailors so forcefully and candidly that he bears quoting:

When the Japs gang up and they are suicidal (using kamikaze tactics), you don't have much chance, for no matter how good a shot you are, you have to shoot everything apart except the propellers of the planes) to keep them from diving into you. Over nine-tenths of the ships lost here are being sunk by suicide planes, boats, or swimmers. That just shows what kind of people we are up against.

Maybe its fair fighting but I don't see it that way. In 24 hours' time right around here, there have been two cans [destroyers] and two LSMs sunk and several others damaged. There have been at least 300 men killed. To them [the Japanese] today a total of 18 planes [have been] shot down around us, according to the radio—I couldn't count them all, but I think I saw most of them go down—out of 18 sent. They lost every plane they sent out, but yet what is 10 planes or 20 planes to one Destroyer?

These patrols are really suffering, but we are doing what we came out here for. We are intercepting the planes and destroying them and, above all, keeping them away from the island [Okinawa] and main anchorage. Only a few are getting through. It is only a matter of time at this rate before every ship will get it, but we will hold these little bastards back at any cost—so help us.[10]

Fortunately, the rate of ship losses that Blanton predicted failed to hold as the desperate picket station battles carried on in May and into June. Losses of destroyer-type vessels (DD, DE, DM, DMS, APD), however, most of which served extensively on the stations, were very high in the Okinawa campaign. Of the 148 ships that took part, 119 were hit and damaged by Japanese fighter planes and kamikazes. Of these 119, 43 ships were sunk or had to be scrapped.[11]

On May 4th, before the main action began on Station #1, LCS *23* was involved in a curious incident that tells us what CAP flyers felt about how safe it was on the picket line ships. Two naval amphibious planes, PBMs, were confined to the station area because one was out of fuel. Two enemy planes flew in an attempt to destroy them, but were shot down by the ships present, and Captain John C. Zahn, tactical commander of ships on the station, thinking that the PBM crews would be more comfortable on a ship, sent LCS *23* to pick them up.

"No, thank you," replied the 'PBMers' smugly, "we prefer to stay where we are."[12]

At 0715 on May 4th, upwards of 50 enemy planes made a particularly vicious attack on the ships on Station #1: *Morrison* (DD *560*), *Ingraham* (DD *694*), LSM(R) *194*, and LCSs *21*, *23*, and *31*. The planes, which came in low over the water to avoid radar detection, attacked all of the ships at once, and although two planes were shot down, four of them dove directly on *Morrison*, striking her vulnerable parts and dropping bombs in rapid order. In effect, tearing the ship apart so that it sank within minutes. There was not time even to abandon ship and practically all the men below decks went down with the ship.

According to W. H. Stanley, crew member of *21,* which was nearby and also under fire, the first two planes hit *Morrison* directly, but the second two, which were seaplanes, landed on the water in front of *21,* leading *21*'s crew and possibly *Morrison*'s to believe that they were Americans. But after "about two minutes, they took off and headed straight for *Morrison,* which was already fighting fires from the two other hits. Just before they reached her, they fired two torpedoes, [which] struck the ship about midway, and both planes followed the torpedoes into *Morrison.* There was a terrific explosion. When the smoke cleared, there was nothing left but fire on the water. The *Morrison* was gone."[13]

Two of the Japanese planes then machine-gunned *Morrison* survivors in the water. Because they were continuously under fire, *21* was not able to pick up the survivors for over two hours. At that time they picked up 179 of *Morrison*'s original crew of 331. Of the survivors picked up, 108 were wounded and only 71 were uninjured. These were heavy losses.

In the meantime *Ingraham,* LSM *194,* and LCSs *23* and *31* were continuously under fire from the swarming and harassing kamikazes. Just as *21* finished picking up *Morrison* survivors, a Japanese Zero dove on them and strafed them. W. H. Stanley has given details: "I could see fire from his machine gun coming out of his wings. But luckily all his shells went over our head into the water. He came so near to us that I could see the pilot's head and feel wind from his propeller. Then just before he would have hit us, he made a sharp turn. He dove straight into the stern of the LSM *194* who was behind us. The bow of *194* was sticking straight up as it slid into the water.

"We [LCS *21*] moved in quickly to rescue the crew. As soon as we reached them, the rockets on the sunken ship exploded. The blast hit the bottom of our ship; it almost blew us out of the water. We bounced and rolled for a few seconds and then settled down. The explosion created a whirlpool, and some of the survivors were sucked down into it."[14] LSM(R) *194* lost 13 men missing and 23 wounded.

At one point in the four-and-one-half hour battle, with three of the ships sunk or sinking and enemy planes still swarming and diving at the ships, Stanley thought his end had come. At that moment the CAP drove off a number of planes. One CAP pilot, who had run out of ammunition, literally 'sat on' a Japanese plane and pushed it down into the water.

Throughout the Okinawa campaign, the men on the picket line ships had nothing but admiration for the CAP pilots and the pilots of the carrier planes who supported their ships admirably and valiantly day after day.

While the actions described above were taking place, *Ingraham* was under severe attack. The ship's gunners shot down six planes, but the seventh, with its 500-pound bomb, crashed into her bridge base. Her forward fireroom was flooded and she was damaged and down by the bow. Fourteen of her men were killed and 37 wounded.

Like *21*, LCSs *23* and *31* were firing continuously, rescuing men from the sinking and damaged ships, and caring for the wounded. Marvin Peterson, *23* crew member, reported that every gun on his ship was firing from 0730 till noon and that the ship was rattling, and asbestos from the engine mufflers was tearing off. That night the crew couldn't sleep because they had wounded men in their bunks and were keyed up and exhausted beyond sleep.[15]

During the battle, LCS *31*, which scored repeated hits on and destroyed six enemy planes, came under attack by an overwhelming force of suicide planes. Earlier that morning the ship's captain, Lieutenant Ken F. Machacek, had had a feeling that something would happen to his ship when the crew was called to general quarters, as a mass of enemy planes zoomed in low over the water.

The first attacking plane came in on the ship's port side and was taken under fire with numerous hits scored. The plane barely missed hitting the conning tower, but its wing cut off the halyard flying the ensign and it landed in the water just 50 feet from the ship. The second plane came in with all the ship's guns on it and passed between the conning tower and the 40mm twin gun just forward of the tower. One wing of the plane tore up the gun, killing two men and seriously injuring another. The other wing cut off the stanchion supporting the fire control director's tub and ripped a large hole in the pilot house.

The plane's fuselage and engine tore off a 20mm gun; the explosion killed two men and injured two. At this point *31* was dangerously crippled by several fires and extensive damage. Using the emergency steering to maneuver, *31* crew got her fires under control and continued to destroy enemy planes, despite drastically reduced firepower. The *31* gunners shot down a third plane about a mile and a half away. The gunners also hit a fourth plane, which swerved and crashed across the main deck aft, spewing burning gasoline over the deck. It tore out the aft fire controlman's tub and the ship's small boat as well as a 20mm gun and ready box. This crash killed two men, injured three, and threw two men overboard.

The fifth plane was taken under fire at 1,200 yards; direct hits were scored, causing it to explode and crash about 25 yards from the ship. The sixth plane was shot down 1,500 yards from the ship.

The *31* picked up its men blown overboard. Later an injured survivor was picked up, and the dead and wounded were transferred to *Clemson* (APD *31*); *31* went on to Hagushi and then to Kerama Retto for repairs. LCS *31*'s losses were 9 killed and 12 wounded. The crew shot down a total of eight enemy planes in the Okinawa campaign, and was awarded the Presidential Unit Citation for their heroic actions against Japanese aircraft on May 4th; her captain, Lieutenant Ken F. Machacek, was awarded the Silver Star medal.

During the first ten days of May, LCSs not on radar picket patrol were active in various ways in and around Okinawa. On May 1st at sunrise while returning from patrol duty, LCS *84* sighted a native dugout with four Japanese in it. They took the men aboard as prisoners, destroyed the boat, and transferred the prisoners to intelligence for questioning.

Two LCSs participated in naval shore gunnery by firing at troops on the beach, as LCSs, along with LCI(G)s, LCI(M)s, and LCI(R)s, had done more extensively at Iwo Jima. On the same day (May 2) LCS *24,* working with destroyers and cruisers, moved along the shore from one area to another observing enemy mortar positions and troop locations and firing at them. LCS *24* also provided night illumination for the firing. For the next two days, *24* fired on enemy troops ashore. At 1334 on May 3rd, *24,* working with LCS *38,* received short bursts of return machine gun fire from the beach but sustained no damage. On the next day, *24* sank a Japanese barge and destroyed a suicide boat.

On May 4 and 5 the crew of LCS *54* was busy around the clock. At 0106 on the fourth, while on skunk patrol with *12* and *53,* the *54* opened fire on two suicide boats dashing between her and *53.* She sank one boat but the other escaped. Later that afternoon, while providing anti-aircraft support in Hagushi anchorage, *54* fired on an attacking plane which dove down vertically on the cruiser *Birmingham* nearby. Later in the evening while serving on Picket Station #10 with LCSs *55* and *110,* LSM(R) *192,* USS *Cowell* (DD *547*), and DM *33,* the *54* shot down one attacking plane and assisted in downing another. This second plane struck LSM(R) *192,* glanced off its fantail and exploded in the water, causing only minimal damage. During that attack, *110* shot off the wing and tail

*Captain Neill Phillips, USN, Commander LCS Flotilla Four.
Photo taken in 1966. Courtesy of Roy Larson.*

of an enemy plane and splashed it. In the attack, however, DM 33 (USS *Gwin*) was hit by a kamikaze and two of her men were blown overboard. LCSs *54* and *110* conducted an unsuccessful all-night search for the two men, which continued into the morning of the next day.

On May 5th and 6th, LCS *23* went on patrol duty along the coast, firing its guns and sending its rockets into troops on the shore. The *23* also destroyed a skunk that was attacking the battleship *West Virginia*. Faithful to what turned out to be one of its 'callings' at Okinawa, LCS *11* picked up two more pilots out of the ocean, one on May 4th and one on May 6th. On May 6th LCS *19* covered LCS *11* about 1,000 yards from the shore of Yoron Shima while she picked up a downed American pilot. LCSs *11, 35,* and *81* shot down enemy planes while on patrol. The one that *35* splashed was attacking an LSD.

On May 10th Captain Neill Phillips, Commander of LCS Flotilla Four, arrived at Okinawa and began duties as CTU 52.9.11, Commander of LCS Picket Supports. Arriving along with the Flot Four commander and his flagship LC(FF) *1082* were 11 sister ships: *65-67, 90, 92-94, 112, 121, 122,* and *123*. All of these ships were part of Flotilla Four, except for *112*, which was the last ship to arrive from Flotilla Three. Two of the eleven ships encountered enemy opposition very soon. The *112* destroyed a mine while entering the anchorage and *67* was under air attack within an hour after arriving. All of these ships were assigned to picket

FINEST ANTI-AIRCRAFT SCORE IN NAVAL HISTORY!

FLOT 4

1,000 KAMIKAZE ATTACKS!

MIGHTY MIDGETS!

JOHN VADAY RM2c

Served on the LCS...85... during the capture and the occupation of OKINAWA

Craig E. Randall Lt. USN commanding officer.

Clifford E. Montgomery Lt.Comdr. Commander Group

Neil Phillips Capt. USN Commander FLOT 4

Flotilla Four staff art work. Using artistic license, a staff artist makes an LCS look like a super cruiser on a certificate awarded to all hands. Courtesy of John Vaday.

line duty or to anti-suicide boat and anti-aircraft patrol or to other duties immediately.

Arriving with Captain Phillips on May 10 was his Flotilla Four staff. Officer positions on this staff included an operations and gunnery officer, a material officer, a communications officer, and four communication watch officers with parallel assignments as flotilla personnel officer, staff secretary, radio material officer, and radar officer. Enlisted positions included twelve radiomen, four signalmen, one quartermaster, two radio technicians, and two radar men; three storekeepers and three yeomen; one motor machinist's mate and one electrician's mate; one ship's cook and two steward's mates.

Like the Flotilla Three staff, this staff maintained a 24-hour radio and visual communication watch for all Flot Four ships at Okinawa. Also like the Flot Three staff, this staff served their 36 individual ship crews and over 2,500 officers and men in every way they could.

In fact members of this staff also did things that, while not particularly important in themselves, boosted the flotilla officers' and men's morale. The staff published a directory of all officers serving on all Flot Four ships at Okinawa—simply a list of names and addresses, but unique and valuable both then and now because it records those who lived the unforgettable Okinawa experience together. Early in July, just before the flotilla was ready to leave Okinawa for the Philippines, the flotilla staff issued certificates to all personnel acknowledging service at Okinawa. Certificates were topped with a drawing of a fantastically attractive LCS—not the LCS of reality but the one of your dreams. That the picture was far from accurate did not bother anyone.

Later in July, soon after the flotilla arrived in the Philippines, the flot staff distributed to all ships copies of a vivid narrative describing LCSs and their battles with the kamikaze planes on picket patrol. This narrative, entitled "The Mighty Midget" and written by James W. Downes, Flotilla Four staff yeoman, made a strong impression on LCS sailors who read it. It gave them a new and broader perspective on what they had been doing at Okinawa. It also gave them a strong sense of pride and a sense of reassurance that a staff yeoman should describe their ships and portray their life and death struggles. It was as if the staff members, some of whom they had looked upon as merely 'paper pushers,' had really been their supporters and even their cheerleaders all along.

Also arriving on May 10 with the Flotilla Four commander was Lieutenant Commander Joseph Dodson on LCS *122*, Commander of Flot Four Group 10.

Commander Dodson, who would soon be assigned to LC(FF) *1079* as his flagship, was accompanied by his staff which included an operations officer, a material and engineering officer, a communications officer, a medical officer, and a supply and disbursing officer. His enlisted staff included rated men who supported his five staff officers.

The sixth air raid of 150 planes on Okinawa came on May 10-11th. LCSs on the picket lines began to feel the full effects of this raid on May 11th when two stations were severely attacked. Curiously, in one of these attacks on Station #5, where two DDs, one PGM, and four LCSs were serving, the only ship to be damaged with heavy casualties was an LCS, the *88*. Other ships on this station were *Douglas H. Fox* (DD *779*), *Harry F. Bauer* (DM *26*), PGM *20*, and LCSs *52, 109,* and *114*.

The attack began with the DDs firing at a Japanese Betty, which was at that time beyond the range of the LCSs' guns. Minutes later, two single engine bombers appeared coming in at low elevation, with one heading toward the destroyers.

Firing from broadside, with all possible guns, LCSs *52* and *88* took this plane under fire, both ships firing steady streams and pounding the plane so hard that the shells seem to swing him and cause him to turn off and go down into the ocean just 25 or 50 feet short of hitting *Fox,* which also had him under severe fire. At this time the second single engine bomber came in toward *88* from astern of the ship's formation. LCSs *88* and *52* took it under fire, and a projectile from one of its guns hit the bomber's starboard wing tip, breaking it off and causing the plane to veer off from hitting *88* amidships.

Gunners on *52* and *88* then made direct hits; the plane exploded in a burst of flame and went down into the ocean about 200 feet from the ship. Just before it was shot down, however, the plane dropped a 200 pound bomb which hit *88*'s stern just forward of its fantail. All members of the aft twin 40mm gun crew, including the director operator were killed, as was the ship's captain, Lieutenant Casimir L. Bigos, in the conning tower.

Two officers and two signalmen in the tower were injured, as well as a man hit by a bomb fragment. Two other men were in a severe state of shock. Casualties totaled nine killed and seven injured. The *88, 52,* and *114* were all strafed by the enemy planes, without casualties, however. A man on *52* was severely injured in the face by flying shrapnel. Battle damage to *88* was serious and disabling. The ship's rudder was jammed at full right. There were fires in the area of impact in which there was an ammunition magazine. There was a large hole in the hull's port side where the bomb struck.

Charles Cullens, *52* storekeeper, described the condition of *88* when *52* went alongside: "It was an awful sight that met our eyes as we pulled alongside to give them protection and assistance. There were three dead men on the after gun, clothes blown off; there were several burned and others killed by shrapnel. The captain bled to death of a neck wound while we were standing by."[16] Arthur Martin, an *88* crew member, recalled, "Instances of individual heroism were too numerous to mention. Of particular note must be the pharmacist's mate, Ernest Stephenson. Our boatswain's mates could be singled out as of immense help along with the engineering officer, Ensign John White."[17]

In this attack on Station #5 on May 11, eight enemy planes were shot down, LCSs *52* and *114* were slightly damaged with one casualty, *88* was severely damaged with serious casualties. One of the other three ships, *Fox, Bauer*, and PGM *20* was damaged. Six days later, however, on May 17, *Fox* was to be hit and damaged by kamikazes causing major damage with 9 killed and 35 wounded. Serving with *Fox* on Station #9 at the time were *Van Valkenburgh* and LCSs *53, 65,* and *67.*

After the attack was over, LCS *114* began the job of towing the now dead *88* to Kerama Retto, but found the job very difficult because of the locked rudder. A seagoing tug then took the ship to Kerama where she waited a month for repair orders in a situation that was anything but restful for the exhausted crew. The crew went "to general quarters on a constant daily and nightly routine; [there] were Japanese underwater swimmers who placed demolition ordinance on the ships' hulls. All ships [were] to have a 24-hour watch aboard, armed with rifles with orders to shoot anything floating in the water."[18]

Also in this highly tense security atmosphere waiting for repairs at Kerama Retto was LCS *31*. Three of the ship's petty officers "came up with a stunt to raise morale. While in training at Pearl the ship had recovered a nylon target sleeve. The sleeve was now resurrected and a pair of tight fitting shorts made from it, just large enough to tightly cover the derriere of one of the petty officers. All members of the crew were sent out from the mess hall. Then, blindfolded, they were allowed to return, one at a time. As each returned, his hands were guided so he could feel the shape of the shorts; then he was allowed one gentle 'pat' as he made a wish!!"[19]

Somewhat later, while *31* was still in the Kerama repair area, it was learned that crew members could each be given a captured Japanese rifle if the ship would offer the Army authorities ashore something in trade. The ship had 20 cases of beer to be used for a future party ashore and was planning to offer 10 of these for the rifles. But when the executive officer went to check on the beer, he found 10 cases of beer and 10 cases of empty cans. It seems that six of the petty officers had been enjoying a daily beer nightcap for some time and had been carefully returning the empties to the cases.

The exec did not want the captain to discover this 'happening', so, as a *31* crew member put it, "A meeting of some of the more devious minds aboard came up with a solution. We would still trade 10 cases of beer. However, the requisition would read '20' cases of beer. The work party that passed the cases over to the Army would consist of the beer drinkers who could put in a good show, as if the empty cases weighed as much as the full ones. The people who received the cases were instructed to keep their mouths shut when they realized that half of the cases were empty.

"The requisition was duly made out, the transaction was completed, the captain was glad to see that all the beer was gone; and everyone got a rifle! The rifles were very inferior. Each one had a ramrod attached that could be used after firing, for the spent brass was frequently not ejected by the bolt action, and had to be forced out by the ramrod. The troops of General Custer had the same kind of dependable equipment when they lost the battle of the Little Big Horn in 1876."[20]

Also on the morning of May 11 an attack took place on Station #15, now known by picket line men as 'Suicide Alley'. Upwards of 150 planes (practically every plane in the sixth raid) took turns diving down on the six ships on that station: *Hugh W. Hadley* (DD *774*), *Evans* (DD *552*), LSM(R) *193*, and LCSs *82, 83,* and *84.* The attack began at 0750 and by 0755, *Hadley* had over 130 enemy planes in her radar plot.

Even though sorely outnumbered most of the time, Combat Air Patrol planes were very active in defending the station and reportedly shot down at least 50 planes. As they had done before, the CAP pilots literally 'sat down on' and pushed the kamikazes into the water.

In this concentrated and severe attack, ships on the station shot down a large number of planes. The two DDs and the LSM splashed approximately 42, with *Hadley* accounting for 23, something of a record at the time. The LCSs shot down at least 9 planes and were credited with 5 assists.

Four of the planes attacking *Evans* crashed into her within two minutes, and parts of four other planes crashed onto her decks. Also a large bomb from one of the planes exploded, and the crippled *Evans* went dead in the water with several fires and extensive flooding of compartments. *Hadley* was also crashed by enemy planes, two of which dropped bombs; one of these was a Baka bomb (a manned glider missile carrying large bombs and making glide speeds of up to 500 knots). *Hadley* had several fires with ammunition exploding and extensive flooding. At one point it was feared that *Hadley* would capsize. The crew was reduced to a skeleton size of 50 to save the ship if possible.

Since all ships on the station were being attacked simultaneously and were forced to defend themselves, the LCSs and the LSM were not able to go alongside the crippled DDs to render aid immediately. At this time LSM *194* destroyed an enemy plane coming in over its stern with just one shell burst from its five inch gun—a remarkable feat!

LCSs *83* and *84* splashed a plane that, when falling, barely missed *84*'s bow. LCS *83* fired at a plane that exploded and sprayed gasoline over the ship. Fortunately the gasoline did not ignite. LCS *84* had a plane splash just 10 feet off its bow, covering the ship with water and flaming gasoline and causing a fire on the bow and in the adjacent gunwales. The fire was soon put out, but one man was blown overboard and another suffered lacerations and was set on fire. Curiously, a wing of the Japanese plane with the number '84' on it crashed on the deck of *84* when the ship's gunners were shooting it down.

Parts of an enemy plane whose tail section *82* gunners had just blasted away started falling on *82*, but the captain maneuvered the ship so that very little fell on the ship, and the plane splashed a 100 yards off the fantail. In this action, one of *82*'s gunners was, for the only time in his life, 'frozen to his gun' and unable to fire. He could hear but was unable to move.

The *84* started to pick up *Evans'* survivors in the water, but was attacked by an enemy plane which their gunners shot down. The *84*, with *82*, finished picking up 47 survivors from *Evans*, 11 of whom were seriously wounded. At 1008 the *84* went alongside *Evans* and started pumping out her compartments and shoring her up. Then they put over power lines and furnished the stricken ship with electricity.

At approximately the same time, *82* went alongside *Evans*, also pumping out water and bringing out the dead and wounded and sending their damage control parties aboard the burning ship. Gene Buenting, an *82* crewman who helped to bring *Evans'* wounded men aboard *82,* furnished these details: "We took many casualties aboard, some injured, bloody and dying, some literally cooked from the broken steam lines in the fire room. Some numb with shock. Those who were not taken from the water were pulled down by sharks who were apparently attracted by the blood. There wasn't a man out there who wouldn't have done anything in his power for his wounded buddies that day—there wasn't a man out there who would bother to throw a piece of canvas over the mangled body of the Jap pilot [of the kamikaze plane that crashed the *Evans*] to keep off the big blue-green flies."[21]

That *Evans* was crowded with wreckage and bodies of crew members was evident when the damage control parties, including *82*'s Chief Boatswain's Mate Paul Kostyk, went aboard: "I had two of our sailors carrying a Hale pump [probably a P500 pump because Hale pumps were not portable] over to the Number 2 fireroom area on the *Evans*, to rig it up for pumping water, when I happened to notice that the sailor I left with the pump was standing in a man's insides. Only the lower part of the torso from the rib cage down was left, minus a leg. I said, 'Hey, look where you're standing.'

"'What do you mean?" he said.

"I said, 'You're standing in someone's stomach.'

"He looked down and got sick."[22]

Dean Shillingburg, *82* crewman, described a wounded *Evans* crew member he helped to treat: "The sailor that Doc [*82*'s pharmacist's mate] had trouble getting plasma into was burned black, crisp like an overbaked pie. He couldn't speak, but he lifted two fingers in the victory sign as they treated him. I'll never forget that. It was the most courage I ever expect to see."[23]

Victor Lother, an *82* crew member and part of the damage control party on *Evans* reported: "We cut the deck in the foc'sle [forward part of the ship] and got, I think, twelve trapped men out of a compartment, and I helped pass them to the *82*. They were burned so bad their skin and flesh stuck to our hands. Not the best thing to remember."[24]

While *82* and *84* were alongside *Evans*, the picket station ships were under occasional fire and, all of a sudden, *82* gunners 'chewed up' the engine and propeller of an attacking plane, which veered right and exploded in the ocean a 100 yards from *Evans*. The *82* gunners, keyed up and overly quick to act, also accidentally punched holes in the bow of *Evans*, setting her paint locker on fire. *Evans* was towed to Ie Shima and later on to Kerama Retto for repairs with a loss of 30 men killed or missing and 29 wounded. Before leaving, she thanked her rescuers. The *82* received this message: "Without you we would never have made it. The deepest thanks from the bottom of our hearts," and *84*, this message: "Thanks for your quick, efficient and timeless help. Otherwise we would never have made it." Both messages were from Commander Robert J. Archer, Captain of the *Evans*.[25]

At about the same time *82* and *84* were giving aid to the *Evans*, *83* and LSM(R) *193* were moving to go alongside the stricken *Hadley*. While trailing *Hadley* just before this, *83* picked up 29 of her crew members in the water. When *83* and *193* got alongside, *Hadley* was in very bad shape—it had no steam, no electric power, no pumps operating; huge fires raging with ammunition exploding; many of its crew in the water and the forecastle crowded with wounded men; two of its main spaces flooded, with the ship settling down in the water with a growing list to starboard.

As soon as she was alongside, LCS *83* put damage control parties over to put out the fires. Her crewmen began to care for *Hadley*'s wounded, taking the

LCS 83, *on the left, alongside* USS Hadley *conducting salvage operations. Severely damaged on Station 15, Hadley received aid from LCS 83 and LMS(R) 193. Note wreck of Japanese plane fuselage in Hadley gun tub. Courtesy of Anthony Roth.*

worst cases to treat aboard their ship. The *83*'s damage control parties rigged a collision mat, which they used along with mattresses to plug up big holes in the sides of *Hadley*. The *83* also provided *Hadley* with electric power.

At the same time *83* men began pumping out thousands of gallons of water from *Hadley*'s flooded fire room, engine room, and other compartments. Tony Roth, *83*'s engineer officer, soon had reason for hope: "After about 15 minutes we all knew that the ship would not sink as long as we kept our pumps going full speed."[26] Roth reported that *83*'s two Hale pumps, which together pumped 1,000 gallons a minute, burned 15 gallons of gas in less than three hours.

Key members of the *83* engineering department succeeded in getting some of *Hadley*'s fire pumps started. All of these efforts by *83* men allowed *Hadley*'s damage control men to work to repair their pipes, isolate leaky pipes, restore emergency pumps, and do whatever else was necessary to keep their ship alive and afloat.[27]

The extent to which *83* helped the stricken *Hadley* is strongly suggested by two statements expressed at the time: one is what *83* engineer officer Roth wrote in his wartime notebook entry for May 11, 1945: "The captain of the destroyer *[Hadley]* said we saved his ship, yes, how well I know." The other is what the captain of *Hadley*, Commander B. J. Mullaney, said to Ensign Daniel Lewis on *83*'s conning tower: "The skipper of the *Hadley* came upon the superstructure of his ship and surveyed the situation. He turned to me (we could not have been more than 20 feet apart) and said 'You are the only thing holding me up'."[28]

Somewhat to his surprise, *83* boarding party member Arnold Nitz discovered, while he was pulling the wreck of a Japanese plane out of *Hadley*'s gun tub, that part of the plane's gas tank was made in Saint Paul in his home state of Minnesota. He was given the part with the Minnesota Mining label on it as a souvenir. Nitz was severely injured later and transferred to the hospital ship *Relief*, however, and his souvenir was unfortunately lost.[29]

During the entire five hours that *83* and LSM *193* were alongside *Hadley*, and while *83* was pumping water out of her, they were pushing her toward Okinawa. After the two ships completed rendering the aid described above, a fleet salvage tug took over and towed *Hadley* the rest of the way to Okinawa. *Hadley*'s losses were 28 killed and 67 wounded.

Although the May 11 attack on *Hadley* and *Evans* and LCSs *82, 83, 84*, and LSM(R) *193* on Station 15 was sustained and devastating in its effects, it marked the introduction of a new defensive tactic of 'mutual fire support' by all of the ships on the radar picket stations. Because the picket ships in early April were so absolutely overwhelmed by the hordes of kamikaze planes attacking them, they were unable to develop defensive tactics to make themselves less vulnerable to suicide planes diving directly at them. The extreme difficulty of dealing with such planes coming in head-on has been vividly described earlier in this chapter by Earl Blanton, *118* gunner, in his ship's encounter with *Luce* on May 4th.

During the early part of April, the support ships and the destroyer-type ships on the picket stations were sometimes stationed at such a distance apart that they could offer no mutual support to each other and were highly vulnerable to attack. Although the two units were later stationed closer to each other and different formations for both units were experimented with, it wasn't until May 11th that 'mutual fire support' was obtained.

Lieutenant Commander Clifford Montgomery, Commander of LCS Group 11, explained: "On 11 May 1945 in Radar Picket Station 15, 'mutual fire support' became more than a generality, but an accomplished fact. During that action many ships were saved from being hit by suicide planes through the assistance rendered by another ship. It had often been observed that a plane headed directly at a ship in a long, low angle run is able to continue closing its target in spite of heavy anti-aircraft fire against its forward surfaces. This happened many times during the 11 May action, but the ships were in such a disposition that a second ship was usually able to bring its guns to bear on the attacking plane. In the cross fire that resulted the planes were readily splashed.

"The LCS disposition that made this mutual support possible was a diamond formation of 1,000 yards diameter. While patrolling the station the two destroyers [that made up the destroyer unit] circled the formation at a distance of approximately 2,000 yards. In this manner the destroyers were permitted to exploit their superior maneuverability while still obtaining the benefit of fire power from the LCSs."[30]

The next opportunity for an LCS to provide support and vital assistance to a destroyer came on the night of May 13 on Station #9 where *87* was serving with *Bache* (DD *470*). Attacked by several planes, *Bache* shot down two, but the third hit the ship's main deck and its bomb exploded, knocking out vital steam and power lines and starting a serious fire amidships. LCS *87* came alongside and put over six hoses and dispatched a boarding party.

The party extinguished the fire which was raging fiercely around *Bache*'s torpedo tubes. The *87* also provided care for the wounded, giving 11 seriously wounded men emergency treatment aboard their ship. The *87* furnished emergency power to *Bache* so that her crew could pump out her flooded engine room and search for casualties. The *87*'s vital assistance kept *Bache* afloat so it could be towed to Kerama Retto for repairs. On this same night, *87* shot down her second enemy plane.

Although there was no raid underway on Okinawa on May 17, a large number of kamikazes attacked Station #9 in the evening. Serving on this station were *Douglas Fox* (DD *779*, *Van Valkenburgh* (DD *656*), and LCSs *53, 65,* and *67.* All ships on the station had been at general quarters for the three previous nights because of enemy planes in the area. Two of the attacking planes were shot down by the destroyers. A third plane was splashed by the combined fire of the LCSs. But the fourth plane hit a gun turret on *Fox*, which set the ship on fire.

Five of *Fox*'s men were blown overboard, and the three LCSs became a search party searching all that night and the next morning in the vicinity of the Japanese held island of Kume Shima. In spite of the long search, the five men were not found. Plane attacks on Station #9 continued the next evening (May 18) with LCSs *53* and *67* providing assisting fire to the CAP, which shot down nine planes in the evening.

The extreme importance of each and every man to the LCSs' guns while on picket duty is illustrated by an incident on *65.* When a kamikaze plane was bearing down on the stern of *65,* one of the two loaders of the after 40mm twin gun froze and stopped loading. The fire from the other loader's gun, however, was able to turn the plane into the ocean only 35 feet from the ship's fantail. Because he continued to load in the face of the menacing kamikaze heading directly for him, Seaman Ellwin Darling saved his ship and his shipmates from certain death and destruction.[31]

Occasionally LCSs in the picket line were accidentally shelled by other LCSs. This happened to *118* serving on Station #7 with *12* on May 16. While both ships were at general quarters, gunners on *12*, directly astern of *118,* accidentally fired eight rounds of 40mm which missed *118* by less than 20 yards. It was reported that a gunner on *12*'s forward 40mm gun fell asleep and accidentally pressed the firing pedal. Fortunately *12*'s guns were not pointed directly at *118.*

On the night of May 20th, LCSs *21* and *121* came under attack by planes flying just above the water. Both ships took the attackers under fire, and a shell from *121*'s aft 40mm gun hit the port bow of *21* near the water line and punctured a hole in the hull. The *21* crew began pumping out the flooded compartment and returned to Okinawa for repairs.

On May 11th a task group of eleven ships left Okinawa for the invasion and capture of Tori Shima, an island 60 miles west of Okinawa that harbored a Japanese radio and weather station. The group was made up of three destroyers, a PCS, a PCE, LST *620*, which was combat loaded, and LCSs *11, 12, 20, 21, 85,* and *89.*

Working under the task group commander on the LST, the ships made landfall at 0511 on May 12, and the destroyers began bombarding the beach. The other ships followed, firing guns and launching rockets. The LST unloaded its Marine troops and cargo. There was little opposition and the island was secured at 0715. After the capture, LCSs were assigned to skunk and anti-aircraft patrol duties in the area.

After they returned from picket line duty with *Hadley* and *Evans*, the *82* and *84* went on anti-suicide boat patrol and were joined by *19*. On May 12, LCS *19* destroyed two skunks off Naha and with *82* and *84,* broke up a possibility serious attack by suicide boats on the ships in the anchorage.

On the night of the 12th, a number of ships in the Hagushi harbor mistook *84* for a skunk and fired 5-inch and 40mm shells at her. Although surprised enough to high-tail it out of the harbor, the *84* crew suffered nothing more than some flying bits of shrapnel.

For their performance of breaking up a skunk attack, LCSs *19, 82,* and *84* received a commendation on May 13th from the commander of Task Group 51, Admiral Richmond Kelly Turner. This statement not only acknowledged what they had done, but gave LCSs the nickname of 'mighty midgets' that was to identify them throughout the Okinawa campaign and beyond:

"To all those engaged in flycatcher [skunk] operations: your alertness and your shooting last night at an elusive and dangerous enemy broke up a coordinated attack which constituted a serious threat to the safety of our forces in the Dodger [anchorage] Area. LCS *19*, LCS *82*, LCS *84* gave an outstanding performance. The LCSs which are our mighty midgets and to all members of the fly catcher group, Well Done."[32]

On May 11, LCS *36* found a suicide boat and discovered a place that was being used to assemble these boats. The *36* destroyed the boat assembly area, thereby preventing further skunk attacks in the Kerama Retto area. The crew converted the skunk into a captain's gig.

In mid-May at least two LCSs were doing double duty during their time off from the dangerous picket lines. At night *82* and *111* were on constant lookout for suicide swimmers carrying explosives and skunks, or on anti-aircraft patrol, or making smoke to screen larger ships. By day these same two ships were firing on the shores of Okinawa at caves, at possible gun emplacements, and even at enemy troops, and providing artillery support for the Army and Marines.

LCS *111* was firing in the Buckner Bay (formerly Nakagusuku Wan) area and *82* in the Hagushi area, where she destroyed several skunks and started a number of fires on the beach. On May 13, LCS *24,* serving on patrol at islands off Okinawa, destroyed a mine, and two days later demolished a new Japanese motorboat. During May LCS *90* patrolled small rivers at Okinawa, searching for one-man submarine pens. They located several but found them abandoned. While on a logistics mission in Buckner Bay, *90* shot down a kamikaze plane attacking her.

On May 17, six LCSs arrived at Okinawa from Ulithi to join their sister ships in the long, arduous battle for that island. They were *68, 69, 91, 95, 120,* and *124.* Like those that had come before, they were assigned immediately to picket or patrol duty.

A number of times in the Okinawa campaign, ships, and even landing craft, were in danger of being blown up or severely damaged by bomb-laden suicide boats or explosive-carrying swimmers. LCS *37* was severely damaged by a bomb from a suicide boat on April 28; LCS *62* engaged in an hour-long battle with suicide swimmers on June 26.

Another ever-present danger was running aground and being vulnerable to air, skunk, suicide swimmer, or shore fire attack. On May 18 the destroyer *Longshaw,* while bombarding the shore, ran hard aground off Naha. She immediately came under fire from shore guns who pounded her mercilessly for hours while other ships tried unsuccessfully to work her loose. *Longshaw* was so badly damaged as to be unsalvageable. Losses were 85 killed or missing and 97 wounded.

Crews of ships that did run aground (as did my ship described below) should thank their lucky stars that they were not attacked. I find it mind-boggling just to think now, over 50 years later, of how close every Sailor (not to mention every Soldier and Marine ashore) was to real danger at Okinawa all the time!

On May 19, Admiral R. K. Turner, Commander, Joint Expeditionary Force, issued what he called a 'splash score' to date for Flotilla Three ships who had been at Okinawa since the invasion on April 1. The score, actually the number of enemy planes shot down by Flot Three ships reporting, was: '50 definitely', '3 probables', '23 assists', making a total of 76. Also destroyed, 21 skunks, 7 in action and 14 on the beach. Since by this time over half of the Flot Four ships had been serving at Okinawa since April 1, a conservative splash score for them would be at least '30 definites', '3 probables', and '15 assists', with at least 15 skunks destroyed. For all LCSs for the first seven weeks of the three month campaign, the total is approximately '80 definites', '6 probables', '38 assists', and 36 skunks destroyed.

Because the waters around Okinawa, and in the Kerama Retto area in particular, covered a large number of coral reefs, LCSs on patrol sometimes found themselves aground with the tide pulling the ocean out from under them at a fairly rapid rate. As the water moved out and the ship became unbelievably quiet, crew members became acutely aware of how vulnerable and fragile they were in a very hostile world. While our ship was on patrol one evening in early May, our crew experienced these same unforgettable sensations, as Richard Lewis, our executive officer recounted:

Soon after I took over as officer of the deck and made the turn to double back down the bay, we ran aground on a reef. No amount of backing and fooling with the engines would help, we were stuck hard. We had become sitting ducks for a suicide attack—if they realized we were aground and not anchored. We stopped the main engines and waited. Everything else functioned normally. However as time passed, the tide began to go out. As the ship's equipment came to the final shutdown, the silence became eerie—you could even hear someone walking on the steel decks one deck below you, and at the other end of the ship.

The ship settled on the rocks into a list to port (maybe 10 degrees), which was unusual—no ship motion, but a fixed position off the level. And when the electricity went off, the darkness became eerie too. Then, of course, the decks and the bulkheads began to 'sweat' from condensation. Since no engine or navigation watches were required, only a few men were detailed for lookout duty; most everyone went to sleep. It was the most quiet night any of us had for months. It was like a giant steel grave or coffin, with the silence of the dead. When morning came, we felt strangely, unusually refreshed. With a little shunting of the engines, we were soon freely afloat and on our way again. We had not been attacked by a suicide squad of any kind, though for a few hours we were nothing but a sitting duck.[33]

The last ten days of May saw considerable activity on the radar picket lines. On May 22, LCSs *14, 17, 18*, and *21*, serving with three destroyers on Station #16, came under attack but without damage and casualties. Three days later, LCS *92* shot down an enemy plane on Station 9, and *122* splashed one plane and assisted in shooting down another. On May 27, LCS *24* and the ships serving with her were attacked; *24* gunners assisted in shooting down the attacking planes. A day later, LCS *115* splashed one plane and assisted in downing another on Station 11A. The next day, May 29th, *122* did the same thing on another station. Around this time LCS *53* and the ships serving with her were attacked by six planes. The *53* splashed one of these, which went into the water just 200 yards astern.

On May 23-25 the seventh kamikaze air raid sent about 165 planes down on the picket stations. A number of the raiding planes focused on Station #15, on which three destroyers and LCSs *61, 85, 89,* and *121* were serving. At 2000 on May 23 station ships went to general quarters as enemy planes approached. One hour later a plane dropped a bomb close to *121*, killing two men and wounding several and causing minor damage. Because the plane was sighted just seconds before it dropped the bomb, none of the ships could take it under fire. The bomb exploded off *121*'s starboard quarter and sprayed the afterdeck with shrapnel. The *121* was also strafed by a kamikaze. During the encounter, she shot down two planes, one of which headed for her and the other for a nearby destroyer.

Enemy planes left soon after the bombing and returned after midnight on May 24. At 0120 many planes began an attack on the station ships. At this time, my ship, the *85,* took three enemy planes under fire simultaneously. No hits were scored on one plane that came in at an altitude of over 100 feet at approximately 175 knots over the bow and then turned off and disappeared. The second plane, moving in at an altitude of just 50 feet at approximately 225 knots, was hit by our gunners as it came over, but then it circled over the other ships and crashed into the sea. The third plane came in at an altitude of 600 feet at approximately 250 knots, and was taken under fire, but with no hits recorded; then it turned off and disappeared like the first.

Attacks on the station ships resumed in the evening of May 24. At 0230 on May 25, another plane came over our ship at 100 feet at approximately 175 knots. It was hit at least once but continued on its flight and disappeared. Again a half hour later, a fifth plane came over and was taken under fire, and it, too, disappeared.

At 0800 the planes returned, although not nearly as many as before. At approximately 0900 an enemy plane flew into a heavy cumulus cloud directly above the ships and dove almost vertically down on *Stormes* (DD *780*), hitting her torpedo mounting, killing 21 men and wounding 6. As did *121*'s crew earlier, *Stormes*' crew put out the fires, took care of their dead and wounded, and the ship moved rapidly into Hagushi anchorage to hospital facilities. At least six enemy planes were splashed by station ships during the action on Station #15 on May 23-25.

In the conclusion of his report on the above action, Lieutenant Craig Randall, *85* captain, suggested that LCSs on this type of duty be equipped with radar controlled directors so their gunners could open fire sooner on planes coming in so close and so fast that there is practically no time to fire. Randall also made an observation about the kamikaze pilots: "It seems that enemy planes have a very hard time spotting surface craft at night or else the pilots do not have the nerve at the last minute to make the suicide dive. At least three planes had an excellent opportunity to suicide this vessel during the last attacks, but the planes passed on without even dropping a bomb or strafing the ship."[34] I believe that, in addition to the failure to see and a lack of last-minute nerve, a third possibility is that the enemy pilots did not discover their target's size until they were just 50 to 100 feet above us and chose not to sacrifice themselves for such a small ship. Whatever their reason(s), my *85* shipmates and I thanked God that the three enemy pilots passed on and failed to attack our ship.

On May 27-29 the eighth kamikaze air raid sent 110 planes down on the picket ships again. Station 15 was a favorite target as before, with a mass of planes attacking LCSs *52* and *61* on the station on May 27. Charles Cullens, *52* storekeeper, described the attack: "It seems like every plane coming down from Japan came our way—planes were everywhere. [As] radar would report each bogey, the guns would swing around and we'd try to spot him, but it was dark. Finally one of them spotted us and headed in. Gunners opened fire. When you fire at night you are immediately blinded, and you give the plane a line of tracers to come in on. He came. We kept firing, pounding him with everything we had. A few yards off, he banked towards the stern and dove in. Every gun that could get a line on him was firing till the last second. There was a loud crash, then a silence as black as night itself. We all thought he had hit the ship. Fire from our guns had exploded the plane as it passed over the ship, so low that some of the men swore they had to duck because the wing would have hit them."[35] Although damage to *52* was slight, two men were killed and 12 were wounded.

LCS *61* assisted *52* in splashing the plane that nearly missed her. As *61* moved to aid *52,* its gunners had to drive off another plane. Then *61* escorted *52* back to Hagushi to transfer her wounded on what turned out to be a very difficult trip: "We [*52*] started back on the longest journey I ever lived through. I wouldn't have given a plugged nickel for our chances of ever getting back—nor would any of the others. For about four or five hours that seemed like as many weeks, we made our way back . . . There wasn't a time during that trip that we didn't have bogeys on our radar. Finally one of them spotted us and came in. We threw up so much flak that he veered off and the *61* opened up on the plane. He turned and dove at her, but overshot and hit the water so close that the bottom of the *61* scraped him as they went over. We got in about daylight—it seemed like weeks."[36]

As the two ships approached the Hagushi area, a plane attacked *61* from very low. By putting on left hard rudder at flank speed, the *61* captain, Lieutenant James W. Kelly, was able to keep the plane from hitting them; it fell into the water just 20 feet off *61*'s bow. The *61* crew were sprayed with water and gasoline and thought at first that their ship had been hit. One man was injured by a piece of the plane's tail; the crew found the pilot's parachute still in its pack on the deck.

On the morning of May 27 ships on Station #5 were attacked by four enemy planes. Serving at this time were *Braine* (DD *630*), *Anthony* (DD *515*), and LCSs *13, 82, 86,* and *123. Braine* was hit in rapid succession by two planes. The first plane hit the ship right behind its #2 five-inch gun mount with a 500-pound bomb, exploding and demolishing the Combat Information Center, the wardroom, the loading room and seriously damaging the whole bridge structure. The second plane, which also carried a large bomb, crashed into the ship's superstructure at the #2 stack, with the plane burying itself in the sick bay and its bomb exploding in a major fireroom below.

The effects of the attack on *Braine* were devastating. The ship was afire with ammunition exploding, her communication system was destroyed, she had no steering and engine control, and her rudder was jammed so that she went around in circles, erratically and uncontrollably, at roughly 18 knots. A third

Seriously damaged and set on fire by two kamikaze planes, Braine *(DD 630) moves in circles, wildly out of control, at 18 knots. LCSs, not visible here, were, at this time, throwing out life rafts and preservers to men from the* Braine *in the water. Courtesy of William Mason.*

plane attacked the station and was splashed by *Anthony* and the LCSs. A fourth plane was shot down by the LCSs.

Since the LCSs could not catch up with *Braine* to help her, they began dropping life rafts and rescuing men who had been thrown overboard by the explosions and those who were abandoning ship. The *86* picked up 45 survivors and the other LCSs picked up a number, possibly as many as 50 more altogether. When sharks began to appear because of the blood from the many wounded men in the water, the *82* crew machine gunned them.

The LCSs had a difficult time picking up survivors in the wake of the uncontrollable *Braine*; *123* was nearly run down by the runaway ship, as was *82*. Curtis Williams, *82* seaman: "When that ship was circlin' out of control, and we were chasin' after him, I remember looking back aft one time. I wouldn'ta' give you two cents for our ship—that thing was bearing down on us, seemed like it was right on our anchor [at the stern on LCSs], and the next thing I knew it was runnin' right alongside and all them shells was goin' off, and Queenan and Burford and myself got down on the deck.

"Then while we were followin' the destroyer, these guys out in the water were screamin' about sharks gettin' them; [later] a fellow [from *Braine*] in a

The fantail of the wildly circling destroyer Braine showing crew members gathered there to avoid the fiercely burning fire in the forward part of the ship. Courtesy of William Mason.

small boat who had picked up a body out of the water asked, 'Can anybody identify this fellow?' Course, this fella was pulled apart and chewed up horribly and that of liked to scare me to death. I said to myself, 'By George, if our ship gets hit, I'm going down with it. I sure ain't goin' to jump in that water.'"[37]

After over an hour of circling madly around, *Braine* finally went dead in the water with fires on her still fiercely burning. *Anthony* and LCSs *82* and *86* went alongside and put fire and rescue parties aboard. The *86* took many wounded aboard for treatment; the *82* crew transferred some of *Braine*'s casualties to *Anthony* and to LCS *123*, which was now alongside.

Incidentally, sending its valuable chief boatswain's mate to direct the firefighting on *Braine* gave *82* an opportunity to show the world that even small, lowly, flat-bottomed amphibious gunboats could have truly professional sailors. Bob Wolfe, *82* seaman: "When we were moored alongside the *Braine*, Chief

Kostyk was over there taking charge, giving orders, getting things organized and everything. I can still hear him barking, 'Get your hands out of your asses! Where the hell's your damage control and fire control at? Grab the hoses and get on those fires!'

"Those sailors were scared before the Chief got there, but they were now in awe of him. And their captain, on his bullhorn, hollered over to the *82*, 'Where the hell'd you get a man like that aboard that damn ship?'

"Our captain shouted back, 'It's a damn good thing for you we've got men like that on this ship.'

"'I guess you're right captain.'"[38]

The arrival of enemy planes in the area forced *Anthony* to get underway to challenge them. LCSs *13* and *123*, now also alongside *Braine*, joined in the fire-fighting with *82* and *86*. The *86* put out *Braine*'s fires forward and in her

LCS 86 alongside Braine *fighting and putting out her fires after the destroyer had stopped her wild circling. Courtesy of William Mason.*

magazines. The other LCSs' fire-fighting teams put out fires in different areas and compartments on the ship.

Although their crew gave it little thought at the time, *86* was in great danger alongside *Braine* because she was tied up next to an ammunition magazine which contained a vault filled with gunpowder that could have blown sky high at any time. Heavy seas pounded *Braine* and the rescue ships. The *86* had her starboard side and one of her 20mm guns damaged.

The four LCSs alongside *Braine* fought her fires for two hours until all of them were out. Then they transferred the wounded to *Anthony*, which took *Braine* in tow. *Braine*'s losses were 67 killed and 103 wounded. These were heavier casualties than those for any other destroyer in the war that wasn't sunk.

In his Action Report for the *Braine* for May 27, 1945, Captain W. W. Fitts made this statement: "Great credit is due the LCSs *123, 86, 82,* and *13* for their splendid work in fighting fires and aiding the wounded."[39]

Station #15 was again the scene of a heavy and determined attack early in the morning of May 28 while the eighth kamikaze raid was in progress. Ships on the station were *Drexler* (DD *741*), *Lowry* (DD *770*), and LCSs *55* and *56*. Just as the attack began, LCS *114* joined the group. Even though the CAP was very active against the enemy planes, *Drexler* was severely crashed by two kamikaze planes in rapid succession. This caused a tremendous explosion, and the ship sank within three minutes. All that remained on the surface were two large oil fires and many of *Drexler*'s crew struggling in the water.

LCSs *55, 56,* and *114* picked up survivors from *Drexler*'s crew, and gave medical attention to the wounded. All hands on the three LCSs worked hard to get the survivors aboard; three *114* men dove over the side to rescue drowning men. All of this took place while all station ships were under continuous air attack. The planes that hit *Drexler* were fast bombers with speeds as high as 350-400 knots in their glide dives. Two of the planes had bomb loads totaling 2,000 pounds with two 500-pound bombs apiece, one under each wing.

In his action report dated 26 June 1945, Commander R. L. Wilson, *Drexler* captain, said: "It is also desired to commend the 'small boys' for their excellent job of recovering survivors. LCS(L) *114,* which arrived during the engagement, picked up about 150 survivors. The other survivors were recovered by LCS(L)s *55* and *56*."[40]

On May 29, the Commander of the Fifth Amphibious Force sent this message to ships under his command: "During the recent attacks this force has again demonstrated its alertness and efficiency by knocking down the majority of Jap planes sent against it. The total for the past two days is now more than 115. Again the pickets, Mighty Midgets, and screen [the ring of anti-aircraft ships stationed closer to Okinawa] have borne the brunt of the attack, and by their sharp shooting and intestinal fortitude have added to the already glorious traditions of the Okinawa campaign. You are licking the Japs and they know it. A hearty Well Done to all hands."

On May 27, LCS *111* went alongside PC *1603* (patrol craft) that had just been hit by two suicide planes. The *111* crew pumped out seven feet of water from *1603*'s engine room and two feet from other spaces so the PC could be towed. The *111* shot down an enemy plane off its port quarter on May 28. On June 6 she entered LSD *Four* for repairs to her screws damaged on coral reefs.

Up until the end of May, LCS *119* had been a lucky ship. She had seen action on the picket lines without damage and avoided serious trouble. On May 21 she was attacked by three enemy planes while returning from duty. One of the planes dove down and strafed her. But in its dive it narrowly missed hitting the ship's bow and crashed into the ocean just a few feet away. Flaming gasoline from the plane set *119* on fire, but this was quickly put out by a damage control party. The two other enemy planes withdrew from attacking and moved off.

On May 28, while *119* was on anti-skunk patrol off Hagushi, her luck changed. Around midnight she was attacked by two enemy planes. She shot down the first. The second circled *119* and crashed right into the engine room areas, spreading fire over the ship and causing ammunition boxes to explode.

Two men, Francis Morgan and Lyle Hayes, were trapped in *119*'s engine room. Both were injured and Hayes couldn't walk. The ladder leading to the only hatch was inaccessible and the men were surrounded by burning fuel. Even though sorely wounded, Morgan carried Hayes through a bomb hole in the overhead, the only outlet in the room. Lieutenant Emil Saroch, the captain, rescued a wounded man from the aft 40mm director's stand, even though the stand was on fire and the ladder to the stand blown away.[41]

'Abandon ship' was ordered. The wounded were the first to go into the life rafts. One officer dove over the side to save a drowning man, and another crewman dove in to rescue a badly burned mate. Because there was no main water pressure, however, and all the pumps were damaged, the crew was unable to control the fire. The *119*'s losses were 10 killed and 18 seriously wounded. The remaining crew worked diligently to care for the wounded and put out the fire.

A salvage tug came alongside to fight the fire and take some of the men off the burning ship. In the meantime LCS *67* came alongside and removed the dead and treated the wounded and pumped out the engine room and other flooded area. The *67* then towed her stricken sister ship back to port.

LCS gunners at Okinawa sometimes found themselves staring at Japanese planes diving at them or cruising uncomfortably close by them when they were unable to fire even a few shells or bullets in their defense. A *93* gunner, Jim Nettles: "I was attempting to unjam the magazine [of my 20mm gun] when the enemy plane appeared and began strafing us. I could see the flashes on the guns from the leading edge of his wing. My mouth dropped open and I stood there as the number two 40mm swung into action. The gun crew managed to get off just eight rounds before the aircraft exploded.

"As I stood there transfixed, I could see the shells exploding against the plane and when the explosion occurred I was knocked off my feet by the force of the concussion. Although the aircraft missed us by only about 20 feet and the explosion covered the ship with shrapnel and debris, not one crewman was injured. I think that downing an aircraft with only 8 rounds is remarkable and quite possibly some kind of record. At the time I was 16 years old and had no conception of the real magnitude of the battle of Okinawa."[42] The concussion Nettles describes did split the seams open in *93*'s steering engine room, which were repaired in drydock.

George Sims, *111* gunner, reacted somewhat differently in a similar situation: The *111* was "laying a smoke screen. A Jap plane cruising just above the water flew by within 50 feet of our ship. I could see the pilot with the cockpit open and his scarf waving; [the officer on watch] told me not to fire [the rifle I was standing watch with]. About that time one of the cooks, Fred Fagy, came by with a bucket of potatoes, and the same plane cruised by again, and the pilot looked at us as if nothing was going on; [then] we saw the plane turning and coming back.

"I remember telling Fred that before he was out of gas that bastard is going to take us, and sure enough here he comes again. The plane was so low that he was at our level and even closer. I got one of Fred's potatoes before the plane got there, and threw it a good bit ahead of the plane, and I remember saying, 'Take that, you tow-headed s.o.b, and Fred was just standing there wide-eyed. I heard the potato hit, I don't know what it hit, but the plane flew in a straight line across the bay into a hill and exploded."[43]

On May 28, LCSs *34* and *35* were assigned to provide a screen against enemy planes and suicide boats and swimmers for PGM *17* beached on a reef in a channel at Uten Ko off the coast of Kouri Shima on the northeast side of Okinawa. This assignment continued until June 3. On May 28 LCS *63* destroyed a suicide boat, and the next day they rescued Captain K. L. Revisser, USMC, whose plane was shot down.

May 30 saw the arrival of 4 LCSs—*70, 71, 97,* and *99*. These four ships were the first from Flotilla Five to join their sister ships in the battle for Okinawa, which was still underway.

On June 1 Lieutenant Commander Byron D. Voegelin, Commander of LCS(L) Group Twelve, in LC(FF) *786,* led LCSs *61, 62, 65, 81,* and *90* into Buckner Bay where they protected large ships against attack by suicide boats and swimmers until June 14th. On June 5 LCS *61* and LC(FF) *786* landed a party on a small island in the bay to search for a Piper Cub pilot. The party was fired on but continued their search until dark.

LCS *62* discovered on June 6 a number of suicide swimmers in a bay at Okinawa and in an hour-long running engagement killed all of them and sank their boat. Over a three-night period (June 6-8), LCS *81,* with the use of radar and alert lookouts, captured three Japanese small boats, took a total of 39 prisoners, and sank a fourth boat which tried to escape.

Working individually, LCS *82* destroyed a Japanese landing barge approximately 60 feet long off the southeast coast of Okinawa on June 5. The next day while on skunk patrol LCS *20* picked up three Japanese civilians from a small boat and turned them over for interrogation. On their way to Kerama Retto on June 8, the *82* destroyed two empty Japanese boats. A week later, while *82* was anchored off Okinawa, Japanese bombers dropped six bombs which landed just 300 yards off *82*'s bow and very close to the battleship *82* was providing smoke for.

Shortly after this, LCSs *62* and *82* strafed Japanese pillboxes, huts, and other targets ashore with 20mm and 40mm fire. On June 4, LCS *11* destroyed an enemy dugout canoe and four days later *87* destroyed a suicide boat. Throughout June LCSs made themselves useful escorting other ships to various places. On June 2, the *121* escorted a group of LSTs to Hagushi and four days later, *82* was escorting LST *849* to Kerama Retto. LCS *99* escorted an LCI to Iheya Shima on

June 8. On the 16th, LCS *14* escorted an LST from Aguna Shima. As late as June 30, the *117* and *118* escorted AOG 25 into Buckner Bay.

On June 3, six LCSs supported landings on Iheya Shima under Commander LCS Group Ten, Lieutenant Commander Joe Dodson in LC(FF) *1079*: *68, 69, 91, 95, 120,* and *124*. This operation was repeated on June 9th with the same ships plus *21* on Aguna Shima. In both instances LCSs strafed the beaches with 20 and 40mm fire and bombarded them with salvos of 4.5-inch rockets. No opposition was encountered in either operation.

The two kamikaze raids on Okinawa in June (the last two raids of the campaign) came on June 3-7 and 21-22. They involved fewer enemy planes than any of the previous raids: 50 for the first and just 45 for the second; the 95 for June being just a fraction of the total numbers in the four raids in May (550) and the four in April (820).

Curiously, in early June at least not all the raiding enemy planes were intent on making suicide dives. "One night two Jap planes flew down suicide alley on an unauthorized mission of peace. Nearing Okinawa they broke in on an air-to-ground voice circuit, speaking English they'd learned in California schools, offering to give themselves up. Instructed to turn their landing lights on, they were intercepted, 'wing escorted' into Naha and taken prisoner. The suicide run was not for them—their ancestors would have to wait."[44]

In spite of this, there was activity on the picket lines in June, and it could be just as serious and devastating as before. On Station #11A on June 3 (first day of the first raid) LCSs *16* and *84* took under fire a kamikaze plane attempting to suicide *16*. The plane was splashed just 30 feet off *16*'s bow.

On Station #16A, also on June 3, *Harry E. Hubbard* (DD 748), *Knapp* (DD 653), and *Prichett* (DD 561) were serving with LCSs *63, 64, 118,* and *121*, with the LCSs in a straight column. The *121* opened fire on a low flying plane as it passed. After circling *118*'s bow, the plane flew back along the port side and was splashed by 20mm fire from *118* just 200 yards from the ship.

On Station #9 on June 6, *Claxton* (DD 571), *Stoddard* (DD 566), *Massey* (DD 778), and LCSs *12, 85, 117,* and *123* were able to fire on and splash all attacking planes before they could get into their suicide dives. In fact *117* was able to pick up a man overboard from *12* while the attacks were going on. On the next day on Station 1, *Anthony* was showered with burning gasoline. Her crew readily put the fire out, but five of their men were blown overboard. They were rescued by an LCS.

Also on June 6 on Station #16A, *118* scored hits on a plane coming down out of the clouds into a suicide dive on *Cowell* (DD *547*). The plane crashed and exploded 200 feet off the port bow of *Cowell*, which evidently never saw or fired at the plane. Although it was never acknowledged, *118* saved *Cowell* from an almost certain hit. Curiously, back on April 16 a situation almost the reverse of this one occurred. The *118* was saved by *Twiggs* (DD *591*) from a possible suicide hit. Using 5-inch fire, *Twiggs* splashed a plane that was diving on the *118*.

On June 10 the ships serving on Station #15 were *William D. Porter* (DD *579*), *Smalley* (DD *565*), *Cogswell* (DD *651*), and LCSs *18, 94, 86*, and *122*. At 0824 the ships were attacked by just one bomb-carrying plane which approached at a low angle and struck *Porter* at the waterline on the starboard side aft and exploded. While there was no evidence of fire, the ship began taking on water and the four LCSs went alongside, two to each side, and sent damage control parties aboard and began pumping water with all available equipment as fast as they could. *Porter*'s crew was also helping with the salvage work; the LCSs were furnishing air pressure and electric power.

This continued for approximately two hours when it became apparent that the pumping was of no avail, and *Porter* would probably capsize and sink shortly. At this time all *Porter*'s crew and all ship's gear and equipment that could be salvaged were taken aboard the LCSs, which now included *19*, also alongside. At 0919 the *86* crew was seriously shaken by a heavy explosion when *Porter* dropped armed depth charges. Beginning at 0925 the *Porter*'s medical officer placed his ship's 29 wounded men, including seven stretcher cases, aboard *86* where they were treated.

At 0926 it was suggested that the four LCSs, while remaining in position alongside, take *Porter* in tow. Because *Porter* was so settled in the water and obviously sinking, the idea was abandoned. At 1115 the *Porter* sank with every member of her crew on board the LCSs. *Porter* Seaman C. A. Williams describes leaving his ship: "But—our ship was sinking. The LCMs (LCSs) came alongside and we went aboard. Those guys were wonderful, giving us coffee, cigarettes and treated us for shock."[45] With approximately 125 survivors aboard, *86* cast off, cutting cut lines to *Porter*. The *122* took 99 survivors and the other ships took approximately 116 of the total crew of approximately 340.

LCSs stand off from the sinking William D. Porter *after rescuing every member of its crew. Although only three LCSs are visible here, four ships—18, 86, 94, and 122—participated in this June 10th rescue on Station 15. Courtesy of Ray Baumler.*

Porter then rolled over to starboard, down by the stern; then it sank slowly with the bow straight up, and disappeared while the hundreds of survivors on the crowded LCSs stared in disbelief.

An interesting sidelight and sequel to the *Porter* salvage and rescue story is that for 44 years, unbeknownst to each other, two men, one from *18* and one from *122,* have claimed to have been the very last man off *Porter* before she went down. Bare minutes before *Porter* sank, Edward O'Meara, on *18,* and Bob Skarin, on *122,* were directing damage control parties with pumps aboard *Porter*. They were both left behind when their damage control parties returned to their ships. O'Meara was forced to jump, against his skipper's orders, at least 10 feet down onto *18.* But Bob Skarin had to get off *Porter* onto another LCS that would put him back (on *Porter*) so *122* could then pick him up.

After meeting Skarin 44 years later at the LCS Association reunion at San Diego in 1989 and discussing all the issues involved, O'Meara admitted to the world that, for what it is worth, Skarin, and not he, was the last man off *Porter* before she sank.[46]

On the day after *Porter* sank, *122* was severely damaged on Station #15 while serving with three destroyers and LCSs *19, 86,* and *94.* Two of the planes that attacked the LCS were splashed and the third did not attack. The fourth

LCS 122 *was severely damaged on June 11 when a kamikaze plane crashed into the base of its conning tower. Note the wheel from the attacking Japanese aircraft on the deck. Courtesy of Ray Baumler.*

plane, even though hit and on fire, crashed into *122* at a crucial place, the base of the conning tower. The fuselage plunged into the radio room and caused a raging fire amidships. A bomb from the plane went right through the ship's port side but did not explode. The *122* suffered losses of 11 men killed and 29 wounded.

Although painfully wounded by shrapnel embedded in his liver, Lieutenant Richard McCool, captain of *122,* courageously rallied his men to face the seemingly impossible job of saving their ship. Under McCool's direction, the crew manned a damage control station and started rescue work. McCool went from one blazing compartment to another bringing men out trapped by flames until he was transferred to another ship as a seriously wounded stretcher case.

For this heroic action McCool was later presented the Congressional Medal of Honor by President Harry Truman.

In the meantime LCS *86* picked up 23 men blown off *122* into the water, many of them badly burned. LCSs *19* and *94* went alongside *122* to fight fires and do whatever else was needed. All hands available from these ships were assigned to fight fire on *122*. The *86* also went alongside and fought fire and cared for a large number of *122*'s wounded crew.

The *86* damage control party aboard *122* worked to salvage as much of the ship's gear and equipment as possible. The party also searched the ship for wounded and trapped men but found none living. After *19* and *94* cast off from *122*, the *86* began towing her while still alongside, but had to stop because the rough seas endangered both ships. The *86* then sent key members of her engineering department on board *122* to help get the ship underway and her electrical equipment going. The engineering party was successful and *122* returned to Hagushi anchorage under her own power.

On June 16, while LCS *14* was on skunk patrol off Naha, the destroyer *Twiggs*, serving nearby, was torpedoed by a kamikaze plane. The plane then flew back and crashed into the port side of *Twiggs* causing severe damage. Expecting to provide help, *14* crew broke out their firefighting equipment, and the ship began to move toward the stricken destroyer; since several ships were moving in, however, *14* deferred. The larger ships were also sending in motor launches to rescue survivors. Thinking that possibly they could still be of some help, *14* lowered her dinghy to rescue survivors.

Two *14* crewmen recorded the incident: "There were about seven or eight fellows hanging off the fantail [of *Twiggs*] waiting for someone to pick them up, when the ship blew sky high. The force of the explosion knocked us to the deck and when we were able to look again, all we could see was burning oil on the water. To this day I can still see those fellows hanging off the fantail. We were unable to see our dinghy anywhere."[47]

"On the fantail of the *Twiggs* we could see a sailor actually heaving men off the stern of the burning ship. Three of our men were in the dinghy and rowed towards the ship, now burning out of the control, and we were now pretty close; when, suddenly, it blew up. As we hit the deck, objects from the destroyer started to land in the water and on our ship. When we stood up after the ship exploded, all there was on the surface was a few oil fires and some floating life jackets with no one in them."[48] Happily the dinghy and the three men were returned the next morning. The dinghy had just picked up three survivors when a motor launch rescued all of them as well as the dinghy just before *Twiggs* blew up.

In mid-June a Flot Five LCS did at Okinawa what her sister ships were doing in the Philippines and Borneo, and would be doing in farflung areas after VJ Day—destroyed mines cut loose by minesweepers, using rifles as well as ship's guns. Working with minesweepers between Okinawa and Formosa, LCS *99* served from June 13 to 20, destroying 10 mines on the first day. Later on in the campaign, after they arrived in early July, LCSs *105, 106,* and *107* worked with the minesweepers doing mine demolition duty off Okinawa.

On June 14, Lieutenant Commander Bryon Voegelin, Commander, LCS(L) Group Twelve, led LCSs in his group to Ie Shima, an island northwest of Okinawa where Ernie Pyle had been killed. These ships were *65-67, 89, 91, 93, 94,* and *95.* Joining them the next day were the rest of the group: *68, 69, 90,* and *92.* These ships provided anti-aircraft support and smoke screen protection for large ships anchored in the area between Ie Shima island and Nago Wan, a bay in northeastern Okinawa. While on this duty at Ie Shima, *92* picked up a pilot from a downed U.S. Black Widow. Also LCS *69* shot down an enemy plane on June 26.

During the remainder of June, individual LCSs engaged in various actions. On June 18, LCS *64* patrolled north of Ie Shima, towing a raft loaded with gasoline drums to be set afire when enemy planes came in within 15 miles, and thus be a target for suicide planes. On June 19, LCS *32* rescued a Marine pilot. Three days later, *62* splashed an enemy bomber. On that same day (June 21), LCS *54* fired on a plane attacking USS *Curtiss* in Kerama Retto. *Curtiss* was hit, and *54* made preparations to provide aid to the burning ship, but was not called.

A few days before the landing on Kure Shima on June 26, *121* landed scouts and raiders to seek ways to gain a military advantage for the landing troops. LCS *Two* participated in the Kure Shima landing. On June 30 LCS *34* took on screening duties, comparable to the duties of Group 12 in Buckner Bay. Throughout June a number of LCSs continued to serve on radar picket stations.

LCSs arrived during June to join their sister ships. On the 8th: *Three* and *98;* on the 18th: *72-74, 96, 100-102, 104, 125.* Included in these June 18 arrivals were two Flot 5 group commanders and their staffs: Lieutenant Commander R. L. Jackson, Commander Group 13 on LCS *96,* and Lieutenant Commander K. E. Curley, Commander Group 14 on *72.* For the first time in the Okinawa campaign, just about an equal number of ships left. On June 2nd: *23-25, 38-40,*

112, 113, and LC(FF) *536*; on the 7th: *111*; on the 22nd: *122*; on the 24th: *20;* and on the 25th: *22.* Most of these went to San Pedro Bay in Leyte in the Philippines for repairs, and or rest and recreation, and for preparation for the invasion of Japan.

In the fighting going on ashore Marine and Tenth Army troops made their strong push against Japanese troops in the south end of Okinawa on June 18. On June 21, organized resistance of the Japanese land forces ceased, and the Okinawa campaign was declared to be over as of July 2nd. Air raids, however, and the threat of suicide boat attacks continued throughout July, and LCSs were rendering aid to stricken destroyers as late as July 29. In fact, on June 22 the day after organized resistance ended, LCSs *34, 62, 81,* and *118* were attacked by a Betty, which was splashed by *62.* The ships were serving in box formation on Station #7 with destroyers that were five miles away.

The extent to which LCSs at Okinawa served on radar picket patrol and on anti-suicide boat and anti-aircraft patrols for April, May, and June can be illustrated by the performance of LCSs *20* and *118.* The *118* served on radar picket stations for 49 days, over half the three-month period. In addition to going to general quarters at sunrise and sunset every day on station, *118* crew manned all of their guns at general quarters 154 times, sometimes staying for hours and days at a time.

LCS *20* served for 43 days on anti-suicide boat and anti-aircraft patrol, going to general quarters 93 times, for just under 86 actual hours. The *20* made smoke to screen larger ships 18 times. In addition, *118* served on anti-suicide boat patrol for 14 nights and participated in 10 harbor anti-aircraft screens; *20* served on radar picket patrol for 32 days, going to general quarters 38 times. Other LCSs spent comparable amounts of time on these two primary patrol duties during the three month period.[49]

The versatility and adaptability demonstrated by LCS crews in meeting the new challenges encountered at Okinawa did not go unnoticed. In his Group Action Report, Lieutenant Commander Clifford Montgomery summed up the achievements through June of the 12 ships in his Group Eleven of Flotilla Four: "26 enemy aircraft destroyed, with credits for 17 'assists' and 1 'probable'; 4 suicide boats sunk and 13 boats and barges destroyed; 41 enemy personnel and civilians captured; 8 ships assisted by firefighting and salvage operations [6 destroyers, 1 destroyer minelayer, and 1 LCS]; 817 officers and men rescued from the water and from stricken ships. It is confidently believed that no other type of ship now in existence could have performed so well the combination of services listed in the above tabulation."[50]

That the troops ashore at Okinawa were aware of, and grateful to, the crews of naval vessels that bombarded beach targets incessantly, supported with gunfire their advancing units, and protected them from hordes of kamikaze planes on the picket lines is evident in this dispatch from the Headquarters, XLV Army Corps on June 20 to All Ships Present: "All of us on the beach have enjoyed working with you and hope to do so again. Best testimony to your work [is found] in statements made by POWs. You have given everything we have asked for and more besides. We assure you that the doughboys have appreciated your help. Our entire gang extends to you our thanks."

As in June, LCSs continued to arrive during July to join their sister ships in the battle for Okinawa, which was not entirely over, especially in the anchorages and water areas around the island. On July 2, seven ships arrived: *76, 103, 105, 107, 126, 128,* and *130*—the highest numbered LCS. Included in these arrivals was Captain J. M. McIsaac, Commander of Flotilla Five and his staff on LCS *126*. Twelve days later (on July 14) the last group of LCSs reported for duty at Okinawa: *75, 77, 78, 106, 108,* and *129*. Arriving on *108* was Lieutenant H. Heine, Commander Group 15 and his staff.

Because resistance by the Japanese on land ended June 21, however, and the Japanese were no longer sending raids of large numbers of planes over Okinawa, almost all the LCSs that had come in April and May had left for the Philippines by July 22. While there, their crews would enjoy hard-earned rest and recreation and begin long and involved preparations for the invasion of Japan scheduled for November. The ships that came in June and early July took over the duties of the departed LCSs and even acquired a few new responsibilities in the process.

Japanese planes were still frequently (almost daily by some accounts) harassing U.S. ships at Okinawa in July. The *86* narrowly missed by just a few feet a hit by a diving plane, while making smoke early in the month. At the same time, *86* reported many enemy planes just 50 to 100 feet directly overhead.

Early in July, LCSs *73, 103,* and *104* were dispatched to Komala Shima off Okinawa because Japanese had been seen swimming to it. On arriving at the island, the ships fired a barrage of shells and rockets into the area where the swimmers had been spotted. Around the same time, the *104* crew was surprised by an unmarked Japanese plane flying low over them in foul weather right after a storm. The plane then changed directions and crashed into the bow turret of a nearby destroyer.

On July 8, LCS 65 picked up two Japanese suicide swimmers who were believed to be planting explosives. They were spotted hiding under crates floating out to sea against the tide. They asked to be shot, but were taken prisoner instead.

Evidently there was still congestion in the anchorages at Okinawa on July 9 when LCS 67 was struck in the fantail and had her anchor cable parted by the freighter SS Ole Rolvaag.

Three days later, 67 reported with LCS 95 for anti-aircraft and anti-skunk patrol and smoke screening duty in Nago Wan, where her sister ships had earlier seen extensive service. On July 1, LC(FF) 368, with Lieutenant Commander K. E. Curley, Commander of Group 14, aboard, and LCSs 2, 70, and 72 delivered eight natives, whose actions were suspicious, to the military government ashore. These men were in a boat near Komala Shima. LCS 78, which arrived at Okinawa on July 14, immediately relieved 95 as Port Director for Nago Wan and Senior Officer Present Afloat representative for that area. The 78 reported that air raids occurred nightly while on that duty.

On July 15, LCS 105 escorted a geographic survey ship to several small islands southeast of Okinawa. The next day LCS 72 was designated standby rescue vessel and anti-aircraft screen for two LSTs aground near the harbor entrance. LCSs 70-74 lent assistance with pumping equipment and other aid on July 21 to APA 200, severely damaged by an underwater explosion. After providing aid for a period of time, the five aiding LCSs were relieved by LCSs 102-104, 106 and 107.

On July 30, LCSs 71, 102, and 105 conducted a search for a downed pilot. They were unsuccessful even though 102, with the aid of a small boat, continued the search into the next day. LCSs 106 and 107 went on July 29 to a screening station to search for a man in the water but without success. At the same time, LCS 70 carried casualties from USS Hamul (AD 20) to medical facilities ashore.

On July 29 on Picket Station #9A, LCSs 125, 129, and 130 were on patrol with Cassin Young, Pritchett, and Callaghan. Callaghan (DD 792) had seen much action and had served at Okinawa since Palm Sunday, a week before the invasion. Ironically, she was scheduled to leave for the States at 0130 the next day. At 0042 she was hit by a kamikaze in her No. 3 upper ammunition handling room. After four minutes, this room exploded and then a bomb from the plane exploded in the engine room. After the first explosion the ship began to sink, ammunition began exploding, and fire swept throughout the ship. At 0253 *Callaghan* sank.

LCSs *125, 129,* and *130* went to *Callaghan*'s aid. Although under fire part of the time, the three ships rescued well over 180 crew members from the ship and the surrounding water. Parties from *125* and *130* fought and put out *Callaghan*'s fires. The *129* offered to fight fire but was not needed. All these ships provided care for the wounded *Callaghan* survivors; they transferred severe cases to a hospital ship at Okinawa.

The *125* did such a thorough job of rendering aid to *Callaghan* that Captain Chester C. Wood, Commander of Destroyer Squadron 64, was moved in a Flotilla Five Action Report to make this comment: "Here is another worthy chapter to be added to the splendid story of the gallant picket support craft. As has happened before, the Commanding Officer, LCS(L)(3) *125*, did everything correctly and left nothing undone."[51]

When *Callaghan* sank, her depth charges went off and shook *130* violently. The *130* tore a hole in her bow from scraping against the submerged stern of *Callaghan.* For his ship's action with *Callaghan*, Lieutenant William H. File, *130* captain, received the Silver Star medal, which was presented by Captain J. M. McIsaac, Commander of LCS Flotilla Five. Lieutenant Brennan, *129* captain, received the Bronze Star for *129*'s part in the rescue.

It is highly appropriate that two of the last LCSs to give aid to another ship at Okinawa should be *129* and *130,* the two highest numbered LCSs. Early in August, the *130* crew demonstrated ingenuity and resourcefulness. They beached their ship, dug out from under their bow, and repaired the hole in their hull.

In summary, during the month of July at Okinawa, Group 14 ships of Flotilla Five (*70-75, 102-107*) provided anti-aircraft screens for larger ships in Buckner Bay; smoke coverage as needed by larger ships; escort duty for ships to Ie Shima, Kimmu Wan, and Hagushi; patrols against suicide boats and floating objects; and net control of a voice circuit for all small craft (a total of 4,000 messages sent). Ships in the group also maintained a schedule of service at harbor entrance control posts.[52]

On August 7 all available Group 14 LCSs at Okinawa were sent to a merchant ship in the anchorage to assist in putting out a fire. Five days later on August 12, LCS *75* assisted the battleship *Pennsylvania*, hit by a torpedo from a Japanese plane. Everett Taber, crew member on the nearby *106*, describes the incident: "We were in position to smoke for the battleship *Pennsylvania*. About suppertime a plane flying about 200 feet above the beach was slowly circling around; one of us on the conning tower said, 'isn't that a Jap Betty?' The plane flew over our heads and dropped a torpedo into the amidships of the *Pennsylvania*. They pumped water all night—the fire ships and other water pumping vessels. We left early the next morning for the Philippines."[53]

At least three of the Flotilla Five LCSs to arrive at Okinawa in June and July—*4, 77,* and *78*—remained there serving different duty assignments until the middle of November. After August 10 the *78* was assigned briefly to serve with the Commander of Amphibious Forces, Group 7, and tour the islands in the area. While serving on radar picket patrol in August, *78* was credited with splashing three enemy planes. LCS *Four* served for a period on secondary harbor entrance control at Buckner Bay. LCSs *77* and *78* rode out two typhoons at Okinawa on September 16 and October 9.

A *78* crewman described the October 9 storm which was especially severe: "Reputed to be the worst in the history of Okinawa, it brought with it a wind velocity of 130 knots causing untold devastation and destruction to both men and ships. A ceaseless, untiring effort on the part of the entire crew of *78* enabled her to ride out the storm with LCS *77* moored alongside, both ships entirely dependent on the anchor cable holding *78* to a mooring buoy. The turbulent waters had previously carried away the dolphin to which the ships had been moored by the bow. In a short period of time, the [area used as a] typhoon refuge of Unten Ko was littered with PCs, SCs, and numerous types of small craft being tossed about by the relentless waves. One LCS went aground; another was thrown up on the beach; everywhere in the haven ships were forced to get underway. Through it all, *78* held fast. When the storm had subsided, an inspection of the cable revealed that all but three strands had broken during the night."[54]

LCS crews met the new challenges they encountered at Okinawa head-on with a number of achievements. Since these achievements have been described in detail above, only two of the crews' more remarkable ones will be mentioned here by way of summary.

LCS crews rescued at least 2,635 men from the water and from the sinking ships out on the bloody picket stations off Okinawa. LCS crews cared for and treated literally hundreds (the exact figure will never be known) of wounded and dying men from 21 stricken ships. Since only one LCS in 12 carried a medical officer and none of the ships had sick bays or even first aid compartments, their contributions were remarkable. LCSs converted their mess halls into emergency rooms and even temporary surgeries in which each ship's single pharmacist's mate worked, sometimes alone, but often with volunteers from the crew, to keep men alive until they could be transferred to hospital ships.

Victory at Okinawa was a giant step forward for the Allied Forces in the long battle for the Pacific in World War II. In effect they had defeated an enemy who literally fought to the last using massive suicide tactics as no other great power had done before in modern history. The Allied Forces had gained a foothold in the Japanese empire itself and had achieved a truly great victory.

The cost of this victory was high, however, especially for the naval forces. The total number of naval ships and craft damaged was 368; 32 were sunk. Naval and Marine aircraft losses numbered 763. Close to 5,000 sailors were killed and over 4,800 were wounded. The Tenth Army had 4,582 killed or missing, and the Marines just under 3,000. The Army and Marines had close to 32,000 wounded, and there were 26,090 non-combatant casualties. As historian Samuel Eliot Morison has commented: "Sobering thought as it is to record such losses, the sacrifice of these brave men is brightened by the knowledge that the capture of Okinawa helped to bring Japanese leaders face to face with the inevitable, and that their surrender in August saved many thousand more Americans from suffering flaming death in an assault on the main islands of Japan."[55]

Naval historians writing during and since the Battle for Okinawa have confirmed that the outer protective ring of radar picket stations around the island was the primary naval battleground in the campaign. The same historians, as well as a war correspondent and commanders of relevant naval forces, have commended and recognized the achievements of the men and the ships who served on the picket stations.

Naval historian George C. Dyer has said, "The main naval struggle was between U.S. radar picket ships, their supporting small craft, and the fighter aircraft on one side and the Japanese kamikaze on the other side."[56]

Commander C. F. Chillingsworth, Jr., Commander Destroyer Division 100, said this about the picket line support ships (primarily LCSs and LSMs): "The heroism, skill and performance of these small ships with a record of big achievements is not only inspiring to those who witnessed their daily deeds of courage, 'guts,' and efficiency, but is writing a chapter of heroism unexcelled in naval history."[57]

Naval historian Samuel Eliot Morison, who was exposed to kamikaze attack at Okinawa, has written: "Radar picket stations were the premier posts of danger in the Okinawa operation. Destroyers and other vessels assigned to this duty suffered tremendous losses, and protected other ships around Okinawa from sustaining even greater losses. By giving early warning of approaching kamikaze attacks, vectoring out CAP to intercept, and most of all by bearing the brunt of these attacks, the pickets gave the finest kind of self-sacrificing service."[58]

"Few missiles or weapons have ever spread such flaming terror, such scorching burns, such searing death, as did the kamikaze in his self-destroying onslaughts on the radar picket ships. And naval history has few parallels to the sustained courage, resourcefulness and fighting spirit that the crews of these vessels displayed day after day after day in the battle for Okinawa."[59]

Admiral Richmond Kelly Turner, commander of Pacific amphibious forces and head of Okinawa expeditionary forces, has written: "By their steadfast courage and magnificent performance of duty in a nerve wracking job under morale shattering conditions, the crews of the ships and craft in the Radar Picket Stations emblazoned a glorious new chapter in naval tradition."[60]

W. H. Lawrence, *New York Times* correspondent serving at Okinawa at the time, has written: "It is no exaggeration to say that these little [radar picket] ships performed a major role in our great victory at Okinawa."[61]

Military historian Hanson W. Baldwin, who has called the battle for Okinawa "The Greatest Sea-Air Battle in History," has this to say about the scope of the battle and the parts played by radar picket ships: "In size, scope and ferocity it dwarfed the Battle of Britain. Never before has there been such a vicious sprawling struggle of planes against planes, of ships against planes. Never before in so short a space had the Navy lost so many; never before in land fighting had so much American blood been shed in so short a time in so small an area.

"The fleet that came to stay, and made Okinawa's conquest possible, gave far more than it received. The simple accolade applied to the brave men of the little ships—they stuck it out with determined valor, is equally applicable to all those at Okinawa, dead and living, who stood, fought, and endured in that greatest battle of U.S. arms. But to the small boys, the spitkits, the tin cans, the little ships of the radar picket line, belongs a special glory. They bore the overwhelming share of death and destruction, they were the thin and bloodstained line that stood between the Sons of Heaven and the domination of the East China Sea."[62]

Endnotes

[1] Sources for factual information: S. E. Morison, *U.S. Naval Operations in World War II*, Vol. 14 (Boston: Little Brown, 1960), 233-282; War History of Flotilla Four; A Factual History of Flotilla Three; individual ship histories, action reports, personal accounts. Source of the chapter title is statement by Morison, 179, quoted in Chapter 9.

[2] Powell Pierpoint, "The History of the War Cruise of LCS(L) *61*," 6.

[3] William Sholin, *The Sacrificial Lambs* (Bonney Lake, Washington: Mountain View Books, 1989), 164.

[4] Arnold Lott, *Brave Ship, Brave Men* (Annapolis: Naval Institute Press, 1964), 194. In Lott's account the rescue ship is *83*; however J. M. Faddis, *83* captain, informed me that Lott is incorrect and *14* was the first rescue ship to aid the *Ward*.

[5] LCS(L) *1-130*, Association Newsletter, Vol. 1, May 1988, 6.

[6] *LCS(L) 14, One of the Mighty Midgets*, 131 pp., n.d., 57.

[7] Letter sent via the Commander, Task Group 51.5, dated May 9, 1945.

[8] *Boston to Jacksonville*, 88.

[9] Ibid.

[10] Ibid., 89.

[11] Sholin, 223.

[12] Walter Karig, *Battle Report—Victory in the Pacific* (New York: Rinehart and Company, 1949), 420.

[13] "Kamikaze, the Battle for Okinawa—Big War of the Little Ships," May 16, 1988, 14.

[14] Ibid., 14-15.

[15] Marvin Peterson, letter to author, undated.

[16] Untitled account of LCS *52* action at Okinawa, 1.

[17] "History of the LCS *88* with Emphasis on May 11, 1945," 5.

[18] Ibid., 6.

[19] "USS LCS(L) 31," 3-4.

[20] Ibid., 4-5.

[21] Rooney, *Mighty Midget—USS LCS 82*, 101.

[22] Ibid.

[23] Ibid., 100.

[24] Ibid., 99.

[25] Ibid., 102; and John H. Coogan, Jr., "The History of the USS LCS(L)(3)*84*," 11.

[26] War Service notebook by Anthony Roth, *83* engineer officer.

[27] Ibid.

[28] Roth notebook, entry for 5/11/45; and Daniel Lewis, letter to author, July 8, 1994.

[29] Arnold Nitz, letter to author, July 6, 1994.

[30] LCS(L)(3) Group II Action Report, 7/30/45, Enclosure (A), 7.

---

[31] John Prunty, "A Tribute to Ellwin W. Darling," 5/19/83, sent with letter to author, Feb. 3, 1994.

[32] To CTU 52.9.1; 52.9.2; and CTG 54 from CTG 51.

[33] "A Coffin near the Graveyard," by Richard Lewis.

[34] Action Report, USS LCS(L)(3) *85* for May 23-25, 1945, Part VIII, 5.

[35] Untitled account of LCS *52* actions; see n. 16, 1 and 2.

[36] Ibid., 2.

[37] Rooney, *Mighty Midget*, 125-126.

[38] Ibid., 127.

[39] William J. Mason, *USS LCS(L)(3) 86—'The Mighty Midget'* (San Francisco: 1992), 146.

[40] Action Report involving the loss of USS *Drexler*, 7 and 8.

[41] James A. Downes, "Mighty Midgets," 7/21/45, 4-5.

[42] James A. Nettles, letter to author, undated.

[43] George W. Sims, letter to author, undated.

[44] Rooney, *Mighty Midget*, 130.

[45] Sholin, 220.

[46] Edward (Vince) O'Meara, letter to author, April 22, 1992.

[47] Eugene W. Scott, "Experiences of a Sailor in World War II and the Korean War," 19.

[48] Frank Korany, *LCS 14—One of the Mighty Midgets*, undated, 70.

[49] "Skunk Patrol & Air Attacks—Record of General Quarters," handwritten list; Earl Blanton, *Boston to Jacksonville*, 136.

[50] LCS(L)(3) Group II Action Report, July 20, 1945, Enclosure (A), 6.

[51] Captain Chester C. Wood, ComDesRon 64, endorsing Flotilla 5 Action Report, Dated July 29, 1945.

[52] Commander LCS(L)(3) Group 14, War Diary, July 10, 1945, 4.

[53] "Memories of Navy Time—April 1944 till July 1946," 4.

[54] "LCS *78* Birthday Booklet," published by *78* crew staff, n.d., 2.

[55] Morison, 282.

[56] *The Amphibians Came to Conquer*, Vol. 2, 1034.

[57] Raymond A. Baumler, *Ten Thousand Men and One Hundred Thirty 'Mighty Midget' Ships* (Rockville, MD: 1991), 60.

[58] Morison, 235.

[59] Morison, 239.

[60] COMPHIBPAC Okinawa Report, Par. II, 18, in Dyer, Vol. 2, 1103.

[61] *New York Times*, July 9, 1945.

[62] "The Greatest Sea-Air Battle in History," *New York Times Magazine*, March 26, 1950, 68.

Chapter 11

Rest, Rehabilitation, and Preparation in the Philippines

As early as July 5 Flotilla One LCSs that had served in the Philippines and Borneo campaigns began arriving at Subic Bay in Luzon. Arriving on LC(FF) *778* with several of the ships on July 7 was Captain Rae E. Arison, Commander of LCS(L) Flotilla One, who as Commander Task Force Group 76.25, organized a close support training program for the LCS crews who would train newly arrived Army personnel from Europe and the United States for the invasion and assault of mainland Japan, tentatively scheduled for November.

Since, however, this training program did not begin until the latter part of July, ships' crews that arrived early in the month were allowed to go ashore in the bay area and to make liberty trips to Manila. On his first time ashore since May 1, Raymond Ross, *60* electrician, learned first-hand from a native former soldier how the Japanese invaders treated the natives. The former soldier, who escaped from the Japanese prison and was now a guerrilla, made his strong feelings known: "The U.S. is too easy with the Japs. They feed them, clothe them and give them cigarettes while we in the front lines were almost starving. People stateside don't know and realize how the Japs treated us, the Jap bastards."

Ross asked, "Did you take Jap prisoners?" A definite NO was the reply, and the native continued, "One former Filipino soldier had formerly worked on a rice farm and had a large family who worked the farm. Now, after four years, he was living in a humble shack with his family, his wife had died. All of his possessions were gone. The Japs had driven off his livestock [pigs and chickens], taken the grain and farm equipment, furniture and household effects, and burned the buildings, for they were 'headquarters for guerrillas.' All machinery and metal was gathered and sent to Japan, even to the extent of rusty nails and sheet metal.

"During the occupation, the Filipinos were paid 75 cents a day for labor, then had to pay 20 pesos for a pack of cigarettes, 15 pesos for a box of matches; any canned food was prohibitive in price. If the Japs found any meager rations

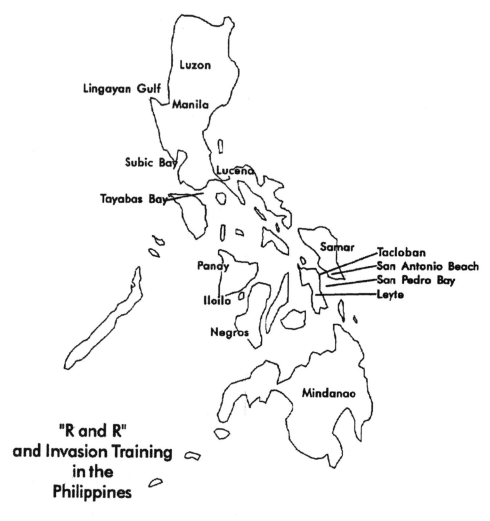

"R and R"
and Invasion Training
in the
Philippines

Flot One Ships at Subic Bay
Flots Three, Four and Five
at San Pedro Bay

on their many inspection tours, the natives would have to give them up or be shot right there. All Filipinos had to bow on sighting a Jap, for failure to do so was cause for a severe beating. About 2,000 civilians were killed in Manila when the Japs tried to make Filipinos wipe their feet on a large U.S. flag flown over main street of Manila and torn down by the invaders."[1]

Later in July Ross enjoyed liberty in Manila: "I walked about the rubble of Manila through the Chinese quarter then back again to the Red Cross Service

Center. Shops were opening daily, offering everything from used nails to Cracanoles and beauty treatment. One is still cautioned not to eat or drink except at supervised and inspected places. The city is very dirty with mud, debris, and human filth. U.S. Army engineers are doing an excellent job in sanitation though."

Ross and several friends sought out night-time entertainment: My friends and I "lit out after chow for the 'night life of Manila'. We stopped at the Reliable Bar—piano and violin music by two Chinamen under torch lights and Coleman lanterns. Had a few drinks at 1 peso and proceeded to the Victory Club Bar where we had a hilarious time after eight pints of whiskey were broke out on the table. The orchestra was very good. The singer was good, too, and sang 'You are My Sunshine' for us. At 2300 we marched off down the middle of the street singing 'I Don't Know Why She's Worth It' while it rained hard." In his diary entry for July 22, Ross has this "Manila girl with 7 live ducks on her head. Moral: good idea for Naval U.S. Headdress."[2]

While returning to Subic Bay over the relatively short distance from Manila, LCS *60,* Ross's ship, encountered very rough seas. All their unlashed gear on deck was washed overboard, including all their silverware.

Most of the LCSs at Subic Bay in July and August participated in the close support training program for the invasion of Japan that their Flotilla commander organized. This program made use of islands and shore areas where invasion maneuvers could be practiced and landing troops be trained. LCSs were assigned to practice in different areas: *28, 29, 45,* and *46* in Lingayen Gulf; *42* in Tayabas Bay in Luzon; *43, 44,* and *60* at Balayan Bay (which was said to be very similar to Tokyo Bay) and later at Lucena; *27* and *47* at Iloilo, Panay, and later, Negros. The other LCSs at Subic did practice training at different places in the Subic Bay area and participated in extensive anti-aircraft firing practice at sea.

L. E. Guillot, *27* officer, provided details: "Our flotilla was spread out over several islands, including Panay and Negros, to practice landings with Army divisions that had just been sent from the States or from Europe. The one we were to work with was from Europe, and their morale was quite low. Our destination was the Japanese mainland, and our particular island was Honshu which contained Tokyo, Osaka, Hiroshima, etc. The landing was set for the middle of September and we would probably be working with minesweepers and underwater demolition people for two or three weeks before the landing."[3]

The close support training program continued until after the Japanese surrender announcement on August 15. At that time the LCS crews in the Subic

Bay were expressing a great sigh of relief that the invasion of Japan would not take place.

While his ship was doing training exercises at Iloilo, Lieutenant(j.g.) Guillot discovered that that little town must have been one of the older Spanish settlements in Luzon because it had a number of the original colonial Spanish buildings as well as many very light complexioned people, including some who were blond. Later on the island of Negros Guillot took crew members from the *27* ashore for sightseeing, beer, and baseball, and for what turned out to be a taste of genuine Filipino hospitality:

> A very large Filipino came up to us and introduced himself and said he was the mayor of that particular village and wanted to know if we would all come to his house for barbecued pig.
>
> The Mayor's house was a two-story job that was about sixty feet square. No window and no screens—just a roof with a few inside partitions. He told me all of the people present were his relatives. Three generations. They were drinking rice wine they called 'tuba'. They suggested we would like it better if we mixed it with our cool beer. It was an experience. His 'relatives' decided just before dark (they had no electricity) that it was time to catch a pig for roasting. That was a floor show. The squealing pig would come running around the house with a bunch of Filipinos follow-ing. Our crew members were cheering everyone—pig and all. It tasted very good, but I am sure the meal back on the ship was better. They later rowed us back to the ship in long outriggers. I told the men to be prepared for their return the next day because there was no such thing as a 'free lunch.' The outriggers returned and we were ready for them. They wanted the works but mostly school supplies. We gave them what we could spare, and they went off happy.[4]

Beginning in late June, LCSs from Flotillas Three and Four arrived at San Pedro Bay between Leyte and Samar in the Philippines from Okinawa where they had been in intensive combat with kamikaze planes and boats for three months since April 1. This was happening at the same time that Flotilla One LCSs were arriving in the Subic Bay area to train troops for the invasion of Japan and to enjoy liberty ashore and in Manila.

Most of the ships that served in Okinawa in April, May, and June arrived at Leyte in groups of various sizes. A Flotilla Three group of 12 ships arrived on June 29, another Flotilla Three group on July 10; parts of two Flotilla Four groups

After arduous duty at Okinawa a fleet of LCSs moves south on the placid, lake-like Pacific Ocean to the Philippines for rest and recreation. Courtesy of Earl Blanton.

(19 ships) arrived on July 14, and another Four group on July 26. My ship, the *85*, was in the group of 19 ships made up from Flotilla Four; directing the movement was Captain Neill Phillips, Flotilla Four Commander. By the end of July, 31 Flotilla Four ships and 26 Flotilla Three ships were anchored together in San Pedro Bay off Tacloban, Leyte. The missing Flotilla Four ships were undergoing repairs of battle damages in rear areas, and the missing Flotilla Three ships were being repaired and overhauled at Saipan and other rear area ports. Also anchored in San Pedro Bay at the time was an impressive array of capital ships—at least 10 battleships, 26 carriers, 5 cruisers, and a number of other combatant ships.

The extreme relief and welcome comfort that the quiet Leyte area afforded those of us in the LCS crews at the time is best expressed by the captain of LCS *35,* whose ship had served in Iwo Jima as well as Okinawa, and by a radioman on the *82*: "In the middle of July the *35* was sent to a rear area, Leyte, for rehabilitation and repairs. Both were very much needed. The men had not had any recreation since early in January and everyone had been under intense strain during the entire period. The number of General Quarters ran into the hundreds and no night passed without one or two. Most of the men had been sleeping in their clothes for months and there was no such thing as restful sleep. To these men can go only the highest praise for their endurance, cooperation and courage. The material condition of the ship was better than most because of an exceptionally alert and active 'black gang' [engineering department] but repairs were needed and several tons of rust required removing from several parts of the ship. Leyte which had been previously scorned for its heat and rain was a very welcome sight to all hands on July 9."[5]

"At Okinawa we had spent most of two months at general quarters, day and night. We were ragged and drawn out tight, and we badly needed rest and time away from the place. At Leyte we went on beach parties at the edge of the jungle on Samar: bologna sandwiches, green beer and 'Old Mold' cigarettes. Wow! We played ping pong and ogled the look-but-don't-touch Red Cross gals (courageous women). Leyte was far from the Waikiki Royal Hawaiian, but it was far from danger too. We relaxed and enjoyed ourselves, got some exercise and plenty of sleep, and basked in the tropical sun."[6]

Also it was at Leyte, probably at the Fleet Recreation Area on Samar across the bay, that, much to their relief, thousands of LCS sailors stepped on dry land

The fleet recreation area at San Antonio beach on Samar Island. This area was used extensively by LCS crews for recreation in the Philippines. Courtesy of Charles Thomas.

for the first time in four to five months. Land that would not rock and roll dangerously at 35 or more degrees, and toward which no kamikaze plane dived and no suicide boat charged.

Although LCSs at Leyte did not participate in close support training programs for troops in invasions, as did the Flotilla One ships at Subic, preparations by LCS crews for future hostile actions were not completely neglected. On our way to Leyte those of us in the group of 19 ships under Flotilla Four Commander Phillips held extensive drills and anti-aircraft gunnery practice every day.

All Flotilla Four ships participated in at least two full days of anti-aircraft firing practice in the first two weeks of August, and all Flotilla Three ships a comparable amount. Most of the LCSs sent crew members to gunnery schools and to classes in recognition training for identifying enemy aircraft. Even the LCSs under repair at Saipan held gunnery practices and exercised at various drills when they could do so.

Not to have at least some gunnery practice at this time would have been highly detrimental, since LCS gunnery crews arriving at Leyte were at the peak of their marksmanship ability. They had faced, and had helped to defeat, the most terrifying of weapons—the kamikaze planes. The high competence of one gunnery crew is evident from this illustration: While on gunnery practice late in the Okinawa campaign, the LCS *14* gunnery crew instantly destroyed the first drone target sent toward it by the LST conducting the practice. The LST then moved farther out from the LCS and released anther drone, which the gunnery crew destroyed in short order. Evidently this wasn't supposed to happen or hadn't happened up to that time. As a *14* crew member reported: "All the guys on our ship were falling all over each other laughing like fools. The officers on the LST were madder than hell."[7]

Flotilla Five ships that had been at Okinawa from late May through July arrived at San Pedro Bay in early August. Several Flot Five ships remained in Okinawa where they continued to serve until mid-November. They would ride out two typhoons while there, on September 16 and October 9.

A great advantage for the LCSs in the safe and quiet Philippines right after the Okinawa campaign was the opportunity to repair damaged ships and overhaul their engines, their guns, and their essential equipment, and make them fully seaworthy again. Almost every LCS at Leyte went into drydock at least once to effect serious repairs—opened seams, leaking rudder posts, leaking steering

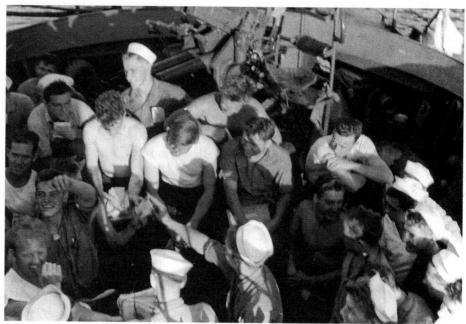

*Happy hour on an LCS anywhere west of Pearl Harbor was spelled "M A I L C A L L."
Most of the time, letters from the United States arrived weeks after they were written,
which made them all the more welcome. Courtesy of Charles Thomas.*

compartments, fouled screws and rudders—or just to scrape and paint the ship's hull. Our ship went into drydock so that our crew could scrape and paint our hull, which sorely needed a new and smooth covering. As first lieutenant I was in charge of this operation, which involved all the boatswains, coxswains, and seamen in our crew—a total of about 20 men. Although the heat and humidity was high, making hot work of our job, we were fortunate to get our ship into a floating drydock in which there was at least some slight breeze coming through the dock's open ends, rather than in a graving dock where there was no chance of a breeze at all. The facilities at Leyte provided all the LCSs their first opportunity since Pearl Harbor to get needed repairs. Every LCS took advantage of the opportunity to get ready for the impending invasion of the Japanese homeland.

The Navy provided facilities for rest and recreation for the thousands of LCS officers and men living for the first time in their lives in highly oppressive tropical heat and extremely high humidity. In addition to ping pong, "green beer," bologna sandwiches, and 'Old Mold' cigarettes, the recreation centers at San

Antonio beach and other areas offered horseshoes, basketball, volleyball, and softball. There was enough interest in softball for several ships to hold a tournament in which teams competed. At one point LCSs *61* and *86* were in the tournament playoffs. Although *86* had an enviable '7 wins-1 loss' record, *61* won in the playoffs and became the flotilla softball champion.

Many of the men who found it too hot to play ball outside took advantage of the extensive picnic facilities to eat lightly and to drink the two beers they were allowed (or many more if they could successfully pretend that their entire crew, not just 30 of them had come on liberty). Different LCSs would take turns delivering liberty parties to San Antonio Beach and in true amphibious fashion would let out their stern anchor and move right up to the pier until they touched bottom. LCTs also served as 'liberty boats'. Those of us in Flotilla Four had no way of knowing at that time that our primary occupation duty in Japan would be ferrying liberty parties from the anchored fleet of ships to Yokosuka, Yokohama, and Tokyo in Tokyo Bay. In a very crude sort of way, we were training for that duty.

Other recreational activities were swimming, until devastating dysentery appeared, movies practically every night on the ships' decks, and reading, with the Navy providing ample material.

Occasionally ships' crews would go ashore on their own, either to 'play tourist' in the nearby villages (Manila was out of reach) or to have a steak-fry or party ashore. Frank Korany, *14* crew member, has written about their crew's steak fry: "We moved the ship around the point of the gulf and pulled it within a few hundred feet of the shore and dropped anchor. The natives from the village on the shore came out in their small boats and paddled our crew, with our food and sporting equipment, ashore.

"We played baseball and started to cook our steaks. When we were ready to eat, there were so darn many kids standing around watching us that we wound up giving most of our food to them. Most of the fellows went back on the ship since it was impossible to eat anything with all of the kids. But some stayed and sat around the fire drinking beer and just shooting the bull. Later the natives paddled the crew out to our ship."[8]

With the help of all these diversions and recreational facilities, officers and men of the LCS crews were adjusting to the incessant heat and the frequent rains which kept the humidity unnaturally high and the ships' interiors damp and their decks and bulkheads wet from condensation. There was, of course, no air conditioning!

Crews of some ships were cutting their sleeves and even the tails off their shirts, and shorts (usually 'home-made') were replacing the standard issued pants. When possible, men were sleeping topside and staying out of the sun during the day. While wishing they were somewhere else, LCS crews were becoming tolerant of their enforced way of life.

What was affecting the morale of the LCS crews at Leyte as much or even more than the stultifying climate was the prospect of invading the Japanese homeland. "We rested in the languid safety of the Philippines while our Pacific Command planned the final assault against the Japanese islands. It was a grim prospect. After what we went through at Okinawa, we looked on an invasion of Japan with deep apprehension, certain it would be the kamikazes all over again, probably worse. With no Navy left, their defense was bound to have 2,000 flyable planes to smash into us. One estimate had it that half the invasion fleet would be lost or crippled. We had no reason to doubt that."[9]

According to Samuel Eliot Morison, eminent American historian who served on the USS *Tennessee*, which came under kamikaze attack at Okinawa, this figure of 2,000 flyable planes is quite low. Here is what he said: "It is simply not true that Japan had no military capability left in mid-August. Although 2,550 kamikaze planes had been expended, there were 5,350 of them still left, together with as many more ready for orthodox use, and some 7,000 under repair or in storage; and 5,000 young men were training for the Kamikaze Corps. The plan was to disperse all aircraft on small grass strips in Kyushu, Shikoku and western Honshu and in underground hangers and caves, and conserve them for kamikaze crashes on the Allied amphibious forces invading the home islands. Considering the number of planes, pilots and of potential targets, all within a short distance of principal airfields, it requires little imagination to depict the horrible losses that have been inflicted on the invading forces, even before they got ashore."[10]

On August 15 a startling announcement raised to the heavens the spirits of the LCS crews at Leyte. THE JAPANESE HAD SURRENDERED! "We received the news about 2100 and for several minutes all was quiet, then suddenly the sky was alight with hundreds of various colored flares and searchlights. Sirens wailed, whistles screeched, and bells clanged. Firefighting ships shot streams of water in the air, and with searchlights shining in the streams and flares giving color to them, a stunning effect was produced. It was all very beautiful and touching.

Some men were very quiet, some went wild, and some fell to their knees and gave thanks to God for victory. It was a night that will never be forgotten by any of us."[11]

According to the captain of LCS *82*, "The excitement was so severe as to require the prescription of medical brandy to all hands. The relief from the prospect of invading the Japanese main islands was tremendous."[12]

W. H. Stanley, *21* crew member, has given his personal reaction: "We couldn't believe it. I felt like a thousand pounds had been lifted off me. A big celebration broke out and guns were firing, shells bursting the air. All this looked like San Pedro Bay was under heavy air attack. It reminded me of the 'Star Spangled Banner.'

> *And the rockets red glare, the bombs bursting in air,*
> *gave proof through the night that our flag was still there.*
> *O, say does that star-spangled banner yet wave*
> *o'er the land of the free and the home of the brave?"*[13]

Although we (a 'we' that included literally thousands of happy men on the many ships, large and small) were excited and even ecstatic about the wonderful news, at times the massive fireworks seemed to get out of hand. A number of us received burns on our necks and arms, but the pain faded almost instantly, and the absolute joy lived on throughout the night.

In mid-August the final group of Flotilla Five ships arrived in San Pedro Bay from Okinawa, where they had been serving from late May through July. Three of the ships would continue to serve there into November.

Although men's spirits and morale remained high the rest of their stay at Leyte, the LCS crews' material condition worsened considerably in early September when dysentery infected the men in epidemic proportions. This debilitating disease spread rapidly, seriously afflicting large numbers of men on many of the numerous ships at Leyte. "Dysentery. It ran though the huge fleet like wildfire. Twenty-five [men] on *35* were really out of action. Temperatures around 104°. A miserable illness."[14]

On my ship at least 20 men were seriously ill with it—three of them so ill that they were transferred to hospitals in the States and did not return to the ship. Several of the men spent two or three weeks on hospital ships in the area. A large number of LCSs and the other ships in the bay were affected. Swimming was prohibited and other activities curtailed. Fortunately, the number of cases began to decrease in the next two or three weeks, and most of the afflicted men returned to their ships.

After the exciting Japanese surrender announcement, there was a great deal of speculation among LCS crew members as to where the LCSs would go and what sort of duty they would have. It was thought, somewhat hopefully, that since LCSs were basically useful only in landing assaults and anti-aircraft defense, they would be sent to the States immediately for decommissioning. That they were useful in many situations, peaceful as well as hostile, and might be very useful in the occupational Navy was somehow conveniently forgotten, or at least not considered out loud.

An amusing sidelight to the rampant speculation at the time was the appearance of rhyming slogans expressing hopeful messages that became part of the sailors' language for at least the next six months:

'Back alive in '45'; 'Out of the sticks in '46'; or 'Leave these Dicks in '46'; 'Be back in heaven in '47'; 'Oh it's The Golden Gate in '48.'

Endnotes

[1] Raymond Ross, Diary, 11-12. Used with permission.

[2] Ibid., 12-13.

[3] L. E. Guillot, *How Did We Ever Win the War?* n.d., 67-68.

[4] Ibid., 68-69.

[5] "Ship's History, USS LCS(L) *35*," by Kenneth C. Huff, captain, 4-5.

[6] Rooney, *Mighty Midget—USS LCS 82*, 131-133.

[7] Korany, *LCSL 14—One of the Mighty Midgets*, n.d., 72.

[8] Ibid., 76.

[9] Rooney, 136.

[10] Samuel Eliot Morison, *Victory in the Pacific, U.S. Naval Operations in World War II*, Vol. 14 (Boston: Little Brown, 1990), 352.

[11] Maurice T. Jensen in *USS LCS(L)(3)86—The Mighty Midget*, edited and written by William J. Mason, 1992, 24.

[12] Rooney, 139.

[13] "Kamikaze, The Battle for Okinawa," 20.

[14] Kenneth Huff, "USS LCS(L) *35*—1945-46."

Chapter 12

Liberty Boats in Tokyo Bay

On September 3 LCS Flotilla Four under the command of Captain Neill Phillips departed Leyte for occupational duties in the Tokyo Bay area of Japan. Except for three ships, *88, 116, 119*, that were undergoing repairs in the States for battle damages at Okinawa, the flotilla was made up of *61-69, 81-87, 89-95, 114, 115, 117, 118,* and *120-124,* going from the tropical Philippines at approximately 11 degrees north latitude for over 2,000 miles north to Yokosuka, Japan, approximately 36 degrees north. Curiously Yokosuka, Japan's large naval base in Tokyo Bay near Yokohama and Tokyo, is at a latitude very close to that of Norfolk, Virginia, America's largest naval base.

Although our ships took on winter clothes for all hands at Leyte before departure, many of us felt the penetrating cold. "En route north from the tropics, our blood was so thinned that we virtually froze on deck during the cool nights, despite winter parkas."[1]

Since our ships would become a sort of victory parade going into Tokyo Bay, passing the battleship *Missouri* to our starboard just nine days after the surrender signing (on September 2), our flotilla commander was very much concerned about his flotilla's appearance and started making preparations a few days ahead of time:

> Our Commodore wanted a snappy looking bunch of ships to show up at Tokyo, and began inspecting the ships in formation with his binoculars. Shortly messages blinked to various LCSs calling attention to sloppy appearance, crummy paint work, sailors lounging against the lifelines. The next day, one LCS was called up to be chastised ('come within hail—have skipper on bridge').

> The Commodore spoke scathingly and at length, critically reviewing that ship's recent administrative sins (crew leaning on lifelines!) and casting aspersions on all its captain's past career—from doubtful parentage to defrauding the government by risking expensive government investments (those sailors at risk should the lifelines fail). Even the pain of that drowned

---

sailor's mother was included, and all this via the Commodore's 'Beach Master' loud speaker, audible to all ears the length of the formations. The lecture ran five minutes, remarkably free of repetitions—a credit to the Commodore's style and endurance. Glum silence as the offending LCS retreated to her normal station.

The next day the performance was repeated almost exactly—almost. It was LCS *62*'s turn; her 'skipper on bridge' was Lieutenant Pfau, a lawyer from Philadelphia, with lots of 'points' toward early release from the service. The commodore ended another magnificent monologue, setting down his loud hailer with a flourish. Pfau picked up his own, and also clearly heard by all the flapping ears in the flotilla, boomed back: "Pardon me, Commodore, I missed some of that. Would you please repeat everything after 'Son-of-a-bitch'?" The old man managed a grin at that, and we heard no more such during the trip.[2]

As our flotilla approached Japan, as long as four or five hours (at 12 knots) before we actually arrived in Tokyo Bay, we were treated to an absolutely awesome sight. Floating in the clear blue sky was an ethereal form, graceful in shape and apparently suspended in mid air. For at least two or three hours we could see nothing but distant nebulous clouds below this elegant form suspended in the blue. Then the magnitude of the immense base became apparent to us. This was the great Mount Fuji. Even the word 'magnificent' understates its effect. It is no wonder that people have worshipped it and perhaps still do.

After this unforgettably romantic spectacle, however, we were subjected to two rather harsh realities. One was that in Yokosuka we would have to find our own anchorage or mooring space in a highly congested and confused anchorage strewn with moving breakwaters and wrecked ships and craft of all kinds. As it would turn out, some of our crews found this situation, particularly the abundance of wreckages, to be highly advantageous.

The second reality was somewhat upsetting to all of us and even degrading to some. While in the Tokyo Bay area, our ships would serve as liberty boats ferrying recreation parties from the larger ships—destroyers, cruisers, carriers, battleships—into Yokosuka, Yokohama, and up the bay to Tokyo. (See "Tokyo Bay" on the Japan occupation map in Chapter 13.) Here is a comment by Earl Blanton, *118* gunner, that speaks for those of us who were upset: "We, the Mighty Midgets, had been reduced to ferry boats to haul the big-ship sailors back and forth on liberty! Why LCSs instead of true landing type amphibious ships I don't know. No question that some type of seaworthy craft was required to navigate the open choppy waters of Tokyo Bay. The main fleet was anchored well offshore, twenty to thirty miles from Yokohama and Tokyo and several miles from Yokosuka. Much too far for whaleboats or gigs heavily loaded with sailors to travel during the typhoon season. The war was over and we sure didn't need any casualties from drowning in Tokyo Bay. However, there is no reason why LCTs or LCIs could not have been used for this duty [as it turned out, LSMs and LCIs were used, but only a very few and for just a short period]."

In a letter to his father, Blanton wrote: "The *118* is a liberty boat for a floating boot camp. The last two days, we were assigned to the cruiser *Chicago*. We have to be humiliated by carrying their boys ashore. They have been out of the states since June, saw two Jap planes and shot down the Navy fighter that was on their tails. To see them and hear them you would have thought that they won the war."[3]

On at least one occasion the humiliation suffered by the crew of one LCS on liberty boat duty was quite real. The LCS *82* captain had the last word, however:

> We would receive a message the night before as to what ship to go alongside the next day. I remember the first assignment we got was a CV (aircraft carrier) with many battle stars and Jap planes to its credit. As we came alongside the top of our mast just did reach the flight deck, and with our five little Jap flags painted on our conn, we drew a large Ha! Ha! and whistles from the CV's crew. One would have thought we were in some foreign Navy. I could see our captain's face turning red.

> Well, we took their party aboard—75 or 85 men crowded onto our deck. It was about 25 miles up the bay to Tokyo. There was a chop on the bay which we headed into, and you know our main deck was just a few feet above the water. Maybe the captain figured these fellows were in a hurry to reach Tokyo, so he rang up flank speed, and of course we could pitch and roll on dry land. Before long a good number of heads were over the side or down in the head. Another time, returning from Tokyo with a party of sailors from a large ship, they were in worse shape, maybe because of drinking the Jap beer and sake, and they said "You guys didn't ride these things all the way over here across the Pacific?" We said, "Brother, we rode 'em anywhere you guys went!"[4]

In spite of this general and sometimes bitter dislike of having to ferry liberty parties from the 'Big Boys', LCS crews adjusted readily to their new world, and

LCS 115 crew members enjoy the Japanese launch they commandeered and named the "Foo Foo Maru." Here they are moving through the Yokosuka Naval Base. Courtesy of Earl Blanton.

even found some things to their liking. A number of LCSs moored to wrecked vessels in the anchorage and discovered advantages they had not contemplated. The *118* moored to a wrecked Japanese PC which was securely attached to two large mooring buoys, thus providng *118* with a firm mooring during the fairly frequent storms and typhoons. For the first time, the crew didn't have to worry about dragging or losing its anchor in rough seas and high winds. The crew was also able to use some of the PC's deck space for storage and repair facilities. They could not use the below-deck areas, however, because the PC was infested with roaches and rats. In like fashion, LCSs *82* and *83* were moored to either side of another Japanese PC, and my ship was moored alongside a Japanese gunboat.

At least two LCS crews, *115 and 118,* 'comandeered' two Japanese harbor patrol boats of about 65 feet in length and converted them into motor launches for their own liberty parties and other transportation needs. The *115* crew gave their boat a name, the 'Foo Foo Maru,' and a radio voice call by adding a '1' to their own—'Tameless 5-1'. They used it to meet the train from Tokyo on many nights in the fall of 1945. Other LCS crews 'commandeered' suicide boats for their own uses. Evidently there were a large number of these boats in fair condition, as well as a large number of one- and two-man submarines in the Yokosuka Naval complex.

Differing from the crews of the 'Big Boys' who were lucky to get ashore even once while their ship was anchored at Tokyo Bay, those of us in the LCS crews had frequent liberty in all three cities—Yokosuka, Yokohama, and Tokyo. We were also relatively free to go on 'spoils of war' scavenging trips on the large Yokosuka Naval Base and to gather such souvenirs as Jap rifles, compasses, and binoculars.

Aggressive souvenir seekers, however, found out the hard way (sometimes from inside a Marine brig) that some of these areas were restricted and were guarded by Marines. Fleet recreation facilities provided in Yokosuka for ships' crews included an enlisted men's club with beer drinking contests, among other activities, and facilities for athletic events. Here LCS crews competed in basketball with a number of teams.

Crew members on liberty found Yokohama and Tokyo almost completely demolished, but Yokosuka practically untouched by the bombers. The reason given for this was that the U.S. Forces wanted to keep Yokosuka intact for their own use during and after the invasion. Crew members on liberty found the Japanese people fearful of them at first, but thereafter respectful (actually overly so) and agreeable. They felt at ease mingling with the Japanese on the crowded streets and in busses and trains.

When I was free, I took advantage of my liberty to look around Tokyo. I saw the Emperor's palace, still completely intact, with its famous imperial carp swimming lazily in the moat. At the palace's front door was a sign: "General Officers Only" since it was General McArthur's headquarters. On another day I saw the huge building that, before the war, had been Saint Luke's Hospital. The large sign on it still bore the official name of the great future world it was to be part of had the Japanese won: "The Greater East Asia Co-Prosperity Sphere Hospital." While wandering in the city one day, I discovered down in the older part of Tokyo, several blocks from the market docks where the LCSs landed liberty parties, a large Buddhist temple which, although completely surrounded by rubble and ashes, was miraculously untouched by bombs or even incendiary fire. The temple, which had housed a Boy Scout troop and other youth groups, was even more intact than Saint Paul's Cathedral in London, which survived almost unscathed while buildings all around it where reduced to rubble by heavy bombing.

In October and November officers and men from the LCSs took excursion trips into the countryside, going to resort places such as Atami on the south coast of Honshu. More popular destinations because they were more accessible to Yokosuka were Kamakura, home of the famous 50-foot high image of Buddha, and Gotemba, a resort town at the foot of Mount Fuji. One weekend another officer and I traveled to Gotemba on a crowded and rather primitive train that wound its way through a series of hills and villages to within a clear view of the majestic mountain that we had seen from the sea.

At the small hotel where we stayed was a personable young man in his late teens or early twenties, a member of the hotelkeeper's family. After a few minutes of conversation we discovered that the young man had been a kamikaze pilot. There he was, however, alive and talking pleasantly to his would-be enemies because the date assigned for his flight to Okinawa (or other designated target area) was September 15, exactly one month after the surrender was announced. He told us that at first all kamikaze pilots were volunteers, but not long after that men were ordered into that service. He was happy the war was over and was planning to go to college. He spoke good English, but when he made this statement he gestured for emphasis, moving his hand across his eyes: "Before we were blind, but now the Japanese are able to see."

Back in Tokyo Bay LCSs were providing ferry service for parties from larger ships to the three liberty ports on the bay. In addition to the liberty parties, LCSs carried passengers, including stretcher cases, from the ships to appropriate points in the bay area for travel to the States. LCSs serving ships farthest out in the anchorage had to add two or three hours to their daily schedule to go out early, sometimes close to dawn, for pick-up and to return from delivering the men to their ships late in the evening. On a typical day at least 26 LCSs would be going to and returning from one of the three ports with parties ranging from 75 to over 100 men. LCSs in effect were serving between 2,000 and 2,600 men of the fleet each day. The number of LCSs ferrying parties each day varied somewhat because LCSs were used for other purposes.

They also served as picket boats, dispatch boats, and utility craft, carrying and distributing provisions and mail for the others LCSs. I recall our ship leaving our berth at Yokosuka at 0300 one morning to go across the bay to pick up a

A change of command ceremony on a Flot Four ship serving in Japan. This took place on the signal deck of LCS 115 at Yokosuka. Courtesy of Earl Blanton.

large load of mail and bring it back to Yokosuka. Some of the ships carried out special occupation assignments such as patrolling "inshore of anchored Japanese ships that were repatriating Japanese troops to prevent repatriates from going ashore by means other than the official repatriation route."[5] On very few days were all Flotilla Four ships ferrying liberty parties.

The many daily trips went smoothly in the mornings when the ships picked up and delivered their parties. In many instances things did not go so smoothly when the ships picked up the men for return to their ships in the afternoons or evenings. Somehow many men in the returning party would be drunk, sometimes uncontrollably so, and fights would break out on the fantail or elsewhere on the ship. Most LCS crews put up with this as best they could, but occasionally, and in some cases routinely, ships' crews would give their unruly passengers a good hosing down. Since LCSs were firefighting ships, they were well equipped to douse the drunken sailors to the tune of 1,000 gallons or more a minute.

Embarking and disembarking the liberty parties was easily handled in Yokosuka and Yokohama. Tokyo, however, was a different story. Differing from the open and accessible harbors of the other two ports, Tokyo's harbor was such a narrow, shallow, winding river that even shallow-draft LCSs turned up mud in at low tide. Formerly used for unloading market goods, the single dock where liberty parties landed was limited in length so that LCSs were forced to nest, sometimes six or more ships deep. And because LCS captains did not want to have to navigate that river over twice in the same day, the nested LCSs stayed put for liberty duration.

One afternoon at the Tokyo dock I was shocked to see the captain of the inboard ship cast off the ships outboard of his ship. Evidently he had gotten tired of waiting for them to leave. Six of them moored together moved with the strong current toward a bridge a few hundred yards ahead. Fortunately one ship was able to get its engines going to save the six ships from slamming into the bridge.

Among the numerous ships that LCSs ferried for were several British men-of-war. Our ship served the crews of three different English ships; we found them congenial and at least acceptably well behaved when they were drunk. In the process of serving them, the *82* struck up a mutually agreeable acquaintance with the crew of the light cruiser HMNZS *Achilles* from New Zealand. *Achilles* officers entertained the *82* officers with sherry and the *Achilles* men introduced *82* men to grog (rum), which they enjoyed a pint of every day. And the two crews participated in other pleasant exchanges.

John Rooney, *82* radioman, recalled taking an *Achilles* liberty party back to their ship: "We ferried one memorable *Achilles* liberty party into Tokyo. Late in the evening, we picked them up for return to their ship. Most of them were fairly topped off, and they were wild and disorderly. As we made our way across the bay, I remember one sailor slipping over the rail. All that kept him from going completely overboard was his blue serge coat, strong as iron, that had a buttonhole caught on a railing hook. He dangled senseless in the breeze for a few minutes until somebody hauled him back on deck. When we reached the *Achilles*, she lowered a cargo net onto our deck—with the smoothness of habit, it seemed—to receive her badly bent and prone revellers and hoist them safely back aboard. There were some world-class tipplers on that *Achilles*."[6]

In September one 'LCS liberty boat', the *61,* which was providing ferry service for the USS *South Dakota*, had her status elevated considerably. Because the *South Dakota* was Admiral W. F. Halsey's Third Fleet flagship, the *61* was no less than an 'Admiral's Barge'. On September 18, the *61,* with a four-star flag flying proudly at her truck, carried Admiral Halsey and Admiral R. A. Spruance, Commander of the Fifth Fleet, from their respective ships to the battleship HMS *King George* for a farewell party given by Vice Admiral Sir H. B. Rawlings, RN. The *61* crew was very well treated aboard the *King George.* "Later over coffee in the flag quarters aboard the *South Dakota,* Admiral Halsey told the captain and the executive officer of the *61,* in reference to the LCSs' achievements at Okinawa. 'Break out your blue jerseys. You boys are first string.'"[7]

As if in response to and confirmation of Admiral Halsey's high compliment, on October 4 the LCS *86* went alongside a burning Japanese ammunition barge in Tokyo Bay. They put their fire fighting party aboard and put out the fire. Before *86* arrived, exploding live ammunition on the barge had killed 20 Japanese and wounded the three American sailors in charge of the barge. The barge broke loose from its mooring after the fire was out and began drifting down on the cruiser USS *Wilkes Barre.* The *86* was able to keep the barge from doing damage to the *Wilkes Barre.* The officers involved and two of her men were awarded Navy and Marine Corps medals for their heroic actions.[8]

With the war over, there was nothing to say and little or nothing was said on the many ship's radios in Tokyo Bay. Yet even so, all LCSs and other ships' radiomen were still required to stand a 24-hour watch. It was so dull on the midnight watch in particular that radiomen began talking to each other anonymously just to keep awake. The various speakers who used fictitious names told stories, sang songs, read poetry, played instruments, told jokes, and whatever. The group, which called itself the 'Bad Name Gang' brightened the radiomen's watches for many early, early mornings until the ringleader, 'Billy the Kid', who was going home, signed off one night and the gang was no more.[9]

At the end of October Flotilla Four Commander Phillips arranged a concert for the flotilla. It was presented in a SeaBee compound ashore and included the Eighth Army Band, an eight-piece Japanese band, and six Japanese women dancers. It was welcomed and well received. With the coming of November the weather was getting colder and fewer of the larger ships were sending liberty parties ashore. Rumors were flying as to what the future held for the LCSs.

The most popular of these was that they would go home; another was that they would work with the minesweepers on mine demolition in the China Seas (what Flotillas One, Three, and Five ships were doing at that very time); a third

Moving past the colossal wreck of the Japanese battleship Nagato *in Tokyo Bay, LCS 118, with its "Going Home" pennant streaming from its mast, points her bow homeward. Courtesy of Earl Blanton.*

was that they would haul rice in their magazines up some river to a famine area in China.[10] Much to everyone's joy the popular first rumor was to come true on December 3; but not before the Flotilla Commander put ten ships to sea for maneuvers and firing practice in mid-November. This was the very last planned practice of any group of LCSs before they returned to the States.

On December 3 the first group of LCSs broke out their 'going home pennants' and joyfully made their way out of Tokyo Bay to the Marianas and eventually to the States. Other groups followed. My ship moved out of Tokyo Bay on January 16 with seven other homeward-bound LCSs.

Endnotes

[1] Rooney, *Mighty Midget—USS LCS 82*, 141.

[2] Ibid., 141-142.

[3] Blanton, *Boston to Jacksonville,* 165.

[4] Bill Ross, *82* crew member, in Rooney, 149-150.

[5] Frederick H. Lamartin, *120* captain, letter to author, September 4, 1996.

[6] Rooney, 153.

[7] Powell Pierpoint, Appendix to LCS *61* Ship's History.

[8] William J. Mason, *USS LCS(L)(3) 86—The Mighty Midget,* 1992, 28.

[9] Rooney, 153-155.

[10] Blanton, 180.

Chapter 13

Occupation and Mine Demolition Adventures

Flotilla One Ships

At the end of August, after the Japanese surrender had been confirmed, Captain Arison, Commander, Flotilla One, departed the Subic Bay area in LC(FF) *778* with LCSs *8, 27, 28, 29, 42, 44, 46,* and *47* for Okinawa. From there they would go north and northwest to participate in the occupation of Korea and North China and in mine demolition operations. Other Flotilla One ships in the Subic Bay area included *30, 41, 43, 45, 48, 50, 58, 59,* and *60.* These ships would arrive at Okinawa somewhat later.

At least one of them, however, LCS *60,* would go to Okinawa by way of San Pedro Bay in Leyte Gulf, the temporary anchorage of scores of LCSs from Flotillas Three, Four, and Five who had served at Okinawa. These ships were also getting ready to move north for occupation duties in Japan, China, Korea, and Indochina.

While leaving the Subic Bay area, the LCSs in Captain Arison's group were advised to proceed westward of Luzon and to take refuge in Lingayen Gulf to avoid a severe incoming storm. Because of the delay, they were late getting to Okinawa and missed the landings at Inchon, Korea, in which they were to take part.

Several of the ships, however, which were running somewhat behind Captain Arison's group, were caught in a typhoon at Okinawa on September 15. With some difficulty, LCSs *45* and *43* rode out the storm in Buckner Bay; *43,* however, in attempting to use her anchor to steady her in the very heavy seas and high winds, lost both her anchor and her spare anchor in the first hour of the storm. With no anchor she was forced to run her engines in reverse at full speed for some time to keep from capsizing.

Raymond Ross, *60* electrician, reported how his ship survived the typhoon in Buckner Bay:

September 15, 2200: Wind gaining velocity. Swells getting larger. 2300: lifted anchor and moved to avoid shifting and swinging into destroyer. 2400: anchor dragging. Raised anchor and moved to keep from drifting into destroyer tender. September 16, 0545: started all main engines—[the ship's] bow [is] on a coral reef—beginning to broach. All engines ahead, hard right rudder and we are free. Strain on anchor parted the steel anchor line. Anchor lost. LCS *60* [must stay] underway until new line is rigged with spare anchor.

Wind still gaining velocity. Rain. 1200: larger ships have left bay for open sea. At anchor with two engines [of the eight main propulsion engines] in reverse to lessen strain on anchor cable. Full fury of storm to strike here tomorrow. Ship quivers from swells striking fantail now. Visibility poor. Typhoon passing within 40 miles at 2200 today. Ship straining furiously on anchor cable with all engines full speed astern. Floating debris striking frequently. Largest was a barge with a derrick broken loose from its moorings. 2330: lost second anchor.

September 17 0400-0800 watch: Heavy seas running. We are riding out storm well. Holding position by backing into wind full speed astern. No anchors left. Ships at sea calling for assistance. 0600: visibility poor—rain, high wind. 1400: tied up to LST. 1900: mooring lines broke loose. Hooked line from LST to our bow. September 18: Today ships were seen aground from the typhoon. PTs, LCMs, and LCVPs were cast fifty yards on the beach high and dry. Minesweepers sitting dry on a coral reef. A merchantman at sea hit a floating mine broken loose from a mine field. Subchasers sunk at sea. Two life rafts from our ship not yet found.[1]

On the way to Inchon from Okinawa the LCSs in Captain Arison's group, *8, 27-29, 41, 44, 46,* and *47,* were approximately 100 miles out at sea when they passed the Yangtze River's mouth, yet even that far out, silt from the river gave the ocean a muddy yellow color. As the LCSs were going to Inchon, the dangerous work that some of them would be doing off Japan, China, Formosa, Korea, and other places seemed almost to be staring them in the face.

An officer on LCS *27* explained: "The trip from Okinawa to Inchon was a pretty short one and without incident. The only thing exciting was the sighting of a few mines floating in the North China Sea. Naturally we [the LCSs] were

China, Korea and
Formosa
Occupation
and
Mine Demolition

sent ahead of the convoy to shoot the things, because that was one of the things we had experience with. It never ceased to amaze me how those things would blow once they were hit by a twenty millimeter shell. Of course that shell would explode itself on impact. Little did we know that most of the time from then on we would be looking for floating mines. Every time some convoy would sight a mine, the powers that be would send us back out to sea looking for mines. I don't know how many times we crossed the North China Sea looking for mines."[2]

On September 16, four days after Captain Arison's group arrived at Inchon, all eight LCSs were put to work searching for and destroying the numerous drifting mines recently sighted in the Yellow Sea off Korea. During the September 16-22 period, the ships destroyed a number of mines by sinking them.

Another duty LCSs had in the Inchon area was preventing Korean junks from carrying surrendered Japanese soldiers home. The U.S. authorities evidently wanted the former soldiers treated and transported as prisoners of war, rather than as free fare-paying passengers. Working on their own, without an interpreter or even a Korean native speaker, LCS crews had difficulty enforcing this rule, as a *27* officer explained: "We would come alongside the biggest junks, send a boarding party aboard, open every compartment, pull out every drawer (we were also told to look for money) and leave. We wouldn't have known a Jap from a Korean. They all looked alike. Anyway, we would always give them one of those 3-foot-long canned Spams—just for their trouble. Weren't they lucky? Some of those junks were nearly as long as we were."[3]

While the eight LCSs in Captain Arison's group were destroying drifting mines in the Yellow Sea off Korea, other Flotilla One LCSs in Okinawa were preparing to move out to begin occupation and mine demolition duties in the north and northwest. On September 21, LCSs *41, 43, 45, 50*, and *58* departed Okinawa for Shanghai. Three of them, *41, 43*, and *45*, would serve on extensive mine demolition operations over the next few months. Also on the same day, LCSs *48, 59*, and *60* left Okinawa for Inchon, Korea.

Here is an account of the last three days of the trip to Inchon by Raymond Ross, *60* crew member: "September 24: Full moon; smooth sailing—turned cooler in past few days. Wearing heavy foul weather gear at night. Using blankets to sleep in for the first time in six months. Sighted and sank four floating mines today. September 25: We have sailed the Yellow Seas for three days now. Daybreak brought us between a chain of islands off the coast of Korea, near Inchon. Refueled in channel. Saw Jap cruisers and oilers in channel. They were flying the Ensign with the Japanese flag below—American officers, Japanese crews. Jap destroyers inferior to ours. September 26: There is a high tide here—some say 9 feet, others say 20 feet. At any rate, there is a very strong current running both on incoming and outgoing tides. When the tide is out, the natives in Chinese junks set out their fish nets where it is high and dry. When the tide comes in, the nets are entirely covered and float their boats away until they are ready to return to the nets again."[4]

Captain Arison and the eight LCSs departed Inchon and arrived in the Tangku, China, area on September 28. The next morning the First Marine Division arrived in Transport Squadron 17, and on that day Commander Flotilla One in LC(FF) *778* and LCSs *8, 27-29, 42, 44, 46,* and *47* led occupational Marine troops up the Hai Ho river to Tangku where they disembarked.

On September 27, LCSs *59* and *60* left Inchon to escort several surrendered Japanese ships—two subchasers, three destroyers, and a tugboat to a place near Pusan, Korea. The *59* and *60* were among the first allied naval ships in Pusan.

While the *59* and *60* were in Pusan, crew members were allowed ashore, and one of them described what was going on there on Sunday, September 30, 1945:

> The Japanese hospital ship [at the dock] is being loaded to the gunwales with Japanese soldiers and wives to be sent back to Japan. On the return trip, slave Koreans and families are being brought home from Japan. The

Pusan, Korea, in late September. Japanese soldiers being marched to a hospital ship to be sent back to Japan, in effect emancipating the Koreans, whom the Japanese had treated as slaves for several years. Courtesy of Robert Amick.

city is bubbling with activity in the reshuffling of people. It is a sad sight to see so many people in transit.

The Koreans have a beaten look and some don't seem to care what happens next, for they no doubt have been herded about for a long time now and are just all tired out. There is no liberty here because there are so many Japanese still in town that trouble may be a result. It is estimated that another eight days are required to embark the remaining Jap soldiers. The streets are crowded with people carrying high piles of belongings on their backs: three, four, and five hundred pounds. Others carry baskets and boxes on their heads. Horses and men pull two wheel carts loaded with grass-mat-covered boxes, most likely household effects of departing Japs.

Because the city has no sewage system, there is a stench blanketing the city. The womenfolk do the greater share of the work—carry a child on their back, bundle on the head, and arms full of belongings. Menfolk go ahead unburdened, women follow behind.[5]

Two days later Ross went sightseeing in Pusan: "The tour was worthwhile even though I couldn't talk to the Koreans or purchase anything. The streets were all well-kept, mostly concrete paving. Sanitation was the most appalling factor in my observation. In addition to the terrific stench, there are flies galore. Children in particular gazed at American sailors with almost reverence. The flies walked up and down their faces, but they didn't bother to brush them off their stolid Oriental faces. Some children followed our party all p.m. saying 'Hello' and 'Thank you'. Farther down the street there was a band playing and a couple of thousand Koreans just returning from Japan and getting the glad hand. There seemed to be children everywhere, on the street and hanging out of every door and window you pass."[6]

Although liberty for the LCS crews was practically non-existent in Pusan, the Army 40th Division, which was in command of Pusan, provided recreation space on the end of a dock and in a warehouse for service personnel. Using the warehouse, the *59* and *60* crews held a volleyball tournament. The *60* crew was the winner.

In late September LCS *47* began several weeks of patrolling the Yellow Sea for free-floating Japanese mines. At about the same time, LCSs *41, 43,* and *45* began extended tours of mine demolition duty, working at first to clear the Yangtse River approaches from Shanghai to Hong Kong, with *41* and *43* moving on to clear the area off Haiphong in French Indochina (now Vietnam) and in the

---

Bonham Straits. This duty continued in other areas for the three ships through October, November, and December, and for the *43*, even into early 1946.

The exact nature of mine demolition duty varied somewhat. Sometimes ships searched for free-floating mines and then destroyed them by gunfire. On other occasions, LCSs followed minesweepers and destroyed all the mines that the sweepers cut loose. Most of the time ships on extended duty worked with the sweepers. It was dangerous work all the time, and difficult work when the sea was rising and the rain heavy and incessant.

Here are two accounts of mine demolition duty by crew members of the *45*, a ship that, as of October 12, had destroyed 100 mines: "Our task was to follow the minesweepers and when they made contact with and cut a mine loose, they signalled the following LCSs. We in turn would spot the mines and blow them up. When a mine was spotted, certain gun crews were called to their stations. Usually it was the 20mm crews plus a 50-caliber on the signal bridge. The first ten mines we blew were spectacular and we watched and cheered in awe at the explosion of each one. Some of these Jap mines didn't explode; we'd knock the horns off and blow the tops off; they just floated there until the lapping waves would fill them with water and they'd sink.

At first we were all serious, but then the blowing of mines became old hat—just routine and we'd all go on about our duties—no helmets, no Mae Wests [inflatable life jackets]. One sunny day when the word was passed for mine disposal I decided to go topside and watch the proceedings. Just about the time the gun crew fired a single shot I, for an unknown reason, put on my helmet. I was the only onlooker wearing a helmet. On the fourth shot the mine blew— sprinkling down everywhere. Suddenly I felt a sharp 'clink' on the top side of my helmet. My ears were ringing slightly and I saw the piece of shrapnel bounce onto the signal deck. I quickly reached for it and picked it up, but just as quickly dropped it, for it was still hot as hell and the jagged edges were razor sharp. The piece of shrapnel was about three inches long and two inches wide. After another minute or so, the full realization hit me; if I hadn't put on my helmet, I would have been dead!! The Good Lord watched over me. I still have that piece of shrapnel, and even though it is mine, it doesn't have my name on it.[7]

One afternoon when the minesweeper cut loose several mines which we proceeded to explode or sink, one mine proved to be either hard to hit or wouldn't explode or sink when hit. I do not remember which officer was conning the ship, but he kept getting closer and closer to this particular mine. I am not sure how close we finally got but I would say it was under 50 feet. About this time some wise guy shouts "Fix bayonets and charge." He no more got the last word out when the mine exploded. There was a big clang as a piece of shrapnel about the size of a dinner plate landed in the middle of the flag deck. It put a dent about 1 1/2 inches deep in the deck. After the officers took one look at the dent, it didn't take much argument to come up with the decision that "Brother, we ain't getting that close again."[8]

After LCS 47 anchored in Inchon Bay, Korea, its crew, weary after several weeks of patrolling for floating mines in the Yellow Sea, was forced to take an unwanted 'midnight cruise' without its captain and with just one engine. Ludwig Edstrom, 47 executive officer, tells what happened:

The Captain went ashore on 'R and R' [rest and recreation] one evening, sure that his ship would be safely at anchor upon his return. This, however, was not to be as a ten-knot tide and a dragging anchor would decree otherwise. Despite playing out a mile of cable, the anchor continued to drag until the 47 and its anchor cable, taut as a fiddle string, straddled the ship-to-shore route of a stream of cargo-carrying amphibious trucks [DUKWs] off-loading supplies from a transport anchored off-shore.

The blinker signal from the transport read, "You are interfering with our off-loading operations. Please move to another anchorage." The 47's engineering officer reported to the exec, "We'll have to make it on one engine. The other seven are spread out on deck getting new rod bearings." With its anchor secured, the 47 slowly backed out into the swiftly ebbing tidal current, which immediately seized the ship and propelled it downstream faster and faster and directly toward an LCI riding at anchor in the darkness ahead.

The 47 hit the LCI broadside, bounced off unscathed and continued its wayward path downstream, missing the other ships, finally dropping anchor at the harbor's edge. The LCI, its bow cable severed and its bow doors sprung, fortunately carried a stern anchor that saved it from an unexpected and involuntary cruise. The LCI crew, after surveying the situation from topside, returned below deck to resume watching a movie in progress.

Later that evening, the 47's captain, on returning from shore, told his exec that the captain of the LCI said, "That exec of yours is not very sociable. He dropped by this evening and didn't even stay long enough for a cup of coffee."[9]

On October 1, Flotilla One Commander Arison and several LCSs escorted the first echelon of 23 LSMs loaded with U.S. Marine troops from the Tangku area to the major city of Tientsin, China. This action and the one on October 5 described below were part of a movement in which a total of 53,000 U.S. Marines were landed in North China to enforce the Japanese surrender and effect the repatriation of thousands of Japanese troops still in the area and to guard against attacks and takeovers of Nationalist China holdings by threatening Red Chinese Communist Forces.

Captain Arison's group of ships moving up the river was greeted by enthusiastic crowds at every village. When they arrived in Tientsin, the crowds were so thick that it was almost impossible to land line-handling parties from the ship.

Four days later on October 5 several LCSs, including the *27* and *28*, provided a similar escort, this time to a number of LCIs loaded with Marine occupation troops also moving up the Peking River from Tangku to Tientsin. Soon after they got underway the *27* crew realized that they were playing a part in the emancipation of the Chinese from the Japanese, who had occupied much of China for years. "Going up the river we passed through several villages. Thousands of ragged and barefooted peasants lined the river's edge waving Chinese flags. They were quite exuberant in their waves and cheers. Some of then even had their brass band out. We really felt like conquering heroes. Two times we saw a dead body along the river bank just below the waving crowds. The people standing very close-by hadn't even bothered to bury it. Human life was so cheap in China.

"Our welcome into Tientsin was very similar to the one we had seen in the news reels of the GIs going into Paris. Only the Chinese didn't try to kiss us. Thank heavens! As we entered the city we got more cheers, but one group of soldiers weren't cheering. We waved at them because we thought they were Chinese. But they were Japanese. About one hundred of our carrier-based aircraft continually flew overhead the first couple of days of the occupation. They must have been trying to impress the people and former enemy."[10]

From October 5 to 10, LCSs *50* and *58* were on mine demolition duty off Shanghai and in the Formosa Strait. During this tour of duty LCS *50* also made shore visits to Amoy and Swatow, China. At about this same time LCS *30*

The LCS 50 mascot knows a really safe place on the ship when he sees one. Courtesy of Charles Thomas.

patrolled in search of gun runners in the Amoy and Swatow areas. On October 4, LCSs *42* and *48* went to Chinhai, Korea, and escorted two Japanese destroyers to Pusan. Two days later the same LCSs piloted a group of LSTs into Pusan.

On several occasions, LCSs were providing a show of strength for the allied forces in Korea where the U.S. forces were outnumbered by the Japanese or the citizens were riotous and unruly. On October 11, when LCS *42* was in Chinkai, there were 7,000 Japanese troops and only 500 U.S. forces. Four days later *41* was at Basan where the natives were riotous and there was a murder almost every night. While at Basan, *41* transported a number of Koreans who were injured in a severe train wreck to Chinkai. Then they took the worst cases on to Pusan for further medical treatment.

During October and November several LCS crews enjoyed liberty in Shanghai when they were not out on mine demolition or other duties. Raymond Ross has provided a glimpse of Shanghai as a sailor saw it in the crucial days after the surrender:

October 18: Went ashore in Shanghai; went shopping and bought woodcarving and jade. Went to YMCA. Had dinner at D.D.'s Russian

Restaurant. Food very good. Service slow. Shanghai is perhaps the most corrupt city in the world. Lots of fun on liberty here. First good liberty since Pearl Harbor.

October 22: Took pictures in Shanghai in the afternoon. Tried to take a picture of coolie and ginrickshaw. He took off. Dinner at New Dollar Cafe. Tea and cakes at another. Visited the Mandarin Club, Shanghai's most exclusive and expensive night club owned and operated by Jimmy James, former Minnesota man. His establishment is most beautiful. Panelled ceiling, gold leaf inlay, heavy silk drapes and curtains, ivory carved screens. Tapestry most beautiful. Tibetan and Chinese rugs. Blackwood tables and chairs beautifully carved. Belgian crystalware. Hammond electric organ. Steinway piano. Moon Gate and Chinese waiters and attendants. Seats 40 couples, no more allowed for the evening. $50 to $60 for a bottle of champagne. $5 for old fashioned cocktail. Visited Wind-On Company, largest department store in China.[11]

Members of LCS 45's crew discovered a bar in Shanghai, operated by a family, and warm and friendly like no other place: "For some reason the 45 crew seemed to have adopted Daisy's Bar as their own. It wasn't very big or fancy and there was nothing to make it different from the other gin mills in Shanghai. But it offered a feeling of welcome, rather than 'How much can we take you for?'

"Daisy's Bar was one of the few bars in Shanghai that was not closed because of a fight, giving some drunken sailor an excuse to tear the place up. Oh, there were several times when it could have happened, but there were usually enough of the 45 crew there to tell them to take it outside and be able to back it up. A number of times since leaving Shanghai I have wondered what happened to Daisy, her husband and her cute little daughter when the Commies took over. They were swell people."[12]

On October 16, Flotilla One Commander Arison on LC(FF) 778 and LCSs 27, 28, 29, 44, and 46 established an anti-smuggling patrol off Mokpo, Korea. On the third day of the patrol LCSs 44 and 46 stopped two Korean motor craft and found 749,000 yen, a considerable amount of tobacco, silks, linen, and miscellaneous merchandize, all contraband. Eight days later (on October 24), LCSs 28, 29, 44 and 46 conducted another patrol and confiscated another considerable amount of merchandise, including 70 gallons of saki.

In the latter part of October, LCSs were engaged in different actions. While in Shanghai LCS *30* liberated English river pilots who had been imprisoned by the Japanese. On October 20, *42* towed a Japanese junk to Chinkai, Korea. Three days later the same ship escorted four Japanese destroyers to Sentinel Island. From there they took four Japanese survivors to Chinkai. For the month of October 20 to November 20, the *28* went on night patrol for drifting mines off southern Korea. LCS *58* served on mine demolition patrol from October 24 to 30.

Throughout October, LCSs *41* and *43* continued mine demolition duty in the Bonham Straits, and as of October 25, LCS *43* had destroyed 60 mines. LCS *45*, which as of October 12 had destroyed 100 mines, continued to clear the Yangtse River approaches of mines and also worked off the Chosen Archipelago. On appropriate occasions, LCS *45* served as a guide ship, directing other ships through mine fields.

On October 30, Flotilla One Commander Arison in LC(FF) *778* and LCS *44* went to Lien Tung, China, to determine if that port would be useful for repatriating Japanese soldiers from North China. Soon after the Commander arrived, crews of the *778* and *44* sounded the Lien Jung harbor. The natives of Lien Tung had, before this, seen only one white man over the past ten years. As the Chinese interpreter explained, however, the local natives would not be afraid of the white U.S. naval men because they had seen and remembered this one man. Although there was some anxiety at the time, the interpreter's prediction turned out to be correct.

The officers of Flotilla Commander Arison's delegation were entertained by the Chinese Nationalist Government authorities at a banquet in the Nationalist Military Barracks. On November 1 the commanding officers of a garrison of 300 Japanese troops at Lien Tung surrendered to Flotilla Commander Arison on board LC(FF) *778.* At the request of the Chinese authorities, the Japanese troops were permitted to retain their arms so they could act as military guards on the local railway.

Also on November 1, LCS *42* left Chinkai, Korea, to pilot LCS *46* into the harbor, but on her way out she was called to Sentinel Island, off which a cargo ship, SS *Bridge*, had hit a mine and was taking on water at a dangerous rate. LCSs *42* and *46* then went alongside *Bridge,* which was very low in the water, and started pumping out her flooded compartments. After they raised her to an acceptable height, both ships stayed alongside, continuing to pump out her holds, and towing her toward Pusan. After they arrived at Pusan, tugboats took care of

The commanding officer of a Japanese garrison of 300 troops surrenders to LCS Flotilla One Commander Arison on board LC(FF) 778 at Lien Tung, China, on November 1, 1945. Courtesy of Charles E. Holtkamp.

Bridge. Also giving aid to *Bridge* were DD *752* and LSM *Five*. These two ships and *42* and *46* received a 'Well Done' for their efforts from Admiral J. C. Kincaid, Commander, Seventh Fleet.

Early in November, LCS *48* captured a 75-foot Japanese motor vessel off Pusan. This vessel had 16 Japanese on it, which the *48* delivered to the authorities in Pusan along with the vessel. On November 18, LCSs *42* and *46* went up the Peping River from Tangku for liberty in Tientsen. On this trip the ships' crews were surprised to find such a major river to be narrow, shallow, and barely navigable, even for flat-bottomed LCSs. On November 20 and 21, LCSs *Eight* and *48* patrolled for floating mines off Kako. In the last ten days of November several LCSs including the *30* were stationed and enjoyed liberty in Hong Kong.

Later in November, LCS *28* served as a pilot ship for the repatriation of Koreans being brought back to Korea from Japan. For this mission, *28* rendezvoused off the southwest coast of Korea with a repatriation convoy of one LSM and three LSTs, and then led the convoy up a river to the city of Kunsan, Korea, eight miles inland. Each LST transported 1,000 Koreans who were billeted on straw mats in the LSTs' well decks. The ships in the convoy negotiated the channel to Kunsan without incident, thanks to a 33-foot tide and Japanese navigational charts.[13]

From December 4 to 9, LCS *42* served on mine demolition patrol, working out in the waters surrounding the islands off Inchon, Korea, and in the Yellow Sea. While in Kunsan, crew members from LCS *27* learned the hard way that keeping a close watch on their pet dogs is an absolute necessity in that city. When a group from the ship went out looking for a pet dog that had not returned to the ship with them, "the Koreans told them that someone had probably caught him, ate him, and made gloves out of his hide."[14]

Through late November and December, LCS *45* continued to serve on mine demolition duty working in the northern Formosa waters and the approaches to Kiirun, Formosa. Later they participated in the Shanghai-to-Korea shipping lanes patrol for free-floating mines. One morning while on this duty, the *45* crew became acutely aware of the hazards of mine demolition work; they found a floating mine on their anchor cable. The *45* completed its extensive mine demolition duty in early January and departed Shanghai for their return to the States.

LCSs *41* and *43* saw a considerable amount of mine demolition duty through November and December. In November, they worked in two areas: at sea off northeast Formosa and off Hoko Island, one of the Pescadores in the Formosa Strait. In December, they worked in an area midway between the Pescadores and the China coast and in the sea areas off Hoko and off Kiirun, Formosa. In these two areas these two Flotilla One ships were working with LCSs from Flotilla Three on mine demolition detail. In late January *43* worked in Yulinhan Bay, Hainan Island, in the South China Sea. In February during which the ship made port in Hong Kong several times, *43* did duty in Gaalong Bay, Hainan Island, and off the northeast coast of Hainan in the Gulf of Tonkin. On April 7, the *43* finally pointed its bow eastward and went home, arriving in the States on May 29.

Also serving on mine demolition duty during November and December were LCSs *30, 42, 59*, and *60*. LCSs *43* and *45* were among the last of the Flotilla One ships to complete their occupation and mine demolition duties and to leave the Japanese, Korean, Chinese, French Indochina, and China Seas areas to return to the States. Groups of Flotilla One LCSs began leaving in November and early December, and one of the larger groups departed for Saipan on December 11. This group of eighteen ships included nine Flotilla One LCSs—*8, 27-29, 44, 46-48,* and *42,* along with six ships from Flotilla Three, one from Flotilla Four, and two from Flotilla Five.

Sea of Japan

Hokkaido

Hakodate

Aomori

Korea

Honshu

Tokyo

Yokohama

Yokosuka

Pusan

Kobe Kyoto

Osaka

Hiroshima Nagoya

Tokyo Bay

Wakayama

Shikoku

Sasebo

Nagasaki Kyushu

Japan
Occupation
and
Mine Demolition

Korea Strait

Flotilla Three Ships

In late September Flotilla Three ships at San Pedro Bay departed Leyte for their first occupational duties: supporting the simultaneous landings and occupations by U.S. troops on September 25 of two places in Japan—Wakayama in southern Honshu and Aomori in northern Honshu (the main island of Japan). The twelve ships of Group 7, scheduled to support the Wakayama occupation, went to Japan by way of Okinawa. The twelve ships of Group 8, scheduled for the Aomori occupation, also went to Okinawa first, and while there on September 16, found themselves riding out a typhoon.

Most of the Group 9 ships, also Aomori bound, were at Saipan, instead of Leyte in early September. They would arrive at Yokohama on September 20 and go to Aomori from there.

What the average individual in peacetime would never give a moment's thought to turned out to be a genuine thrill for the men on the LCSs sailing out of Leyte. "The first time at sea in peacetime brought a great thrill to all of us. All the sailing we had ever done heretofore was done in complete darkness with not a shadow of a light showing. But at night all the ships turned on their navigation lights. Not only were we allowed to burn navigation lights, but all our port[hole]s would be opened and we could smoke topside which was unheard of after darkness.

"So it was a great holiday for all of us that night, and the officer conning the ship was also happy as no longer did he have to vigilantly watch the ship ahead of him through binoculars, but now he could guide in the lead ship's stern light. It was a good sight to see, and burning navigation lights really made you realize that the lights went on again all over the world. To that last statement a seaman standing by added, 'With the compliments of the United States of America, the lights go on again all over the world'."[15]

Soon after the surrender announcement on August 15, the Navy established a point system specifying the requirements for immediate release from service. A number of LCS men had enough points as soon as the system went into effect, and as the LCS *36* captain informs us, their eagerness for release knew no bounds: "While at Okinawa the men with enough points urged me to put them ashore as they didn't want to go to Japan and would sleep on the ground if need be in order to speed up their return home. At Okinawa we found the same crowded receiving stations filled with men awaiting transportation back to the United States. Seeing just how badly they wanted to get off, we had their orders written, put them ashore and gave them our blessings and off we went."[16]

The eleven ships of Group Eight (LCSs *11-22*), which found themselves riding out a typhoon off Okinawa beginning September 15, were caught in the same storm that Flotilla One ships were caught in.

The difference between the ships' situations is that the Flotilla One ships were able to ride out the storm in Buckner Bay at Okinawa. The Flotilla Three ships were forced to ride out the typhoon on the open sea. Much of the time the Flotilla Three ships were so completely the victims of the raging mountainous seas and high winds that they did not or could not know where they were.

Here are three personal accounts, by crew members Frank Korany of the *14*, Dick Halstead of the *18*, and W. H. Stanley of the *21*, of ships struggling to survive the typhoon of September 15-17 off Okinawa:

> The typhoon was right behind us as we neared Okinawa. All the LCSs were traveling in columns and we just kept going in a circle off the coast of Okinawa. The waves kept getting bigger and the wind seemed to be blowing from all directions. Most of the time we couldn't see all the ships traveling with us.

> The waves got so big, a decision was made to run with the storm. Two men were required to man the ship's wheel. Every time a wave hit the stern of the ship, it would knock the ship sideways and the helmsmen would have to wheel like hell to bring the ship around before the next wave hit the stern, or the ship would flip over.

> The men in the engine room were busy shifting engines. Every time the ship's screws came out of the water, the men had to slow the engines; when the screws were down, the men had to accelerate the engines. The only thing that kept our ship upright was the fact that all our fuel, ammo, and supplies were locked up tight in the holds and tanks below. We had just taken on a full load before leaving Leyte.

> The waves were getting bigger. It was almost impossible to get to the forward compartment now. When the ship's bow would raise up into the air, you would be struggling to get uphill, hanging on to the ship's frames on the inside bulkheads, then the bow would go down and you would try to hold yourself back to keep from sliding along the passageway. Sometimes the ship would go down into the valley of a wave and the ship traveling 1500 feet behind us looked like it was sliding down a hill. Just when it looked like the following ship was going to hit our stern, our ship would raise up and we would be looking way down into a valley at the ship ahead of ours.

> I was really concerned this time. I had been lucky so many times before and was wondering if my luck was going to hold out.

> The men on watch were starting to look beat out. Craig had been wrestling the wheel almost constantly for two days. The storm was pushing the

ship farther away from Okinawa and the waves seemed to be pushing the ship forward instead of coming from all directions. The wind had started to die down and the waves to get smaller. The sea was full of floating debris. We had to keep a sharp watch for all kinds of floating objects. Some were huge in size. A lot of things seemed to have been washed off the decks of other ships.[17]

Halstead reported on what was happening on *18*:

We were going broadside to swells and rolling pretty heavy. It kept getting rougher and rougher; swells were longer and higher, wind was stronger. We took four foot of water on our port side; it almost washed the guys overboard. Began wearing life jackets all the time when topside. After we learned that we couldn't anchor in Buckner Bay, we wandered around all Sunday west of Okinawa, rolling and pitching something awful.

We were less than 50 miles from the center [of the typhoon]. Swells were at least 70 foot high, wind at least 70 or better. Spray looked like snow drifting. We were taking as high as 35 degree rolls; this scow is only supposed to take 37 1/2 degrees; I was plenty scared, in fact scared to death. Against suicide planes, you had a chance. Here you had the whole ocean against you and it was mean looking.

We turned around to have the wind behind us, until 0730 when Captain Aylward [Flotilla Commander] decided to change course; so we started going broadside of 25 or 30 foot swells. The first swell hit us and I thought we were done for. We watched [LCS] *19* behind us; she was rolling so far that you could see about two feet of her bottom on port side. We were rolling just as bad, so we were scared.

Within a few hours, things were much calmer and the crew's fears were over. Going into Buckner Bay later, the *18* crew saw a YMS and two LSTs high and dry on the beach.[18]

According to *21* crew member W. H. Stanley: "When our [ship's] bow went down, it was about 45 degrees down, and when it came up, it was about 45 degrees up. All at the same time the ship would roll about half way over on its side and pause for a moment, creak, and shake as if it was going to break apart before it started back. There is no way to tell how frightful this was. Every face was pale and not much talking going on. I believed everyone was praying. I know I was. We could not hold a course. When we were finally able to shoot the stars, we found we had been blown 200 miles off course."[19]

On September 22, LCS Group Seven *(31, 32, 34-36, 51-56)* under the command of Lieutenant Commander Frank Stone, departed Okinawa to join Amphibious Group Eight of the Fifth Fleet. These ships were among the first U.S. naval vessels to support the landing at Wakayama and the occupation of the Osaka-Kobe-Kyoto area of Japan on September 25. Relative to this upcoming 'tour' of Japan, Lieutenant Commander Stone originated this message to ships in his group at Okinawa: "The Gunboat Special Tour to the mysterious Orient and Land of Cherry Blossoms is now officially on. There will be a slight additional charge for those with enough points who do not want to go home."[20]

Group Seven ships entered Kakanoura Bay to land at Wakayama "behind a group of old Liberty ships ballasted with cement and crewed by volunteers. Since we [LCS *51*] had shallow draft, we followed them in hoping to be too shallow to hit any mines."[21] On the way in, however, the LCSs did have to steer clear of one mine that was quickly destroyed by a sweeper.

Lieutenant Joseph Sansone, *36* captain, gives his impression of the situation as his ship moved up the Japanese coast on its way to the landing at Wakayama: "Our first impression of it was no different from that of any of the many other stands we had seen in the Pacific. The rugged terrain, high mountains and a windswept coast confronted us, and the first thought that came to us was to thank Almighty God that this was a peaceful invasion and not one which would require bloodshed, as the terrain forebodes many years of fighting in order to half-way occupy this part of Honshu. Looking to the south and west of Kii Suido [a bay separating the islands of Shikoku, Honshu, and Kyushu] the terrain looks as though no landings would be possible under any circumstances. The coastline of the islands of Honshu, Shikoku and Kyushu are rugged with many hills and apparently no decent beaches to launch a large scale invasion."[22]

Although the action at Wakayama was a bona fide landing of a large number of U.S. troops who would occupy a major area of Japan, to those men used to hostile landings, it was quite unusual. According to Lieutenant Sansone, "this landing and occupation differs from the wartime landings and assaults in practically every way possible. In the first place, no ship manned its guns and the supporting ships and the landing troops were greeted by large numbers of Japanese onlookers along the shore. The atmosphere was friendly, almost jovial. The ships' officers were ordered to have their men in clean clothing, white hats and shined shoes. The LCSs were warned to be on the lookout for skunks but to report the skunk's presence before taking action against it. At Okinawa they fired first and reported later. At night all ships had all lights on, ports open, with movies and smoking going on topside."[23]

The landing for the occupation of the Osaka-Kobe-Kyoto area through Wakayama went off without incident. After the landing, LCS crews were allowed ashore. Lieutenant Kenneth Huff, *35* captain, reported on what he saw in Wakanoura, Wakayama's port town, and in Wakayama: "Wakanoura is a small port, unbombed, and a suburb of Wakayama, bombed flat. Kimonos, flat-chested women, short people, lots of grinning and smiling, sliding panels for doors, mats on the floor, dainty gardens, shrines and monuments, parasols, narrow streets, sandals or clogs left outside the doors; utterly destroyed Wakayama; the few cars running on charcoal burners; cigarettes used instead of money."[24]

Although six of the Group Seven ships (*32, 35, 36, 53, 55*, and *56*) were assigned to the Seventh Fleet as of October 19, all ships of the group stayed in the Wakayama area performing assigned duties throughout most of October. These duties included serving as harbor entrance control vessels, patrolling and screening against possible aircraft or small boat attack against anchored larger ships, keeping Japanese fishermen out of restricted areas, and rounding up fishermen who violated rules concerning proper distances from anchorages. "A few audacious Jap fishermen who insisted on fishing in restricted waters learned quickly to remain in proper territory when the lesson was punctuated with rifle fire."[25]

During their stay in the Wakayama area, LCS *52* went to Tokashima to pick up the body of a downed flyer. At least two LCSs (*34* and *35*) reported the necessity of taking refuge in small, sheltered water areas from typhoons which passed nearby Wakayama. On October 25, LCSs *31, 34, 51, 52, 54*, and *57* (ships still assigned to the Fifth Fleet) arrived at Nagoya. On October 27, LCSs *32, 35, 36, 55*, and *56*, assigned to the Seventh Fleet, departed Wakayama for Shanghai arriving there on October 31.

On September 25 at the same time that Group Seven ships of Flotilla Three were supporting the landing and occupation of Wakayama in southern Honshu, LCSs from Groups Eight and Nine were supporting the landing and occupation at Aomori at the northern tip of Honshu across Aomori from the southern point of Hokkaido. In other words, Flotilla Three LCSs on September 25 were simultaneously supporting landings and occupations at the north and at the south ends of Honshu, the main island of Japan proper.

Participating in the Aomori action under the command of Flotilla Three Commander Aylward were LC(FF)s *485, 536,* and *988,* and LCSs *11, 12, 14, 16, 22, 25, 38-40,* and *109-112.* In the landing the LCSs covered Red Beach and Green Beach and provided screen protection and fire support for the landing of the 81st Infantry Division. That the Navy had already been at work in the area was proclaimed by a sign on one of the waterfront buildings: "Welcome U.S. Army 70B Seabees."

Immediately after the landing, LCSs were assigned to standby for fire and salvage work and patrolling and screening duties. For most ships, these assignments were of brief duration; however LCS *22* did patrolling against aircraft and small boat attack in the Aomori area until October 18. Like the action at Wakayama, the landing and occupation at Aomori went off without incident. LCS crew members who went ashore at Aomori found that the city almost completely destroyed by bombs and the one big building still standing, the railroad station, was filled with Japanese soldiers being shipped to their homes.

On October 4, several Flotilla Three LCSs served as support vessels for the landing and occupation of Hokadote in the lower part of Hokkaido, the most northerly large island of Japan. Three of the LCSs participating were *16, 110,* and *111.*

After the Aomori and Hokadote landings a number of the ships in Groups Eight and Nine arrived in the Tokyo Bay area on October 9. When she moored there, LCS *14* found herself docked alongside LCS *13* which had been in the bay area since mid-September and had been put to work carrying liberty parties from larger ships to Tokyo, Yokohama, and Yokosuka, and would be doing this until October 24. This is what Flotilla Four ships in the bay area had been doing since mid-September and would do for the next three or four months. To this writer's knowledge, LCS *13* was the only Flotilla Three ship to provide ferry service for liberty parties from larger ships in the Tokyo Bay area. Maybe her number had something to do with the assignment!

Group Eight and Nine ships, some of which had to take refuge at least part of the time from a typhoon closing in on the general area, caught up on their logistic needs while in the Tokyo Bay area. They also allowed their crews to go ashore for liberty in Tokyo, Yokohama, and Yokosuka, Japan's largest naval base. "This was once the world's heaviest populated area. But now only mass destruction. While we [LCS *21*] were tied up to the docks, little children came to us carrying pasteboard boxes and begged us to dump our leftovers from our food trays in their boxes. This was a pitiful sight. The kids had nothing to do with the war. Yet they had to suffer. We gave them candy and some other food items. I'll never forget their faces. They spoke no English; yet they could say 'chocolate', 'Yankee'."[26]

Group Eight and Nine ships next went to Sasebo, a city on the southern Japanese island of Kyushu fairly close to Nagasaki, where the second atom bomb was dropped. They arrived there on October 28, and the town served as the base from which LCSs went out in different directions on mine demolition duty. In fact, the first LCS to go out from Sasebo was *13*, which served from October 28 to November 16 on mine demolition duty and destroyed 47 mines in the Korean Strait off the island of Iki Shima.

On October 6 LCS *111*, with several other LCSs, went out from Sasebo off the Korean coast on similar duty and in three days destroyed 46 mines. LCS *21* left Sasebo on November 7 for mine demolition duty and in eleven days destroyed 109 mines. "Late one evening the sweepers ran into a large [mine] field and cut them loose. They had to be destroyed before nightfall. We shot our way into the field and then shot our way out. This went on until it was getting dark. We used our battle lamps and spotlights to retreat from the area. Some of the mines got so close when we exploded them, the ship rocked."[27]

On November 9 several LCSs, including *14*, went out from Sasebo into the Korean Strait. "The paravanes, led out by the sweepers, overlapped so they would not miss cutting any mines. There was one sweeper for every LCS. In the distance was a small sailboat occupied by one man who was to show where the minefield was. We [LCS *14* crew] couldn't believe it since we couldn't see land in any direction. The sweeps started to move and the mines started popping up all over the area.

"The sweeps cut so many mines the first hour, it kept us busy shooting at the mines all day. Sometimes the mines would come up so close that we would have to back away to fire at them. We even had some to come up behind the ship. It was a wonder we didn't hit the mines with the ship's screws. When you went below, the effect of the mines going off was the same as if your head was stuck in a steel barrel and someone was hitting its side with a ball bat."[28]

Mine demolition duty at this time caused problems for LCS crews. Since dependable detection of mines required experienced lookouts, ships with a number of newly arrived seamen replacements right out of boot camp were at a disadvantage. And this was true of a number of LCSs at the time. When the sea was rough and the ships were rolling 30 degrees or more, the mines bobbed up and down and were very hard to spot and to fire at. One LCS reported just missing hitting three mines hooked together which were barely visible from the surface. When several LCSs were working close to each other in dense mine fields, men and ships were in great danger of being hit by rifle or gunfire from nearby ships.

After their turn at mine demolition, LCS *14* crew members went ashore in a village on the island of Iki Shima in the Korean Strait: "As we walked by one of the buildings, a voice from a second floor window wanted to know where we were from in the States. I [Frank Korany] told him I was from Detroit and asked him if he knew where that was. He replied, 'I sure do. I went to dental school there in Ann Arbor, Michigan'."[29]

Beginning in late November, Group 8 and 9 LCSs on mine demolition duty worked out of Kiirun, a city in northern Formosa, convenient to Formosa Strait, where the sweepers and the LCSs were cleaning out mines. Because it funnels vast amounts of water between the East China Sea and the South China Sea, Formosa Strait, between China and Formosa, has seas to compare in roughness with few other places on earth. Both the winds and the seas are high much of the time, and the waves were more like huge rollers than anything else, making it very difficult to control small ships in the Strait.

The first three LCSs, *11, 13*, and *18*, to go out off Kiirun in the Strait on November 28 went, first for a two-day practice session and then for four days of work. LCSs *11* and *18* returned to Kiirun on December 4 but *13* continued to work in the Strait until December 19. On December 5, LCS *18* went out again, working this time with Flotilla One LCSs *41, 43*, and *58* in rough water off the Pescadores Islands in the Strait. These ships returned on December 9.

LCS *22* went out on demolition duty in the Strait with five other ships on December 8. This group ran into very rough seas; while they were out, five of the six ships lost their anchors. The ships returned on December 12. LCS *18* went out on December 11, working this time with three YMSs and LCS *55* along the Formosan coast. While they were out, LCS *55* was damaged. The ships returned on December 16.

Also serving on mine demolition duty during November and December were Group 8 and 9 LCSs *12, 16, 19, 20, 23-25, 38, 39, 110, 112*, and *113*. Some of these ships served with the LCSs mentioned above.

While LCS *14* was working a minefield with the sweepers in the Strait on December 5, a crack in the ship opened up in the rough sea and the ship began to leak badly. A change in the propeller pitch at this point further opened up the crack to a full sized hole, and *14* was forced to go into the nearest port at Hoko, largest of the Pescadores Islands.

Evidently LCS *14* moored to a dock in Hoko was such a curiosity to the Chinese people on the incoming inter-island ferry boat that they all rushed to one side and capsized the boat. Many of the passengers were injured and a number were trapped in the boat lying on its side. Members of the *14* crew helped people out of the water, and several crew members dived into the water to save those who were trapped. With the assistance of crew member Korany, the *14*'s pharmacist's mate delivered a baby from a woman passenger on the spot.[30]

Group 8 and 9 LCSs not on mine demolition duties engaged in other activities in November and December. A number of them took advantage of drydock and repair facilities, particularly those stationed in Shanghai. As we have seen, LCS *18* served as escort for a damaged sister ship. LCS *111* served a group of YMSs at Yokkaichi near Nagoya in Honshu by providing them mail and logistics services from November 17 to 30. LCS *21* took over from a group of Marines the job of guarding storage buildings on a dock in Sasebo. They did this from December 28 until January 25 so the Marines could go home right after Christmas.

During November and December, Group 7 Ships (*31, 32, 34-36, 51-57*) were, like Group 8 and 9 ships, primarily engaged in mine demolition activities. Using Nagoya, Japan, which half of the ships had gone to on October 27, and Shanghai, where the other half went on October 31, as their bases, Group 7 LCSs performed extensive mine demolition duties in different areas. LCS *31* worked off the coast of Nagoya and later off from Inchon, Korea. One day while working off Nagoya, *31* raised her anchor only to find a mine entangled in it. "If the anchor were pulled up against the ship, there would be a vast explosion. So while the ship steamed slowly ahead to keep the mine from contacting the ship, Gunner's Mate Kurlenicz hung from the anchor guard and unbolted the anchor so it fell free into the water with the mine."[31]

LCS *32* spent a month (from November 20 to December 20) on mine demolition duty in the extensive minefields around Formosa. Working out of Nagoya with Flot One LCS *42* from December 4 to 10, the *34* did demolition duty in the Yellow Sea along the Okinawa shipping route. Like *32*, *35* served on demolition duty for a month (November 19 to December 19) off Kiirun, Formosa, much of the time in rough seas producing 35 degree rolls.

The *36* also did duty off Formosa for a week at a time out of Shanghai, "blowing up tons and tons of mines," according to one crew member's account. The *53* worked for some time off Formosa in the weeks before Christmas. Also serving on mine demolition duty during November and December was LCS *56*. On November 29 the *56* lost a gunner's mate to an exploding mine, although the ship suffered only minor damage.

That it was no 'bed of roses' for LCSs serving in and around Korea in November and December is succinctly expressed by the writer of LCS *34*'s history: "The problems of scarce provisions, supplies and personnel along with the necessity of shifting anchorages frequently due to swift and highly variable currents, caused no end of trouble at Korea."[32]

Group 7 LCSs did service other than mine demolition duty in November and December. On a number of occasions the *53* served as a pilot vessel for convoys entering mined areas. On November 20, LCS *57* with *28* went to Kunsan, Korea, to take soundings of the harbor. In mid-November LCS *31* guided LSTs through the swift current of 30-foot tides that swept into the narrow harbor entrance at Mokpo, Korea. These LSTs were returning Koreans who had been slave laborers in Japan to their homeland.

As Christmas approached, Flotilla One and Flotilla Three LCSs, which had been doing occupation and mine demolition duties in and off from Japan, Korea,

LCSs docked in Shanghai across from the famous Bund. In the foreground are a Flot Three ship, 36, and a Flot Five ship, 73. Courtesy of Charles Thomas.

China, and Formosa, made preparations to return home to the States. Those wonderfully long and curious going-home pennants with one foot for each man aboard became the order of the day. A number of ships bound for the States left from Sasebo (both before and after Christmas), others from Inchon, and still others from Tsingtao, China. The largest single group (of 14 ships—5 from Flotilla One and 9 from Flotilla Three) arrived on December 21 in Shanghai where there were already some LCSs stationed. The crews of the ships spent Christmas and enjoyed liberty in Shanghai.

Flotilla Five Ships

On September 17 all Flotilla Five ships at San Pedro Bay, Leyte, got underway for occupation and mine demolition duties in roughly the same areas where Flotilla One and Three ships were serving.

Flotilla Five ships arrived at Okinawa on September 22 to be separated into groups going to Sasebo, Nagasaki, and just a few days later to different points in and off the coasts of China and Korea. On September 24 the first group of LCSs arrived in Sasebo. On their arrival, *104* learned that only two other U.S. naval ships had arrived there before them, a destroyer and an LSD.

Almost immediately the second group of ships was sent on to Nagasaki, only 40 miles from Sasebo. Both the ships remaining at Sasebo and those serving at Nagasaki had the primary duty of escorting large Japanese barges out to sea and seeing that the Japanese dumped all their shells and bombs overboard. In effect, they participated with other naval ships in enforcing the disarming of the Japanese.

The ships assigned to Nagasaki also served on skunk patrol, since there was still the danger of possible attack. Beginning October 2, LCS *105* put Marine troops ashore to occupy different places near Nagasaki. To do this the *105* took aboard 50 Marines who went ashore to establish military authority in the villages of Konoura, Nanatsugams, and Pomi-Yuma over a three-day period. LCSs also served as harbor control entrance ships at Nagasaki.

While at Nagasaki LCS crew members saw first-hand the terrible destruction of the second atom bomb. LCSs *103* and *104* remained in the Nagasaki area until November 3, with both ships, along with *106*, doing harbor control duties. A *106* crew member recorded what he saw and what his ship's harbor entrance duties were: "Devastation of Nagasaki was almost unbelievable—three feet of rubble for miles and miles. An occasional chimney standing. A small aircraft carrier blown up on the beach. Areas to the south of the main blast somewhat protected from the direct blast still had a few buildings standing.

"As Harbor Entrance Control Post, our job is to intercept incoming ships and to advise them of the minefields and proper routes to follow to safely enter the harbor. For three days we anchored about three miles out and worked at this job. Communication was difficult because of all the different Allied nationalities involved. We used international Morse signalling methods if we learned that the personnel aboard the incoming ship did not speak English. We survived and passed through about 300 ships with about 15 different languages."[33]

On October 6 LCS Group 13, made up of *2, 3, 96-101, 125,* and *128-130* arrived at Kure, a city near Hiroshima. LCS *100* reported having to enter Kure harbor single file through a narrow channel with many Japanese guns on the hills pointed at them. Because they were like 'sitting ducks', the ship's crew was happy that the occupation was a friendly one. On October 10 to 14, crew members from these ships toured Hiroshima and witnessed the destruction.

Some of the ships dispatched from Sasebo went to various places in China to provide a show of force in support of Chiang Kai-Shek's forces against the Chinese Communists. Among the cities they went to were Tangku, Shanghai, Nanking, Hankow, Anking, Tientsen, and Tsingtao. In some instances they joined Flotilla One ships, which were also showing force in these same places.

On their way from Sasebo to their assigned port in China, LCS *106* may have taken their title of 'Mighty Midget', earned at Okinawa, a little too seriously, as signalman Gene Taber reported it: "Our captain had noticed a line of ships stretching from one end of the horizon to the other and all brightly lighted with running lights. The captain asked me to find out who the ships were and where they were bound. Without hesitating, I wheeled a signal light toward the lead ship and gave him the customary wartime signal of 'AA..AA.' The signal interpreted properly means 'Unknown ship answer or we will open fire.'

"My answer was immediately on the way. 'F7 F7'. I Rogered and closed out and told the skipper we had just challenged the Commander of the Seventh Fleet. With no hesitation, our captain asked me to find out what ships were in company with the Seventh Fleet. Three hours later the signal guy was still sending ships' call letters bouncing the signals off the clouds even after they had gone out of sight—Battleships, Cruisers, Battle Cruisers, Carriers, Destroyers, Supply Ships and all. What an Armada for three or four little LCS ships to challenge."[34]

Fighting Amphibs 295

During February and March the last two of the six months that the ships were in advanced areas, LCSs went to places in China and Korea for different duties and to the surrounding sea areas for mine demolition duty. Like Flotilla One and Three ships, LCSs working off the coasts of China and Korea found the seas very rough and the weather bad much of the time.

LCSs *104* and *106* encountered these conditions while anchored in the Gulf of Pohai in China. The high waves that washed over the ships' sterns forced the aft compartment hatches open, flooding both ships and bringing them very close to sinking. While on mine demolition duty in the North China Sea, several LCSs, including *75*, found the seas very rough and very difficult to work in.

In addition to rough seas ships sometimes encountered very cold weather. "Ice on the front of the ship 12 inches thick, blown there from sea of salt water— pretty cold. Mine hunting in the Yellow Sea." In spite of the extreme cold, the *106* crew found a trip they took into China highly memorable: "most unforgettable [was] the trip 500 miles up the Yangtze escorting LSMs loaded with United Nations Relief and Rehabilitation Agency supplies for the starving people in the Hankow area."[35]

From October to late March Flotilla Five ships had a variety of duties. Like Flotilla Four ships serving at the same time in Tokyo Bay, LCSs *104* and *106* carried liberty parties from the large ships in the Gulf of Pohai to Tientsen and Tangku. Working out of Shanghai, *104* and *106* escorted LSTs carrying repatriated Koreans to Mokpo, Korea, through the North China Sea. LCSs in the Korean area also did harbor patrol work and by their presence also provided a show of force to the Korean Communists.

On November 11, LCSs *96, 97,* and *100* were underway to Haiphong, in French Indochina (now Vietnam), where they would operate as control vessels and pilot ships for LCIs and LSTs carrying Chinese troops from the port of Hongai for transportation to Formosa. Also beginning on November 11, LC(FF) *368* and LCSs *70-75* began mine demolition duty in designated areas. LCS *75* and other ships participated in a special hydrographic survey between Nanking and Hankow from November 11 to 30.

In late November LCS *77* arrived from Okinawa and was soon busy ferrying Chinese repatriates to points in China. While serving at Tientsin, China, in early December, the captain of LCS *105* became Senior Officer Present Afloat, relieving LSM *432*. On November 21, LCS *78* arrived in Inchon, Korea, from Okinawa and, like the Flotilla Three ships' crews before them, discovered the extremely difficult tides in the area. In early December, *78* served as a pilot vessel escorting LSTs carrying repatriated Koreans up the treacherous and shallow Silver River to the port of Kunsan.

On December 9, the LCSs in Group 13, *97-101, 125, 126, 128-130,* broke out their going-home pennants and began their long trip to the States by way of Subic Bay in the Philippines. LCS *96* stayed on to work with the Group 14 and 15 ships in the advanced areas until April.

In January while in Kunsan, members of LCS *78*'s basketball team, along with their shipmates, built a gymnasium for themselves and for other ships' teams in the area. Play started in 'Kunsan Square Garden' just six hours after the gym was completed. The *78* 'Salts' scored several wins, playing teams from an LST, an LSM, and four Army companies. While in Tsingtao in January and February, the Salts won a place in the semi-finals in a 'major league' basketball tournament there.

That there was entertainment and recreation for LCS crews in both Kunsan, Korea, and Tsingtao, China, at this time is evident from this *78* crew member's light-hearted account: "While at Kunsan we were given two parties for the ship, one by the Red Cross and the other by the Army. The Army party was a celebration although we didn't have anything to celebrate. A 'big head' was had by all. A little states-side life was offered by the extravagant 'Monte Carlo' club.

"Tsingtao was a major improvement over Kunsan. Some of the fellows had girl friends there. The only requirement to date one of the Russian girls was knowing Joe Stalin personally. Tsingtao had sports events for the sports-minded, but the majority of the fellows preferred hiring rickshaws and heading for the downtown area where all the excitement occurred. About two minutes before liberty expired, the fellows started back. This time the coolie would be riding and the swabbie pulling the rickshaw."[36]Some LCS crew members enjoyed being tourists and seeing the real China: "We [*106* shipmates on tour] visited Pieping making the trip by train—passed great expanses of the Great Wall of China—went through many peasant villages. Could not believe the crudeness and poverty of the Chinese communities. Visited both the Summer and Winter Palaces in Pieping. Hired a charcoal driven auto for the weekend—tried Saki for the first time. Hired a guide named Yuen C. Wu. Had races in rickshaws with drivers with bare feet on ice-covered streets. Cashed a $20 bill and received a suitcase full of inflated Yen. Back home to Tientsin."[37]

While LCS crews were able to enjoy entertainment and recreation in selected places in China and Korea, they had to depend on a very sluggish shipboard mail service. On January 27, at a very exciting mail call on the *78*, Merl Riggs received 65 letters from the States!

As late as February and March, Flotilla Five sailors were enjoying liberty in the same Shanghai in which Flotillas One and Three men enjoyed their Christmas. It was still an oasis—for liberty, the closest thing to the States in the Orient. "We arrived here on February 13, it was the first time all of us had seen Shanghai with the exception of our Salty Signalman Weir. To get to Shanghai, we must take a sampan, that's a dehydrated ferry. The city is much the same as any large city in the States with plenty of fresh milk, ice cream, night clubs, and Chinese! A night of good liberty costs about $20,000. Don't get excited, that's Chinese national currency. Everyone has his own favorite 'Gin Mill' or night club, if you prefer. The Chinese girls are comparatively pretty and a ten-minute stroll across town to the French settlement proves to be worthwhile. Prices are high with a 50 percent tax on all articles. And the OPA hasn't caught up to the Rickshaw boys yet either."[38]

On March 3 LCS *78* became what *61* had been while serving as a 'liberty boat' in Tokyo Bay in September—an 'Admiral's barge'. "The *78* went out to the entrance of the Whang Poo River to bring Rear Admiral T. G. W. Settle into Shanghai for a conference. There were 50-some persons in the group, including a captain in the British Navy, and a bunch of foreign diplomats. We received a message from the Admiral later congratulating us on a clean, smart ship."[39]

Throughout the six-month period (October through March) that Flotilla Five ships were in the advanced areas, a number of ships served on mine demolition duty in the seas off Japan, China, and Korea. LCSs *104, 106*, and others exploded and sank a large number of mines off Korea. LCS *75*, working with *104* and other ships, demolished mines in very rough seas off Mokpo, Korea. In February and March, *78, 96*, and others on three occasions destroyed free-floating mines on the Yangtse River patrol.

Some crews had extreme difficulty getting particularly stubborn mines to explode and/or sink. LCSs *78* and *102* fired 1400 rounds into one horned mine and hit it many times before it finally sank. These two ships were on mine demolition duty on at least three occasions over the six-month period. Flot Five ships that served on mine demolition duty included these LCSs: *70-75, 78, 96, 102, 104, 106, 126, 128*, and *130*.

As this April 12 message tells us, the Flot Five Group 14 commander was very proud of his ships and their crews. Their duties, though often arduous, were not always glamorous and exciting: "Our part in the war was a big one and you played it well. Things that we did may have seemed trifling or unimportant at the time, but each was a step toward victory or to a long lasting peace. The Navy and the people of our country can be proud of the mighty midgets of this unit. You, too, should be proud with a feeling of a task well done. May you all have marked success in future assignments. Lieutenant Commander K. E. Curley, Commander LCS Group 14."[40]

After six months service in the Japan, China, and Korea land and sea areas, three months longer than most of the other flotilla ships, the remaining Flotilla Five ships began their journey home. On April 18, four more ships, *103* and *105-107*, made the same move. Soon thereafter the few remaining ships followed.

After the Japanese surrender LCS crews had hoped, out loud when possible, that since their primary purpose was to provide fire support for invasions, they would be of little or no use in the Japanese occupation and could thus go home. According to the statement of the 'Operational Use of the LCS(L)(*Three*)' in the authentic *Allied Landing Craft of World War II,* the LCS crews were not too far off course: "To provide close-in fire support for landing operations and to intercept and destroy inter-island barge traffic."[41]

As we have seen in the preceding chapters, however, LCSs proved themselves very useful during the occupation in a number of ways. And they served an important military purpose by providing a show of strength to both the Chinese Communists and the Korean Communists and in support of Nationalist General Chiang Kai-shek by appearances in over a dozen crucial ports in China, Korea, Formosa, and French Indochina.

Endnotes

[1] Raymond Ross, Diary, 17-18, used with permission.

[2] L. E. Guilott, *How Did We Ever Win the War?* n.d., 72.

[3] Ibid.

[4] Diary, 18.

[5] Ibid., 19.

[6] Ibid., 19-20.

[7] Gil Nadeau, *45* signalman, letter to Richard Rhame, n.d.

[8] Richard A. Blake, *45* crew member, letter to Richard Rhame, August 27, 1990.

[9] "The Midnight Cruise of the LCS *47*," LCS(L) *1-130* Association. Newsletter, Summer '91, 11.

[10] Guilott, 76 and 78.

[11] Diary, 21.

[12] Blake, letter.

[13] Ludwig Edstrom, *28* officer, letter to author, September 28, 1992.

[14] Guilott, 80.

[15] Joseph Sansone, "Tells How LCS Convoy Sailed to Jap Shore," Lebanon (Pa.)*Daily News,* September 22, 1945.

[16] Ibid.

[17] Korany, *LCS 14—One of the Mighty Midgets,* n.d., 84-85.

[18] Dick Halstead, Diary, 35-39.

[19] W. H. Stanley, "Kamikaze, the Battle for Okinawa—Big War of the Little Ships," May 16, 1988, 20-21.

[20] Radio message, Action LCS Group 7, September 22, 1945.

[21] J. Gebhardt, "A Brief Account of the Travels of USS LCS(L) *51,* June '44-February '46," 3.

[22] "Invasion of Japan is Sight-Seeing Journey,"*Daily News,* Lebanon, (Pa), October 16, 1945, 10.

[23] Ibid.

[24] Informal chronology of LCS(L)*35,* 1945-46, 1.

[25] "USS LCS *53* History," 4.

[26] Stanley, 22.

[27] Ibid., 23.

[28] Korany, 99-100.

[29] Ibid., 102-103.

[30] Ibid., 113-114.

[31] "USS LCS(L) *31*" n.d. 6.

[32] "History of LCS *34,*" p. 1 of Chapter 2.

[33] Everett E. Taber, "Memories of Navy Time—April 1944 until June 1946," 5.

[34] Ibid.

[35] Ibid., 6.

[36] "LCS *78* Birthday Booklet," 6.

[37] Taber, 6.

[38] "LCS *78* Birthday Booklet," 7.

[39] M. L. Riggs, "Diary of My Experiences aboard the LCS(L)(3) *78,*" 1.

[40] Radio message from LCDR K. E. Curley to Group 14, April 12, 1946.

[41] (Annapolis, MD: Naval Institute Press, 1985), Supplement 1, 47.

Chapter 14

"Out of the Sticks in '46"

Although most of the LCSs did not begin their voyages home until December '45 and January '46, LCS sailors began leaving for discharge or separation the previous September. According to the Navy's point system, older married men with longer service records were the first to be released, and this took effect in late August. Many LCS sailors were 'back alive (in the States) in '45' while their ships and their less fortunate shipmates had to wait until '46 to get 'out of the sticks'.

Needless to say, the released men were eager to leave. Some of them had difficulty waiting for transportation scheduled to take them to the States. The fairly rapid release of what were in many instances the most skillful and useful men in the LCS crews sometimes worked hardships on ships serving in advanced areas. Even though some flotilla commanders held on to their ships' engineering officers as long as was legally possible, ships on occupation duty had to give them up with no adequate replacements immediately in sight.

Our ship met this need by appointing one of its other officers as acting engineering officer. Since as damage control officer I worked closely with our enigneering officer on firefighting and damage control equipment, which included gasoline engines, electric motors, and pumps, I became our ship's acting engineering officer. Because my qualifications were limited, I depended rather heavily on my leading motor machinist's mate and electrician's mate, who were highly competent and had been well trained by my predecessor. When we arrived at Pearl Harbor on our return trip to the States, I was relieved by an officer with an engineer designation.

LCSs on mine demolition duty in waters off Japan, China, Korea, and Formosa lost many of their most experienced seamen lookouts, in some ways the most useful men for that duty on the ship. Many of their replacements were young men fresh out of boot camp who began asking about when they could go home soon after reporting aboard.

Before some Flotilla Four ships left Tokyo Bay for the States, they were given a departure inspection by Flotilla Commander Neill Phillips. The inspection included a fire drill, as Lieutenant Peter Beierl, *82* captain, relates: "The pumps roared to life, the water blossomed over our bow like N.Y. harbor fire boats on parade. Everything was going swimmingly. Then wham—the starboard hose pulled out of its fitting at the manifold and became a writhing 3.5-inch snake. Who's standing there to be swept into the water? The Commodore and his yeoman, of course. Hauled back out of the dirty harbor a few minutes later, we thought he'd be spitting fire. But in fact, all was cool and calm, and the *82* was allowed to leave. In retrospect, perhaps he was glad to be rid of us."[1]

LCSs began leaving the advanced areas in December, and by May and June, all of them had left and were back in the States. The LCSs, with their going-home pennants trailing behind them, and their crews in the best of spirits, left Japan and China and other areas. These high spirits were dampened somewhat when a number of the ships ran into engine trouble that delayed their arrivals in the States by days and sometimes weeks.

The number of ships in Flotilla Three that had breakdowns was evidently large. "Of the ships that left Tsingtao (China), around 36 or so (from Flotillas 1, 3 and 5), I [Joseph Gebhardt, *51* officer] think only the *51* and *52* made it back without some sort of breakdown."[2] And these were just some of the total number of ships having breakdowns.

Ever since they left the States, many LCSs had been running their eight main propulsion engines for long periods without overhauls. Some engineering departments had worked on their engines while underway, a real challenge, especially if there was a sea running. Engine overhauls were made on some of the ships while they were at San Pedro Bay in the Philippines. That was back in July and August, however, four or five months earlier.

Lack of engine overhauls was of course only one of a number of possible problems. On some ships corrosive salt water coolant had frozen the clutches used to clutch individual engines into the two engine-quads that turned the ship's two screws. Several ships, probably a number of them, 'limped' into Pearl Harbor with only two or three operative clutches even though all eight engines ran. Problems affecting the main engines also affected the two generator engines providing the ship's electrical power. Also some ships' systems were showing defects not reparable at sea. Several ships discovered that Freon, a refrigerant gas, was leaking from their cooling systems, causing the refrigerator temperature to rise dangerously.

Although we were serving as the flagship, with Lieutenant Commander Joe Dodson, Group 10 Commander in command of our group of eight homeward-bound LCSs, our ship was one of the 'limpers' into Pearl with six frozen clutches and only two operative. One distinct advantage of having eight main propulsion engines and eight clutches is that we were not really completely broken down as long as one engine and its clutch were going. When the *85* got into Pearl Harbor, our new engineering officer and I (the supply officer) discovered that we could not get new complete clutches from the Supply Depot because they were Title B equipment. We had to order every separate part of the six clutches, piece by piece ad infinitum.

In spite of all these problems (and there were more), ships' crews were determined to make it to the States on their own. LCSs helped their sister ships in every way possible, providing power for sister ships in port, even exchanging engineering officers, machinists mates, and engine parts in mid-ocean. Ships' crews used their ingenuity to the fullest to constantly keep their ships moving. Victor Lyon, *99* officer, reported what some ships moving homeward did to keep going: "After spending some 30 days repairing our engines at Eniwetok, we were ready to proceed to Pearl Harbor, but of course the convoy was long gone. We had made it about halfway to Pearl when the LCI accompanying us broke down in about the same manner we had broke down coming into Eniwetok. The LCI rigged a sail and with its three or four engines on the one screw made the best possible speed and within about four days we arrived at Johnston Island, low on water. We were prepared to ask for water as we handed over the lines, but they beat us to it and asked if we had water we could spare. This helped make up our minds to get underway at first light the next morning."[3]

Charles Thomas, *35* signalman, explained how his ship operated underway without electrical power: "The *35* left Shanghai with only one generator functioning and now the only generator still operating quits. When the engineer officer orders it shut down for repairs, the ship is without electrical power. The main propulsion diesels do not require power, but the pilot house steering mechanism does, and the steering must be done manually in the after steering room by two men who have become experts at this very uncomfortable job. Electricity also powers the pumps cooling the propeller shafts. The engineers solve that problem by using a Handy Billy pump fifteen minutes out of each hour to flush the shafts with cool water. Without electricity, cooking is impossible. The cooks serve cold cuts.

"Battery power is our sole source of illumination also. The crews' mess hall has red lanterns operated by batteries. For running lights at night two men suspend more battery-operated white lanterns from the main mast and stern. Hand-held red and green lights to show port and starboard are kept available on the conn. Long periods at sea are telling on the temporary nature of the *35* and her sister LCSs. Other ships in the convoy also begin a series of breakdowns early in the voyage. One ship, the *30*, experiences repeated engine problems almost from the beginning. Several other ships join the ailing list as the voyage progresses."[4]

Ships crossing the International Date Line had duplicate days. A few crews had two Christmases, but made do with one Christmas dinner; a few others two New Year's Days, but one celebration was enough.

On their return home, LCS sailors enjoyed playing tourist and hiking on the high coastal cliffs at Saipan. Here in the distance are the 'suicide cliffs' that Japanese soldiers and civilians jumped off of rather than surrender to the U.S. forces in the battle for Saipan. Courtesy of Charles Thomas.

The LCS *61* crew held a double celebration on November 29 at sea. It was the first anniversary of their commissioning and Thanksgiving Day. Here from their Thanksgiving dinner program is an expression of thanks that puts into words what many of the returning LCS crews felt at the time: "On this 'Homeward Bound' Thanksgiving and First Anniversary Day, we truly have much to be thankful for. Wherever we have sailed or fought there has seemed to be some Divine Power guiding and protecting us. And so, it behooves all of us, on this day of thanks to bow our heads and thank Almighty God for the many wonderful privileges of living and seeing us safely though the year."

Crews of six LCSs bound for Seattle from Tokyo Bay enjoyed a close-up glimpse of the romantic past when they ran alongside, within hailing and 'camera-clicking' distance of a large square rigged sailing vessel, the *Pamir*, on her way with a load of wheat from the United States to New Zealand.

All of the LCSs returning to the States stopped at some of the same ports they visited going out. Crews of some ships stopping at Saipan saw ships being readied for atomic bomb testing at Bikini Island. Dick Halstead, *18* crew member, was highly impressed by the physical efficiency of naval facilities at Eniwetok: "Arrived at Eniwetok on February 16 and it was then that I saw the Navy work very efficiently for the first time in my life. All thirteen of us [Group 8 of Flot Three plus their group commander's flagship] were fueled and watered by 1600." Ships traveling with the *18* were also breaking down. "Two days out [from Eniwetok] the first breakdown of LCS *50* occurred. For two or three days she would get fixed up and we would begin to make speed and she'd break down again. At last she got running okay and for three hours we made good time when LCS *17* had something happen either to their shaft or propeller forcing them to use one quad. LCS *11* towed them 2 days; LCS *14* for 2 days; LCS *20* for 1 day; and LCS *16* for 2 days."[5]

Although LCS sailors still thought highly of Pearl Harbor and Honolulu (after all, both were part of the USA!), they were not eager to have liberty in Honolulu on the way back. They wanted to get home. One sailor, Richard Kreider, *10* quartermaster, whose ship didn't stop there on the way out and who kept hearing about the wonders of Honolulu and Pearl, was very disappointed. "Honolulu was just one big Coney Island. Everyone was out to get the sailors' money. Between getting your picture taken with a hula girl, pin ball machines, movie machines, and pictures of naked women, there was little else. All the souvenirs were sky high."[6] Kreider did like Waikiki Beach.

Happy the ship that boasted a friendly and competent barber! On this ship, the 35, smiles on the faces seem to say that this was the case. Courtesy of Charles Thomas.

Officers on my ship enjoyed a surprise reunion at Pearl Harbor with Jim Littlefield, our first executive officer who was so completely debilitated by seasickness on the way out that he was transferred off at Majuro. He became a public relations officer on Admiral Nimitz's staff headquartered at Pearl Harbor and squired us around the island in a jeep.

Unfortunately LCSs going home had to 'drive defensively' to avoid collisions, the same as they did going out to war earlier. "We were less than 50 miles off the California coast heading due east. The ships [in our group of LCSs] had formed up into a single column and we would be entering the San Diego harbor after daylight. At 0340 a large unidentified commercial ship, heading south, cut through our convoy and nearly collided into our port bow. Our captain took instant evasive action and a collision was avoided. What an ironic twist this would have been. To travel halfway around the world and back again, blacked out mostly, in all kinds of weather, under all sorts of adverse conditions and then to be sunk by some damn tanker in sight of our homeland."[7]

LCSs entered the United States using practically every major West Coast port on their return from the war—Seattle, Portland, Astoria, San Francisco, Long Beach off Los Angeles, and San Diego. The greater majority of the ships, however, came into Portland and Astoria and San Francisco.

Those LCSs that entered San Francisco Bay in early December got the full treatment: a hero's welcome to Navy ships and men who served in the Pacific war. There were signs on the hills overlooking the harbor: "Welcome Home" and "Well Done." There was a third large sign at Treasure Island: "Hi Mates, Welcome Home." Out in the harbor were fireboats shooting streams of water and tugboats loaded with bands playing and friendly people singing popular and patriotic songs to welcome the sailors home.

As the returning LCSs entered the West Coast harbors from early December until April and May and even later, whether or not there were 'singing welcomers' and streams of water from fireboats still there, LCS sailors cheered and wept or just stood silently, completely overcome by powerful emotions. Those ships making port in San Francisco rolled in on the Pacific sea swells under the magnificent Golden Gate Bridge with hills on either side and the city of San Francisco on the right.

My ship arrived in a group in March. We went under the fairy tale bridge at sunset (a glorious experience in itself), and anchored for the night off Alcatraz Island. I stayed aboard ship as officer of the deck. The next morning our group moved across the bay to an anchorage off Sausilito. When I went ashore for the first time at Sausilito, I knelt and kissed the ground. I then took a bus to the city, and while riding through part of Marin County to the Golden Gate Bridge, I looked off to the left across the bay and there it was, what we had been fighting for—a city of white buildings glistening in the morning sun. Then the familiar song came back to me:

> *O beautiful, for patriot dream that sees beyond the years. Thine alabaster cities gleam, undimmed by human tears! America! America! God shed his grace on thee, and crown thy good with brotherhood from sea to shining sea.*[8]

Earl Blanton, *118* gunner, puts his sentiments into words: "Being home [in San Diego] was a great feeling. Once some of us [Blanton and a few shipmates] rented a hotel room just to sleep in a bed, but it was so quiet and strange, we didn't sleep well. We had plenty of money so we hit the restaurants and ate all sorts of food that we had been denied for so long. We had all-night liberties and didn't return to the ship until the last minute, hanging on to the sweet stateside sights and people. We were so glad to see American people in American clothes speaking American English that at times we just sat and stared. In my continuing quest to see the 'country', I bought a bus ticket to some town (whose name I don't remember) two or three hours north of San Diego. I simply rode the bus up and turned around and came back, rubber necking all the way."[9]

Although these two instances of homecoming celebrations may be slightly extreme, all returning LCS sailors were excited by the experience. After all of their unique, 'never to be repeated' experiences of the last two years, returning home was the greatest experience of all—there would be nothing else quite like it, ever.

Underlying the high spirits of the jubilant homecomers was the feeling of loss for those shipmates who had been killed. Recently a former crew member of DMS *Aaron Ward*, who lost a number of shipmates on Picket Station 10 off Okinawa on May 3rd, felt this loss so strongly that he held a memorial service for his lost shipmates in a boat on the waters of what had been Station 10.

In their excitement at the time, perhaps only a few of those returning took time to reflect on how their LCS experiences had matured them. When they reported earlier to the Solomons base for LCS training, most of the enlisted men were boys in their late teens just out of high school or newly released from jobs on farms or in factories or drugstores or eating places. They had all been to boot camp and some had been to service schools.

Most of the men who became LCS junior officers—the five on each ship who served under the captain—were generally known at the time as 'college kids', and after they earned their commissions, as 'ninety-day wonders'. Only a few of these new LCS crew members, officers as well as men, had been to sea, or even on a boat or ship of any size for more than a few hours at a time.

Yet they all returned home as seasoned first class seamen in the truest sense of the term: They had survived typhoons with 70-foot swells and sailed on some of the roughest waters in the world; they had demonstrated courage in fighting against the kamikaze planes at Okinawa and in other combat actions and in invasions in the Philippines, Borneo, Iwo Jima, and Okinawa; they had worked and lived in extremely crowded conditions on a small flat-bottomed gunboat designed for close-in fire support in invasions, but destined to serve much of its time on the high seas; they had demonstrated skill in firefighting and salvage work on larger ships as well as small ones; and they had demonstrated compassion by rescuing thousands of men from the waters and from stricken ships and then caring for hundreds of the wounded. The LCS crews who went out to the war as boys came back as men.

Before the ships reached their 'final destinations' for decommissioning and mothballing, a number of officers and men would leave the ship and a lesser number of new people would come aboard. Within three weeks after arriving in San Francisco in early March, my ship lost its captain, its executive officer, its gunnery officer and 20 petty officers and nonrated men. At the same time it acquired a new captain, from another LCS, a new officer, and 10 enlisted men. On other ships these changes would have happened earlier or later and, perhaps, over a longer period of time, rather than, seemingly, all at once.

In preparation for decommissioning and mothballing, LCS crews were reduced from 6 to 4 officers and from 65 to approximately 35 enlisted men.

The loss of half the crew in a matter of weeks was sometimes sad, and even painful, for remaining crew members who, without the points for release, would have to decommission and help to mothball the ship with green officers and men right out of boot camp. The attitudes of the new personnel toward their assignment to an LCS varied considerably. The engineer officer who relieved me as *85*'s acting engineer officer at Pearl Harbor had a positive attitude and turned out to be one of the most competent officers on the ship. An Annapolis ensign assigned to replace the *111* communications officer in San Francisco promptly announced "there's nothing to running this tub." When the *111* went on what turned out to be its stormy decommissioning voyage to Portland, "the new ensign finally made it to the bridge [for duty] while the ship was in the Columbia River."[10]

From their various West Coast arrival points the LCSs moved in two directions. A number of ships went north up the coast to Astoria and Portland, where they would be assigned to shipyards for mothballing and then be decommissioned by a skeleton crew and moved to Tongue Point, Oregon. Other ships went south down the coasts of Baja California and Mexico through the Panama Canal, 'back through' for former East Coast ships. Then they moved east across the Gulf of Mexico around the Florida peninsula up to Jacksonville and then down the St. John's River to Green Cove Springs for mothballing and decommissioning. A number of the eastbound ships made several stops, including New Orleans, where they enjoyed their liberty to the full.

The then silent mothballed LCSs at Tongue Point, Oregon, and Green Cove Springs, Florida, were not destined to remain in place for decades as units of the Reserve Fleet to be activated for service in future wars and international conflicts. Beginning in 1946, the same year the ships were mothballed and stored, 51 LCSs were stricken from the Navy Register and sold—most of them for scrap metal but some to private individuals and to fishing companies. In 1951 the selling was stopped and most of the remaining ships were loaned or transferred to foreign countries: Italy, Okinawa, France, Japan [which received 50], Korea, Taiwan, Greece, Thailand, and the Philippines. In 1958 and '59 Japan returned 27 of their 50 to the United States and the United States turned over the remaining 23 ships to Japan.

Several of the countries receiving LCSs used them in, or transferred them to, other countries. The French used their LCSs for duty in Indochina, and one ship, the former LCS *96*, was transferred to three countries and served in the navies of Japan, Vietnam, and finally, the Philippines.

Ironically Japan used a number of the LCSs turned over to them as targets to be sunk by rockets, bombs, and naval gunfire. Approximately a dozen of the sunken LCSs lie in a 1,000-fathom-deep ocean area about 70 miles southwest of Tokyo, which was the ultimate target of the Allied Forces in the Pacific Ocean war.[11]

Endnotes

[1] Rooney, *Mighty Midget USS LCS 82*, 163.

[2] "A Brief Account of the Travels of USS LCS(L) *51*," 3.

[3] "Some Notes About USS LCS(L)(3) *99*," 10.

[4] *Dolly Five—A Memoir of the Pacific War*, 394-395.

[5] Dick Halstead, Diary, 63-64.

[6] "USS LCS(L)(3) *10* Log," Personal log, 138.

[7] Blanton, *118* gunner, *Boston-To Jacksonville (41,000 miles by sea)*, 192.

[8] Verse 3 of "America, the Beautiful" by Katherine Lee Bates.

[9] Ibid., 193.

[10] Letter from Charles Rhoades to Bill Reid, n.d.

[11] For the material in these last four paragraphs I am indebted to Raymond Baumler, *Ten Thousand Men and One Hundred Thirty "Mighty Midget" Ships*, (Rockville, MD: 1991), 66-73.

Bibliography

Note: Unpublished sources and references, as well as published ones, are cited in the notes following each chapter. Book length publications used as sources and references and recommended for further reading are listed below.

Bartley, Whitman S., *Iwo Jima: Amphibious Epic*, U. S. Marine Corps Historical Branch (1954).

Baumler, Raymond A., *Ten-Thousand Men and One-Hundred Thirty 'Mighty Midget' Ships* (Rockville, Maryland: 1991).

Belote, James H. and William M., *Corregidor, The Saga of a Fortress* (New York: Harper and Row, 1967).

Bertoch, Marvin J., *The Little Ships* (Salt Lake City, Utah: 1989).

Blanton, Earl, *Boston—to Jacksonville (41,000 Miles by Sea)* (Seaford, Virginia: 1991).

Dyer, George C., *The Amphibians Came to Conquer—The Story of Admiral Richmond Kelly Turner,* Vol 2 (Washington, DC: Department of the Navy, 1972).

Foster, Simon, *Okinawa 1945: Final Assault on the Empire* (New York: Sterling, 1995).

Guillot, L. E., *How Did We Ever Win the War?* n.d.

Karig, Walter, *Battle Report—Victory in the Pacific* (New York: Rinehart and Company, 1949).

Korany, Frank, *LCSL 14—One of the Mighty Midgets*, n.d.

LCS(L) Landing Craft Support (Large) (Paducah, Kentucky: Turner Publishing Company, 1995).

Lott, Arnold, *Brave Ship, Brave Men* (Annapolis: Naval Institute Press, 1964).

Mason, William J., *USS LCS(L)(3) 86—"The Mighty Midget"* (San Francisco: 1992).

Morison, Samuel Eliot, *History of United States Naval Operations in World War II* (Boston: Little Brown), Volume 13, *The Liberation of the Philippines,* 1959; Volume 14, *Victory in the Pacific*, 1960.

Rielly, Robin L., *Kamikaze Patrol—The LCSL(3) 61 at War* (Toms River, New Jersey: 1996).

Rooney, John, *Mighty Midget—USS LCS 82* (Phoenixville, Pennsylvania: 1990).

Sholin, William, *The Sacrificial Lambs—The Entire Story of the Japanese Kamikaze Attacks Against the US Fleet in WW II* (Bonney Lake, Washington: Mountain View Books, 1989).

Surels, Ron, *DD 522: Diary of a Destroyer* (Plymouth, New Hampshire: Valley Graphics, Inc.) 2nd edition, 1996.

Thomas, Charles, *Dolly Five: A Memoir of the Pacific War* (Chester, Virginia: 1995).

Thurman, Paul, *Picket Ships at Okinawa* (New York: Carlton Press, 1996).

Appendix

LCS(L) Sailors Killed in Action

LCS shipmates who gave to their country everything in their power to give:

USS LCS(L) 7

Henry A. Averell
Frank M. Best
Emil R. Bowman
Henry S. Burgert
Israel L. Garcia
Earl J. Hardin, Jr.
Ellis A. Hawkins, Jr.
Joseph F. Hendron
Willie J. Jackson
Clayton A. Laird, Jr.
Lee R. McDonnell
Kenneth L. Mills
Willard M. Neely
Kenneth C. Pack
Robert I. Raaflaub
Cozzie N. Simpkins
David H. Stephenson
Thomas H. Strickland
Kermit Leon Stott
Robert E. L. Sutton
Thomas D. Thornhill
George E. Trammell, Sr.
Herbert A. Webb

USS LCS(L) 15

Norman Ankenbrandt
Richard D. Brunner
Richard W. Burnett

Walter R. Butter, Jr.
James A. Canode
Francis V. Cincera
Willie L. Conklin
John Dibattista
Olin O. Hammer
Marvin L. Hiles
Samuel Krainovich
Arnold W. Reif
Leo A. Renz
Macon L. Thomason
Lawrence E. Underwood

USS LCS(L) 25

Wallace E. Smith

USS LCS(L) 26

Alvie C. Arnold
Milton N. Bachman
Casper A. Bacrowski
Richard L. Bartz
Edward Bayus
Donald V. Bearison
Alvin F. Beczynski
Howard W. Bedford
Ulysses M. Bendy, Jr.
Albert S. Bellofatto
Horace E. Blair
Norbert H. Bleau

Paul E. Boyer
Arvel B. Clark
Harold L. Clark
John E. Cooper
Vernon H. Frey
Calvin R. Jones, Jr.
James H. Nix
Chester A. Oddell
Carroll D. Pipes, Sr.
Howard T. Priest
Arlo R. Schellhardt
Walter E. Smith
Stanley Swierk

USS LCS(L) *27*

Louis J. Rodriguez
George O. Turner
James D. Whaley

USS LCS(L) *31*

Howard E. Allman
William L. Cooperider
Robert L. Cupton
Norman E. Gunter
Paul J. Petitt
Clyde Stevens
James O. Watson
Paul K. Willey
Marshall C. Wyvell

USS LCS(L) *33*

Edward C. Gertz
Craig D. Keistler
Rudolph W. Koepke
Johnie F. Nicely
Glenn L. Shade

USS LCS(L) *49*

George Apostolos
William O. Barlow
James E. Canley

Robert J. Caton
John H. Clay
Francis W. Collom
William P. Comer
Roger F. Court
Sam H. Deakins
Edward A. Decker
Henry O. DuPont
John M. Eastridge
Arnold H. Ferguson
Elmer C. Glenn
Elijah Hayes
Paul A. Kiger
Peter G. McGrath
William McLaughlin
David Mehanna
Victor L. Raymond
Harold A. Scribner
Sylvester M. Sikon
George W. Spahr
Lois Szkochek
William E. Travers

USS LCS(L) *52*

Spencer Burroughs
James L. Hawks

USS LCS(L) *56*

John F. Cooper

USS LCS(L) *57*

Samuel Chick
Andrew Schmidt

USS LCS(L) *88*

Casimir L. Bigos
Leon E. Caldwell
Stanley J. Hosick
Julius H. Pontecorvo
Harry J. Puls

George E. Riehm
James R. Robert, Sr.
Abram D. Schwartz
Cecil B. Wetzel

USS LCS(L) *116*

Willie Barnes, Jr.
Jasper C. Caldwell
Andrew J. Campbell, Jr.
Homer A. Clapper
Edwin Delaney
Bill J. Edds
Sam Ellis
Charles W. Francis
Michael C. Gaynor
John Gibson
Billie T. Harris
John E. Maloney
Lloyd B. Paugh
Bernard J. Riser
James M. Roberts
Leo Taylor
Malcolm E. Thomas

USS LCS(L) *119*

Donald W. Adams
Orvel O. Dawson
Aubrey L. East
John P. Ekers
Robert E. Emerson
Billy F. Mullennix
Donald L. Sarbaugh
Waid D. Smith
Robert E. Smitley
Charles E. Stephens
John G. Sutton
Oliver S. Wiseman
George W. Wood
Lois A. Zabinski

USS LCS(L) *121*

Sidney P. Baker
Harry J. McCleod

USS LCS(L) *122*

Nicholas F. Black
Charles L. Downs
Dan A. Hedrick
Charles W. Higgins
Ernest M. Kelly
George A. Murphy
John F. Peoples
Douglas Robertson
Frank C. Salemo
MacDonald Thomas
Jay F. Wiseman

LCS(L)s Sunk, Damaged, and Casualties—February 1 through December 31, 1945

Ship	Date	Cause of Damage	Place	Type of damage	Casualties Killed	Wounded
7	Feb. 16	Suicide Boat	Philippines	Sunk	23	13
26	Feb. 16	Suicide Boat	Philippines	Sunk	25	13
49	Feb. 16	Suicide Boat	Philippines	Sunk	25	23
27	Feb. 16	Suicide Boat	Philippines	Major	3	22
33	Feb. 19	Shore Batteries	Iwo Jima	Minor		6
48	Feb. 25	Raft Explosion	Philippines	Minor		12
20	Apr. 1	Shore Batteries	Okinawa	Minor		4
36	Apr. 9	Suicide Plane	Okinawa	Major		5
57	Apr. 12	Suicide Plane	Okinawa	Major	2	8
33	Apr. 12	Suicide Plane	Okinawa	Sunk	5	29
115	Apr. 12	Suicide Plane	Okinawa	Minor		3
51	Apr. 16	Suicide Plane	Okinawa	Minor		3
116	Apr. 16	Suicide Plane	Okinawa	Major	17	12
15	Apr. 22	Suicide Plane	Okinawa	Sunk	15	12
37	Apr. 29	Suicide Boat	Okinawa	Major		4
14	May 3	Air Attack	Okinawa	Minor		2
25	May 3	Suicide Plane	Okinawa	Minor	1	7
31	May 4	Suicide Plane	Okinawa	Minor	9	10
52	May 11	Suicide Plane	Okinawa	Minor		1
88	May 11	Suicide Plane	Okinawa	Major	9	7
121	May 23	Bomb Near Miss	Okinawa	Minor	2	5
52	May 27	Suicide Plane	Okinawa	Minor	2	7
119	May 28	Suicide Plane	Okinawa	Major	14	24
122	Jun. 11	Suicide Plane	Okinawa	Major	11	28
22	Jun. 24	Air Attack	Okinawa	Minor		1
28	Jun. 26	Gun Explosion	Okinawa	Minor		1
8	Jun. 28	Shore Batteries	Borneo	Minor		5
56	Nov. 29	Mine Explosion	off Formosa	Minor	1	
14	Dec. 5	Very Rough Seas	Formosa Strait	Major		

Totals: 5 ships sunk; 9 major, 15 minor damage; 164 killed, 267 wounded. Major damage is that which requires over 30 days for repairs. Source: Ray Baumler, *Ten Thousand Men and One Hundred Thirty "Mighty Midget" Ships,* p. 54, and ship histories.

LCS(L)s Awarded the Presidential Unit Citation

Ship	Place and Date of Action	Commanding officer
USS LCS(L) 31	Okinawa May 4, 1945	Lt. K. F. Machacek, USNR
USS LCS(L) 51	Okinawa Apr. 16, 1945	Lt. H. D. Chickering, USNR
USS LCS(L) 57	Okinawa Apr. 16, 1945	Lt. Harry L. Smith, USNR

LCS(L)s Awarded the Navy Unit Commendation

USS LCS(L) 21	Okinawa May 4, 1945	Lt. J. C. F. Geib, USNR
USS LCS(L) 32	Iwo Jima Feb. 19-26; Okinawa April 1-June 17, 1945	Lt. J. M. Evans, USN
USS LCS(L) 82	Okinawa May 11, 1945	Lt. Peter G. Beierl, USN
USS LCS(L) 83	Okinawa and Ryukyus Islands May 3 & 11, 1945	Lt. James M. Faddis, USN
USS LCS(L) 84	Okinawa and Ryukyus Islands May 11, 1945	Lt. J. A. Naye, USNR
USS LCS(L) 86	Okinawa April 18-June 21, 1945	Lt. Howard N. Houston, USNR
USS LCS(L) 118	Okinawa and Ryukyus Islands Apr. 1-June 6, 1945	Lt. Peter F. Gilmore, Jr., USNR
USS LCS(L) 122	Okinawa June 10-11, 1945	Lt. Richard M. McCool, USN

Information from *United States Navy and Marine Corps Awards Manual,* Dept. of Navy, SECNAVINST 1650.1D

Index

All ships' names are in capital letters.

OLE ROLVAAG, 240
Osman, Lt. Stan, 61
Osterland, Lt.(j.g.) Frank, 122, 173-74

PA 208, 140
Pack, Woodrow, 97
PAMIR, 305
PC 1603 attacked, 229
PENNSYLVANIA, 241
Peterson, Marvin, 205
Pfau, Lt. W. F., 260
PGM Nine, 202
PHILLIP, 115
Phillips, Capt. Neill, 40, 46, 153, 207,
    251, 253, 259, 267, 302
Pierpont, Lt.(j.g.) Powell, 183
Powers, William A., 97
PRICHETT, 240
PRINGLE, 182
Profitt, Don, 75
PURDY, 172-73, 176
Pyle, Ernie, 183, 237

Quimette, Raymond, 171

Randall, Lt. Craig, 223
Rawlings, Vice Admiral Sir H. B., 267
Reifsnider, Rear Admiral L. F., 193
RELIEF, 216
Revisser, Capt. K. L., 231
Rhame, Lt.(j.g.) Richard, 72, 77-78, 79,
    81, 84-85, 110
Rhoads, Joe, 79, 82
Richards, Captain John K., 16
Riggs, Merl, 298
Rooney, John, 19, 25, 183, 266
Roosevelt, President Franklin D., 172

Ross, Raymond J., 85, 110-111, 114, 115,
    247-49, 270, 272-73, 274, 278-79
Roth, Tony, 216
Royal, Rear Admiral F. B., 80, 105

SALT LAKE CITY, 135, 143
SALUTE, 111
Sanders, Cmdr. W. H., 198
SANGAMON, 196-97
Sansone, Lt. Joseph, 124, 137-38, 287
Saroch, Lt. Emil, 229
Satota, Micheal, 139
SCRIBNER, 161
Settle, Rear Admiral T. G. W., 298
Shillingburg, Dean, 214
Shuldenrein, Morris, 130, 131-32, 171
Sims, George, 230-31
Skarin, Bob, 234
Slama, Richard, 188
SMALLEY, 233
Smith, General H. M., 131
Smith, Lt. H. W., 175
SOLACE, 142
SOUTH DAKOTA, 266
Spruance, Admiral R. A., 267
Stanley, W. H., 52, 204, 257, 285-86
STANLEY, 177
STARR, 162
State, Lt. L. A., 117
Stephenson, Ernest, 211
STERETT, 170
STODDARD, 240
Stone, Lt. Cmdr. Frank, 122, 132, 153,
    287
STORMES, 223
Sweeny, Lt. J. J., 128